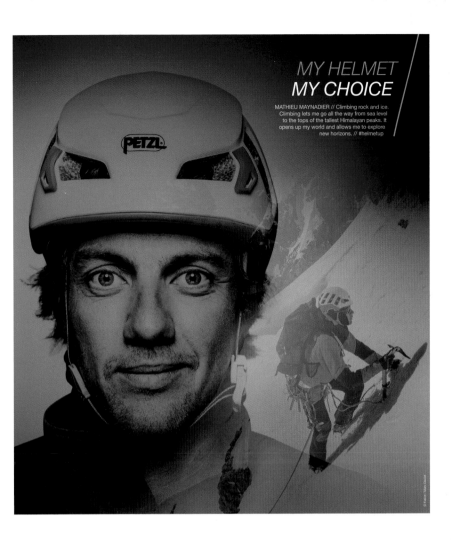

MY HELMET
MY CHOICE

MATHIEU MAYNADIER // Climbing rock and ice.
Climbing lets me go all the way from sea level
to the tops of the tallest Himalayan peaks. It
opens up my world and allows me to explore
new horizons. // #helmetup

METEOR

Lightweight helmet with enhanced
protection for mountaineering,
climbing and ski touring.
petzl.com

Access
the
inaccessible®

THE
ALPINE JOURNAL
2019

Sharp-dressed men. Summiteers on the first ascent of Mount Foraker:
Thomas Graham Brown, Charles Houston and Chychele Waterston,
the former pair dressed in tailor-made wind-suits made of Grenfell cloth.
Peter Foster's biography of Graham Brown is reviewed on p330.
Waterston, born in Edinburgh and a teacher in Andover, Mass, was the
father of actor Sam Waterston. *(National Library of Scotland)*

THE
ALPINE JOURNAL
2019

The Journal of the Alpine Club

A record of mountain adventure
and scientific observation

Editor: Ed Douglas

Production: Jane Beagley

Volume 123

Number 367

Supported by the
MOUNT EVEREST FOUNDATION

Published by
THE ALPINE CLUB

© 2019 by the Alpine Club

THE ALPINE JOURNAL 2019
Volume 123 No 367

www.alpine-club.org.uk

Address all editorial communication to the Hon Editor:
Alpine Club, 55 Charlotte Rd, London, EC2A 3QF
email: journal.editor@alpine-club.org.uk

Address all sales and distribution communications to:
Cordee, 11 Jacknell Rd, Dodwells Bridge Ind Est, Hinckley, LE10 3BS

Back numbers:
Apply to the Alpine Club, 55 Charlotte Rd, London, EC2A 3QF or,
for 1969 to date, apply to Cordee, as above.

First published in 2019 by The Alpine Club
Typeset by Jane Beagley, Vertebrate Publishing
Printed and bound by Novoprint SA, Barcelona

A CIP catalogue record for this book is available from The British Library

ISBN 978-0-9569309-8-9

Front cover: Climbing the Castle on Janukhot during the British attempt
of 2014. The peak was finally climbed in 2018, as described in this issue
of the Alpine Journal. *(Simon Yearsley)*

Endpapers
Front: Micha Rinn high on the schist prow at the top of *Perfect Storm*,
on the Miage face of Mont Blanc, proving that if you look hard enough,
there are still amazing new routes to climb even on famous mountains.
(Simon Richardson)
Back: Looking out from the tent at the second bivy during the first ascent
of the north-ridge and north face of Latok I. From left to right: Ogre II,
Ogre I and in the distance in the centre of the image the Kunyang Chhish
massif. *(Tom Livingstone)*

Foreword

If the past, as L P Hartley[1] wrote, is a foreign country, where people do things differently, then the future is an undiscovered continent. No doubt people there will also do things differently, and it's tempting to wonder what alpinists fifty years in the future will make of the bizarre photograph that appeared in newspapers and on television all over the world this May, of a long, snaking queue on the summit ridge of Everest. Will they be appalled that such things were allowed? Or will they simply see it as a step along the road to a wholly commercialised mountain? Perhaps by then there will be a pressurised cable car or funicular, an easy way down for those tourists who still bother to walk to the top, much as climbers now rely on the cable car at the Aiguille du Midi in the Mont Blanc range. Perhaps 2019 will seem a more innocent age, where life was simpler.

It wasn't just Everest attracting negative headlines. News that guiding companies want to place bolts and ladders on K2 to safeguard paying clients also caused alarm, at least among mountaineers, since the story didn't get anything like the same public attention. This infrastructure would take the rocky ground left of the infamous bottleneck of K2, which is over-hung by enormous seracs. This was where Fritz Wiessner went in 1939, when he almost climbed the mountain. Not surprisingly, plans for a K2 *via ferrata* raised concerns about the impact the growing high-altitude guiding industry is having on the ethics of the sport. It seems many more climbers these days are jugging fixed ropes than climbing for themselves; lacing the mountains in this way is proving lucrative for local expedition organisers, especially in Nepal. It seems pretty unarguable that while a few dozen alpinists are climbing in the Himalaya in great style, many more are using the tactics – and then some – more familiar from the era of siege expeditions.

Does this matter? The Matterhorn and other famous peaks have been compromised in some shape or form for the benefit of paying customers. More than a century ago, when developers were planning a railway to the summit of the Matterhorn, Martin Conway organised opposition through an English branch of the League for the Preservation of Swiss Scenery, which Edward Whymper joined. But Whymper refused to condemn the project publicly. For Whymper, it was for the Swiss, not outsiders, to decide what they did with their own country even though he deplored the idea and 'should look upon any Swiss concerned in such a proceeding with very much the same feeling of abhorrence as I should upon a person who murdered his mother for the sake of gain.'

Perhaps in the modern era we don't have the luxury of Whymper's *laisser faire*. Another observation that climbers of the future might make about

---

1. Leslie Poles Hartley, whose career offers hope to late flourishers everywhere, was named for the Club's president Leslie Stephen. Virginia Woolf loathed him.

Everest in 2019 is the amount of snow and ice on the mountain, because it's practically certain there will soon be a lot less of it. As Jacques Morey and his co-authors explain in this year's *Alpine Journal*, global warming has stripped metres of glacier from the bottom of many popular routes in the Mont Blanc range; the same is happening in the Himalaya. Studded throughout this edition are references to the immense impact the changing climate is having in glaciated mountains around the world. Like it or not, climate breakdown is one of the hallmarks of our era. Fixed ropes, bottled oxygen, helicopter taxis: none of it feels like the correct response to this crisis. The ethical appeal of alpine style lies in self-reliance: in doing the most you can with as few resources as possible. That seems a better message for our age.

Happily, there is much to report in this edition of the *Alpine Journal* that shows the true spirit of alpinism is alive and kicking. Once again, it has been a pleasure to work with an amazing and wide range of writers and photographers, art historians and scientists, critics and correspondents, and above all climbers, who make this book what it is. I want to thank in particular Rod Smith, who as assistant editor takes care of the 'In Memoriam' section despite his many commitments. We are currently on the lookout for more regional correspondents to help transform the Area Notes, so if there is somewhere you'd like to write about, then please do get in touch.

Ed Douglas

Correction

In last year's article 'Challenging the Mountaineer's Gaze', there were errors in the references to W W Graham. Far from publishing 'no account of his exploits', Graham wrote several articles, including one for the *Alpine Journal* (vol XII, 1884). He did not sit out the monsoon, but was active in Garhwal, although quite what Graham did there is a matter of debate. And while it's correct Graham was blackballed from the Club, this happened in 1882 before his Himalayan expedition and he remained on good enough terms to contribute his article and information on his Alpine season a year later.

Contents

HISTORY

AREA NOTES & MEF

REVIEWS

IN MEMORIAM

ALPINE CLUB NOTES

This year's section frontispieces celebrate the bicentenary of John Ruskin's birth and include the seven John Ruskin works in the Alpine Club Collection.

High Asia

The Lyskamm from the Gornergrat
John Ruskin, 1844/49.
Watercolour and bodycolour. 17.1cm x 25.1cm.
Gifted to the Alpine Club by Charles Warren.

MALCOLM BASS

Janhukot

Paul Figg, Malcolm Bass and Guy Buckingham acclimatising on Kedar Dome.
(Guy Buckingham)

The road ends at Gangotri. Minibuses and taxis jostle for space to turn around or disgorge their passengers into the narrow street. It's a busy, lively place, full of the excited energy of Hindu pilgrims making the journey of their lifetime to the headwaters of the sacred Ganges. Some will be content to bathe and worship at the temple here, but many will start the long walk up the beautiful pine-scented track towards Gaumukh, the Cow's Mouth, where the river pours out from the snout of the Gangotri glacier.

Beyond Gaumukh the going gets rougher and the crowds thin out. But the well-watered meadow of Tapovan under the north face of Shivling is an ideal campsite, and will usually hold several clusters of tents: trekkers, spiritual seekers, yogis, gap-year backpackers and alpinists. The peaks around the lower third of the Gangotri glacier are, with good reason, well known and much climbed. Shivling, Meru, and the Bhagarathis are elegant in form, cast in good granite, with the odd shale band for spice, and accessible. Many great routes have been climbed here.

Follow the glacier upstream past Shivling though and the names, if they have names at all, become less well known, Kharkachund, Swachand and Mandani Parbat until, 35km from Gaumukh, the glacier ends in a beautiful cirque of distant, mysterious mountains. It's not unreasonable to say that the snowmelt from these peaks is the ultimate source of the Ganges. The four 7,000m summits of the Chaukhamba ('four pillars') massif make up

3

Ganga Aarti in Rishikesh on the journey up the Ganges. *(Guy Buckingham)*

most of this 16km horseshoe skyline and there are two un-named 6,000ers on the ridge. Janhukot (6805m) forms the northern end. Only three lines have been climbed from the Gangotri glacier on these mountains and only the summits of Chaukhamba I and II have been reached. Chaukhamba III has been climbed, unofficially and to just shy of the summit, from the other, south side.

It has taken my friends and I a long time to begin to understand how to climb in these mountains. Until last year I had been to the head of the Gangotri glacier three times and hadn't reached a summit. In 1995 Julian Clamp and I were at 6,300m on the north-west ridge of Chaukhamba I, completely overwhelmed by the enormity of our situation. Two weeks out from our base camp 25km down the glacier, overtired and underfed, and with lifelong friendships falling apart amongst the rest of the team down on the glacier, it was all too much for us. We turned and fled. But these mountains seared themselves into my memory. One peak in particular stood out: the elegant, unclimbed pyramid of Janhukot.

Also referred to as Jankuth or Januhut, Janhukot first came to the attention of mountaineers during the prolific 1938 Austrian expedition to the Garhwal led by Rudolf Schwarzgruber. They photographed but didn't attempt Janhukot. In 1989 Indian climbers Prashanta Roy, Atanu Chatterjee, Sushanta Majumder and Dibya Mukherjee made an attempt but I don't know how far they got. An Austrian team made an attempt on Janhukot in 2002 but heavy snowfall prevented them reaching the foot of the mountain.

In 1998 I was back on the upper Gangotri for an attempt on the west face of Swachand that ended the morning after Julian Clamp and I sat though a six-hour rock-fall bombardment at our second bivouac. Helpless and unprotected on a snow ledge we thought we were going to die. Three rocks ripped through the tent but, by some miracle, we survived. We climbed two pitches the next morning, then both of us burst into tears and we abseiled off.

Janhukot seen from the east from Meade's/Chaukhmaba col. The 2014 and 2018 descents dropped into the cwm on the left edge of the shot. *(Malcolm Bass)*

Yet I couldn't get the image of Janhukot out of my mind: there aren't many unclimbed, good-looking, granite peaks of 6,800m in the world. So in 2004 I organised an expedition to try and climb it. We went in the post-monsoon season and got hit by two heavy snowfalls. Trekking up the glacier was arduous and required snowshoes. Our New Zealand friends Pat Deavoll and Marty Beare climbed the broad couloir in the middle of the west face and reached the south ridge at about 6,500m, still a long way horizontally from the summit. Here Pat was struck down by severe altitude sickness, the only safe course being descent. Our long sojourn on the upper glacier hadn't done enough to acclimatise us. Paul Figg, Andy Brown and I reached about 5800m on the south-west buttress on the right-hand side of the face before the threat of more bad weather sent us scurrying back down. Then it dumped snow again and we only just managed to get our kit and ourselves back down from base camp.

By now Janhukot was attracting other suitors. Bryan Hylenski, Anindya Mukherjee and friends made attempts in 2010 and 2011 from the east side, where it is easier to gain the south ridge, but both attempts ground to a halt against the sustained difficulties of that ridge.

In 2014 I was back yet again with another veteran of the upper Gangotri, Simon Yearsley. By then we had learned enough to have a decent chance. We had worked out that we needed to acclimatise on the easy slopes of Kedar Dome just above base camp, and not head up the glacier until we were ready for the climb. We also knew that climbing there in spring means there is still enough consolidated snow on the glacier to ease the journey. What we still hadn't learned was how long the south ridge was.

We had a delightful trip. Going early in the year meant the range was quiet. We climbed well and the feeling of remoteness with just two of us 18km out from our base camp was exhilarating. But we made two mistakes. Having climbed the south-west buttress and reached the south ridge we went for the summit from a bivouac at about 6,300m, leaving our tent and sleeping bags. This was too far for one day. And we stayed right on the crest of the south ridge where steep mixed pitches in 'The Castle' at over 6,500m slowed us down. So evening came as we reached over 6,600m, with a lot of ridge between us and the top. We're comfortable climbing in the dark, but a strong evening wind sprang up. Exposed on the crest, we couldn't keep warm. So, wisely and sadly, we went down. By the time we got back to our

Paul and Malcolm on day two. *(Guy Buckingham)*

tent we were so cold that our thinking was slowed. I suffered some frostbite in fingers and thumbs. We were comfortable then, and still are today, that we made the right decision, but it was a painful one. Despite all the hard work and not getting to the top, this expedition in 2014 with Simon was one of the best trips of my life: two old friends doing something we love in a strange and wonderful place. On medical advice we drank a lot of rum on the journey home.

I can only get time off for long expeditions every other year, so it was 2016 before my thoughts turned back to Janhukot. One of my friends said: 'You climbed most of it didn't you? No point in going back now.' But that wasn't how I saw it. For me Greater Ranges alpinism is about reaching summits. Close isn't good enough. I knew that no matter how fulfilling our journey had been Simon and I had not climbed the mountain. The rum had worked: I had only lost a couple of millimetres off each thumb. I had hooked up with a super-psyched and highly experienced new climbing partner, mountaineering instructor Guy Buckingham, and we set our sights on Janhukut.

It was not to be. We learned Bryan Hylenski was renewing his campaign on the mountain, and that he and John Miller had already made arrangements for an attempt later that summer. So we let them get on with it, changed plans, and went to Himachal Pradesh. The winter of 2015-16 was unusually dry throughout the Himalaya, and consequently Bryan and John found Janhukot in terrible condition. The south-west buttress was bare rock so they attempted the Deavoll-Beare couloir but became the seventh team not to reach the summit.

In May 2018, Paul Figg and I were back at the beautiful Sundenvan base camp beneath the south face of Shivling. Guy had joined us and was revelling in the beauty of his first trip to the Garhwal; he had yet to experience the joys of the 18km approach to Janhukot. I have spent a lot of time at Sundenvan and it has become a place of great peace and joy for me. I love the slow pace of base-camp life, the long rambling conversations, the time to read and think, and the plentiful sleep. I love the sound of the wind and the distant roar of the cook-tent stove. Joining us on this trip was outdoor photographer, cameraman and back-country skier Hamish Frost. A good base camp is a place of physical and emotional warmth, a place of safety and rest, a haven in which to prepare for, and recover from, challenges up high. This was a good base camp. We were ably supported by our excellent liaison officer Vikram Ghiyal, sirdar Anoop Tamang, cook Santabir Sherpa, cook's assistant Hari Singh, and Pemba Sherpa who would support Hamish with the filming.

Good health is vital for successful expeditionary climbing, and we were lucky that the stomach bug that most of us caught only lasted a couple of days. Then the four Brits and Vikram acclimatised by spending two nights at increasing altitude on the convenient and gentle snow slopes of Kedar Dome. Our normal two-day post-acclimatisation rest was extended by a couple of days to let a period of bad weather pass. Then we were off.

Janhukot is not visible from base camp, and naturally Anoop and Vikram wanted to see the mountain we had all come so far to climb, so they joined us for the trip up the glacier. Hamish and Pemba planned to stay at the foot of Janhukot for a couple of days to film and take pictures. A light-hearted, holiday atmosphere prevailed as we trekked towards our mountain, with safety in numbers and the journey fresh and new for most of us. On the afternoon of the second day and three weeks into our trip, we finally saw Janhukot.

It looked good: the south-west buttress was well plastered in snow and ice. On previous attempts we had spent one or more days under the face scoping the line and watching for objective hazards. This time we had our evening meal, rested for a couple of hours, and set off at 1am on the half-hour walk up the subsidiary Maindani glacier to the foot of the route. This tactic had the advantage of reducing time away from the good food and lower altitude of base camp, but it meant we set off still rather weary from the approach.

There was no sign of a holiday atmosphere at 1am. This was more like a funeral march. The huge task ahead, the early hour, the darkness, and our tired legs dampened our spirits and we shuffled slowly along in silence. Hamish

Looking down at the Gangotri glacier from the second bivouac. *(Guy Buckingham)*

seemed the only one with any life in him as he dashed around filming.

'I feel fucked,' I said.

'Well, that's a great start,' Hamish replied.

As the snow slope steepened beneath the bergschrund we said goodbye to Hamish, leaving him filming our glacial plod. As the angle steepened my feeling of exhaustion grew. I wasn't feeling positive. 'If I can't walk up snow at 5,100m how am I going to be able to climb ice at 6,800m?' Then Guy led us over the bergschrund and everything changed.

A gusty wind was blowing as we began soloing up the lower part of the buttress, following ramp lines up and right. Waves of spindrift poured over us. Snow stung our faces. The world was reduced to the size of our headtorch beams. Our nervous systems began to crackle and spark as we became fully awake to the challenge. Dull leaden fatigue was replaced by energetic drive. Careful foot placements over loose rock ribs and trail break-ing in the deeper snow: at last we were climbing, exulting in the move-ment. Up and up we went as the sky lightened, although the west face itself remained in shadow. Although Janhukot is made of good, solid granite there is still some rock and icefall on the west face in the afternoon, and we wanted to be at the bivouac site that Simon and I had used in 2014 well before noon. This site, at about 5,800m, is well protected beneath an over-hang, and is off to one side, away from the main fall line of the buttress.

Then, as it became fully light, it became clear to me that I didn't know where we were. Guy, never having been here before, was calm about us being a bit lost. Paul had the excuse that he was last on the route 14 years earlier and couldn't really be expected to remember much. So it was all down to my fallible memory from fours years ago. Surely if we kept going upwards all would be well?

Paul Figg just below the summit. *(Malcolm Bass)*

A short abseil down from a rock rib into yet another gully shook my confidence further: we hadn't abseiled at any point whilst climbing the south-west buttress in 2014. The sun continued to rise and swing west but there was nothing else to do except keep climbing the easiest line. And as we turned a rock wall on the right, I recognised something: a place where Simon had stopped for a shit in 2014. We were on the right track and five minutes later I spotted the bivouac site. We were there at about 11am. I can't remember how we spent all those hours at the bivouac. Above, the route climbs a narrow gully, the fall line for anything from the top part of the buttress, so stopping before noon made sense. We were anyway satisfied with 700m of height-gain. Digging the ledge and setting up the rope system took some time, then I guess we cooked, dozed, chatted vaguely. I would have listened to an audiobook on my iPod for what prove to be the last time. Then we would have crammed into the tent and slept fitfully.

In the first dim light of morning we made horrible instant coffee then carefully dismantled the bivouac, stuffed everything into our packs, and roped up for climbing. But I wasn't careful enough. A small stuff sack went tumbling down the mountain: my headtorch, sunglasses, ordinary glasses, back-ups for my contact lenses, spare gloves, iPod and earplugs had all gone. I very nearly cried. I am badly short sighted and have a terror of not having spare optical aids with me. Luckily Guy had an extra torch, and I could wear my snow goggles against the sun. But nothing could replace my iPod, my most effective form of temporary escape. And without earplugs I would be defenceless against Paul's snoring; no wonder I was stressed. I asked to be excused from leading for a couple of pitches as I collected myself. I must have been in a bit of a state because the long-running, and well-deserved cascade of jokes about me dropping stuff on every big climb didn't start up again for at least another hour.

We didn't do very well on the second day. After I dropped my kit nothing further went wrong, and my morale rose again. But while we seemed to be climbing well enough, we just didn't make much upwards progress, nowhere near as much as Simon and I had on our last attempt. Hard grey ice wore us down and we ground to a halt at the first half-decent ledge we reached in the late afternoon at about 6,300m. It was a joy to sit in the warmth of the sun and gaze down at the glacier. The night in the tent was less enjoyable.

It is always a delight to reach the top of a shadowed face and emerge onto a sunlit ridge. At a stroke, your world doubles in size. And so it was on day three when we emerged at the top of the buttress onto the south ridge and into the morning sun. The ring of Chaukhamba peaks dominated our new vista. We sat down and allowed ourselves a brief pause before pressing on along the ridge. We still had a long way to go: the summit was over a kilometre away and 400m higher.

We stayed right on the crest. Icy sections of gently rising ridge alternated with steeper rocky sections through gendarmes. We passed the bivouac Simon and I had used in 2014 with no sign now that we had ever been there. We passed the point where the south-east ridge, the start of our planned descent, sweeps up to join the south ridge. Clouds bubbled up, as they did every afternoon, from the jungly foothills beyond the Chaukhamba skyline where bamboo shoots had saved Shipton and Tilman from starvation. But this afternoon the clouds didn't settle again as they usually did, instead advancing towards us, menacingly, obliterating first the Gangotri glacier, then the lower part of the south ridge. Lightning flashed in the cloud mass and the air grumbled. We were not in a good place to meet a storm, partway along a long horizontal section of sharp ridge. We dithered. I started leading us along the ridge to the potential safety of a rocky outcrop about 300m away, but suddenly felt we would be too slow to outrun the storm. So we turned tail and starting digging into the ridge crest but hit hard ice too soon; we would be too prominent if we stayed there.

So Guy, veteran of many miles of Swiss Alpine ridges, took the bit between his teeth, and pushed on to the sanctuary of that distant outcrop. Alas, there was no sanctuary to be found there but the clouds had luckily halted to the east of our ridge: some invisible force of meteorology holding them at bay. Even so, we still needed somewhere to sleep. Then a chance glance over the edge provided the answer. A rope's length down the west face, at the foot of the outcrop on which we stood was a bowl of snow the size of a basketball pitch. Its outer edge was 20m high and its base was perfectly flat. We abseiled gleefully down onto it, not even needing to stamp out the tent platform. Cupped safely here, harnesses and helmets off, we rested well and made plans for the summit the next day.

We were now just below the rocky cockscomb of The Castle, the feature that had forced our retreat in 2014. Our plan this time was to traverse the top of the west face about 100m below The Castle then cut up through some less steep rocks onto what we hoped was the final section of the south ridge leading to the summit. Before night fell we had spotted a gully leading from the end of the traverse up through these rocks and Guy took its picture. We were at 6,500m: 300m to gain.

It's 5am. I simultaneously register the alarm and the sound of snow on the tent. I peer out of the door to find thick cloud and heavy, wet snow. Which, incredibly at this altitude, turns into sleet and then rain. Rain at 6,500m! We can't head up in this: we'll get soaked and freeze. We are all tense. The possibility of another failure hangs in the air. The fear of being wet and cold at this height eats at us. The prospect of sitting it out crammed in this tiny tent is grim. We put off the decision till 7am at which time little has changed, except it's got a bit colder and rain has turned back to snow.

'It's just like Scotland.'

'At 6,500m though.'

'Yes, but still just like Scotland.'

'I'm turning back if I get wet.'

'I'm not sitting in this fucking tent all day.'

'It's just like Scotland.'

'It is.'

'Sod it. Let's go anyway.'

So we did. We crossed a bergschrund to leave the snow bowl and I led off across the traverse in what I hoped was the right direction, but the fog was so thick I was just guessing: it really was just like Scotland. We fumbled blindly on until the vague shapes of some cliffs appeared through the murk. There now seemed to be several gullies. We looked at the photo on Guy's camera then back at the vague shapes. It didn't help. We tried to match up features from the bright camera screen with miserable reality. They didn't match. Then the fog cleared and for a moment we thought we saw the ridge. Then all was grey again.

'I think it's that gully by the black striped wall.'

'Really?'

'Perhaps. I'm not sure.'

In the end I think we guessed.

The climbing in the gully was good. Rocky sidewalls offered gear placements. The steepest section was narrow so we could chimney up. We could only see half a rope's length ahead. We were moving very slowly now, with long pauses as we bent double to get our breath back. Something about the gully felt right but it could still terminate at a dead-end at any moment.

Descending the south ridge from the summit on evening of day four.
(Guy Buckingham)

If it did, would we have the energy to try another way? We became desperate that the gully would run up to ridge and kept shouting at the leader:

'What can you see? Does it go?'

'Don't know.'

The gully turned to the right and grew narrower. Surely it wouldn't close off now?

'Come up and see.'

We gathered at a small col, on the ridge. The Castle was below us. A beautiful snow crest ran up into the clouds. We moved together up this ridge. I fell through a cornice and my legs briefly dangled down the east face, which seemed unfair. Guy was leading at this point and he's much bigger than me. I was in the middle and carefully following his footsteps. Luckily my centre of gravity and, critically, my ice tools somehow remained above the break. The others didn't know I'd fallen until they heard me swearing with relief. Our hopes rose twice, and were twice dashed by false summits. Yet the third one somehow looked different. We stopped on a rocky promontory on the west side of the snow ridge. Forty metres of classically shaped snow ridge ran up to a point that might just be the summit. Guy and Paul kindly suggested that I, in recognition of my long service on this mountain, should lead us to that point. I took some ice screws and set off.

I stuck in an early ice screw to protect the belay, then climbed the steepening ridge till it grew icy at 25m and I felt the need for another screw, then another soon afterwards. Five metres to the high point: was it the summit?

Descending from the summit in the evening of the fourth day. The tent is visible in the snow bowl below the snow arête. *(Guy Buckingham)*

Thick clouds were blowing over the ridge, intermittently hiding Guy and Paul at the belay. I couldn't see beyond the highpoint until the very last moment. Then, finally, I saw the ridge drop steeply away. This was it. This was the summit. We'd made it. The wind was too strong for my words to carry, so I raised my arms in the classic victory salute, then made a two screw belay and brought Paul and Guy up.

We were still in a very serious situation. It was 5pm, an hour of daylight left. The altimeter read 6,822m, 17m higher that the official height. We were 23km away from and 2,300m above base camp and the nearest people. Our planned descent was to reverse the upper part of the south ridge before descending the east side of the mountain and the ridge would be no easier on the way back down. But I had a strong instinct that everything was going to be okay. Maybe it was partly the illusion of safety in numbers, more likely it came from well-founded confidence in the evident strength of the three of us as a team. We don't normally do summit hugs. The time to celebrate is when we are all safely down. This time we broke that rule.

As we started back down the ridge the high clouds finally parted and all the high peaks of the Garhwal were suddenly revealed. The glaciers and foothills remained shrouded in cloud but warm evening sunlight blessed the peaks. We were tired but not wrecked, our palatial campsite was only 300m below, and Guy had presciently made v-threads on the way up, so we were able to savour the moment, aware that nothing in our future alpine climbing might ever match it. I was slow and cautious down the ridge; with the adrenaline gone I felt like a premonition of the stumbling old man I will soon become. But then the abseils took us efficiently down through the darkness, and having retrieved Paul from the bergschrund above the snow bowl, we were soon all safely gathered in.

The next day, our last on the mountain, took us back down the south ridge to its junction with the south-east ridge. A few abseils down this, then down to the top of a broad gully on the east face, which we climbed down into the baking heat of the high eastern glacial basin. Sun-struck and still buzzing, we plodded down this, weaving around crevasses back to the Gangotri glacier. As the rush of joy from success and safety wore off, the long slog back round the toe of the south ridge to our tent on the glacier became purgatorial. In the five days that we had been away, the glacier had suffered horribly in the heat: pools of knee-deep slushy water and great cracks forming in its normally smooth surface. It made me sad to see my old friend so sick. These places we love will soon be gone. And what then will water the plains of northern India?

Even though it was only 3pm when we completed the circle and got to the tent that Hamish and Pemba had left for us, I was wasted and went straight to bed, stirring only to eat our last dehydrated meal. We all slept superbly that night. Next day we got up early again, hoping to complete most of the ice walk before the sun did much damage. But there hadn't been a freeze overnight, and we were sinking to our knees almost immediately. Guy had found new reserves of strength and sped on ahead, Paul and I stumbled along behind. It wasn't much fun, but we knew all we had to do was put one foot in front of the other and we would eventually make it back to base camp. Then, just before the worst part of the journey where the ice gives way to tottering piles of moraine, we saw them, four figures in the distance coming out way. Hamish, Pemba, Vikram, and Anoop, alerted by our Inreach text saying we were down, had come up from base camp to help us down the last few kilometres. With them they had bought *jeera* potatoes, fresh chapatis, Tang and chocolate. After a joyful reunion we sat on a boulder looking up the Gangotri glacier and ate too much, too fast. Then we stood up, shouldered the packs, and set off together back down the Ganges.

Acknowledgements
We would like to express our thanks to the Mount Everest Foundation, Rab UK, the Thomlinson Trust and the Montane Alpine Club Climbing Fund for financial and equipment support. Malcolm Bass is sponsored by Montane, Petzl, La Sportiva and Lyon Outdoor.

Summary
First ascent of Janhukot (6805m) Garhwal Himal, 3-7 June 2018 by Malcolm Bass, Guy Buckingham and Paul Figg via the south-west buttress to south ridge (3000m, ED, Scottish IV).

TOM LIVINGSTONE

Latok I

Aleš Česen, Tom Livingstone and Luka Stražar. *(Tom Livingstone)*

I have always wanted to 'go big' in the Himalaya. The idea of climbing a technical alpine route at high altitude enthralls me. When I was a young climber, I absorbed stories of bold climbers questing high into the unknown in the Greater Ranges. I knew these were the ultimate proving grounds, high-altitude climbing on impressive, remote mountains. Finally, this year, I thought it was time to find out just how much adventure they'd hold. And I hoped I wouldn't be found wanting.

Slovenian alpinists have a strong reputation. Straight-talking, quiet and solid climbers, they regularly climb hard alpine routes without any fuss. When Luka Stražar attended a BMC International Winter Meet in Scotland a few years ago, I shared a few beers and belays with him, although we never tied in together. We crossed paths in Europe and Alaska over the course of the following years and when he approached me in early 2018 with the idea of a trip to Pakistan, I readily agreed. With Aleš Česen we planned to trek up the Choktoi glacier in the Karakoram with the infamous Latok I (7145m) in mind.

Stuffing gear into duffle bags as we prepared for our Pakistan trip, I reflected on my journey to this point. As far back as 2010, while a student at Bangor University, I was climbing as much as possible. The relaxed life-style and proximity of brilliant trad climbing in Wales certainly helped my progress and I was permanently psyched. I enjoyed it all, from long days at Gogarth getting pumped high above the waves to classic ticks in the Llanberis Pass. Lectures were simply necessary short interruptions between parties, climbing and madcap adventures. We even got a chance to test the length of our climbing ropes on the notorious bridge swing.

After university, the world opened up and suddenly there weren't even short lecture breaks between climbing sessions. All day, every day, I could climb uninterrupted, and with a healthy level of ambition and enthusiasm my climbing prospered. I looked objectively at my ability and experience, identifying the areas where I was lacking. I became firm friends with the 'Gogarth grip': pumped forearms and a frazzled brain from fighting up a Gogarth route, which usually includes loose rock, steep climbing and a crashing sea.

I also climbed in the Alps, summer and winter. To stand beneath a 1,000m north face without bivy gear took a lot of self-belief. To look up at a technical pitch, with ice smears and tenuous hooks, was another test. I always took my time to rack up, mentally preparing for the battle ahead. I climbed with several strong partners, on classic routes like the *Walker Spur* and the *Pierre Allain* on the Petit Dru, both in winter. I explored the wild side of Mont Blanc, climbing *Divine Providence* on the Grand Pilier d'Angle. These routes were a sequence of progressively more demanding forays outside my comfort zone, each one a mental and physical test, each harder, longer and requiring more self-belief.

After every big trip, be it to Alaska, Patagonia or Canada, I always returned to the UK. Good friends and great climbing lured me back but between climbing in Scotland in winter and trad climbing in North Wales, I was grateful for how well these experiences prepared me for bigger mountains: fiddling in gear where others might not look and battling through storms in Scotland proved useful skills.

*

I travelled to Pakistan in July, my first visit to the Himalaya, meeting Aleš and Luka en route. After four days of walking through the barren, dusty Karakoram mountains, we finally rounded a corner of the glacier and saw our goal: Latok I. 'Oh shit,' I said, 'this is the real deal.' The scale blew me away. These mountains were the biggest objectives I'd ever seen. I could stack two of the mountains I'd climbed before into one of these: two Grandes Jorasses, or two Cerro Fitzroys. Routes were measured in days, not pitches. Luka and Aleš have climbed many times in the Greater Ranges, and I was grateful for their support and advice. The impressive mountains around our base camp needed little introduction: Latok I, II and III; the Ogre I and II: so many stories of epics, near misses, and endless days 'on the wall'.

Latok I's most famous feature is its north ridge. A huge, knuckled spine, it runs from the summit ridge all the way to the glacier 2,400m below. Its formidable reputation began in 1978, when four of history's best American alpinists, Jim Donini, Jeff Lowe, Michael and George Lowe spent

Above: Climbing at night for stable snow conditions, the team made rapid progress on day one. *(Tom Livingstone)*

Right: Luka Stražar leading on the first day. A lot of this ground was moderate ice where the trio could move together. *(Tom Livingstone)*

26 days on the ridge, climbing higher and higher, battling storms and mixed weather, only to retreat a few hundred metres below the summit. In the following 40 years, dozens of teams have tried to better their impressive effort, but without success.

In 2017, a team of three Russians endured a 15-day epic on the north ridge, suffering several storms and poor conditions. Two of the climbers had digits amputated due to frostbite. I knew my Slovenian friends were tough but thankfully we all agreed we didn't want any epics. 'I think there is a better way than the full north ridge,' Aleš said to me when I climbed with him and Luka in February, sampling Slovenian Alpine climbing. 'We should plan for seven days on the mountain,' Luka added. I agreed with their ideas and instantly we developed a strong partnership.

The day we arrived in base camp, two Russian teams started up the north ridge. We wished them luck but tried not to think about them as we acclimatised. We didn't want to be pressured into a decision and launch too early.

One of the Russian teams bailed after eight days but the other, comprising Alexander Gukov from the 2017 attempt and and Sergey Galuzanov, continued for 10 days, battling storms and deep snow, all whilst at nearly 7,000m. By then we were nervous for their safety, since they only had five days of food. We then watched from base camp as for several days in a row they made summit attempts. When they finally began their retreat Sergey fell to his death rappelling, leaving Alexander stranded at around 6,000m

without the means to descend. Impressively, Alexander survived a six-day storm, finally rescued on a long line by a Pakistani army helicopter on his 19th day on the mountain. When Alexander landed back on the glacier, Aleš said, 'I've never seen someone so close to death, but still alive.'

*

After this event, we debated our options. We were still motivated to attempt the route, but with a different style and on a different route to the Russians.

'Let's keep an open mind,' I said. 'We can start climbing without too much commitment.' We all agreed, and anxiously watched the forecast. A stable weather window looked to be arriving in a couple of days.

We left base camp on 5 August at 1am, bright stars creating a patchwork of light above. The north side of Latok I stood in total darkness, tall and ominous. As we soloed over the bergschrund, my pack pulling against my shoulders, I was absorbed solely in the white circle of light from my head-torch. I swung and kicked into chewy, soft ice, trying to be as efficient as possible. An enormous amount of climbing towered above my head but as the hours passed I focussed only on maintaining a steady rhythm and the white light in front of me. We bivied early that day, finding a small flat section in the notch of the north ridge safe from stone fall as the sun moved onto the face.

Aleš Česen route finding on complex terrain during the second day.
(Tom Livingstone)

Aleš Česen high on the face. *(Tom Livingstone)*

Left: Stražar and Česen at the second bivy, cut into a precarious snow mushroom. *(Tom Livingstone)*

The alarm chimed merrily on the second morning and together we start-ed the process of getting ready. The stove burst into life, then porridge, water and packing our bivy before I led us up and right, over ridges of snow and through deep runnels of ice. Our rack was the bare minimum: a few ice screws, cams, wires and pitons. We would simul-climb for a hundred metres or more and then quickly pitch harder sections. One stretch of the ridge required weaving and ducking under cornices and snow mushrooms, always wary of the threat above our heads. That night's bivy wasn't so comfortable, barely big enough for the three of us to lie down.

The third day took us higher up the north ridge and then we traversed rightwards, reaching the col on west of the summit on the fourth day. Luka led us silently over much of this ground, the rope arcing miles before the next screw. As we crested the col between the north and south sides of Latok I, we slumped into the snow, exhausted with the altitude. We'd reached over 6,500m and every step, every swing required more energy. Aleš led us as we side stepped across easy-angled snow on the south side until we all began to bonk, hanging from single ice-screw belays and breathing heavily.

We barely slept that night. Heavy spindrift and gusts rocked our single-skin tent continuously, and we frequently thumped its walls to shed snow as the hours of darkness crawled past and the sky brightened. Luka had

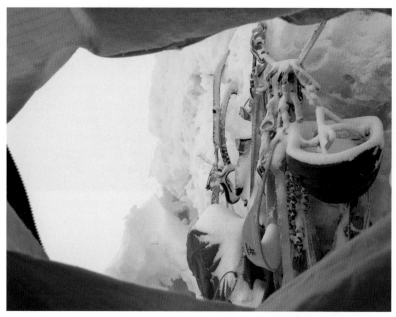

During the storm that almost turned the team back just 300m from the summit. *(Tom Livingstone)*

nearly been trapped on a mountain in Tibet a few years ago and was worried we'd have a repeat experience. All thoughts of the summit had gone and we simply debated, between heavy breaths, about how to get down.

By mid morning, however, the clouds had thinned and the summit only 300m above our bivy looked to be within reach again. Once more it was Luka who racked up and began kicking into the snow slope, ignoring the heavy spindrift avalanches tumbling down runnels either side of him. Aleš and I followed on the other end of the rope, exhausted, hypoxic, but determined. The wind-blown snow and clouds crashing over the summit felt more akin to Scotland, I reflected grimly. Except we were crossing the 7,000m mark in the Karakoram.

When I shuffled onto the summit cornice, taking my turn after Luka, I couldn't see the view because of racing clouds. But the satisfaction of being there was all I needed; the relief was absolute. Up until a few hours ago, I hadn't dared believe we could climb this mountain. It was such a monumental objective for us, and the biggest route I'd ever tried. I knew this point only marked halfway and that arriving safely back in base camp was our true goal. But right then, on the summit, I was totally content.

*

Livingstone leading high on the face. *(Aleš Česen)*

As always, the descent was a long and tiring experience. On the sixth day, we reversed our route back to the west col, and then dropped down towards the north ridge. Only at night, with the safety of colder temperatures, did we plunge down into the darkness, abseiling again and again from V-threads in the ice. I weighted each anchor with caution, watching it carefully, before sliding down the ropes, over and over and over again. Slowly, the sky began to brighten and we reached our first bivy, on the notch of the north ridge, just as the sun crept towards the horizon.

We slumped onto our bivy platform from the first evening, the roughly cut ledge still obvious in the snow, and lay there, faces turned to the imminent sunrise, waiting for warmth and light and relief. Aleš fell straight to sleep, Luka and I laughed as our brains exaggerated shapes and colours, the snow looking brighter and faces appearing in the lichenous patterns on the granite around us. After six days and six nights of concentration, hard physical effort, high altitude and abseiling through the previous night, it wasn't surprising we were exhausted.

Finally, the morning sun burst over the horizon, flooding us with heat. I felt the light prickle my cheeks and I wriggled my cold toes and for a few hours, we slipped into a deep, satisfied sleep for a few hours. The final 800m of abseiling back to the glacier could wait for a short while as we dreamed of base camp and home.

DAVE CUTHBERTSON & JOHN BARRY

Hagshu: Unfinished Business

The imposing north face of Hagshu climbed in late September 2014
by the Slovenian team Aleš Česen, Luka Lindič and Marko Prezelj.
Their line was just to the right of the left skyline, the last chapter
in a long story that began with Cuthbertson's story.

In the winter of 1986, I was halfway though my assessments to become
a mountain guide. Sitting in the Glenmore Lodge bar with my pal and
co-guide, Mike 'Woofer' Wooldridge, he made me an offer.

'JB and I are going to India to look for some missing friends. Do you
want to come?' John Barry was at that time principal of Plas y Brenin
in Capel Curig. Four young instructors from the outdoor centre, Mike's
brother Dave, Ian Kerr, Ian Fox and Steve Briggs were drastically late
coming home from an expedition to Kishtwar. They had seen a picture in
the *Alpine Journal* of a huge face on an unclimbed peak called Hagshu. The
four lads had gone lightweight, hired no porters, travelled discreetly and
aimed to climb in the best style. They had left few traces of their progress
through the villages of northern India. Due back in Wales in September,
by the start of October fears for their safety were growing. By November,
Mike and Ian Fox's brother Chris were making search arrangements with

help from British officials in Delhi. Their plan was to ski into the Hagshu area, by then heavily snowed up, to the hamlet of Abram, the closest habitation to Hagshu in the Zanskar valley.

Heavy snow now blocked the roads and vehicles, even trucks, would not be running. From notes found at the Brenin and overheard conversations, it was clear the four lads had been aware of travel restrictions due to any late-lying snow in early summer, so had decided to travel north by train to Jammu, hire trucks as far as the small town of Kishtwar and then walk in along the Chenab river, through Machail and Atholi, passing under Kishtwar Shivling, and then up the remote Hagshu Nullah. From the col of the same name, at the head of this vast valley, they would start looking for their mountain. Deep November snow made the ski search impossible and even getting to Atholi was a superb effort from Mike and Chris but to no avail. They returned bitterly disappointed without any news. Mike was now inviting me to help renew the search the following June, along with JB and Issie Inglis, ski instructor and all-round mountaineer, who was also working at the Brenin.

Assembling at Heathrow, we emerged from Indira Gandhi airport into the chaos and heat of Delhi, taking taxis to the home of the British military attaché in Delhi. John Pearson was open about our challenges, some bureaucratic, most logistical, but he had been a great help to the families so far, and official letters were given to us, so 'doors could be opened' if necessary. The Pearsons kindly looked after us as we made forays into the city for supplies, but then we had to leave the comfort of the embassy for the station, the dusty evening light making the maelstrom of people, cows, vehicles, bicycles even more surreal.

Travelling by train has always excited me, but this journey was something else and I don't think I slept much. In Jammu, we repacked our luggage and hired a truck for the next leg of our mission to Kishtwar, on the south side of the mountains. I hadn't really experienced this sort of expedition, journeying by truck over mountain passes, through valleys and small towns. It was really fascinating but unpredictable. The roads were really rough tracks suspended precariously above immense drops into deep valleys. Mud and broken-down vehicles created hazards for our driver, sometimes blocking the way. Watching locals replace a driveshaft on a truck, in the open at night, was incredible. These were resourceful people.

By morning we had pulled into Kishtwar. Along the way, at every opportunity, we had made enquiries about the missing men: had they been seen going through here? Did they talk to anyone about which way they were going? There was nothing to be gleaned: they had clearly been very discrete. We caught a crowded bus but were soon disappointed to be brought to a stop by an impassable section of the road. We unloaded the baggage, hired a few porters, and started our journey on foot along the Chenab. The powerful river, twisting and turning, gouging out the rocks and soil of its banks, was an amazing sight, but after three days, the novelty began to wear off. We turned north up a quieter tributary, glad to be free of the

constant roar beside us. At the police post at Machail, a friendly police officer called Abdul Magid showed us the record book, which clearly proved the lads had passed this way. Apart from that, there was no trace. Continuing along the river, we headed for Atholi, where we knew, from Mike's recce, a bridge would take us over the river to Suncham. Here our maps showed we would soon turn up the Hagshu valley.

At home, the families had done everything they could, even turning to a medium for clues. The medium claimed one of the lads was still alive and after seeing maps of the area, had pinpointed to a spot high up in a side valley, away from our intended route. There was no way we could ignore the prediction, and just before reaching Suncham, the valley lay before us. We had already agreed two of us would divert on a search mission, while the others would continue towards the Hagshu La. We hired a local man, who took his sheep up to this spot every summer for grazing. Issie and I followed him up a steep path for two days, bivouacking among trees. Eventually we reached the summer pasture, but found only a few stone walls.

There was no point lingering so we sped down and two days later were re-united with JB and Mike at the entry to the Hagshu Nullah. Here we found the remnants of winter snows, deep and soft. Our gang of porters were feeling exposed and weren't keen on continuing. We tried to keep them going, breaking trail sometimes in thigh-deep snow. The Hagshu La

Above: The expedition on its way to Hagshu, with Cuthbertson still smiling. *(Smiler Cuthbertson)*

Left: Trekking in Zanskar, nearing the Pensi La. Barry's interest in climbing Hagshu began with the mysterious disappearance of four Plas y Brenin instructors. The road was empty of traffic after an avalanche tragedy on the Zoji La. *(Smiler Cuthbertson)*

(c5300m) beckoned. Hopefully we would see the peak and perhaps some clue about the lads. Despite the snow it was very hot, the sun reflecting off into our faces. Several porters melted away, dropped their loads packs and returned down the valley. Even so, after two full days we made camp on the Hagshu La, pitching our tents in the early evening, disappointed not to be able to see much of our surroundings in the late afternoon cloud. A storm broke later but fortunately was short-lived.

Next morning it was still cloudy, but when I opened the zip of my tent, a group of what I took to be Zanskaris in the long maroon robes of monks were approaching the col from the far side in strange, winkle-picker-like shoes with the toes curled up and laced with what looked like straw. They passed our three tents in silence and vanished into the mists on the Kishtwar side, never to be seen again. After breakfast we searched around the col looking for clues, some sign that the boys had been here or where they might have gone.

It was hopeless. Snow was still falling slowly and softly from thick, cloudy skies and we had to admit, there was nothing to see here now. Next morning, the sun was out and we could at last observe our surroundings. On the south side of the col, a ridge led up to a rocky peak we now know is Chiring (6100m). On the north side, our views were obstructed by rock walls and ridges, but we knew Hagshu should be somewhere in this direction.

We couldn't be certain the lads had come this way at all. Had they approached their objective from a totally different place? It was a hopelessly huge area. We had scant information from the UK, and almost none here. We could only conjecture. Had they run out of time and decided to drop down into Zanskar? It would be a quicker way back to civilisation. At that time of the year, the road from running south from Kargil into the Zanskar valley would be free from snow. At Kargil you could turn east to Leh or west to Kashmir.

Without much hope of success, we continued north, descending for a couple of days to the Zanskar valley, cajoling our porters a little further through more soft snow and crossing dangerous rivers. It was tough going. On down the huge valley we went and then suddenly, turning a bend, we saw a wonderful sight a few kilometres up a side valley to the north. There it was, Hagshu, with its beautiful, icy north face glistening in the sun. Sitting there, taking it all in, we realised we now had a problem. Our time in India was running out and we didn't have the time or energy to get up that valley and anywhere near the foot of the face to continue the search. Reluctantly, we decided to continue down to the road junction, surmising that if the lads had followed our route, they too would have been short of time, and would, like us, have descended to the Zanskar valley and gone out that way. So there was still a chance we could learn something about their disappearance.

Dropping further down the valley, through more deep snow and still more river crossings, our journey was harder and longer than we imagined, so we were grateful to be pitching tents on flat, grassy ground, where stone walls surrounded a few solitary houses. This was Abram, also known as Hagshu village. The inhabitants comprised a couple of families, six adults and three children. They made us very welcome but had no news of any British climbers before us.

Next morning we discovered that no trucks had passed through Abram since the previous summer. We thought it strange and hired four of the local men from the village with their horses to carry the baggage. From the map, we could see we had to cross the Pensi La, our exit from Zanskar into Ladakh before crossing the famous Zoji La (3528m) into Kashmir. The prospect of a night on a houseboat beckoned before the night bus to Delhi. We figured on a maximum of a week's travel: it would take us 11 days. It didn't take us long to realise why. Approaching the Pensi La, we would regularly cross avalanche cones that had buried the road.

We trekked on for three days: or was it four? I was losing all sense of time. An old Zanskari soldier, also headed our way, tagged along; he was full of interesting conversation. At night he and his companions would slip away from our bivouac spot and return with masses of brushwood. Soon there would be a cheerful fire to huddle around. The Pensi La was heavily snowed up on the north side but clear on the south. Even so, there were no trucks and it took two more days before we turned a bend in the valley to see the famous landmark of Rangdum monastery perched on its knoll. As we approached we found a tiny one-roomed stone-built house occupied by a

Into Zanskar. *(Smiler Cuthbertson)*

little old man. He told us the monks were away. He offered us some tea but it was the salted butter variety and I found it difficult to get the liquid down despite a burning thirst.

Our route now lay over the Zoji La, but we heard of a terrible disaster there the previous autumn during a freak storm. Many trucks, buses and cars had been travelling in a convoy along the rough road above a huge gorge on the Kashmiri side of the pass. A truck broke down, stopping all vehicles, bumper to bumper. As repairs commenced, an avalanche poured down on the stationary vehicles, sweeping most them over the cliff and into the gorge. At least 80 people were killed. From the timing, if the lads had been involved they would have been at least a month late on leaving their base camp for the UK. That seemed unlikely but could it be true?

Our crossing of the pass was an eerie one. By now, seven months after the disaster, much of the debris had been removed but the snow still lay deep at the summit. We walked through deep channels cut a vehicle's width through the snow. A single JCB was at work and as we watched, it exposed the grill of a buried truck. Down below in the gorge, hundreds of feet lower, I could see a truck suspended in a clump of trees. We were relieved to drop down the hill and it wasn't long before we were clear of snow and were soon on our way to Srinagar in the back of a truck. We spent two days on a houseboat, replenishing our energy on Dal Lake, relishing the comfort but disappointed that we hadn't achieved much for the families. A tedious 29-hour bus journey, delayed by aggressive Indian troops looking for gun runners, delivered us back to the Pearson family for a lengthy debrief. Soon we were back at our day jobs, but seeds had been sown. It didn't take long before we were planning our return, to search once more for JB's friends and perhaps climb the huge face of Hagshu.

At this point, I'll leave JB to tell the story. His writing shames my meagre attempts. A version of this appeared in *A Passion for Mountains* (2014): essays written by British mountain guides and edited by the guide Hannah Burrows-Smith.

*

Some time in the 1980s, *writes John Barry*, the *Alpine Journal* published a black-and-white photo by Stephen Venables of a mountain in Zanskar. She was a beauty and virgin. She was called Hagshu. I showed the photo to four mates. They, much taken, convened at the pub that same evening for a planning conference. And 30 seconds later had decided to go, had it all figured; all over but the shouting. The shouting went on for some time after closing, became several decibels more vehement and, in as far as any remember, met with rather less accord. As these things often go.

They went to climb Hagshu. They never came back. Damndest thing you ever heard of. Searches were mounted. We found signatures at the police post at Machail and later a diary: bits of a tent; a lock of hair; scraps of clothing; a broken campsite; but nothing conclusive and never enough to hazard a narrative, or plausible explanation. The only thing for certain is that they'd disappeared.

It was on the search Smiler writes about that I saw Hagshu for the first time. This was no ordinary hill. It's about the best-looking bit of vertical geography on the planet. Ama Dablam, Alpamayo, Thamserku and the Matterhorn: contenders all, but no cigar. Hagshu's the mirror-on-the-wall fairest and unclimbed by any of a half-dozen possible lines. Or was then. What I saw, from a smart-ish potential base camp, rendered Venables' photo pedestrian. Here it was, now in glorious Kodachrome: a vision of primordial, pyramidal, near-equilateral splendour; a shimmering edifice; a wee stotter. And there and then I thought, maybe even said, 'Gotta have a go.' And by that face. Right there. In the middle. And straight on up the hey-diddle-diddle. Perverse perhaps, to call the disappearance of mates a beginning, but that's the start of this tale.

So began a pilgrimage, a mini-series of adventures, misadventures, scrapes and escapes and escapades, attempts, essays, farces, failures and fuck-ups such as you wouldn't credit. We gave it several goes, ardent suitors and fantasists that we were. Typhus did for us one go. Or typhoid, I forget. On another we ran out of gas, or maybe guts: mostly the same thing. This go was the best because we got it on. Except we didn't, quite. Went something like this. Don't recall the year. But it was Heathrow to Delhi by Aeroflot. Remember them? Went via Moscow, as they always did, and easily the most dangerous part of the entire trip.

The team was what may politely be termed eclectic. Let's hear it for

Smiler: pathological optimist, Pollyanna and Pangloss all rolled, somewhat untidily, into one. Nicest man you ever did meet. And, as the soubriquet hints, Smiler smiled. A lot. Near as damn it, a pretty much permanent, all-but-360-degree latitudinal grin circumnavigated his head in a wrap-round, enamel-plated wonder of the universe: the physical evidence of the Nir-vana-land of near-permanent optimism that The Smile's owner inhabited; a smile so wide that you wondered if there had at some stage been a surgical intervention. Except no surgeon could have wrought this blinding Colgate of physiognomy. Even better, all this was weather-proof. Indeed close to universally proof against all circumstance and human misfortune. Good man to have on a rainy day. The verbal manifestation of this pathology was a vocabulary of fantastical, of *surreal*, optimism, albeit limited in scope and variety. As far as Smiler was concerned, all humanity, all existence, the entire universe and beyond, anything and everything in the human register could be captured in two phrases, two phrases that served universal office for all of mankind's existential and lexical needs. They were: 'Grite!' (For 'great': he's a Brummie.) That was pretty much standard; covered 90% of everything and would certainly embrace mere inconveniences like flood, contagion, plague, disease, avalanche or sundry cluster-fuck. An impressive span, I think you'll agree. If things were better than that, for example if it wasn't raining or he wasn't broke, then things were 'fockin' grite'. The sophist or pedant might describe this as a simplistic view of the universe: a limited take on the complexities of the human condition. The generous might argue that to smile in permanent defiance of all reason is a gift to humanity and – yep – Smiler is a gift to humanity.

Then there was Jan, Jan-the-Crow. (Don't ask.) An old (both senses) Marine mate, he was a fellow traveller in more madness and scrapes than you could shake a fist, stick, cudgel, blowpipe, boomerang, spear, pistol, rifle, 105mm howitzer or anti-aircraft missile at, and Jan had up-close-and-personal acquaintance with all of those. He is possessed of, some might say 'by', what is probably the finest criminal mind in Europe. Had he been Russian he would by now be a billionaire oligarch. He'd own a Premier League club, or all of them, and be paying barristers zillions to sort out his byzantine affairs and *affaires*. But he Devon, so it was Plymouth Argyle on Saturdays and Diamond Lil's of an evening. Bad-est twinkling-eyed man you ever did meet. Also nails. Also as kindly and as generous as Christ-mas. Far as I can judge the history of it, he won the Falklands back all but single-handed, returning be-medalled and be-trophied, of which trophies pride-of-place goes to a brand-new Mercedes that Jan liberated from some Argentinian general in Stanley the day after the surrender, acquired with a cheeky, 'General, I am the victor, you the vanquished. Out: you won't be needing this anymore.'

That's the 'we' of this tale. Good team to have around; to be around; to be part of.

There was a four-hour delay to our flight from Moscow, time we invested in an excursion to the bar. All the other passengers seemed to have beaten

The idyllic base camp below Hagshu. *(Smiler Cuthbertson)*

us to it, as well as the crew. The passengers were drunk. All of them. So too the crew: all of the crew. The bar went 'Wild East', the full Vladivostok, in less time than it takes to order, 'Tri vodka, pazhalsta'. This is what it must have been like when all those dodgy billion-dollar gas and utility deals were going down the other side of Siberia. Here at the bar I'm not sure if it was supply and demand, or demand and supply, novel concepts to a Russian at that time, but booze flowed freely and was consumed apace. Glasnost looked distant then.

Somehow we got to Delhi alive unbeaten and with throats unslit, both skills in which Jan was an expert. Next day was Delhi to Jammu by train and then on to fabled Srinagar, ignoring, as always, dire FCO warnings. (Note to climbers: always ignore FCO advice. It is mostly alarmist and usually wrong.) After hitching a lift on a Leh-bound truck we crossed the Zoji La to Kargil and two lorry-top days later we rolled into Zanskar, a place as wild, remote, beautiful, and brutally hospitable as anywhere on earth. We disembarked at Abring, leaving the Sikh driver and his mate balancing a primus and an enormous pressure cooker on his knees. And on top of the pressure cooker, a large rock blocked the pressure valve: no effete, western safety-culture nonsense for these boys. They bounced on down to Padam cooking breakfast, a movable, if precarious, feast, while we scouted round for some likely lads to porter, and after some time had, by sign and histrionic, recruited a couple of very likely lads, and a yak and two ponies. (An LO may have been handy, but we were unofficial, illegal and skimping.)

Nearby a Genghis-lookalike farmer toiled to till a barren dry-stone-walled field. He and we apprehended each other with quizzical regard. We were contemplating survival on the vertical: a thing, a game, of utter irrelevance, because we could. He contemplated a hardscrabble struggle on the horizontal: a thing, no game, of existential imperative because he had no choice. Not for the first time the metaphysics of mountaineering sat uneasily on my western conscience: the philosophical bollocks of it all.

It had started to snow and was late. We'd go tomorrow. We asked the farmer if he'd mind if we pitched our tent by a wall that afforded some shelter from the storm. He insisted that we slept inside, in his parlour, by his fire. We spread our cushioned mats on the mud floor, a little humbled and slightly embarrassed by our host's hospitality as we nestled into our riches of soft pile and pneumatic down. Come morning, we found ourselves alone in the house, to discover the entire family, hubby, missus and a couple of kids, outside in the yard in a snowstorm all huddled under the same yak skin and a foot of snow. Seemed they had wanted to give us westerners some privacy. I tried to imagine the roles reversed in Snowdonia. Next day, first parade, we loaded up, saddled up, booted up and headed up to re-find that potential base camp I'd spotted on our search. We ambled under cobalt skies and alongside a silver stream and talked of bear and of snow leopard.

Towards the end of the second day we found it. 'Potential?' Check the thesaurus for synonyms for idyll: paradise, Avalon, Nirvana, Shangri La. This camp was all these and more. Add any superlative takes your fancy and you don't come close. This was veriest heaven: grass; sky; mountains; a stream; tent-spaces football-field flat; boulders baby-bum smooth for lounging. If heaven is half as fine as this I'd better start minding my manners. This was a place to spend time: to spend your *last* time. And in no time we had our camp, two tents and a tarp in our very own Elysium. And there, up the road apiece, was Hagshu.

At dawn she was luminescent, by dusk luminous. If you had commissioned Rodin to do you a mountain this is what you'd have got, but only if he was on form. She wore a come-hither look. The faecal wasteland that is Everest wears an only-if-you-can-afford-me-and-can-stand-the-stink look. K2, an if-you-got-the-balls look. Where Everest acquiesces, Hagshu winks. Where K2 threatens, Hagshu beckons, flaunts. And whereas Everest exacts its toll in treasure, and K2 in blood, all Hagshu wants is a flirt, and a two-step. If you can step the measure you get to climb. When folk ask 'Why do you climb?' I show them pictures of Hagshu and of that base camp. If that doesn't do it, then there's no point: nothing will. Hagshu, as Jan's Janner has it, is 'proper job'.

Perhaps it's not a great hill. To be a great hill, a mountain must, I think, inspire fear, or awe. Everest is not a great hill, except in the narrow sense of dimension. K2 is. It holds the cards and knows it. Inspires fear and knows it: has you grasping and gasping for excuses. Everest has you grasping for your bus pass. No one goes to K2 lightly; you go as a cortege. The world goes to Everest as the world goes on holiday. You do Everest; K2 does you. To stand at Concordia and gaze at K2 is to look into your soul and to ask, 'Do I have it?' And then to doubt that you do. To stand at Tengpoche and gaze at Everest is to be a tourist. To stand at our little base camp was simply to be privileged. Our pristine, unspoilt little beauty up the road stirred frisson rather than fear.

A couple of days and a reconnaissance later we assembled at the foot of the north face under an unavoidable, slightly overhanging and doubt-fuelling bergschrund, loins girded, tooled up, psyched up, geometrically central and plumb-bound on a line that would have met with Signor Comici's or any surveyor's approval: slap bang on the isosceles median from bottom to top. The first 30ft – okay, make that 20ft – consumed all but about two of my entire stock of calories. By the application, somehow, of three axes, I got, somehow, onto the face proper. Some start. Twenty-and-a-bit feet of three-thousand-and-quite-a-bit-more and I'm already knackered.

From here we went arrow-straight for the summit. There can few things finer than having an unclimbed Himalayan face to yourself. The not knowing what's round the corner, not knowing if the next three feet, never mind the next three thousand, are possible. Not knowing if you can climb the next three feet, which is not the same thing. Not knowing where the next breather lies, or belay waits. Not knowing if this is madness, if this is, indeed, your last time: all that accumulating uncertainty draining, drip, drip, your well of courage. I love that timeless moment when you are out front and trying to hold the line: Blake's 'holding infinity in the palm of your hand and eternity in an hour.' You are Vitruvian man, four-square and spread-eagled and grasping at the farthest corners of a world of a *graffito impasto* of snow on rock, a spanning of all of the universe, or the only bit of it that matters to you, that being those few feet to your immediate front. Anything more than an inch below your feet is history: done, dispensed with. Anything more than an inch above your reach is future, maybe even tomorrow and you hope you have a tomorrow. And framed and bounded by the span of your spread-eagle the world, your world, climbs with you, move by move, inches by inches, while below Zanskar waits and whispers, 'That a man's reach should exceed his grasp – or what's a heaven for?'

We fought the hard yards, cruised the easy ones; grabbed, galloped, gambolled, gavotted and gambled – and won. Made mighty height. Pitch followed pitch with little drama beyond the sheer, unalloyed, naked, 100%-proof exhilaration of it all. Sure, we got lucky but, this day, we were good. We were shining.

Little drama that is, except maybe this: towards the end of the day I was bringing up Smiler. The pitch had been a full rope length and about Scottish V with next to no gear: a mind-concentrator; a soul-searcher. Smiler seemed – I couldn't see him – to be making good progress. Then, of a sudden, the rope went tight, as in 'Smiler plus big-hill paraphernalia' tight. The belay was good, or I wouldn't be telling you this, and all held fast. A little later, as he pulled over onto the stance all teeth and perma-grin, I waited for some comment, some remark, word, perhaps, of a slip. After all, a fall from a Himalayan north face is not exactly the quotidian stuff of a weekend's crag-

First view of Hagshu. *(Smiler Cuthbertson)*

ging and must surely earn a token acknowledgement. I examined his face
for some betrayal, and in its absence asked:
  'You come off mate?'
  There was a pause, and the smile widened to an aperture-dazzling blinder.
  'Took a flyer mite. ... Fockin' grite!'
  It was now dark and past bivy-time. There was a prow of rock stuck out
proud like the bows of a battleship. It offered possibilities, not much more.
We plundered those possibilities, arranging ourselves about the prow, Smiler
and me either side, and an uncomplaining Jan, (personal code: 'never, ever
whinge') bent round the bow like a ship's fender. Nowhere was the ledge
more than two-foot wide, but pegged and pitoned we were safe if not comfy.
Charles Blondin acrobatics with the stove allowed a cuppa. Then sleep.
Sort of.
  Dawn. More stove balancing and more tea. Do we procrastinate? You
bet. Bravado's gone absent. There's a collective afraid-ness. We procrastinate for several cuppas more and then, tea-fortified and courage collectively
screwed to the sticking place, we go at it for day two. Lines of faith are
followed and faith finds good fortune. (Amazing, though, how tortuous a
direct line can be.) No banter at all now. Work to be done. I led; Jan led;
Smiler led. We lead all three, a mutualisation of afraid-ness.
  But if we got no banter we got gusto. And gusto's sometimes worth a
foot; and a foot is sometimes the difference between up and down, done or
dead. The force is with us again and we go like a train. Hagshu, she doesn't
lie. We get lucky every pitch. Couloir leads to corner, leads to snow slope,
leads to pitch of mixed, leads to buttress, leads to couloir. I won't claim it's

Under the north face. *(Smiler Cuthbertson)*

seamless but it goes. Sometimes it goes all Tommy-Cooper-ish 'jus'-like-that'; sometimes it goes only with a liberal dab of gusto. But always it goes. Always there's a hold, an unlocking move that works, a slice of rock that surrenders, an axe-compliant chunk of ice, an accommodating splodge of snow and always a belay and something, if only vestigial, to tie to. You can call it high-mountain savvy. Or you can call it luck. Let's call it luck.

'Round there, mate.'
'Traverse right, mate.'
'Over there by the crack, mate.'
'Fuck that!'
'Cracked it! Fockin' grite!' (Guess who?)
'I'm knackered. About time we bivied.'
'Don't look great bivy ground.'
'There's always one.'
'Well you find the bugger. Smart-arse.'
'This'll do.'

Cut for an hour and get a feet-over-the-edge ledge, and a peg and a nut and a screw for a three abreast-ish, beggars-can't, needs-must bivy. Eat something. Guzzle tea. Ponder the stars and the madness beyond and think of – Jeez! What is it exactly that you think of? And sleep. Sort of.

A snowflake! There's times when to be awoken by a snowflake's lover-like

Smiler, still smiling, belays John Barry across the bergschrund. *(Smiler Cuthbertson)*

The straightforward initial pitches of Hagshu's north face. *(Smiler Cuthbertson)*

nose-tweak would be the sweetest awakening imaginable. But here it fell some way short of a cuddle. I half-woke from a half-sleep. It was snowing lightly. I dozed. Now it was snowing heavily. I dozed. Now it was heaving down in torrents of spindrift avalanches, channelled straight through our bivy by some monstrous conspiracy of fate, weather and geology. Windy too. Spent the rest of the night shedding increasing accretions of snow. Words shared are few. Each is lost in his own unspoken, unspeakable anxiety. Anyway what was there to say? Grim for one is grim for all.

Some semi-conscious huddling time later, a starless black night dawned a reluctant day of undifferentiated grey. I dug for the stove and, against all odds, got it going. The night before, a star-spangled Zanskar had been a thousand feet beneath us. Now it was nowhere to be seen. I was aware of Jan stirring: the ritual shedding of snow, the punching outwards from the inside of a still zippered bivy-bag. Snow in a sleeping bag is a wet bag, and a wet bag is white-flag time. There was a tentative unzipping, a hand carefully brushing, a nose sniffing and Jan appeared on the end of the nose.

A council-of-war ensued. We had plenty of fuel and fuel is water and water is life. Some food. But you can go hungry as long as you don't go thirsty. Let's sit it out until tomorrow. There followed a long, doing-nothing day and the hopeless piling of hope on hope. And then into a second night, morale sustained by brew and biscuit.

John Barry leading steeper ground.
(Smiler Cuthbertson)

Avalanche! Smiler, who like us all, is cocooned and over-the-head-zippered in his bivy-bag, is swept off our half ledge by all-invading snow in a spluttering, thrashing, Dervish-desperate dance. Banshee yells jerk us from our half-sleep. There's no sign of Smiler, but inchoate exhortation tells us he is somewhere below. We find him in a torch beam and drag him up by the anchor ropes, still fully mummified, get his head out, dust him off, administer encouragement and a biscuit and restore him, worryingly damp, badly shaken and re-zippered to his bivy spot. He's unhappy. Sure as hell he wasn't smiling.

By morning all hope was fled. I woke, if, that is, I had slept, to a continuing maelstrom. As I coaxed the stove, Jan rolled over and from the depths of his bag began the mountaineer's reveille snow-shedding ritual. At last a face appeared cowled like a monk by his red bivy bag. He made a big show of scanning the horizon, which was all of a foot away. The situation asked for few words. There was no longer any hope of up and not much of down. It was hard to see how things could be worse. While I struggled for something semi-heroic to say, fumbled for words that might pass into posterity as something less than abjectly craven, Jan, with shrugged insouciance, an interminable dramatic pause, and with the affected resignation of a man about to down the first pint of a summer's evening at the local, uttered a spectacularly laconic, incongruent, insanely chirpy and faux-philosophical:

'Yer matey, s'nodda a *bad* o' loif.'

Where he found the spirit is an enduring mystery and source of wonder. Zeno and his Stoic mates might have approved. Retreat was the unspoken and unsolicited call. We packed as desperate men pack and set up an abseil. I went first. At times like this it takes less courage to be the messenger. As I prepared to step into the void, I remembered the words of mock encouragement of a sergeant instructor on my first night jump 20 years back when learning how to parachute from Her Majesty's aeroplanes.

'Gentlemen. Night jumps: piece of duff. Like jumping from nothing into fuck all.'

We knew that today 'fuck all' was Zanskar somewhere beneath, but it could have as well been the moon. Here at least we had gravity on our side.

We threw the ropes to wind and void, unable to see little beyond their first 10ft. Where had they gone? Where would they take us? Would there be a stance at their end? Or anywhere in between? Or an anchor? Then we abseiled, from nothing into … you got it. How many? Ten? Fifteen? Twenty? Who's counting? We'd know when we were down. It'd be flat. Once you can handle, but 10 times and you're running low on guts. But we were absurdly, beyond-deserving lucky. Abseil after abseil the ropes came compliantly down on first summons and without snag. And every time we found anchors to suit our dwindling hardware. Or a spike would volunteer. Something. Fifteen times equals miracle. Could be there is a god.

Some time toward evening we sensed ourselves on the lip of the bergschrund, the spot from which we'd set out in blithesome hope three days before. Now there was no anchor, or none that in our beaten state we could think to conjure and our supply of hardware was exhausted. We remembered it was 30ft feet. Or 20ft. Chucked our sacs over and on hearing no report prayed for feet of forgiving new snow, and on a count of one-two-three we jumped. Into and onto Zanskar. The landing was neck-deep and soft: never have three been so happy to be buried alive. We laughed like madmen. And Smiler said – well, you know what Smiler said. For once it was spot on.

So we get down, obviously. This isn't posthumous. A trudge back to base camp for a final night in a blizzard-besieged paradise, but paradise still, and then we're down the road, passing through Abring where the same farmer toiled. And I thought … Because he must … Because we can … The absurdity. The idiocy of it all, the sheer, unutterable daftness. I couldn't recall who said life is a great cosmic joke played on itself. But he had a point.

At the road a single half-cocked thumb stopped the first truck and we clambered atop and roared off toward Srinagar for a bath. I was still lost in the magical realism of it. That Marquez didn't know the half of it. But trying to make some sense of it as we settled into the rooftop box for the 20-hour trip across Zanskar, about to get twaddle-bound, Jan ushered in some sense.

'See-mate-I-told-'ee. S'nodd-a-bad-o-loif.' (Which may be transliterated as: 'See mate, I told you. It's not a bad old life'?)

The end? One day someone will. Someone may have. If not, it belongs now to the boldest: which ain't me any longer. A couple of grand, 30 seconds planning and some courage. Stand at the foot, look up, count to three and go. Go straight and do right by her. She never lied to us. And she let us off. As Jerry Lee nearly said, 'Hagshu? You broke my heart, you broke my will, but what a thrill.'

Bad weather trapped the team within striking distance of the top.
(Smiler Cuthbertson)

*

Smiler continues: The route has now been done, but maybe, only maybe now, I'll return one day. I often thought of calling JB and Jan to suggest: 'Let's have another crack?' Things (and life) got in the way. Hagshu became a dream unfinished. The alert we may have missed the boat came with news that Mick Fowler and Paul Ramsden were thinking about the unclimbed face as a project. Mick had seen Hagshu on one of his many trips and now, after some research, had decided it was time to try. They faced an unusual situation when too many permits were granted for Hagshu, all well documented in the *Alpine Journal*. Aleš Česen, Luka Lindič and Marko Prezelj, three excellent Slovenian climbers, were also intent on going for the north face. As is his nature, Mick avoided any conflict and they climbed Hagshu's north-east face, with the Slovenians achieving a two-day success on the north face a few days before. Looking at the photo of Aleš embarking on the steep ice, just above where JB, Jan and I had got to in 1990, shows what great climbers they are, doing the complete new route on the north face in one very long day, for which they were awarded the Piolet d'Or.

• Dave 'Smiler' Cuthbertson died after a short illness on 2 May 2019. His obituary appears on page 363.

West Nepal

Dom and Täschhorn from Zermatt
John Ruskin, 1844/49
Watercolour over pencil. 45cm x 50cm.
Victoria and Albert Museum.

JULIAN FREEMAN-ATTWOOD

Karnali Country

A Summary of Peaks over 6,000m on the Tibetan Frontier of Far North-west Nepal

Kaqur Kangri centre, Myung Thang Kang left and
Lalung right of centre from 6419m. *(Bruce Normand)*

Far west Nepal has, until recently, been the least explored area of the country or indeed of the Himalaya in general, with the exception of parts of Bhutan and Arunachal Pradesh, traditionally referred to as the Assam Himalaya. This overview, a guide for those interested in the mountain geography of far north-west Nepal, is confined to the border mountains of what was once the administrative Karnali Zone and is now, under Nepal's 2015 constitution, Karnali Pradesh: 'Karnali Country'. More specifically, it covers the Tibet-frontier districts of Mugu and Humla, collating what I've gleaned on 13 expeditions and journeys to Nepal's wild west.

It does not include Dolpo to the east of Mugu, or Jumla to the south, which includes Kanjiroba (6883m), visited in the 1960s by the prolific explorer John Tyson. Nor does it cover Darchula district, on Nepal's far western border with India and previously explored by Tyson and Bill Murray. Hereabouts lie the 7,000m peaks Api, climbed in 1960, and Saipal, climbed in 1963. Much more is known and has been written about these mountain areas than the Tibetan frontier peaks 30 miles or so further north: the subject of this article.

In total, along or close to this border, there are around 93 peaks over 6,000m of which, at time of writing, 33 have been climbed and 60 remain unclimbed. There are yet more peaks between 5,750m and 6,000, many of which are extremely interesting and often more technical than the higher peaks yet are so numerous that I haven't tried to enumerate them. I have also included some ranges, like the Nyalu, a little more distant from the frontier itself, and some of the *lekh*, a term used for alpine country that does not hold significant snow through the summer, unlike a *himal*.

All the mountains below are at present completely closed for climbing from the Tibetan side of the border. All heights, with some exceptions, are from the Finnish-Nepal government 1:50,000 map series and are in metres. I have confined the account of the region's climbing history, more or less, to first ascents or first attempts. I have used the Tibetan word *la* for a mountain pass rather than the Nepali equivalent. As it is largely a 'Bhotia' region, I thought this apt. But I have used the Nepali word *khola* for a river valley. I refer to Tibet, as opposed to China. To those who understand such matters, the reason is clear and intended as a mark of respect to the Tibetan people.

We begin on the western fringes of Dolpo near Mugu and continues west to Hilsa on the Tibet border, south of Gurla Mandhata (7694m) and the sacred sites of Lake Manasarovar and Kailas: a distance of about 225km. To access section one as below, the township of Gamgadhi is the jump-off point, now accessible by road, at least when isn't blocked by landslides, or by air in a STOL aircraft from Nepalgunj on the India border to Talcha airport, just 4km from beautiful Rara Lake, the largest in Nepal.

On foot, Gamgadhi to Mugu takes three and a half days following the Mugu Karnali Nadi, passing the confluence of the Namlan Nadi, which flows from Dolpo, at Tiyar. Further north and 6km south of Mugu village itself, the Mugu Khola meets the Chham Khola from the east. This valley gives access, none too easy, to the south side of the eastern Kanti Himal via the Chyargo La (5150m) and then the Yala La (5414m) of northern Dolpo. This is particularly wild country and the Chyargo La is only passable during the late monsoon or post monsoon. A longer journey would be from Shey Gompa to the south-east but that would certainly not be possible in early spring. Both sides of the Yala La are within Shey Phoksundo National Park, accessible via Shey Gompa and the airstrip at Juphal.

SECTION ONE: YALA LA TO KOJI LA

Kanti Himal
Known as the Rongla range in Tibet, this section of the Himalaya extends from the Yala La westwards to the Koji La (5495m), a distance of some 29km. In this sector three 6,000m peaks have been climbed but 14 remain unclimbed.

Just north of the Yala La on the Tibet frontier is Yara Chuli (6236m), unclimbed but now listed as open, although Nepal's tourism ministry includes it in the neighbouring Palchung Hamga Himal and suggests an approach from Shey. Ministry caravan routes should be treated with a large dose of

Section One: Yala La to Koji La.

Lalung Kangri on the left, 6293m centre and Yara Chuli from above the Yala La.

Close-up of south-west face of 6293m from near Yala La.

salt in remote regions. This sector is attainable from the Mugu side (from the west) by mule trail over the Chyargo La as mentioned above. The peak's Tibetan name is Sur Lung Kangri and it's located at 29°41'22"N 82°49'44"E.

Going west 2km from Yara Chuli is an unclimbed peak (6293m) on the true left bank of a major icefall descending from Tibet into Nepal's Chyandi Khola. On the true right bank of that glacier at 29°43'09"N 82°47'55"E is the unclimbed Changdi (6623m), Tibetan name Lalung. This should not to be confused with the Chandi Himal 100km further west. The Finnish map marks this peak as Chandi without a 'g'. Changdi, which is the official name, is an open peak and at present unclimbed. To access it from the south there is a formidable icefall to overcome. Routes on the south face look uninviting, but possible. The east ridge from the Tibet border above the icefall is certainly feasible if you can get there. Changdi/Lalung was first photographed from Tibet in 1997 by a Japanese expedition making a reconnaissance of the highest peak in the Rongla range: Kaqur Kangri (6859m),

Kaqur Kangri (6859m), 6095m and 6030m far right. *(Luke Hughes)*

which is a Tibetan name. This is the same peak as Zazi Kangri (Chinese) and Kanti (Nepali).

Yet before we get to Kaqur Kangri, which lies 4km north-west of Lalung, there is another unclimbed border peak on Nepal's 'open' list close to the west of Lalung and called Kaipuchonam (6329m). This peak is at 29°43'32"N 82°47'00"E. The Kaipuchonam Khola running up to it from the Chyandi Khola seems unexplored. Two more unclimbed 6,000m peaks (6093m and 6218m) form the border just east of Kaqur Kangri.

In October 2002, a Japanese team led by Toyoji Wada made the first ascent of Kaqur Kangri from the Tibet side via the east ridge. (This peak is incorrectly labelled Kubi Kangri on Google Earth. Kubi Kangri exists, but far to the west in the Changla Himal. It is also incorrectly labelled on Wikipedia.) Kaqur Kangri, called Kanti Himal in Nepali, is on Nepal's list but is quite technical and serious on the south side and remains unclimbed from Nepal. A recce was done by Sadao Yoshinaga's expedition in autumn 1998 but no safe route could be seen on the 1,800m south face.

A kilometre to the north-west of Kaqur Kangri is another unclimbed peak now on Nepal's open list called Myung Thang Kang (6449m). This peak is hard to reach from the Mayonithan Khola to the immediate south of Kaqur Kangri and is probably best approached from the Koji Khola, leading to the Koji La, further west.

West of Kaqur Kangri lie three not particularly prominent unclimbed 6,000m peaks. The most interesting peak (6014m) is on a promontory just a kilometre from Kaqur Kangri's 1,300m west face. The next permitted peak west of here is Takla Kang (6276m) 29°45'40"N 82°41'43"E. Again, the caravan route suggested by the Nepal ministry, via the Takla Khola, is convoluted and time-consuming. It is more accessible from the Koji Khola.

Kanti East (6516m) in foreground, Takla Kang centre left and 6273m fluted centre. *(Bruce Normand)*

Koji Kang North (6275m) on the left from the Koji La. *(Julian Freeman-Attwood)*

The border now runs a little north and north-east towards the Koji La. There is another prominent unclimbed peak (6273m) and after that two more unnamed peaks (6030m and 6095m). We then arrive at Koji Kang North (6275m), now on Nepal's open list and Koji South (6159m). These lie either side of the Koji La 29°49'35"N 82°42'52"E and were both climbed in 1997 by the Japanese led by Sadao Yoshinaga while hunting their route to Kaqur Kangri prior to its first ascent in 2002. The routes taken were obvious ones running up from the pass in respectively opposite directions.

The Koji La was an important trade route in old times between Mugu and the Changtang, the 'north country' of Tibet. It is now infrequently used except, we were told by smugglers. I led a trip to Mugu and the Koji Khola in 2007 with Luke Hughes, Nick Colton and Phil Wickens, trying to find a route on Rongla Kangri (see more on that peak below) and climbed a peak just under 6,000m near the pass leading into Tibet's upper Rongla glacier, which had not been visited before.

Section Two: Koji La to Namja La.

SECTION TWO: KOJI LA TO NAMJE LA

Kanti Himal

Following the border from the Koji La (5495m) to the Namje, or Namja La (4907m) is some 31km. This sector includes nine 6,000ers that have been climbed and three that remain unclimbed. The main valley route that serves all the peaks of the Koji Khola, the Kojichwa Khola and on up to the border at Namja La itself is the valley running north from Mugu village: the Namje Khola. All the main summits lie to the east of this khola, although to the immediate west at 29°44'46"N 82°28'20"E is a spectacular natural rock arch first photographed by Ed Douglas on our expedition in 2009. In 2018 a rock-climbing team led by Anna Torretta attempted to climb this arch but without success.

From the Koji La, the Tibet frontier runs north-west, then west and then back north. The major peak on this border close to the Koji La is Rongla Kangri (6647m). This peak gives its name to the whole range from the Tibetan point of view and its main summit lies completely within Tibet. I had thought I'd been given a permit for it from the Chinese in 2007, following a permit issue for a 7,000er in the Assam Himalaya, only to find Rongla Kangri was also refused. The mountain's south summit lies on the Nepal border and is itself now a permitted peak named Kanti East (6516m). The first ascent of both these peaks was made by Bruce Normand solo [*Editor's note:* Normand narrates his remarkable 2018 season on p70.] in November 2018 by a route on the Tibet basin side of Kanti East via its north-east face and from there by a linking ridge from the south summit to the main summit of Rongla Kangri. The next 6,000er on the border (6275m) was also climbed by Normand at the same time as Rongla. Immediately

South face of Kanti East (6516m)
on left with Koji Kang South on right.
(Julian Freeman-Attwood)

North-east, Tibet face of Kanti East
and Rongla Kangri (6647m) centre.
(Bruce Normand)

Rongla Kangri (6647m) centre far back and Kanti East in front of it. 6275m right
and Churau far right. Kojichwa South (6264m) in foreground. *(Mick Fowler)*

west again is a smaller unclimbed summit (6272m), followed by Churau
(6419m), Normand's next solo summit in November 2018, at 29°50'06"N
82°38'25"E. This is incorrectly named Kanti on the Finnish map, but this
name only pertains to the main peak Kanti, aka Kaqur Kangri, 15km east.

Any traveller continuing up the main Namja Khola past the entrance of
the Koji Khola arrives in only 3km to the entrance of another valley, the
Kojichwa Khola. This remarkable side valley has some serious objectives.
In October 2008 a Spanish team led by Alvarez and Fernandez tried to
climb Kojichwa Chuli via the Kojichuwa La (5550m) without success and
the following spring attempted Mugu Chuli, which they found too serious.
Julian Freeman-Attwood, with Ed Douglas and Nick Colton, had done a
recce into here in spring 2009 just after the Spanish and climbed a sub-
6,000m peak on the Khola's true right bank. Also on the true right bank at
29°49'10"N 82°36'59"E is a spectacular unclimbed peak (6047m) and then
another (6137m) about a kilometre to the north-east.

Mugu Chuli (6310) showing Fowler route and descent over Kojichwa South.
(Julian Freeman-Attwood)

6259m left and on the right 6047m in Kojichwa Khola. *(Julian Freeman-Attwood)*

After this recce, we showed Mick Fowler photos of a safe technical line on the north-west face of Mugu Chuli (6310m), some 3km further north again, which Fowler and Dave Turnbull climbed in 2011. Their descent was over a peak called Kojichwa South (6264m), also a first ascent and also now a permitted peak. These peaks could both be seen close up by Bruce Normand from Churau's summit. North again is another inspiring, unclimbed and unnamed mountain (6259m) before the last of this sector's 6,000ers, the permitted and unclimbed summit Kojichwa Chuli (6439m) which lies a kilometre to the north. was attempted via the north-west ridge by Ohnishi in 2009 but without success and again in 2010.

Section Three: Namja La to Kang La.

Between here and the Namje La is a ridge of no great interest, more or less part of the Tibet plateau with no peaks breaking the 6,000m mark. The nearest thing to it, 6km south of the pass, is a mountain called Kaptang (5965m). This is a permitted peak first climbed in 2009 by the prolific explorer Tomatsu Ohnishi with two others via the north face, prior to his attempt on Kojichwa Chuli as mentioned above.

The Namje La is much used by Tibetan and Bhotia traders, probably the busiest until you reach the Lapche La far to the west. The author saw sometimes 80 laden yaks in a single day arriving into Mugu in 2007. In those days, eight miles into Tibet, was an area trucks can get to where goods were transferred onto pack animals. Now vehicles can get as far as the pass, and some way down into Nepal but not all the way down to Mugu village, which at 3,000m is as low as yaks will go before returning over the pass. Below Mugu, mules, horses and laden sheep take over. This 'Bhotia line' extends across the southern side of the whole Himalaya, a cultural watershed between ethnic Tibetans and peoples from the south.

SECTION THREE: NAMJE LA TO KANG LA

From the Namje La (4907m) to Kang La (5358m), as the border goes, is 17km. In this sector, the Kangla Himal, there are two 6,000ers, both climbed, one of them not quite on the border. This is a wild area of the Tibet frontier oriented mostly east to west. The first reconnaissance was Yoshinaga's trip, following the recce of Kanti's south face. North of Mugu they trekked northwest into the Takya Khola and over a col (5100m) into the Gorakh watershed. They made a recce to the Kang La itself but did not go far into Gorakh Himal, travelling a short distance up the Kanla Khola. They then descended

Bhandar Lekh (6024m) centre background from Kang La. *(Julian Freeman-Attwood)*

Kangla Kang (6130m) from Kang La. *(Julian Freeman-Attwood)*

through the grazing grounds of Bholbihan to Nepka, the only significant village in the Take Khola. It seems they were the first foreigners into the village. Here the Take Khola becomes the Loti Karnali Nadi, which two days' trek downstream joins the ancient mule trail from Jumla to Simikot.

In the area just north of the 5,100m col mention above, there are two sub-6,000m peaks climbed by a German expedition (Christof Nettekoven, Nils Beste, Franz Friebel et al) in October 2017. They also went on to climb the one 6,000er in the Kangla Himal. These peaks were Sunkala Topi (5865m), their own name, and Lekh Fett (5767m).

Kangla Kang (6130m), named Pratibandhit Lekh by the German expedition, lies at 30°00'17"N 82°25'15"E. I had attempted to get to this peak in spring 2015 with Phil Bartlett, Nick Colton, Ed Douglas, Crag Jones and Skip Novak, but encountered the worst spring snow for at least a decade. We could get no further than the Bholbihan Khola before the Nepal earthquake happened and our Nepali crew needed to return to their families. In late May 2017, the author and party finally set up an advance base on the Kang La (5358m) and attempted the north-west ridge to 5,700m, defeated by endless poor weather, snow and wind. In autumn the same year, the German expedition succeeded and completed our route.

I have added within this Kangla sector, an extremely impressive peak called Bhandar Lekh (6024m) at 29°49'26"N 82°17'50"E. This is an unofficial name that appears on Google Earth and is unlikely to be the local name. This peak is east of the Loti Karnali Nadi and thus within this Namje La to Kang La sector. In December 2016 American climber Jack Bynum walked solo from Simikot without porter assistance via the Margor La to Nepka, the same route taken by the author in 2013, and on to a base camp at the foot of the mountain's north spur with c1700m of vertical interval to the summit. He soloed the peak, often exposed and quite technical, in three days and then traversed the mountain by rapping nearly 1,500m down the south-west face, landing back in the Loti Karnali Nadi, with the last two days without water due to lack of fuel. This was a very notable ascent.

SECTION FOUR: KANG LA TO BHOLBIHAN ICEFALL

From the Kang La (5358m) to the Bholbihan Icefall is around 18km and features the Gorakh Himal. In this sector there are five 6,000ers, none of them climbed. The Gorakh is the least accessible of the north-west *himal*, oriented north-west to south-east. There are two access points: one via the Kangla Khola, which only gets the traveller to one of the main summits, Gorakh Kang, and unlikely to yield a safe route to that peak. The other is via the Bholbihan Khola.

Starting at the Kang La the next border peak 2km west is Ngomodingding (6133m). It is unclimbed, not on the permitted list, and with a reasonable route only from the Tibet side. This has been referred to as Kangla II, but this is incorrect. The name is Tibetan and referred to by Sven Hedin during his Tibetan travels in 1906-8.

Some 4km further west is Gorakh Kang (6254m) at 30°02'46"N 82°20'04"E. It is unclimbed and on the permitted list. Whilst it gives its name to the range, it is by a short margin not the highest peak in the Gorakh Himal. Its Tibetan name is Absi, again mentioned by Hedin and visited, though not climbed, by the Japanese from the north during the Kubi Kangri expedition of 2007. As this peak is not accessible from Tibet, it would have to be tackled either via the icefall at the head of the Kangla Khola and then via the west face, or to the same west face via the Bholbihan Khola.

From this point onward, any peaks in the Gorakh Himal can only be

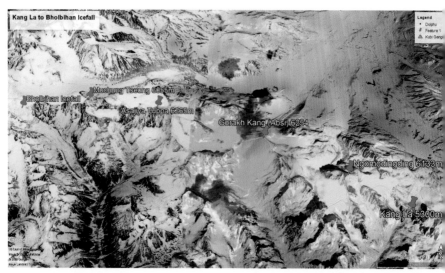

Section Four: Kang La to Bholbihan ice fall.

East face of Gorakh Kang (6254m) left
and Ngomo-dingding (6133m) centre.
(Christoph Nettekoven)

Assajya Tuppa (6265m) south face.
(Julian Freeman-Attwood)

Tibetan, north side of Absi, aka
Gorakh Kang. *(Atsushi Senda)*

accessed by way of the Bholbihan Khola. The author and others made the
first ever recce into the khola in 2013. The route to this and all points west of
here is from the airstrip at Simikot, also reached from Nepalgunj on STOL
aircraft. A trek down the Karnali and then a left turn into the Loti Karnali
Nadi brings you to Nepka village. We were the second party to visit Nepka
after Yoshinaga; it's an extremely poor region with few porters and those
that may be for hire are badly equipped. Simikot to Bholbihan with mules

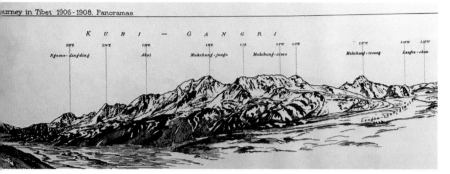

Sven Hedin's 1906 sketch map of main range Ngomo-dingding to Langtachen.

Mukchung Tseung (6088m). *(Julian Freeman-Attwood)*

is an eight-day trek through some fine primary forest, although it should be said that slash and burn deforestation is a real and continuing problem in Nepal whether in or out of a national park.

The problem here is that the Bholbihan Khola is impossible to access with mules, at least for the first mile and even with a few porters from Nepka the going was extremely taxing over boulders covered in lichen and roots and with thick thorn bushes. Once through, the valley opens out and is fairly easy going but wild. After 14km, you reach the snout of the Bholbihan glacier and at this base camp a 'cwm' opens to the north to give a view of the broad south face of the next 6,000er, and highest of the range, Assajya Tuppa (6265m). This is unclimbed and on the permitted list. Its Tibetan name is Mukchung-Jungu. There is a col at about 5,400m at the base of the east ridge, on the border, giving access to a glacial basin within Tibet that links with the col marking the head of the Kangla Khola mentioned earlier. From this border col Assajya and Gorakh could possibly be climbed.

Section Five: Bholbihan ice fall to Chang La.

Assajya has an unnamed west peak (6055m) and 2km on again is another peak (6088m) that I dubbed 'False' Gorakh, since it was incorrectly named Gorakh on some maps. Its Tibetan name is Mukchung-Tseung. This brings us to the Bholbihan Icefall and the west end of the Gorakh Himal and to east end of the Changla Himal.

SECTION FIVE: BHOLBIHAN ICEFALL TO CHANG LA

Between the Bholbiham Icefall and Chang La (5293) is some 38km of border and 15 unclimbed 6,000m peaks in the Changla Himal. Four more have had ascents. The two peaks immediately west of the icefall are firstly unnamed (6198m) and then Langtachen (6284m). Neither of these is on the permitted list and both are unclimbed. It would be a convoluted but feasible journey to get to Langtachen's north face, which is in Tibet, via the Bholbihan Icefall. Previously the author tried to get to the west face of the peak via the Lurupya Khola. This was reached more directly from Simikot via the lower Dojam Khola from where the rest of the Changla range is accessed. In 2012 myself, Ed Douglas, Nick Colton and Phil Bartlett entered the Lurupya, probably the most beautiful valley we had seen or visited in Nepal, heavily forested with great oaks, wild and magical. After some days this brought us to Langtachen's west face but were disappointed to find no reasonably safe or unthreatened route.

The whole of this section along the Changla Himal and the Chandi Himal further west comprise the headwaters of the Yarlung Tsangpo, which becomes the Brahmaputra as it flows from Tibet into India. Discovering the exact source of this mighty river impelled various foreign expeditions to roam south-west Tibet from the mid 1800s, and the approximate source

Top left: Langtachen (left) and 6198m from the Laruppya Khola.

Top right: View from Laruppya La to 5894m. (Julian Freeman-Attwood)

Above: South side of Gave Ding (6521m), British 2011 attempt to 6,000m right-hand ridge via couloir. (Ed Douglas)

Right: Fowler-Ramsden on Gave Ding from 2015.

Gave Ding north face. *(Mick Fowler)*

Kubi Kangri (6721m) from Tibet.
(Atsushi Senda)

was known by 1900. Sven Hedin accomplished perhaps the most scientific work in 1906 by measuring flows at the Kubi Tsangpo's confluence with the Chemayungdung Chu, some 12km north-west of present-day Larue township. Hedin found the largest flow was from the Kubi Tsangpo, originating in the Changla Himal, hence Kubi Kangri, which he named as the source of the Yarlung Tsangpo. Nevertheless, the Chemayungdung Chu, *chu* meaning water or stream, is longer by some 30km, originating in the Chandi Himal and the Angsi glacier, which is backed up by Tibetan tradition as the true source, which the Kubi Kangri glaciers are not. So despite its lesser flow, the Chemayungdung Chu is now the accepted source of the Yarlung Tsangpo, both by tradition and also for being the furthest point upstream from the Bay of Bengal. The most concise work on the whole matter, discussing whether a river's source is defined by length, flow, or tradition and which ultimately showed Hedin to be incorrect, was by the Indian ascetic and explorer Swami Pranavananda as a result of extensive travels in the region in 1936 and 1937.

The Changla Himal now bends north from Langtachen with the border passing over three unnamed and unclimbed 6,000ers (6202m, 6122m and 6223m) before landing on Gave Ding (6521m) at 30°07'32"N 82°09'56"E. A name given to another nearby peak by Hedin, Gave *Ting*, refers to another mountain just 4km to the east and entirely in Tibet. The Atsushi Senda map put the peak Gave *Ding* at the position given above. In 2011 Freeman-Attwood, Douglas and Colton made the first recce into the south fork of the Lachama Khola, off the Chwa Khola, the main drag to the Chang La and into Tibet. This south fork took them into unknown country to the south of Gave Ding. It also led them to a pass, the Lurupya La (5200m), which linked to the Lurupya Khola subsequently explored by them and mentioned above. They tried a route on Gave Ding's south ridge via a steep couloir gaining the ridge but were forced back by bad weather at around 6,000m. Mick Fowler and Paul Ramsden made the first ascent of Gave Ding in 2015 via the north face. This was, with Jack Bynum's climb, the most impressive done in the whole area to date and more technical than either Bynum's route or indeed Fowler's own fine route on Mugu Chuli, involving 1,500m of climbing over five days on steep mixed ground followed by a day of rap-

Gave Ding east summit and 6223m beyond from summit of Gave Ding with
Gave 'Ting' in centre across glacial basin. *(Mick Fowler)*

ping on V-threads virtually the whole way down. They rightly received the
Piolet d'Or for this climb. There is another quite distinct unclimbed peak
(6045m) forming a part of the long west ridge of Gave Ding.

The earliest visitors to the Lachama Khola and the north side of Gave
Ding were members of a Japanese women's expedition in 1983 whose goal
was the first ascent of Kubi Kangri (6721m), Nepali name Lachama Chuli
and Chinese name Kubi Dongdong. This is the second-highest peak along
the Tibet border in the scope of this article, after Kaqur Kangri. At that time,
Kubi Kangri was misidentified on earlier maps as Changla Peak, which is in
fact up near the Chang La itself. The Japanese were unsuccessful but it has
to be said the Nepal side of the range hereabouts is unrelentingly steep with
no obvious good routes.

Kubi Kangri's only ascent so far was in 2007 from the Tibet side, led by
Atsushi Senda. This is the trip that also made a recce of Langtachen and an
attempt on Absi. The ascent of Kubi Kangri was up a straightforward route
via the south-east face and east ridge and is now on Nepal's permitted list
along with its north peak Lachama North (6628m), still unclimbed. The
border carries on north for a kilometre to a prominent unnamed and unlisted peak (6581m).

From here to the important trading pass of Chang La, the peaks are all
unclimbed and difficult to access on the Nepal side, although easier on the
Tibet side. The problem is that there are very few good access points onto
the Tibet side. The border heads west, then north-west with seven unnamed
6,000ers: 6233m, a significant peak 6506m, followed by 6391m, 6122m,
6210m and 6133m, the latter at 30°13'29"N 82°07'39"E. The border is
then uninteresting for about 5km before passing over 6222m and landing
on Changla (6563m) itself, aka Chemayungdung Phu, and on finally to its

Section Six: Chwa Khola to Limi Valley.

distinct west summit (6162m). Changla was also first explored by the Japanese women's expedition of 1983 and then visited in autumn 1998 by Tomatsu Ohnishi. That year his team made the first ascent of Changla's west summit, which is the closest to the Changla pass. In late September 2010 another Japanese team led by Hirofumi Kobayashi with Seiya Naka-sukasa, Yuta Shibayama, and Naoki Yamaguchi reached the main summit via the north face and north-east ridge.

SECTION SIX: CHWA KHOLA TO LIMI VALLEY

The distance from Chwa Khola to Halji in the Limi valley is some 40km and comprises the Nyalu Lekh. In this sector are five climbed 6,000ers and 10 unclimbed.

We now diverge briefly from the Tibet frontier to look at the Nyalu Lekh and associated peaks running through the Nyalu La westward and beyond to Ardang on the south bank of the Limi valley. Geographically, if not polit-ically, this is the main Himalayan divide. It is truly arid and anywhere north of the Nyalu La 30°09'48"N 81°42'26"E is trans-Himalayan in character.

The closest 6,000er to the west of the Chwa Khola, approached via the Lor Khola, is a peak called Chhamsacka (6246m) at 30°06'01"N 82°55'27"E. It lies just 10 miles in a straight line north of Simikot and was photographed in 2011 from Gave Ding in the east by the author, who then did a recce of it from the west, via the Hepka Khola, in 2015. The first ascent was in autumn 2016 by Becky Coles and Simon Verspeak via a fine route on the east ridge. They found fixed rope and tent platforms from an earlier unknown attempt. They also found another name for this peak, Lasarmu La, although this sounds rather more like the pass to the north of the mountain running

Chhamsacka (6246m), aka Lasarmu La, from the east. *(Julian Freeman-Attwood)*

6098m on left and 6010m right. *(Paulo Groebel)*

Nyalu Kang (6265m) right and Nying Himal (6140m) left. *(Julian Freeman-Attwood)*

Nyalu Kang's north side left and Nying Himal on right from Aichyn. *(Paulo Groebel)*

into the Thanmuche Khola on the Hepka side. Be that as it may, immediately west of Chhamsacka is another fine mountain (6028m) that remains unclimbed. The Hepka Khola is the next valley west of Simikot, oriented north to south, and I was surprised nobody seems to have travelled further up it than Hepka village prior to 2015 when I made my reconnaissance. This khola would give access to 6028m and to the south side of the Nyalu Lekh itself.

6194m far left and 6010m far right from Nyalu La. *(Ed Douglas)*

Ardang's (6034m) north face with Limi valley below. *(Ed Douglas)*

The north side of Nyalu Lekh is much more glaciated then the south, has better climbing routes, and can be accessed in two ways: via the Nying La (5448m) at 30°13'29"/81°53'07", again from the Chwa Khola, thus going anti-clockwise from Simikot; or over the Nyalu La, thus going clockwise. Both approaches end up on the Nying glacier in the upper Nyalu Khola.

Looking south from the Nying La, you see peak 6065m, which a French team climbed by the south face in autumn 2018 and unofficially named Phasang. South from there are two unclimbed peaks: 6084m and 6022m.

At the east end of the main Nyalu Lekh ridge is another peak (6150m) and then Nyalu Lekh itself (6265m), the highest of the range. Some 2km west, Nying Himal (6140m) sits at the far west end of this group. All are unclimbed and unlisted.

There are three more unclimbed 6,000ers to the west of the Nyalu (Nying) glacier: 6098m, 6010m, and 6053m. The next peak (6194m) was climbed by the French team in 2018 via the west face and southwest ridge and was unofficially named Limi Koti.

The last two peaks accessed from here have both been climbed. These are just north of the Nyalu Khola. The first is Aichyn (6055m), aka Ashvin, which was first climbed by a Japanese team who made the first ascent in two groups in very early September 2015. French guide Paulo Grobel, who had already got to know this area well, was en route with his team to do just the same thing when they met the Japanese returning. Disappointed, they made the second ascent of the mountain via the west ridge just three weeks later. The day before, they made the first ascent of Aichyn North (6025m), only just south of the Chandi Himal, which features in section seven.

There is one 6,000er to the west of the Nyalu La: this is Ardang (6034m), aka Chyoro Ri, which is on the permitted list and as yet unclimbed. Again Paulo Grobel made a reconnaissance of the Phupharka peaks just west of the pass in 2013 and had wanted to climb Aichyn that year but was thwarted by heavy spring snow. Instead they headed across the Phupharka country and over into the Limi valley to Halji monastery and back. An interesting journey with an eye on climbing Ardang as well but bad weather persisted. In autumn 2017 Mark Bielby and Emily Ward attempted Ardang's north side without success but climbed a peak below 6,000 metres.

SECTION SEVEN: CHANG LA TO LAPCHE LA

We are back now on the Tibet frontier. The border between Chang La and the Lapche La is c40km and includes the Chandi Himal. There are two climbed 6,000ers here and nine that remain unclimbed. All this region is very dry, windy, trans-Himalayan and in essence the traveller is on the Tibet plateau, all of which lies at only a little less than 5,000m anywhere west of the Chang La or north of the Limi valley

In fact, Survey of India maps drawn in 1930 show the Tibet border from Changla to Nalakankar some 18km farther south than today's frontier, just where the Nyalu Lekh range lies. Yak herders in the Limi valley used to take their animals north for grazing. Early maps gave the name Changla to the mountain in the position of today's Kubi Kangri (that is, south of today's Changla) and Nalakankar to a peak in a position within the Takphu Himal (section eight), south of present-day Nalakankar as well. In 1961 the border demarcation agreed between China and Nepal drew the line farther north, and eventually Nepal opened two peaks to climbers along the frontier, with the new names Changla (section five) and Nalakankar, thus reinforcing that Nepal controlled access to this area and not the Chinese.

Continuing westward along the modern frontier, just west of Changla are two unclimbed unnamed 6,000ers (6030m and 6254m). The next peak is the highest in the Chandi Himal, not Chandi itself but Kananu Pukari (6256m), called Ganglung Kangri in Tibetan. Less than a kilometre south of it is another unnamed peak (6171m). Four kilometres west on the border is Chandi (6142m) itself at 30°21'33"N 81°57'05"E. This is on the permit list and is

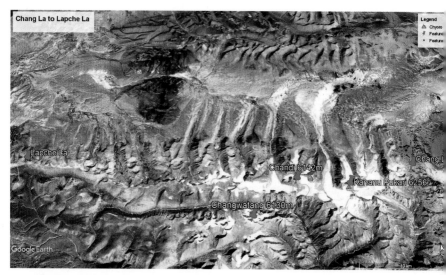

Section Seven: Chang La to Lapche La.

Kananu Pukari (6256m) left and Changla (6563m) far right. *(Paulo Groebel)*

Peaks from section seven: A is Changwatang, B is 5988m and C is 6022m in Chandi Himal. *(Guy Wilson)*

unclimbed, lying north of the Nin Khola, which runs parallel to the border. If we continue along the frontier there is an unnamed peak (6022m), a climbed peak (6024m) and finally 6069m and 6025m, the last 6,000ers on the border for the next 45km. In 2013 Guy Wilson and party from the UK climbed 6024m mentioned above. They also attempted 6069m unsuccessfully.

Just south of the border here and south of the Nin Khola is Changwatang (6130m), which is at 30°19'35"N 81°53'18"E and on the permit list. This peak lies only 4km north of Aichyn North climbed from the south by Paulo Grobel as previously mentioned. Ohnishi and party first climbed Changwatang in late June 2000 and it was again climbed in 2008 and 2011. There is an unnamed and unclimbed peak (6076m) 3km west of Changwathang and from here to the Lapche La is 25km.

Section Eight: Lapche La to Hilsa.

Til Kang (6369m) east face on left and Takphu Himal (6395m) right. *(Ed Douglas)*

SECTION EIGHT: LAPCHE LA TO HILSA

This final section, from the Lapche La (5018m) to the village of Hilsa is some 50km and includes the Nalakankar Himal, incorporating the sub-range of the Takphu Himal. In this sector there are 10 climbed 6,000ers and two that are unclimbed.

The Lapche La has a motorable track running over from the Tibet side and then south past the upper Limi Valley, over the Nyalu La and may soon link with Simikot. One day this road may in turn link with that at Gamgadhi. Whatever the pros and cons of roads, they will inevitably have an impact on remaining timber resources and ancient forest on the Nepal side of the Nyalu range. Whoever wins or loses with road building, and there are of course some of both, there is plenty of robust research on Himalayan

Takphu Himal left and Peak 2 (6521m) on right. *(Julian Freeman-Attwood)*   Til Kang's west face showing line of first ascent. *(Bruce Normand)*

roads that shows environmental degradation as a result.

From the Lapche La to the Nalakankar La, the most north-westerly point of Nepal and just 12km south of Manasarovar, is a distance of 25km. The border to this spot undulates in typical Tibetan plateau fashion at between 5,000m and 5,700m. After the Nalakankar La the border bends more or less due south and then after 8km there is a peak on the permitted list called Nalakankar (6062m) at 30°21'26"N 81°23'57"E climbed by Ohnishi in 2000 and described as easy. They also ascended Nalakankar South (6024m), a kilometre to the south.

The final group in this overview is the Takphu Himal, overall a part of the Nalakankar range.

If you also count peaks that lie entirely in Tibet but within this group as a whole, there are nine 6,000ers in the Takphu Himal. Starting in the north is Takphu North (6142m) and on permit list. The first ascent of this was by a German Alpine Club expedition in October 2016 that climbed the south-west ridge from the upper part of the Takphu North glacier.

The next 6000er is unnamed (6153m) and at the far back of the Takphu North glacier, with a linking col to Takphu North, climbed in the summer of 2016, just prior to the German expedition, by a Japanese team led by Tetsuji Otsue. The Japanese also climbed a peak (5920m) just to the east of the main col at the head of the Sakya glacier that leads over into the Syogan Khola and down to Til village in the Limi valley. Bruce Normand made the second ascent of the 6153m peak in October 2018, part of a British trip led by Julian Freeman-Attwood in October 2018 that climbed the following peaks to the south.

The next peak south is Takphu Himal (6395m) and on the permit list and climbed on 11 October by Bruce Normand, Ed Douglas, and Christoph Nettekoven by the west ridge from a col linking it to a peak in Tibet. This unnamed Tibet peak (6521m) is at 30°16'43"N 81°23'28"E, was climbed on 18 October, solo by Bruce Normand via the south-east face and with a descent to the same col mentioned above.

The next peak on the border, also on the permit list is Til Kang (6369m). This dominates the head of the valley from Til village and also dominates,

Normand's line climbed solo up Peak 1 (6613m). See also following article.
(Bruce Normand)

along with Takphu Himal, the head of the Sakya Khola. Til Kang was
climbed from the Tibet side on 15 October via the west spur by Bruce
Normand and Ed Douglas, who accessed the glacial basin at its foot via the
Sakya glacier and Sayogan col.

Following this ascent Bruce Normand made three more first ascents solo.
These included the west spur of 6422m, which is on the border and historically
referred to as Takphu's highest peak. It is only the highest if you are counting peaks on the frontier rather than in the group as a whole, which includes
Tibetan peaks. It is also the summit once called Nalakankar prior to map
changes referred to in section seven.

The highest in the group as a whole, also climbed by Bruce Normand,
is unnamed (6613m) and at 30°15'03"N 81°22'25"E, climbing it via the
north face from the glacial basin that dominates this side of the range.

There are two outlying unnamed peaks in this group (6042m and 6055m)
that lie away from the border to the north east of Takphu North. Nick Colton
and Attwood climbed 6055m at 30°20'12"N 81°26'54"E in October 2018.

South of 6422m, and on the border, is a named peak Kandumbu (6219m).
This is still unclimbed. Finally, there is one more unclimbed peak (c6180m)
within Tibet to the west of Kandumbu. The border now runs for 10km
inexorably downhill south-west to Hilsa (3640m) on the Karnali river,
one of the gateways for devotees visiting Kailas.

*The author would like to apologise in advance for any inaccuracies, or for inadver-
tently omitting the name of any persons, expeditions or explorations in the areas
involved.*

JULIAN FREEMAN-ATTWOOD
& BRUCE NORMAND

First Ascents in West Nepal

The east face of Til Kang above base camp in the Takphu Himal
in far north-western Nepal on the border with Tibet. *(Ed Douglas)*

The Takphu Himal, *writes Julian Attwood*, is a delightful knot of 6,000m
peaks in Nepal's extreme far west just 15km south of Gurla Mandhata
(7694m), which towers over holy Manasarovar in Tibet. The holy mountain
Kailas, sacred to Buddhists, Hindus and followers of Bon just a little further
north. My companions on this journey were Nick Colton, deputy CEO of
the British Mountaineering Council, Christof Nettekoven from Germany,
a mountain explorer and chronicler, writer and editor Ed Douglas, of this
parish, and last, but by no means least, the Scottish physicist and climber
Bruce Normand. Bruce has possibly made more first ascents of 6,000m
peaks than anyone alive and after this post-monsoon period on Takphu and
beyond that is even more likely to be true.

Takphu is best approached via the Nyalu La (5001m), which we reached
in late September after four days walking from Simikot with a mule train.
It would have been three except for the disappearance of our mules in the
Chungsa Khola. Until mules have crossed a threshold like the Nyalu La,
their thoughts are of home. Our mule drivers gave chase and eventually
found 14 of the 16 animals, meaning the others would carry a but more
weight, no doubt unhappy with the shirkers who bolted.

From Nyalu La, our route dropped into the Talun valley, at the top end
of the fabled Limi valley with its ancient monastery at Halji, founded in
the 11th century by Rinchen Zangpo, and another at Til. Our plan was to

The Karnali river, flowing south-east through Humla during the approach.
(Ed Douglas)

approach Takphu via the plateau above the Limi valley, rather than from Til or Halji down below. Previous expeditions in this area in 2008 and 2016 had been prevented by villagers from entering the mountains or fined on their return. Our route thus took us past the grazing grounds of Traktse and up onto plateau proper. Wild ass and Tibetan antelope were seen. On 6 October, some 100km from Simikot, we established base camp at 4,982m in front of a glacial lake near the terminus of the Sakya glacier. Local herders had already abandoned summer grazing and gone down to their villages in the Limi valley.

As detailed in the previous article 'Karnali Country', the frontier at Takphu is oriented north-south, and this group of peaks is part of the longer Nalakankar range that runs up to the Lapche La in the north and down to the township of Hilsa on the Karnali river in the south. Hilsa has become the main entry point for pilgrims, mostly Indians, to Kailas, following the earthquake that severed the Friendship Highway. For now, the only way to Kailas was via air to Simikot and then, since most Hindu pilgrims from India weren't about to walk five days to Hilsa, being ferried in a fleet of helicopters to the border.

Our arrival at base was greeted with snow and some wind. I had a filthy hacking cough that never left me on this trip. Straight in front of base camp was unclimbed Takphu Himal (6395m) on the right and Til Kang (6369m), for which we had a climbing permit, on the left. It seemed there was no safe way onto Til Kang from this side: a band of seracs threatened the whole of the east side above the true left bank of the Sakya glacier and the east ridge wasn't accessible. It looked like this peak needed to be tackled from

The fluted bulk of Saipal (7013m) on the south side of the Karnali, trekking north towards the Limi valley. *(Ed Douglas)*

the unseen Tibetan side, starting from a glacial basin we knew to exist there.

As for Takphu Himal, that could be accessed via the Sakya glacier and turning right into what I called the Takphu North glacier. This had been ascended twice before, first by the Japanese in 2016 and a month later by a German team. Their activities are detailed in the earlier article.

On 8 October, Bruce, Ed, and Christoph did a recce up the Takphu North glacier, scouting a route up Takphu Himal from a col linking that to another mountain we called P2 (6521m), a high peak within Tibet; three of the five peaks within this group were unnamed, hence the 'P' tags in the process Bruce made the second ascent of the previously climbed 6153m.

The weather was not at all the settled affair you might expect after the monsoon, with the mainly westerly airstream punctuated with a less settled south-westerly flow. It also was abnormally cold. While the others were on the Takphu North glacier, Nick and I, with me coughing and spluttering, headed north to recce a remote pair of peaks (see p69) and dump a tent and gear at about 5,400m by a small moraine lake. After a day back at base camp, Bruce, Ed, and Christoph set off back up the Takphu North glacier on 10 October. Meanwhile, Nick and I returned to and occupied our tent by the lake.

The following day was a cloud-scudding affair, cold and blustery, with visibility coming and going; one of those days that's too good to renege on a plan but too cold with the wind chill to have hands out of gloves for more than a moment. Nick and I had a fairly ruthless trudge of a climb, not technical at all but on one section surmounting some hideous scree and

Bruce Normand at the Nyalu La (5001m) and the start of a more Tibetan plateau landscape. For details of the peaks see top photo on p64. *(Ed Douglas)*

boulders, to get onto the south ridge of 6055m. There was no protection from a continuous south-west wind of perhaps 35 knots. We gained the rounded top in early afternoon and quickly headed down. Nick had slightly frost-nipped toes with his single-layer boots.

The others, meantime, had a hard slog from their tent in soft snow, taking some three hours to ascend 330m to the col at 6,130m below Takphu Himal. This brought them to the easy-angled west ridge, which they ascended in bad visibility. The top was reached about noon, and with no inclination to stay long they descended with some route-finding difficulty into their glacial basin and spent the night there, returning to base next day after a night of heavy snow. Christoph also had some frost damage to some toes.

After a rest day, Ed and Bruce started off for Til Kang on 14 October. The plan was to climb this mountain together and then Bruce might go on and solo what he could of the nearby Tibetan peaks. To reach the Tibetan glacial basin on the far, west side of Til Kang, they crossed the pass at the head of the Sakya glacier went over into the upper Sayogan Khola, keeping as much height as possible and traversing some tricky ground to camp at the Tibet border col at 5,700m. This col separates Til Kang, north of the col, from P3 (6422m) to the south of it. (P3 is the peak once called Nalakankar before the Nepal frontier was moved to the north and the name Nalakankar was applied to another summit on the new border. See p69.)

On 15 October they climbed the west spur of Til Kang, a little to the right of some large seracs. The route was serious rather than technical, mostly 45° to 55°, and they reached the top at 1.30pm. The weather remained cold,

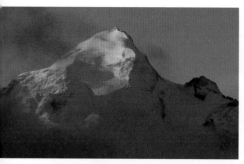

Close-up of the north face of Ardang, above the Limi valley. *(Ed Douglas)*

Bruce Normand setting out for Takphu, the peak on the right. *(Ed Douglas)*

Right: Ed Douglas and Christof Nettekoven on the summit ridge of Takphu with the elegant 'tuning fork' of P2 (6521m) behind. *(Bruce Normand)*

and now it was Ed's turn to sustain some frost damage. They both spent the night back at the col after a great effort. Ed returned next day to base while Bruce remained alone in the glacial basin, that morning heading south from the col to P1, the highest peak in the range (6613m), some 2km away. He climbed the peak by the north face, with some difficulties toward the top of the route. Views in the western distance included Nanda Devi in the Garhwal. The following day, 17 October, he climbed P1's neighbour P3 (6422m) and on 18 October mopped up the last of this tight group, Takphu Himal's neighbour P2 (6521m) before continuing on Takphu Himal itself, making the second ascent of the peak a week after the first. He then returned to his tent at the col and thence to base camp the following day. We had begun to get concerned but this had been a seriously fine effort by any standard: away for six days and out on a limb, alone in wild, high country. Even then he wasn't done, as Bruce himself now explains.

Sometime in 2015, *Bruce Normand writes*, I 'discovered' on Google Earth some unclimbed mid-6,000m border peaks going by the name Takphu Himal, in the furthest north-western corner of Nepal. At the time I was not convinced how attractive they were, given the long and expensive approach from Kathmandu, but I pointed them out to my friend Christof Nettekoven. Christof was excited, particularly that two of the Takphu peaks were on the Nepali Ministry of Tourism's permitted list and unclimbed: Til Kang (6369m) and Takphu Himal (6395m). It didn't escape my attention that the Takphu cirque contains three higher summits 6613m, 6521m and 6422m, the first two located on the Tibet side of the border. It hadn't escaped Christof's attention that British explorer Julian Freeman-Attwood seemed to have already visited every other valley in far west Nepal. So when when JFA contacted me in spring 2018 about something unrelated, I had to ask him about his autumn plans. Takphu, he said. To avoid disappointment all around,

To reach the west face of Til Kang, a day-long high traverse took Normand and Douglas around the base of the east and south aspects before climbing to a col in the upper right of this picture. *(Ed Douglas)*

I brought both sides together and a truce was arranged: Julian had the best logistics, Christof didn't have many committed people and I would come along as middleman. In the end, Julian's team consisted of old friends Nick Colton and Ed Douglas while Christof and I came alone, so five of us met around the JFA gear stash at the Marshyangdi Hotel in late September.

At our first expedition meeting, Julian's usual cook Prem became severely unwell, an apparent stomach illness that was soon properly diagnosed as a heart attack. With Prem recovering in hospital we were lucky in quickly finding a replacement, the irrepressible Ngima, who joined our sirdar Lhakpa. The three of us travelled by bus to Nepalgunj while the rest of the team flew, and we all left together for the 45-minute flight from Nepalgunj to Simikot. (There's a reason west Nepal is expensive.) In Simikot I was introduced to Rinjin Lama, a kind of all-powerful factotum, baggage-handling contractor, airport facilitator, guesthouse owner, *cuisinier,* warehousing specialist, kerosene and egg-dealer, and muleteer discipline enforcer. He knows everyone. Despite some of our gear barrels arriving two days late, Rinjin soon had everything on the road to catch us up with the minimum delay.

The weather was miserable when we arrived at base camp but next day we woke to crystal-clear views of the east faces of snowy Til Kang and rocky Takphu. Even so, I was on my own for a glacier recce. The two problems that plagued our expedition were coming into focus. One was that

'The cirque of the conquerables': Til Kang's west face is on the right, Takphu centre and P2 left, from the summit of P1. Normand climbed all these peaks, plus P3 out of shot, in four days. *(Bruce Normand)*

Ed had given us all some kind of flu, and while he, Christof and I largely recovered, Julian and Nick were laid low for the entire trip. The other was weather: Nepal post-monsoon usually has cloudless blue skies, mild winds, firm snow and icy glaciers but 2018 saw a cold, moist and unstable airflow throughout October. In the far west this exacerbated the results of a major snowfall that hit the Indian Himalaya in late September, piling up 60-80cm of loose snow on all our glaciers. I slogged around the slopes above base camp discovering this while a cloud wall hung persistently over Til, as it did for the rest of the month.

Christof, Ed and I aimed first for Takphu North, ploughing a deep track up the glacier behind Takphu, up its north side and onward to the summit 6153m. As would become standard, the winds got up during the day and clouds moved in to ensure a less than photogenic finish. However, we did get a decent view of the north-facing slope leading to the col between Takphu and P2 (6521m), which would be our route to Takphu. Two days later we were back with the gear and rations for a night out, re-ploughing our blown-in track to set a camp at 5800m. Next morning was sunny but windy, and since we were in deep shadow and deeper snow for three hours, the resulting deep freeze damaging everyone's toes. Reaching firm snow and weak sun at the col (6150m), we strode up the west ridge with renewed enthusiasm, grabbing photographs of the spectacular backdrop: Til Kang,

P3 (6422m), on left and P1 (6613m) centre, seen from above west face of Til Kang with Normand descending the easier summit slopes. *(Ed Douglas)*

P3 (6422m), P1 (6613m) and the triangular east face of P2. Unfortunately, the wind and cloud closed in, and the summit photos show a grey and miserable moment. We beat a hasty retreat to high camp, where joy at a first summit was tempered by numb-toe concerns and several hours of snowfall. The snow stopped but the wind blew all night, causing us yet another slog to get back to base camp.

Julian and Nick had been to their 6,000m top but realised they were exhausted by illness. Christof's numb toes bothered him enough to stop climbing too. Only Ed and I, who had damaged our toes enough before, were ready to tackle our other targets, which meant hiking around the south side of Til Kang to gain the glacier basin ringed by all five of our peaks. First we crossed the col (5300m) separating the Sakya Khola from the valley south of Til Kang that drops to the village, finding reasonable snow conditions for all but the last 100m before dropping into a deep, rocky basin. At the 5,000m contour we decided to traverse a ledge in a rock buttress, and after some scrambling and a strange rock 'tunnel' were rewarded with a route straight into the glacier basin below our target col. Some snow-covered moraine walls, several hundred metres of lower-angle but crusty snow and a final steep gully at nightfall brought us onto endless flat ground, where we dug our tents into a metre of powder.

Normand on Til Kang's summit with
P2 on left, Takphu Himal on right and
Gurla Mandhata (7694m) behind.
(Ed Douglas)

The Dhaulagiri range seen from
6265m during Normand's second
expedition of autumn 2018 to the
Rongla of Mugu district. For more
details of objectives in this area,
see 'Karnali Country', p45.
(Bruce Normand)

Next day dawned bright and stayed that way. From Takphu we had seen that the 'walk-up' option on Til was the 45° snow face beside the west ridge. Ed and I traded painful trail-breaking duties to the base of the face, where I took over with some major wallowing. Fortunately the snow became firmer as we climbed, until the upper half was fine firn and we topped out at 1.30pm to enjoy excellent views of Gurla Mandhata to the north, far beyond across the Tibetan plateau to the northeast, to India in the west and over the known and unknown ranges of Nepal to the south and east. This was certainly the finest panoramic day of the expedition but the stiff wind soon pushed us down again. Our glacier trail had blown in completely and following it was possibly harder than making a new one.

Next morning, Ed was finished and headed back to base camp. I aimed for P1 (6613m), which would have to be climbed by its north face, skirting a serac zone on its left side, traversing towards a rock band at 6,400m and finding a way through that to exit slopes. The day started trail breaking down the flat glacier and avoiding some minor crevasses. The lower face was in excellent condition and progress was rapid. Deeper snow around the serac zone persisted into the middle face but conditions were mostly fine and the snow firmed up as I approached the rock band. The gullies to the left appeared almost vertical for 20m, so I kept traversing until I found that the shortest gully section had a rock ridge on its left side. Launching up this, I found myself doing 10m of vertical ice, which, thanks to the rock, was quite easy to stem. The problem was the exit, which was loose 60° snow over looser blocks. A different descent would be needed and the slopes to my right looked more promising. I finished the last 200m on good snow, crossed the mini-cornice at its narrowest point and walked 200m up low-angle firn to the summit. The views were extensive, but again the wind was strong and high cloud had blown across the region, making the light disappointingly poor. On descent, I found excellent 50° with a couple of sideways steps over

The real Kubi Kangri range from Rongla. *(Bruce Normand)*

rock bands to avoid my vertical section. As some afternoon sun returned over P2 and Takphu, I regained the glacier with daylight to spare but once again the wind had blown my trail in. I was back at camp well after dark.

The following morning dawned grey but I was in fact under Til Kang's usual cloud and the sky was otherwise clear. I headed down the previous day's trail, now rock hard, to stop beneath the col between P3 and P1. A mix of good, firm going and shin-deep post-holing took me to the col, from where I traversed around to south-west-facing firn slopes before zig-zagging to the summit of P3. Once again the wind was up and high clouds were spoiling the light, if not the views. This time my trail on the glacier was still in excellent shape, making for a quick hike back to camp.

With one peak left to complete my quintet, I was out early and quickly descended my trail before crossing the glacier to gain the scree below of the south face of P2. After 200m of shale, I made good progress up 35° firn and ice slopes, except when compelled to take pictures and then warm up my hands in the cold wind. This stopped when my camera shutter jammed at 6,000m, denying me photos from what turned out to be the best day of all. Just as I reached the summit crest, the wind died completely. Here the snow was steep enough that a front-pointing traverse was required in places, but the summit had a minor flat spot in the otherwise knife-edge ridge. I continued along and down the low-angle summit crest, dropping into our col from a week earlier. Being at heart a Scottish-trained Munro-bagger, I used the beautiful afternoon to carry on up to Takphu and enjoy the experience this time. The 360° views were indeed excellent, but there is no photographic proof. This time I descended more good firn slopes on the south face of Takphu to reach the basin beneath Til Kang, needing to cross

Kaqur from 6430m. Chandi is on its right. *(Bruce Normand)*

only a few hundred metres of deep powder to reach windblown snow and then our old track under the west ridge. This worked quite well for a change, delivering me back to the col camp at dark.

Next morning there was little left to eat and no reason to hang around. Intermittent clouds and wind accompanied me as I dropped down from the col, across the snow slopes and through our rock-ledge traverse. I had to dig deep to find some energy to climb the 5,300m col, where the winds were again strong and cold, then found firm going in the windblown remains of our old prints all the way to the bottom of the glacier. The guys were delighted to have me back so that now we could go home. The muleteers had already arrived, a day ahead of schedule, and Julian put up a spare tent to save me drying and pitching mine in the dark. Next day we packed up and headed down the Sakya Khola, trading over the next five days the high plateau for snowy peaks, alpine forests and then the terraced fields lining the Karnali back to Simikot. In one big clean-up evening, Rinjin inherited a lot of used gear and unused food and next day saw us enjoying breakfast and lunch in Nepalgunj followed by dinner in Kathmandu.

Rongla Himal

I had plans for a mini-expedition after Takphu but a confluence of circumstances led to all three of my partners having to cancel, leaving me in Kathmandu fully acclimatised, fully alone and with four weeks to kill. This solo situation hadn't come as a complete surprise, and some Google un-Earthing had, even with the required margins of safety, revealed Rongla Kangri as a worthwhile target. Christof and Julian were quick to provide positive reinforcement. After a few days to round up paperwork, a few hours to work out the transport and a few minutes to pack what I could carry, on 31 October I headed on my way back west.

This second venture started with two and a half days on public buses: from Kathmandu to Surkhet to Manma and thence to Gamgadhi, with one total gearbox failure and two punctures spicing up the experience. My pack leaving Gamgadhi was about 25kg but given my agenda, the added complication of a porter seemed unwise. I set a conservative pace up the pretty canyon of the Mugu Karnali for two days, then on the third day the valley turned north and at Mugu village opened out into high pastures either side of the river. I found the grazing trail through a cedar forest up the Koji Khola and ended the fourth day at the lake at 5,000m directly below the Koji La.

Next day was one of partial rest, of moving my camp out of the howling wind and of visiting the Koji La (5470m). Despite this being an entirely off-limits crossing into Tibet, it sported quite a well-marked trail to the flat, icy glacier. The south face of Rongla was vertical, banded red rock and from a distance the entire cirque offered no obvious ascent routes. So in the morning I set off underneath the south-west face, planning to cross the west ridge and find out if a route could be followed up the north-west face. However, this ridge turned out to be vertical mud, so I returned to a valley fork and climbed the next peak west from Rongla. A glacier hike to 5,800m, a 400m face of 45° firn and 500m along the north-east ridge brought me to a summit I measured at 6,265m. The wind was moderate and the sky cloudless, affording spectacular views across both Tibet and Nepal. The north-west face of Rongla had a steep, rocky finish, so the south-east-facing cirque was going to need a more detailed inspection after all.

With the weather remaining excellent, I set off early next morning intending to summit that day. I met the sunrise on the Koji La and continued north-west. High-altitude cloud streamers started blowing by but evaporated again within two hours. The glacier flattened out and met the cliffs at 5,800m, but there was indeed an option on the far left side of the cirque: climbing 45° firn all the way to the top of the sub-peak Rongla South (6516m). From there I dropped about 75m down a low-angle ridge and then hiked up snow slopes to the true summit of Rongla Kangri (6647m) at 1.45pm. I was treated to views from Gurla Mandhata to Annapurna, far out over the red plateau of Tibet and across the jagged white carpet of Nepal.

The eighth day was a rest day, which turned cloudy and cold. For the ninth day I had considered climbing a peak above the southern wall of the Koji Khola, but I had no desire to push my soloing luck on north-facing snow-covered glaciers, as opposed to south-facing icy ones. Instead I climbed just high enough to recce Churau (6419m), the somewhat dramatic, double-peaked mountain west of 6265m. Then I moved my camp an hour down-valley. Sunrise next morning found me well on my way up, but a hidden glacier trench forced me to change plans from the direct south face to the east ridge. On another perfect but significantly windier day, I reached the ridge with only a little heavy trail-breaking then followed it over a sub-peak to a final 45° snow climb. The views once again stretched north-west across the many unclimbed border peaks and south to the Dhaulagiri massif. From this angle, several peaks in the Dolpo ranges were visible beyond the impressive Kaqur Kangri (6859m), reinforcing my earlier thoughts of giving these a closer look.

Day 11 brought cloud and snow showers on a strong wind and so I walked out to Mugu. This meant a 2,000m climb to cross into Upper Dolpo, and the canyon was unrelentingly steep. Locals were moving their families, animals and bags of a root-like plant down for the winter. Beyond the treeline it was cold and windy, and parts of the river were frozen completely solid. I no longer had the time or energy to get to the peaks east of Kaqur, nor did I have enough body-fat left to stay warm, even at 4,000m. On the thirteenth day I reached the Chyargo La (5150m) and stared across to Kaqur, Chandi Himal (6623m), aka Lalung Kangri, and the Upper Dolpo ranges, seeing no trace of a trail below me. Despite the attraction of the unknown, with three 6,000ers already under my belt and only three days of food left, this was clearly a target for a later expedition. I retraced my steps, arriving in Gamgadhi at the end of my fifteenth day out and spent the next 55 hours relaxing on another scenic bus tour back to Kathmandu.

Acknowledgements
The authors would like to thank the Mount Everest Foundation and British Mountaineering Council for their support in the Takphu Himal expedition. Bruce Normand thanks Julian Freeman-Attwood for the years of experience and logistical expertise that made the Takphu expedition possible.

Alps

The Mountains Opposite Vevey
John Ruskin, 1846?
Watercolour over pencil heightened with white. 15.5cm x 24.8cm.
Bequeathed to the Alpine Club Library by Charles Warren.

SIMON RICHARDSON

The Dream Traverse

Micha Rinn climbing the '6b crux' on the granite section during day three
of the first ascent of *Perfect Storm*. *(Simon Richardson)*

Dreams can be dangerous things I reflected, slowly making my way up the debris-strewn Miage glacier on the south side of Mont Blanc. Very dangerous, especially when the dream has been 25 years in the making. One hundred metres ahead of me Micha Rinn was making an excellent job of finding a way across the moraine-covered ice. The Miage is the longest glacier in Italy and the scenery was more reminiscent of the Karakoram than the Alps. Over 700m wide and hemmed in by the steep walls of the Aiguilles de la Tré la Tête and Punta Baretti the scale was huge with the summit slopes of Mont Blanc glistening with fresh snow 3,000m above. Our packs were heavy with food for five nights and the weather forecast was good for the next three days. I was nervous and apprehensive, but little did I know that we were heading for one of the most momentous climbing experiences of our lives.

I first passed this way in August 1993. Guy Muhlemann and I had climbed the Bonatti route on the Red Pillar of Brouillard, before continuing up the Brouillard ridge and bivouacking below the final slopes of Mont Blanc du Courmayeur. We arrived at the summit early next morning and left the crowds on the Bosses Arête on the descent to the Col de Bionnassay. The weather was perfect and our route was the grand finale to a superb couple of weeks of Alpine climbing that included a long desired ascent of the Walker Spur. We were fit, moving smoothly and felt completely at home in the mountains. Why did we have to go down? Wouldn't it be wonderful just to carry on climbing? And why go to the Greater Ranges when you can have long multi-day adventures on Mont Blanc itself? Ahead the east ridge of the Bionnassay beckoned, but instead we dropped off the col and headed down the Miage glacier to our car and the long drive back home to Scotland.

The dream of a Greater Ranges experience on Mont Blanc stayed with me, and I resolved that next time I climbed the mountain, I would not hurry back down. The logical extension was to traverse the Aiguille de Bionnassay and continue over the Dômes de Miage to Les Contamines. The big question was what ascent route to choose? For aesthetic reasons it had to be something on the Italian side. The Peuterey Integrale was the obvious choice but I was intrigued by the Miage face. Over 1,100m high, it is often referred to as the forgotten side of Mont Blanc, although there is good reason for its neglect. Apart from the Tournette Spur, which was the original route on the Italian side of the mountain, the other routes on the face are rather unappealing and threatened by huge seracs.

On the right side of the face however, there are three 700m pillars running up the west face of the Brouillard ridge. Similar to the better known Brouillard Pillars above the Eccles hut on the east flank of the crest, the upper third of the pillars transition from granite to schist. Incredibly, the left-hand pillar was first climbed by the Gugliermina brothers back in 1901. During their groundbreaking three-day expedition, they gained the untrodden Pointe Louis Amédée (4460m) and continued along the 2km Brouillard ridge to the summit of Mont Blanc. Their ascent has faded into obscurity: modern guidebooks credit the first traverse of the Brouillard ridge to Young,

Looking down to the Quintino Sella hut after the reconnaissance on day two of the west face of Pointe Louis Amédée. *(Micha Rinn)*

Jones, Blodig and Knubel who started from Col Emile Rey. But the Guglierminas had already traversed most of the ridge ten years before.

It was over 80 years before the pillars were visited again. In July 1983, Giancarlo Grassi climbed the prominent Red Pillar (TD-), the rightmost of the three, and the following April ascended the *Fanta Couloir* (TD), the deep cleft to its left. Grassi descended the *Fanta Couloir* after both these climbs. Two years later, the irrepressible Patrick Gabarrou ascended the prominent gully of *Lune de Miage* (TD) to the left of Guglierminas' pillar, and continued to the summit of Mont Blanc. Gabarrou was back in January 1989 to attempt the thin ice line to the right but retreated in a storm near the top. Although the route was incomplete it was called *Himalamiage* and graded ED1. As far as we knew, these climbs were unrepeated, and nobody had set foot on the face for over 29 years. Between these routes lay the untouched triangular central pillar. In some ways it is the most logical line of all, a tapering tower of granite leading to a slender prow of schist rising all the way to the summit of Pointe Louis Amédée. It was a priceless piece of real estate: a perfect unclimbed line high on the Italian side of Mont Blanc.

So what better than to combine this pillar with a traverse of the Brouillard ridge to the summit of Mont Blanc followed by a descent over the Bionnassay and Miage? I called the project the 'Dream Traverse' and had little difficulty in selling the idea to Micha Rinn from Germany. Micha and I had struck up a strong partnership in recent years with new routes in the Alps, Scotland and Canada, and I knew the plan would appeal to Micha's sense of adventure. We both knew that the Dream Traverse was an ambitious undertaking, and more difficult than anything we had done together before. It would demand a unique set of qualities: fitness, acclimatisation, snow-free conditions on the pillar and a long spell of settled weather. We reckoned that early August was the best time for an attempt, and the Dream Traverse became our focus for summer 2018. It was a bold plan, not least because we

Simon Richardson climbing the granite section of *Perfect Storm. (Micha Rinn)*

were putting all our climbing eggs into one basket and there were so many factors that could lead to failure. Fortunately, Tom Prentice was happy to help me out on the fitness and acclimatisation front, and during July we had two glorious weeks mountaineering in the Valais, climbing a multitude of 4,000ers. And Micha, as part of his instructor work for the German Alpine Club, acclimatised on the Goûter Ridge of Mont Blanc.

Planning is everything. Micha and I talked long and hard about the optimum tactics for the Dream Traverse. We estimated that with some inevitable bad weather along the way, the trip would take us seven to eight days. At first we thought that if we were trying to reproduce a Greater Ranges experience, we should avoid huts and take a tent. The advantage of a tent was that we could stop at any time, assuming we found somewhere to pitch it, but in the end we decided it was more practical to use bivouac huts. Only the Durier hut, situated between the Bionnassay and Miage, is guarded and offer any possibility of a meal or restocking supplies.

There's a good reason why nobody had been to the west face of Pointe Louis Amédée for nearly 30 years and as Micha and I branched off the Miage glacier early in the morning on 10 August we soon discovered it. Glacial retreat means access to the Quintino Sella refuge has become one of the most difficult approaches in the Alps. The 100-year-old bivouac hut is spectacularly positioned on a small ledge on a rocky spur 1,400m above the Miage glacier, but the problem is reaching the rocky spur itself. We had two choices: front point up the steep and chaotic lower glacier, or climb the spur from its foot. We chose the latter but were soon challenged by unprotected glacier-polished slabs of dirty schistose rock. Two long and lonely pitches eventually led to an exposed scramble up grass, rock and rubble, and eight hours later we arrived at the spectacularly positioned hut. Even though the refuge only receives three or four visits a year, a building team with helicopter support has recently restored it. A new roof and outside walls protect the original interior with graffiti by the Italian pioneers carefully preserved on the walls.

We had not seen our route close up, so next day we climbed the ugly glacial snout guarding access to the upper Mont Blanc glacier where we had a full view of the Miage face and Pointe Louis Amédée. The approach to the pillar is threatened by huge hanging seracs high on the face, but fortunately they did not look as dangerous as we feared, and there was only one icefall avalanche track across the glacier. Global warming, which is decimating the Alps at an alarming rate, had worked to our advantage and made the largest seracs recede. Across the glacier, our pillar looked enticing with fresh snow from the recent storm burning off in the mid-morning sun. A line of cracks ran up the right side of the granite section, but it was difficult to assess just how difficult the upper schist prow was going to be. It looked very steep, but we hoped that was an optical illusion.

Leaving the hut at 4am next morning, we crossed the bergschrund below the pillar at dawn. Awkward route finding over glacier-smoothed slabs slowed our momentum low down, but once we gained our line of cracks we made fast progress for 200m up stretches of perfect granite to where the angle steepened. I climbed a hanging groove and traversed left below an impending corner and handed over the rack. Micha, it must be said, is an excellent rock climber, so I was a little alarmed when he ground to a halt a few metres above, at the foot of a rounded and unprotected crack. He came down and silently I took the gear and started up a hidden groove to the right. It was steep and difficult to protect, but it was a typical British rock climbing pitch that weaved from left to right and accepted the odd wire or two. Above it was still steep, but the rock was more featured, and Micha shot up through an overhang and galloped up the wide cracks above. I joked that he had made the 6b crux pitch look easy, which was something of an exaggeration, but at least we were now moving again.

Pitch followed pitch, and as we climbed higher we had to dodge verglas and streaks of ice. By late afternoon we were hopping across snow patches to gain the upper schist prow. We were hoping this would not be as formidable as it looked and fortunately the rock was surprisingly solid and well furnished with holds. After six long pitches I found an abandoned pair of gloves and a series of abseil slings. We later discovered these originated from Gabarrou's descent after his *Himalamiage* attempt in 1989.

Near the top, the prow reared up in a 40m vertical headwall of impenetrable schist. It was without cracks and appeared to be unclimbable. Micha probed up to the right and ended up perched on a knife-edge ridge staring down into a black void. By now it was nearly dark and the wind had become very strong, so I had a look below the headwall and found a small, levelled rock platform. This was Gabarrou's high point and bivouac site, but exposed to the full force of the gale. A little lower we found a slightly more sheltered spot. I settled into a buttock-sized seat and Micha perched on a larger down-sloping ledge. In the howling wind there was no chance of melting snow so we burrowed deep into our sleeping bags and made the best of the situation.

The wind was worrying. We knew from the outset that we would not encounter eight perfect days, but the forecast had promised another 24 hours of good weather. This would allow us to complete the pillar, traverse the Brouillard ridge, climb over Mont Blanc and descend to the shelter of the Vallot hut. Micha had a tough night on his sloping ledge but I managed to sleep a little. Every time I woke I peered nervously through a crack in my bivouac bag to check if the sky was still clear. The stars had lost their twinkle when we started to pack our sacks an hour before dawn. Rather ominously, the wind was even stronger, the sky was starting to cloud over and it was cold. We climbed back up to the knife-edge ridge to the right of the headwall and abseiled down an overhanging wall to a ledge. Micha traversed a hanging shelf on the right and I set off up an overhanging groove of precariously jammed blocks. I whimpered with relief when I gained a platform near the crest of the Brouillard ridge. We had climbed the pillar but it felt a hollow victory. Our route was far from over, and by the time Micha came up it had started to snow.

The scene changed from summer to winter in a matter of minutes. Everything was draped in white. The bad weather had come in a full 12 hours early, and we were now caught in a major storm on the most remote and committing place on the mountain. But there was nothing for it but to press on over the summit of Mont Blanc and down to the safety of the Vallot. I set off in the lead, but snowed-up rock slowed our pace and it took an hour to reach the summit of Pointe Louis Amédée. By now the entire ridge was covered in 15cm of snow and the wind was howling. Visibility was reduced to 50m but I felt at home: it was just like winter climbing in the Cairngorms on a bad day.

The ridge narrowed and we abseiled into a notch. Further on the route was barred by a smooth rounded crest. With dry rock it would have been a breeze, but draped in powder with a buffeting wind it was a different matter. After some humming and hawing, I found a way up a steep cracked wall on the east side of the crest. It was a pitch straight from the Northern Corries in December. Beyond it, the ridge seemed endless. In limited visibility each obstacle arrived out of the gloom as a new surprise. Eventually we reached a spectacular rime-covered pair of pinnacles. I vaguely remembered this abrupt obstacle from 25 years before and knew there was no alternative but to climb up and over them using sharp edges and deep cracks that had to be dug out from beneath the snow.

Micha was becoming disoriented. 'I can't see anything anymore,' he complained as he stared directly into the horizontal blowing snow. I was surprised he was not positioned with his hood into the wind.

'Just look the other way,' I suggested.

'What on earth are we doing here?' he wailed. I'd never seen Micha falter

Simon Richardson negotiating icy slabs near the top of the granite section of *Perfect Storm. (Micha Rinn)*

in the mountains before; his distress alarmed me. Was this the first sign of hypothermia? 'We need to carry on,' I replied firmly. I tried to give the impression that everything was under control but Micha's sentiment was absolutely correct. We had gone beyond the point of no return. We were now completely committed; our only option was to reach the Vallot hut that day. Our clothes were damp and we were becoming dangerously cold and tired. Surviving a night out in this maelstrom was inconceivable.

The ridge continued over more steep rock steps interspersed with easier snow. The wind became stronger, the snow deeper and the visibility less. By late afternoon we were on the upper part of the ridge and searching for the summit of Mont Blanc de Courmayeur. I had been here three times before but always in good weather. I remembered a broad open summit area and then an easy romp to the top of Mont Blanc but now we appeared to be traversing along a corniced edge. With visibility down to a few metres it was impossible to find the true summit. I sheltered behind a granite bluff and waited for Micha to join me.

'We need to take a bearing,' I screamed into the wind. Opening the zip on my rucksack, my gloves were so frozen it took me a full five minutes to pick up my compass and hold it securely in my fingers. I realised suddenly it was now me who was getting close to the edge. We hadn't eaten for two days and I was cold, tired and thirsty. Above all I was mentally exhausted. I'd led through the storm for a full 10 hours and now my concentration

was slipping away. It would have been easy to guess the way to the summit of Mont Blanc from here but despite my fatigue I knew we had to be disciplined and navigate properly. Our survival depended on finding the Vallot. We couldn't afford to make a mistake.

Great mountaineering partnerships succeed when leadership passes seamlessly from one climber to the other. This was such a moment. I was completely spent and Micha knew it. Now was the time for him to take control. Somehow he managed to extract his mobile phone from his jacket, take off his gloves and turn on the GPS. He located our position, took a bearing from the screen and set off into the white, breaking trail towards the summit of Mont Blanc.

The snow was knee-deep and it was further than I remembered, but eventually we reached a flat area and realised we were on the top. It was so different to before when there had been crowds of people all around. This time there was no sign of anything at all: we could have been on a remote mountain in the middle of Antarctica for all we could see. Worst of all, there was no track in the snow indicating the way down. Micha's GPS led us to the start of the Bosses Arête, which was well defined at first, so we knew we were on the correct path. The route veers north-west 150m below the

Above: Micha Rinn on easier ground.
(Simon Richardson)

Left: Micha Rinn at the top of the route's granite section approaching the upper schist prow.
(Simon Richardson)

summit but disoriented in the wind and snow we left the ridge a little too high and started descending its northern flank. The slope steepened and twice we nearly walked over serac walls. Around us slopes were avalanching and the light was beginning to fade.

Micha checked our position on the GPS and shouted we were close: it was only 700m in a direct line to the hut. But we couldn't descend directly from where we were and had to traverse horizontally across the slope to avoid a series of ice cliffs above the hut that Micha remembered from three weeks before. Laboriously we contoured west through thigh-deep snow to regain the correct track. I was extremely cold and tired. I'd been continuously wiggling my fingers and toes the last few hours to keep them alive but was now beginning to lose the fight. My energy reserves were almost spent and I knew determination and willpower alone were not enough. My body was running on empty. It was a terrifying feeling; I now know what it means to be staring into the abyss.

Every time Micha stopped to check the GPS the hut was always 700m away.

'Surely we can go down now?' I begged but Micha was steadfast in continuing our slow traverse, wading through the nightmare of blowing snow. Eventually his GPS told us we were back on the correct track and we could start heading down. Minutes later the aluminium box of the Vallot loomed out of the storm. As we wearily climbed up the metal ladder to

Above: Simon Richardson climbing through the storm on the Brouillard ridge during day four. *(Micha Rinn)*

Right: Simon Richardson on day six after two nights trapped in the Vallot hut, climbing the classic east ridge of the Aiguille de Bionnassay. *(Micha Rinn)*

gain the door of the hut my mind was numb. I was too far gone to register emotion. Once inside it was clear we were in a terrible state. Our Gore-Tex jackets were covered in a 3cm-thick layer of rime and the shafts of our ice axes had swelled with ice to the size of marrows. It took 20 minutes to untie the icy ropes and take off our harnesses. We were too tired to eat or drink and simply collapsed into our sleeping bags on the floor.

An hour later the emergency radio crackled into life asking whether we had seen three Italian women who were missing somewhere on the mountain. Later we learned the awful news that they had perished on Mont Blanc du Tacul that night. The storm raged for another 36 hours. It was below freezing in the hut but a brief lull allowed us to thaw our gear, eat, drink and enjoy the delicious sensation of being safe and secure.

Most climbers would have been happy to call it quits at this point. We had climbed a magnificent new route on the south side of Mont Blanc and traversed the Brouillard ridge in a storm. But Micha is no ordinary climber and he knew as well as I that our job was still half done. To complete the Dream Traverse we had to ignore the temptation of descending via the Goûter hut and continue over the Aiguille de Bionnassay.

The storm finally blew itself out late on the second night. It was our sixth day on the mountain, and we were happy to leave the confines of a

hut rapidly filling with climbers en route for the summit of Mont Blanc. By the time we left it was 8am and rather late to start climbing the Bionnassay but the sky was blue and the temperature still low after the bad weather. We climbed the spectacularly corniced east ridge in 45 minutes but soon dispelled any illusion of competence by losing the route descending the south ridge towards the Col de Miage. We had telephoned the Durier hut over a week before to say we expected to be passing this way and arrived to a marvellous welcome, gorging ourselves on a huge lunch before surprising the young *guardienne* by explaining we planned an early start next morning. We wouldn't be descending to the valley as our route was still not yet complete. With our supplies now exhausted, she gave us two loaves of bread and a huge chunk of cheese.

The connection between the Durier hut and the Dômes de Miage is long and rocky and it soon became clear we were tired and moving slowly. But there was no rush. We had been told the Dômes traverse had recently been declared impossible due to badly iced ice slopes on the descent to the Col de la Bérangère, which meant we had the mountain to ourselves. We carefully down-climbed the 'impossible' section on steep hard ice and arrived at a deserted Conscrits hut for coffee and cake early in the afternoon. To prolong the experience we spent the night at the Tré la Tête hotel, walked down to Les Contamines next morning and by a combination of hitchhiking and numerous buses returned through the Mont Blanc tunnel to retrieve our car from Val Veni.

It has taken me several months to come to terms with our adventure on Mont Blanc last summer. I was bang on the mark when I reflected at the beginning of our outing that dreams could be dangerous things. But the Dream Traverse will live in my memory as one of the most profound experiences of my climbing life. On the surface it was a brilliant technical success; we certainly achieved our goal of a Greater Ranges experience. But deep down I still feel a little troubled. I know we were pushed to the very limit. We made some good mountaineering decisions along the way but ultimately it was the strength of our partnership that saw us through. To succeed through strength and fitness is one thing, but to win through due to shared trust in your partner is something else. The rewards are infinitely greater.

Summary

An account of the first ascent of *Perfect Storm* (ED1, 700m) on the west face of Pointe Louis Amédée followed by a traverse of Mont Blanc, Aiguille de Bionnassay and the Dômes de Miage, 10-17 August 2018.

BEN TIBBETTS

The Ultra Royal Traverse

The west face of Mont Blanc at sunset from Semnoz. *(Ben Tibbetts)*

For many years I had been interested in extending the *Royal Traverse* (Dômes de Miage-Bionnassay-Mont Blanc) into the 'Ultra Royal': an end-to-end traverse through the centre of the Mont Blanc massif. Starting on 21 April 2018, Colin Haley and I finally made the 'first ascent' of this route in a 32-hour non-stop push from Champex to Contamines, filming and photographing the project as we went. During our long day out we skied and climbed 89km with 6,800m of height gain. This epic route can also be broken down into five or six reasonable stages of ski mountaineering to provide an extraordinary journey between comfortable refuges, through the heart of the massif.

Katherine Richardson first explored the crucial passage of the *Royal Traverse* to Mont Blanc. In the summer of 1888, guided by Emile Rey and Jean-Baptiste Bich, she made the first crossing of the Aiguille de Bionnassay. The *Alpine Journal* recorded in 1889: 'It has been reserved for a lady to accomplish the traverse of an arête which had hitherto been found impracticable, and to prove that it is possible to pass from the S. ridge of the Aiguille de Bionnassay over the summit of the peak straight along to the Dôme [de Goûter]. Thus a splendid high-level route has been opened up, which has long been aimed at.' At a time when misogyny was widespread, the editor had the good grace to acknowledge that Richardson's 'ascents are, perhaps, the most noteworthy events of the past season in the Alps.'

Sébastien Montaz-Rosset and Colin Haley skinning up the Argentière glacier.
(Ben Tibbetts)

Three months previously, while training for this project, I was caught in a massive avalanche. After skiing an open slope, across the valley from Mont Blanc, I was waiting on a blunt rib, a spot that I thought was safe, as my friend Lara followed me down the same slope. Everything above us released in an avalanche 300m wide. I was swept into a tree and buried upside down under two metres of snow with a dislocated shoulder. Stuart, Lara's husband, found me and dug me out within minutes, though my airway had been blocked and I was already losing consciousness. Lara was swept 400m but unhurt.

This event haunted me throughout that winter, posing dark questions about my motivations in the mountains. No matter how significant a project might seem, that accident had cauterised my appetite for risk. I had no interest in setting some record time for this line across Mont Blanc but the aim was still to complete it non-stop, a goal that in itself carried quite enough risk. Moreover, my desire to record our odyssey was nearly as strong as my wish to finish the story and to that end I carried a substantial camera. This, as Colin noted, weighed more than all our safety equipment put together.

We reached our starting point, the little chapel above the lake at Champex in Switzerland at the northern end of the Mont Blanc massif, just before midnight. The scene was lit by the dull orange glow of a street lamp. I put the camera on a wall and set the video to record. Colin shifted uncomfortably from foot to foot as I read out a poem: 'Wild Geese' by Mary Oliver. You do not have to be good, she says. 'You only have to let the soft animal of your body / love what it loves.' It was as close to a prayer as I would allow myself. The sense of this poem had shifted for me several times in the 15 years since I first heard it. Now the words echoed with me through the first lucid hours of toil, imploring me to question my motives.

*

'I had some very good moments and some very bad moments back in 2012,' Seb Montaz said, looking across to the Aiguille d'Argentière. He had met us in the middle of the Argentière glacier and now Colin, Seb and I were clustered on the Col des Cristaux, seven hours after leaving Champex. Colin was getting cold and seemed anxious to carry on, but while we were in sight of the fateful location I was curious to hear Seb's memories about a similar traverse that Kilian Jornet and Stéphane Brosse tried in 2012. They had left Contamines at the southern end of the massif early on 16 June with the aim of reaching Champex that night. However, when they reached the south face of the Col des Cristaux in the afternoon they found the snow was already too warm and decided to stay the night in the Requin hut. They set out early next morning. 'Kilian and Stéphane wanted to meet me at the top of the Aiguille d'Argentière at 7.15am, and as usual they were exactly on time. I could see them skiing down there [on the glacier] and they arrived at 7.15. We had a short stop. I remember this bird, it was a bit like a symbol, it was flying around us for a long time. We left walking in crampons. They were walking sideways and I was looking at them. Kilian was to the left. I saw this really nice ridge going up into the blue sky. I thought, oh I need to shoot that … so I stopped. From where I stopped I noticed that it was all overhanging. Kilian saw me stopping so he turned around and suddenly realised he was walking on empty stuff. I think the cornice was 10m over the south face, it was enormous. Two seconds after he said to Stéphane, "Come here!" At this precise second a break went between them … and I'm afraid Stéphane was on the wrong side. He fell with the whole cornice. Unfortunately I was recording that, but probably the camera saved my life that day. I don't know which track I would have taken … Stéphane's or Kilian's?' Though I met him only once Stéphane was an inspirational figure, not only in the close-knit world of ski-mountaineering racing but also for the ambitious projects he achieved in the high mountains. It was his idea to traverse the Mont Blanc massif and the beautiful logic of the line inspired me.

In June 2013 Misha Gopaul and I climbed from Chamonix, over the Dôme du Goûter and descended toward the Piton des Italiens. We were heading over to Bionnassay, for the second time, to try and recover the skis and sacks we had abandoned when we were rescued by helicopter a month earlier. On the ridge we crossed paths with a friend, Bastien Fleury and a young star of French steep skiing, Vivian Bruchez, as they prepared to descend the vertiginous north-west face of the Piton. Back then I had rarely mustered the courage to ski steep slopes and I was blown away by their precision and tenacity as they made short jump turns down the face and disappeared out of sight. It never occurred to me that I might ski with Vivian in the future, let alone descend new lines or once again try the Ultra Royal traverse.

A month earlier that year, on 15 May, Misha, Ally Swinton and I set off from Contamines at 2am with the hope of traversing the Dômes de Miage and Bionnassay to Mont Blanc. Our initial objective, the classic *Royal Traverse*, was preparation for the longer project once conditions improved: to finish in Champex, the line inspired by Kilian and Stéphane's attempt. In the spring of 2013 however, good stable weather never arrived. We were frustrated by relentless weeks of difficult conditions. On 7 May, Ally and I had managed to sneak up the *Lagarde* route on the north face of Les Droites but the weather window was only a matter of hours and on the summit we were enveloped in the brooding clouds of an oncoming storm.

Around 13 May we saw another weather window developing, not quite as long as we hoped, but adequate for an initial attempt. We set off on 15 May, initially making good progress. By the time we arrived at the Durier hut however, nestled in the col between the Dômes de Miage and the south ridge of the Bionnassay, we were already several hours slower than planned, having broken trail in variable snow much of the way. The weather was not as good as forecast and a rising wind was blowing plumes of spindrift off Mont Blanc. We reached the summit of Bionnassay at 12.30pm already tired. As wisps of cloud began to gather on the ridge ahead we started to accept we might only make it to the Dôme du Goûter. Ally set off breaking trail down the east ridge towards the Col de Bionnassay. Misha and I rested a few minutes longer before setting off. I took an image of Ally, far along the ridge beyond us, and then he moved out of sight behind a spur of rock. We followed in his tracks for a couple of hundred metres until they ended at a small step in the snow. I stopped and looked at the step for a few moments before I realised what had happened.

'I could see the ridge was a cornice,' Ally recalled, 'so for obvious reasons I stayed a few metres below that. The snow had a very slight crust on top, but the consistency felt fine. Silently and unexpectedly I fell onto my side, and for half a second I couldn't grasp what was happening. I then immediately noticed the slope I was lying on was cracking up and the crest of the ridge was moving away from me. In these first few seconds I tried so hard to crawl and swim my way to the top of the slope that was going with me, the top was only a metre away and even though I gained some ground it was too late. After these few seconds I knew I was going down. I was then thrown off a cliff band and into the air. All I could see was white. Whilst freefalling, in this white room, I remember actually feeling gutted that this was the way I was going to go. I knew something was about to happen and that it was going to hurt, and I wasn't really looking forward to it. I banged into some sections of rocks, and kept thinking that something worse was about to come. After hitting the rock section I was dragged down and washed around. My mouth filled with snow once and I can remember spitting it out

Haley approaching the Col des Cristaux at sunrise. *(Ben Tibbetts)*

and it immediately filling up again. I had to put my fingers in my mouth to unplug it. Suddenly it was all over and I was sitting upright looking around at my new surroundings. I couldn't believe how lucky I was. I couldn't stop swearing at myself,and just being quite angry with what had happened.'

Misha and I stayed on the ridge and had enough reception to call the rescue services. It was a terribly long 20 minutes though before we saw Ally staggering down the glacier 600m below us and realised he had survived the avalanche. We waved and shouted and could see that he was okay but it was another 30 minutes before we heard the spine tingling sound of the helicopter rising up the valley to pick him up. We considered whether we should reverse the route or try to protect ourselves with a rope along the remaining delicate ridge. Then, as the weather began to deteriorate rapidly, the helicopter returned and winched us off.

*

The evening before we departed for Champex I was preparing food and charging batteries, checking and rechecking forecasts. All predicted unseasonable temperatures. I hadn't slept the previous night and the mental haze compounded my anxiety. Though our timing was meticulously planned around snow stability there still seemed too many unknowns; too much potential for marginal decisions that, on such a long route, would leave us wide open to 'human bias'.

Colin Haley and I left Champex on the stroke of midnight and settled into a sustained rhythm, skinning up the long Arpette valley, over massive snouts of recent avalanche debris, and up to the Col des Écandies. For the previous five years I had been interested in trying this traverse again, but variable and thin spring snow-packs had always put the project on hold. It was only a couple of months earlier that I had the idea of reversing the route and trying the project from north to south to allow us to traverse the most crucial slopes: the Col des Cristaux and Bionnassay, in frozen conditions. From the beginning of winter I had been discussing the idea with Colin and hoped he might join me on the project. Though he is best known for his long and hard ascents in the Greater Ranges, he is also an excellent ski mountaineer. Though our ideas on risk and safety equipment were slightly different, I thought his laconic humour and quiet determination might be a good foil to my nervous and obsessive character.

Crossing the Trient plateau, a steady breeze kept us moving. We chatted intermittently, slowing only slightly to unwrap a bar or adjust boots. The moon had already sunk below the western horizon and we moved under a vast canopy of stars towards a notch in the mountains that we could barely discern. At the Fenêtre de Saleina, Colin stopped to take off boots that were already giving him sores. I twitched impatiently as we were already a little behind schedule: Seb Montaz planned to meet us below the Argentière hut in just 30 minutes. At the Col du Chardonnet we forfeited crampons for the sake of speed and dragged our way up a fixed rope, our boots groping and slipping on little steps in the steep icy slope. We crossed the border back into France and carved lazy turns down the icy slopes, the lamp-lit surface rushing towards me quicker than my drowsy faculties could comprehend.

Teams were already starting up the great north face climbs. There were headlamps on the *Lagarde* and *Czech* routes on Les Droites, and several parties in the *Couturier* couloir on the Verte, each buried in their own games and struggles. Seb had left the village of Argentère at 2am to ski up in the dark and join us for the first half of the day. Just after 5am we met him in the middle of the glacier by a prominent rock. He had picked up three bottles of water from the refuge and was now upon us with the camera, asking a few questions and taking clips of video. Colin took off his boots to adjust his socks again. As we set off up the glacier the half-light of dawn filtered over the walls around us. I skinned in circles around Seb and Colin taking a few photos and clips of video. I quickly realised I should have left this to Seb as the slight extra exertion left me smashed with fatigue for the next hour. We climbed slowly onto the steep slopes of the Col de Cristaux and finally crawled into the sunlight halfway up.

At the Col, Colin, Seb and I discussed whether to ski or climb down the south side. Given our fatigue, my marked lack of lucidity and the hard crispy snow, we decided it would be safer to down-climb the slope. Colin headed off quickly and I followed. The snow had a hard crust and I rushed

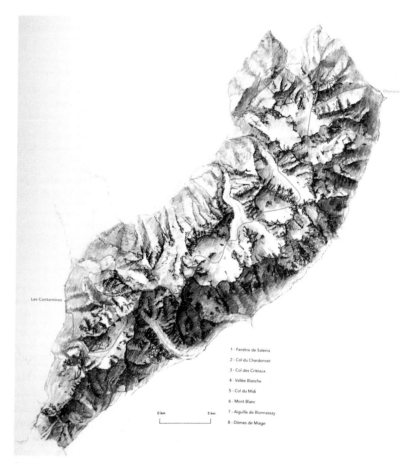

1 · Fenêtre de Saleina

2 · Col du Chardonnet

3 · Col des Cristaux

4 · Vallée Blanche

5 · Col du Midi

6 · Mont Blanc

7 · Aiguille de Bionnassay

8 · Dômes de Miage

0 km   5 km

Drawn map of the Ultra Royal route from Champex to Les Contamines.
(Ben Tibbetts)

down until unexpectedly my foot plunged through a crusty layer and with my downward momentum I almost somersaulted down the slope. Colin was moving like a lizard and had already darted out of sight. I stopped for a moment to calm myself, looking at the cliffs below before setting off again more slowly.

We gathered once more on the glacier and then skied out into the sunshine and onto the Mer de Glace. It was now 9.30am and as the temperature rose, battalions of skiers poured down the Vallée Blanche. At 12.30pm we reached the Col du Midi and found Vivian Bruchez basking in the midday sun, surrounded by eight litres of water, a litre of coke and a stash of cold pizzas. It was our only resupply of food in the whole traverse. Until this point we hadn't stopped for more than 15 minutes at a time; the effort and dehydration were catching up with us. Colin and I gorged ourselves whilst stripping off our boots and drying our fetid feet in the sun. Colin grumbled about his sores and muttered something about stopping there. I didn't really believe what he was saying so made some manipulative appeals to his tattered pride. We dressed our heels with new bandages and over an hour slipped by before we finally began to move again. Seb left us to return back to the valley and Vivian assumed the role of shepherd, and the tiring business of recording pieces of video that we might later piece together.

Into the evening the long icy summit slopes of Mont Blanc poisoned my well of enthusiasm. There was a cool breeze from the south-east that was irritating and I was appallingly tired. Nineteen hours into the adventure and I could barely move 10 paces before collapsing, my lungs rasping on the brittle air. Throughout the day tiredness had come in waves, each one over-whelming me more vigorously than the last. On the final few hundred metres to Mont Blanc I seemed to develop narcolepsy. We had breezed up the same slope – literally, with 80kph of wind – just three days earlier on a recce. This time, I bent over my poles, closed my eyes and the whole world dissolved into a miasma. After half a second, or perhaps half an hour, I would wake with a start. I peeled my eyes open to see my boots and crampons on a blinding bright golden surface. I turned my head upwards. Vivian and Colin were still just several paces ahead of me, each buried in their own struggle.

By the time we had rushed and stumbled down past the Vallot hut the sun had set most beautifully but I barely had the energy to appreciate the vibrant hues or the incredible view. This wave of lethargy subsided as we lost altitude but I could feel how deeply I had already pushed my body. I looked over to Bionnassay and the Dômes de Miage beyond, and in the gathering magentas of dusk it now seemed almost impossible that we could still make it to Contamines. In the gloom their jagged ridges seemed far higher and more fearsome that I remembered. Colin expressed some doubts, striking a chord with my own, but I heard myself wittering on about how the ridge would be fine in the dark. I had been over Bionnassay four times previously and should remember the way. We put a rope on to pass a few crevasses and then dropped down past the Piton des Italiens as the light failed.

From the Col de Bionnassay I broke trail for a spell, stamping footsteps into the narrow snow crest. We were likely the first people that year and it was tough work. As I slowed Vivian took over and continued for another hour to the summit. Colin seemed to be trailing some way behind, his lamp-light weaving from side to side in the darkness. When he caught up I shoved the camera in his face and he muttered vacantly 'definitely not the chilled ascent I would like right now.' He was struggling with the aggressive waves of fatigue I had on Mont Blanc. With steep slopes on both side and a knife-edge to walk on, it wasn't a great moment to fall asleep.

With nightfall our progress had slowed dramatically and when a breeze picked up I was soon cold. At the summit I noticed, with disembodied concern, that one of my crampons had almost fallen off. I slowly carved out a platform to refit it, muttering to myself. We began the descent slowly but soon found ourselves peering into the dark trying to work out where we should go. Though both Vivian and I had been there several times previously,

Ally Swinton below the rock step on the south ridge of Aiguille de Bionnassay, first climbed by Florence Crauford Grove et al in 1865. *(Ben Tibbetts)*

the darkness and a veil of tiredness made it tricky to find the correct line. We eventually found the top of the steep rock step and the rappel anchor. I gingerly clambered down, vaguely remembering the circuitous route down the buttress. Vivian and Colin began to descend on our 6mm rope with a 4mm tag line. At each rappel they seemed to take an age to untangle the lines and I got cold and frustrated waiting for them at the bottom. Down the ridge towards the Durier hut I looked across at the looming mass of the Dômes de Miage ahead of us. I couldn't work out why it looked so huge. They started to tower above us in ghastly shapes. I watched my conviction waver as firm reference points began to crumble. Sleep deprivation was pulling apart any coherent sensory experience of the world. Sound and sight were becoming separated in time and space; voices echoed around my head well after they occurred and in the dark the rocks and snow began morphing into animals, buildings and great machines.

At the Durier hut we found a couple sleeping. Despite our hushed tones they woke and offered us the use of their stove. My head swirled with broken ideas as to how we could or couldn't climb the massive 300m that remained. In 20 minutes we made several litres of hot water but were all still shivering despite having all our clothes on. Colin murmured that he wanted to sleep a little. I wanting nothing more but insisted we carry on before we lost the plot.

We left the Durier hut at 3am and made our way, ever so slowly, up the crenelated Miage ridge. Over the next few hours my senses became madly disoriented and reality and memory blurred. When Colin or Vivian spoke I had to focus all my attention to catch the words and juggle them into

Misha Gopaul on the south ridge with Mont Blanc behind. *(Ben Tibbetts)*

meaning. It felt akin to the first moments having woken up after a general anaesthetic, staring up, once again, at the bright lights of a hospital ward. These long distance challenges provide a kind of mental and physical experience that I can barely access in normal life.

As I denied myself sleep for yet another night, mind and body seemed to have become temporarily liberated into another dimension. The risks, though, associated with moving along steep ridges and faces in the dark whilst deeply fatigued, are all too obvious. Perhaps, however, these risks, for some of us, are crucial in reinforcing an urgent desire to hold on to the dear earth, to stay alive, to purge complacency and cherish every quiet moment of valley life. Up high, with the mind burning brightly along crests of rock and ice, it seems our stupid conceits can sometimes be sublimated through suffering. For in those rich, painful hours they become metamorphosed into self-knowledge by that powerful alchemy of deeply lived experience.

When we finally reached the valley the sun had risen again on another clear day. It was difficult to express any joy at our achievement as we hobbled up to the church in Contamines 32 hours after leaving Champex. The only liberation was from slow relentless suffering, from movement. It took two days of sleep for my senses to recover and it was several more before the experience sank in and amnesia washed away the pain. I actually felt content, for once, that we had closed the story.

Vivian Bruchez cast a pool of light on the Col de Bionnassay, with the Aiguille ahead of him. *(Ben Tibbetts)*

Summary

Ultra Royal Traverse (6800m, AD, III). From Champex head up the Val d' Arpette to Col des Ecandies. Traverse the Plateau de Trient and Fenêtre de Saleina to the Col de Chardonnet. Descend to the Argentière glacier, passing under the refuge and then climbing up the north-east slope of the Col des Cristaux. Descend the south-west slope and down to the Mer de Glace, depending on conditions either on skis or via the path and ladders under the Courvercle hut. Pass under the Requin hut and up the Vallée Blanche, highly crevassed in summer, to the Col du Midi. Climb the three Monts to Mont Blanc, descend the Arête des Bosses, pass under the Dôme du Goûter down to the Col de Bionnassay. Ascend Bionnassay via the east ridge. Descend the south ridge to a steep rock step. Down climb or rappel this and continue to the Durier hut at the Col du Miage. Climb the north-east ridge of the Dômes de Miage: one rappel if heading south to north. From the Col des Dômes descend the Tré-la-tête glacier or, if conditions allow, via the Armancette glacier and paths down to Contamines.

• This article forms a chapter in the new book from Ben Tibbetts, *Alpenglow: the Finest Routes on the 4,000m Peaks of the Alps*. See *www.bentibbetts.com/ alpenglow* for more information.

Fresh Horizons

The Mouth of the Rhône from Lake Geneva
John Ruskin, 1846?
Watercolour over pencil. 16.8cm x 22.6cm.
Courtesy of Birmingham Museums Trust.

WILL SIM

Avellano Tower

The climber, the gauchos, their horse and its luggage. *(John McCune)*

A few years ago, on a grey autumn's day in Llanberis, my friend John Crook came round. With no surprise to anyone who knows John, he came armed not only with enthusiasm to find any dry rock available in the penetrating drizzle but with a stock of fresh stories from far-flung adventures that had come to pass since we'd last seen each other. That evening, sat in my little house on Snowdon Street, John showed me hundreds of photos of exploratory climbing in the Andes and Patagonia that had me squirming on the sofa with jealousy and excitement.

Here he was hacking through jungle to remote, unclimbed crags, or else exploring huge dolerite columns, like a photo-shopped Giant's Causeway, climbing big Andean ice faces, and best of all, a vast, conical tower, more a big wall, in a remote, almost untouched range of Chilean Patagonia. The legendary Jim Donini had introduced John to this spectacular wilderness. John had been kicking his heels in El Chaltén waiting for a weather window with Dave Brown, who had been in contact with Jim. Did they fancy 'something a little different?' That was back in February 2014, and they made some brilliant first ascents, with and without Jim, including a 300m first ascent on the Tooth. It was what they saw across from them that made their jaws drop: a pristine wall of vast proportions, the east face of South Avellano Tower, which to their knowledge had never before been attempted.

John McCune, John Crook, Paul Swail and Will Sim on the first ascent of the east face of South Avellano Tower (900m, E5 6a). *(Ruth Bevan)*

John and Dave set off in the middle of the night with food and water for two days, having scoped out a line of continuous-looking grooves leading to halfway ledges and felt optimistic. But the granite was like that on El Capitan, glacially polished and smoother than expected. Before long they were lowering to the ground. At dawn, they were already trying another groove, but were met with the same fate. A third attempt got them established on the face but it was a circuitous route and they made little vertical headway. Back on the ground, thwarted once again, they spent an afternoon starting up at the monolith that had beaten them back, contemplating their failure: they were going to need reinforcements.

John and Dave were back in December, just ten months later, with Andy Reeve and Will Harris, to try a direct line up the centre of the face. This more substantial effort required a new approach to Avellano, across the huge, rough Lago General Carrera in a small, overloaded boat. The gauchos took their gear 30km up the beautiful Avellano valley from the south-east and the team then made multiple load carries through glacial rivers, marsh, forest and moraine to the base of the wall.

Things started well, and they made good progress up this central line, but their attempt was thwarted by a cold storm that blanketed the wall in snow that took too long to clear. Returning to collect their gear, they found their

Line of the first ascent from base camp.
(John McCune)

Will Sim following high on the wall.
(John McCune)

first 80m of fixed rope gone. A car-sized flake had peeled off from high on the wall, slicing through the rope and leaving blocks of granite strewn over ledges below. Dave made a heroic lead to reach the lines above and so allow the recovery of the team's gear. After that, Avellano was laid to rest for a while, although an American team did make an attempt in January 2015.

Three years later, in January 2018, John was returning for his third attempt and I was going with him, along with John McCune, Paul Swail and Ruth Bevan. Jim Donini and his wife Angela offered wonderful hospitality and although the weather in December had been poor, conditions slowly improved the closer we got to the wall. It took us ten days from arriving in Chile to reach our base camp and during the rough boat ride across Lago General Carrera we became separated, with John McCune, Paul and myself on one side of South America's second-largest lake and John Crook and Ruth on the other with the gear, unable to cross back due to high winds and tall waves. Thankfully a local gaucho gave us shelter until next morning.

Having regrouped on the north shore of the lake, we trekked up to the mountain over the next four or five days with our new friend Luis the gaucho and his horses. For the last two or three days we needed to help relay loads on stretches that were too rough for the animals. The weather was sill cloudy and we didn't get a chance to see the wall until we were nearly at base camp.

Paul Swail low on the face of South Avellano Tower (900m, E5 6a) during the first-ascent push. The summit of the tower can be seen far above. *(John McCune)*

This proved to be an idyllic spot, with running water and plenty of wood. John McCune and I built a handy lean-to for extra comfort and sheltered cooking. And while we were making ourselves comfortable, the wall was finally drying off sufficiently for us to climb. We made quick progress on John's original line, setting ropes to the halfway ledges over the course of two days. Poor weather threatened to arrive by the end of the following day, so we made the decision to go for it. We reached the top of the fixed lines by daybreak and attacked the headwall in two pairs.

The rock became more varied, with some loose flakes and areas of exfoliating rock. There was some high-quality climbing and amazing positions, particularly where we had to avoid a big wet corner for a couple of pitches. John followed steep and strenuous cracks up the left wall of this to a ledge, before looking up in dismay at what appeared to be a dead-end. Paul Swail then set off up a wild-looking groove, overcoming increasingly unlikely terrain. But after managing to place a peg in a very awkward position, he made steep moves through a roof on chicken heads to an outrageously exposed traverse that brought us back to the top of the corner. From here I made a long, bold traverse back right over compact black rock to reach a viable-looking groove. An intricate pitch led to some burly lay-backing around a roof, and before long we were pulling onto the north face, where easy ground led to a final ramp. This provided a great finale, with 200m of high-quality but straightforward climbing. Almost to our disbelief we had found a way up the wall and topped out that afternoon at around 5pm, as the famous Patagonia wind swept in. The rain started as we were halfway down. Ruth traced our progress from base camp with radio contact throughout and had made us pumpkin curry and cheesecake for our return.

Paul Swail pulling through the roof on the crux pitch. *(John McCune)*

Our route was a thousand metres and every pitch had gone free: E5 seems about right, give or take a grade or two. We were all nicely shocked that our main objective had been achieved after only three days' effort: we had half-expected it to take us 10, taking into account the bad weather, and had come equipped with portaledges to give us options. I think the fact that we knocked off the South Tower so fast was partly due to the luck of the weather changing for the better just when we were ready to launch. But it was also due to the groundwork that John, Will Harris, Dave Brown and Andy Reeve had made in the previous attempts. Thanks boys.

With two weeks of food left in base camp and spirits high, it was nice to know that anything else we climbed was a bonus, yet there were plenty of plums for the picking. Once our bodies had recovered from the South Tower, myself, John and Paul made the first ascent of a beautiful route on an attractive mountain we came to know as Cerro Square Face. The climax of this fantastic route was a dreamy, splitter crack that felt about E5 6b and seemed too good to be true. We strolled around on the windless summit for a few minutes in Patagonian heaven before beginning the descent.

A few days after that John, Paul and myself made another first ascent, a classic alpine spur sporting a worrying final tower, which we had heard rumours of being attempted previously by an American team. Sure enough, after several hundred metres of what felt like serious ridge traversing, the final tower reared above us. I was dealt the sharp end and after some scary steep fist jamming through more death-blocks than I care to admit, I rolled on to the summit after completing yet another fantastic, virgin line. We called it the Mestizo ridge.

Our last climbing of the trip was spent trying to repeat our own route up the South Tower's east face, but going more direct in a section where we'd spotted a crack through binoculars. Unfortunately it wasn't to be as the

After finishing the expedition at the Avellano Towers, the team moved on to the dolerite towers of Cerro Colorado just south-east of Lago General Carrera. *(John McCune)*

Ruth Bevan climbing at Cerro Colorado. *(John McCune)*

heavens opened on us halfway up the wall. It was the only day of the trip that the forecast was wrong, but we couldn't complain given the trip we had had. We reversed the load carrying of the approach and met up with Luis and his horses for the walk out to the lake. Hunger had well and truly set in now that we had exhausted nearly all of our provisions, but we didn't care, we'd just had three weeks of dream climbing in a barely explored Patagonian paradise.

Summary
First ascent of east face of South Avellano Tower (900m, E5 6a), *Last Gaucho* (E5 6b) on Cerro Square Face, north-east of main towers, and the high-quality *Chicken Run* (600m, E2) on an unnamed formation adjacent to Square Face.

SEBASTIAN WOLFRUM

The First Ascent of Geli Kuh

Looking north along the main ridgeline of the mountain range during
the descent from the summit of Geli Kuh (2995m), the highest
non-volcano in Iranain Baluchistan. *(Sebastian Wolfrum)*

It was hot in the ready room of the fire brigade at Gosht, a small town
in south-east Iran. I could feel sweat running down my body. Iranians
seem to enjoy recreating inside the weather of the opposite season. During
visits in summer I have frequently been in homes cold enough to resemble
the Arctic, while in winter one has to endure temperatures inside of 35°C
and more. Now it was winter and the Gosht fire brigade had offered to host
us for the night in their overheated station. My Iranian friend and climbing partner Mojtaba Vasou was looking at me. Noticing my discomfort and
clearly suffering himself, he said: 'I am really happy we are here.' I myself
could not have been happier to be embarking on a project we had dreamed
of for a year and a half. We continued sorting our gear on the floor as five
firefighters peered over our shoulders with expressions of total bafflement.

Geli Kuh is a remote 'ultra', a peak with a prominence of over 1,500m,
and at 2,995m the third-highest mountain in Baluchistan. Investiga-
tions about this area had brought to light extremely little information; we
had only established that nobody really knows anything about the peak.
Although Iran is a country full of mountains, mountaineering activities are
mostly confined to three areas: the Alborz, the Zagros and the mountains
south of Kerman as well as a few famous outlying peaks. Contacting Ali
Moqhim, a writer from Tehran, who keeps a list of Iranian first ascents,

119

we found out that Geli Kuh had indeed never been climbed. Looking at Google Earth images revealed the mountain to be the culminating summit of a long range of peaks with a relatively steep west face. It was this west face of the mountain we were planning to climb.

On 1 January 2019 we left the fire station and made our way to Bondaran, 60km north of Gosht and 7km southeast of Geli Kuh. As is the custom, the head of the village invited us to his home. After formally introducing ourselves and explaining our goal, we were able to make enquiries regarding water sources. With Baluchistan experiencing one of the worst droughts in history, having not received normal amounts of rainfall for over six years, all of the rivers were dry. After a lengthy discussion and us trying to explain where we would want to establish our base camp, we were told that nowhere close to the mountain had any water but a small hamlet slightly closer that the village did have a spring, which we could use.

On we went to Jegari. The head of this settlement greeted us enthusiastically and we were shown the spring about a kilometre down a valley,

Above: Rock art in the gorge leading towards the mountain. The lower sections of these gorge are used by local shepherds to access high pastures to the north-west of the Geli Kuh range. *(Sebastian Wolfrum)*

Left: Mojtaba Vasou on the saddle of the first approach ridge with the summit of Geli Kuh in the distance. *(Sebastian Wolfrum)*

offering the merest trickle of water, albeit of good quality. With haste often typical of Iranians, we were soon left alone. Our first task was to establish just where we were exactly. We made a rapid ascent of the steep hill to our east, overlooking our position by about 400m, where we realised we were even further from our mountain than we had thought, and that any approach to it would have to cross over a shoulder of this hill.

Next morning we started early, crossed the shoulder and dropped down into a dry riverbed to the south of it. Following this upstream for over two hours, sometimes climbing to the side of it in order to pass dry water-falls. The course of the riverbed twisted and turned around seemingly end-less corners. Further up we found interesting rock art of unknown age. Having reached a confluence we had identified the previous day, we set off to ascend one of the long ridges running eastwards to the face of the mountain. This soon turned into a succession of pinnacles and rock spikes of intrusive igneous rock of questionable quality.

After reaching the first minor summit on the ridge, we were confronted with a choice of options. In front of us the ridge dropped to a col where it turned right and steepened over further pinnacles to reach another summit before dropping again slightly to the bottom of the face. Deciding against this route we continued to the col and descended north into another dry

Mojtaba Vasou on one of the countless easy rock steps on the first access ridge leading to the west face of Geli Kuh. *(Sebastian Wolfrum)*

riverbed and followed this upstream for about a kilometre. Here, much to our joy, we heard water running from a spring only to find it was salty and undrinkable. We then climbed steeply up a ridge that had appeared benign from afar but which turned out to have yet another long Aonach Eagach-like section. Finally, we reached the summit of this. Here we sat down and surveyed once more the face with our binoculars. We decided to try to climb the steep ridge running directly towards us from an area immediately to the right of the summit.

And so we set foot on the granitic face, first crossing a prominent white band of fresh stone fall then scrambling up with increasing difficulty to the foot of the ridge. We climbed unroped for some time, the initial ridge offering difficulties only up to about V Diff. Eventually, however, we came to a steep corner and tied in. The challenge on some of these lower pitches was to find a handhold not already occupied by a variety of thorny plants: dead thorny plants. The severe impact of the ongoing drought was everywhere around us. At one time, clearly, a wide variety of flora had been growing in the crevices of the rocks right up to the summit ridge. All of it was now dry and dead. I had never before seen such a profound lack of any kind of life in the mountains. Even birds were absent. The only vertebrate we saw was a small lizard.

Climbing on we came to two large towers. It was past 3pm and with sunset at 5pm we had no choice but to turn around. Darkness overtook us on the second pinnacle ridge. Ascending to the col of the first ridge we had climbed, we decided not to traverse it but rather head down into another valley to the south, which, or so we thought, would bring us back to our

The granitic 500m west face of Geli Kuh as seen from the summit of the second access ridge. We followed the most natural line, the steep ridge just to the right of the centre of the face. Once this merges with the face some 100m underneath the summit we continued our ascent straight up. Three individual summit towers can be made out, the true one being the one on the right. *(Sebastian Wolfrum)*

original valley. After about two hours, we had to admit to ourselves that we must have reached the wrong river. We went on and on, the gorge twisting and turning between steep walls before finally being spilled out 2km to the south-east of the tent, which necessitated crossing several intervening ridges to get back to it. The night looked on this with indifference from a sky pregnant with meteors; the silence was profound and complete.

Early next morning the head of Jegari greeted us walking round our tent. A drawn-out conversation ensued and it became increasingly clear that we had already run out of time to try for the summit. After about two hours of talking we were urged to take down the tent and stay in the hamlet's guest room instead. We eventually agreed to this, although it would add yet another 2km to our approach to the face.

Jegari is home to several families, all of whom live in permanent canvas tents, the only buildings made from stone being a small mosque and the guest house, an arrangement not at all uncommon in these parts. The settlement has had electricity for only six years and the locals live a simple life revolving around livestock farming. They are severely affected by the warming trends of the last years. Soon the usual scenes developed; we were asked the same questions over and over again by a multitude of people arriving from nearby settlements. Our goal was met with an air of slight suspicion although in an amiable and well-meaning way. Several times we were asked if we had come to search for gemstones. None of them had ever seen a mountaineer.

Sebastian Wolfrum and Mojtaba Vasou on the summit of Geli Kuh, where the pair built a cairn. *(Sebastian Wolfrum)*

Passing the day in this fashion we planned to leave at 3am the next morning, allowing us to be at the white band in good time for a summit bid. At midnight, I was woken by a wild howling sound. A violent storm, heavy with sand, had begun. Stepping outside I had trouble not being blown over. We couldn't climb in these conditions: even crossing the first hill into the access gorge seemed completely out of the question. We had no choice but to wait.

At 6.30am the wind finally abated. The going was still arduous but not impossible and so we started at once, marching and climbing as fast as we could until we reached the white band at 10.30am. Here we lost no time and started to climb the 500m of granite separating us from the summit. Soon we had reached our previous high point and bypassing the towers on the southern side we continued up the ridge. After another pitch, we found ourselves underneath a large roof. On both sides of it smooth walls stopped our progress. Descending again we were fortunate to find a steep chockstone-chimney going off to the right. This turned out to be both the crux and the key to the route. Once through it we were able to rejoin the ridge by an exposed traverse over a detached flake. The last 200m up to the summit area were over easier broken ground up to about Severe. We packed the rope away and soloed up. The true summit is a 10m tall tower on the eastern side of the broad summit ridge. Immediately after we had set foot on it our phone rang. One of the locals had insisted on us taking his local network SIM card for emergencies and now wanted to enquire how we were getting on. We built a cairn in which we left a short yellow sling and then abseiled off the summit tower. With darkness approaching there was no time to linger.

From below we had spotted an easy way down from the col north of Geli Kuh. This we reached traversing over and around several outlying summits. An unproblematic scramble led us back to the white band and as the last light faded we traversed along it back to the starting point of the pinnacle ridge. Here, back on known ground, we stopped for an extended break. Night fell around us and we looked back at the summit, now a black silhouette against the first stars, sitting in perfect silence for a long time.

Finally we rose and started on the long way back, crossing the first pinnacle ridge and descending into the riverbed. Instead of going up to the next ridge, we continued down the gorge, this time absolutely certain it would be the right way. But the going was no easier than on the pinnacles we thus avoided, thanks to a large number of dry waterfalls, some of which had to be abseiled.

At 11pm we walked back into Jegari, by now fast asleep. In the guest room a *sofreh*, the traditional Iranian cloth that is spread for a meal but also used to wrap up food, had been left for us. Unfolding it we found freshly baked bread inside. We sat and ate, and later, despite our tiredness, we lay awake for some time, staring into the dark of the room, dreaming aloud about other climbing objectives in this area, for which we both have developed a deep affection.

The success of this ascent would have been impossible without the generous help of the locals of Bondaran and Jegari. Had they not shown us the only available water source far and wide, our undertaking would have been impossible. It is to them this climb is dedicated.

The Mountain Environment

Lake of Lucerne and Uri Rotstock
John Ruskin, undated
Watercolour over pencil and ink. 35cm x 54.5cm.
Bequeathed to the Alpine Club Library by Charles Warren.

DOUG SCOTT, IAN WALL
& JONATHAN WESTAWAY

The Everest Mess

*The following is a speech delivered by Doug Scott on 6 June 2019 to a tourism indus-
try conference held in Kathmandu in the aftermath of headlines about overcrowding
on Everest and its environmental impact.*

I have been lured to the Himalaya many times, to be in the landscape and
with mountain people. I suspect it's the mountain people more than any
other factor that brings visitors back time and again. I was immediately
struck by how warm and hospitable Himalayan people are when I started
visiting, twice in 1972 and again in 1975. Between these visits, Nepal's first
tourism master plan was drafted.

The first to visit the Himalaya were bands of nomads during the archaic
period 40,000 years ago, but since I've only got half an hour I better move
on. There is hardly a Himalayan valley that hasn't had in residence nomads
but also sages, saints and holy men seeking peace and quiet from the mad-
ding crowds. The *mani* walls are evidence of the devotion practised in the
Himalaya and also the holy caves, gompas and monasteries. Most of the
caves seemed to have been inhabited by Padmasambhava and Milarepa.
Did anyone know the Himalaya better? What great tour guides they would
have been.

I'm sure these Buddhist saints would agree with William Blake, 'Great
things are done when men and mountains meet; This is not done by jostling
in the street.' The Himalaya is a magical place. Although now old and feeble
and unable to climb peaks I still have an excuse to come out checking on
Community Action Nepal's projects and still get above the treeline.

No wonder the Himalaya have been called the abode of the gods. Europeans were first lured here in the 17th century. They were also holy men but
this time Jesuits and definitely not there to commune with nature as they
found the Himalaya inhospitable places of desolation and horror: they were
seeking the legendary patriarch Prester John and his lost Christian kingdom.

Then came the British from India to trade with Tibet and also China by
the back door: Warren Hastings, Bogle and potatoes. The British arrived in
ever-increasing numbers: explorers, cartographers, geologists, plant-hunters
and the first Himalayan tourists. By 1856, as Ruskin put it, 'mountain gloom
gave way to mountain glory.' The mountains after Wordsworth, Coleridge
and Keats were now appreciated aesthetically.

Then came mountaineers. With the Alps worked out, they arrived in the
Himalaya seeking new challenges and new routes. Why? Because new routes
are where it's at. Why? Because there is more uncertainty as to the outcome

when setting off where no one has been before. There are still more peaks over 6,000m unclimbed than climbed. There is much to do everywhere for serious mountaineers except on Everest, which is now climbed out.

After the mountaineers came high-altitude tourism, the collectors and those who regard the Himalaya as an athletics track, racing up mountains. More about Everest later.

The problem of mass tourism destroying the very thing everyone signs up to experience is becoming familiar in the Himalaya. No one goes to the popular areas these days to find solitude. The Himalaya is no longer a place of peace, serenity and spiritual renewal due to the constant distraction of fellow trekkers. It's now hard to make your trek a walking meditation at the height of the season, when you're jostling on the trail. My personal experience recently in the Everest region was that there are so many trekkers they are backing up along the trails and causing delays. It's hard to take a photograph now without another trekker getting in the shot. A disappointed friend of mine visiting in April found the tea-houses and lodges to be like fast-food joints, where they want to get people in and out as fast as possible.

How to reverse this situation and return to the most beautiful and dramatic mountain landscape on the planet, to a place where mountain people are not overwhelmed by the sheer number of visitors, and the visitors are not so disappointed?

Quotas

Would it be wise to work out the carrying capacity of the Everest and other popular trails by gathering together a consortium of shrewd men and women from many disciplines with expertise in environmental impact, tourism, and with knowledge of local people? And then apply quotas. If so, how can this be achieved without causing offence to the visitor and not reduce the income to the local people?

Helicopters

There have been many insurance frauds committed over the last ten years or more, centring on the demand for helicopters to evacuate trekkers for fraudulent reasons. Helicopter companies, agents and hospitals have grown rich at the expense of the insurance companies and ultimately, the trekker. Some French insurance companies have already started to refuse to insure their nationals for travel in Nepal. Other countries are planning to follow. We all remember how quiet Nepal was during the Maoist insurgency, when the foreign minstries in many countries recommended travellers avoid Nepal. No insurance equals no trekkers equals no problem. Continuing on this path will solve all problems of overcrowding and associated environmental issues.

Everest and Other 8,000m Summits

Before 1986, there was one expedition per season per route, which was wonderful, with time and space to be there, communing with the mountain as well as each other. In those days you just had to wait for an opening.

After 1972 we had to wait again until October 1975. But we didn't mind waiting. It was part of the experience. Now, people are impatient and want to rush to achieve their goals and move on. It's especially good when coming down; the best part of any climb is when you're just off the mountain, out of danger, before having to deal with porters and so forth: clear head, returning strength, internal dialogue slowed down, space between thoughts. All have seen Nirmal Purja Magar's recent images from Everest where now the climber may be one of a thousand people at the base of mountain. And with 500 people on the mountain there's no chance to commune with the divine in nature, nor with one's inner self.

Why should Everest be treated any differently to Mont Blanc or the Matterhorn? We must respect the fact it is the highest, a world heritage site, considered to be of outstanding universal value and to many, the abode of the gods, and in particular Miyolangsangma, the deity of the Sherpa communities.

We have to discuss not only how to protect this sacred mountain, and all mountains, but also protect what is sacred to mountaineering. Respecting the style of the first ascent. Given the large number of people now being attracted to the summit of Everest by the original route and the inevitable deaths, it seems necessary that the number of permits will have to be limited, once the carrying capacity of Everest has been calculated, as is done on Denali, the highest peak in North America. But how to protect the mountain from the tyranny of numbers and at the same time accommodate those who have come to rely on Everest and other popular mountains for their income?

Here are suggestions from Sherpas, western climbers and other interested parties. Our charity CAN only helps where help has been asked for and where it is really needed. We are not donor driven: telling the villagers what we think they need. Similarly, I make these suggestions on behalf of friends in Nepal who have asked me to do so, since the commercialisation of Everest and other Himalayan peaks is largely unplanned and uncontrolled.

Consider making it a stipulation that a permit for Everest will only be given to those who have climbed at least one, if not two other 7,000m peaks elsewhere in Nepal first. If not, at least return to checking client competence. We used to have a letter from the Alpine Club to verify our competence as climbers.

If no restrictions are put in place then will have to allocate teams to certain days: not all on the one most favourable. This will not go down well with those stuck with bad weather periods.

Refuse to allow agents to operate on Everest who have previously been shown to be incompetent and have cut costs by employing inexperienced staff, placed both staff and clients in danger, and have brought incompetent clients with little or no experience who rush on when they should turn back, driven by overwhelming ambition. We hear of fights breaking out at base camp, of teams stealing each other's oxygen.

Increase the permit fee for the general well being of the mountain and the people who live around it and work on it.

To counterbalance the above restrictions, use peak royalties to improve the working environment of the local guides by ensuring full insurance cover but also setting up a welfare and compensation board to cover accident and death to ensure financial help to bereaved wives and children.

Establish a fairly remunerated mountain rescue group from an elite core of Sherpa and other local mountain guides on stand-by to assist with rescues. This same group could be employed to fix ropes at the beginning of each season and to remove them at the end of each season. We should pay Sherpas and other guides well for collecting, sorting and recycling rubbish and waste from off the mountain and glaciers.

If Everest hopefuls have to climb elsewhere in Nepal before qualifying for an Everest permit, then this will enable others in Nepal to benefit from high-mountain tourism and not just those in the shadow of Everest.

Is the promotion of mountain tourism compatible with the enjoyment of high-altitude tourism? There is so much else to discuss on this including encouraging the dispersal of tourists to less visited areas. And possibly at less visited times of the year. There is work here for local mountain guides and sirdars to explore new trekking routes, especially now it becomes more difficult to find treks away from new roads and jeep tracks.

There is also work to be done developing capacity in previously untrekked regions to enable local rural communities there to benefit from mountain tourism, inducting homestay and lodge owners, guides and so forth into the art of sustainable tourism and supporting them to tap into government funding.

There are many success stories here in Nepal: leading the world with animal conservation, and in particular the increase in rhino population; vast areas of afforestation, when at one time we all thought Nepal would end up a mountain desert; success in encouraging trekking lodges and expeditions to use other sources of fuel and not the last of the Himalayan juniper; vastly improved literacy; establishing and maintaining peace following ten years of Maoist insurgency; devolving power to the grassroots level; and how wonderful it is to start seeing some streets of Kathmandu free of litter and parts of Thamel free of traffic. Perhaps one day we will be able to drink water from the Bagmati.

Fixing Everest can be done, and with the resourcefulness and resilience of the Nepali people, it will be done.

*

Why Is Fixing Everest So Hard?
The 2019 Everest season, *writes Ian Wall,* was one of the most controversial since the mountain was first climbed in 1953, on a par with the tragedy of 1996 and the deaths of 16 high-altitude workers, buried in a serac avalanche in 2014. Heavy media coverage has prompted questions and a demand for change. Under pressure from negative headlines and foreign expedition operators, several 'consultation' meetings have been held in Kathmandu to

try to gain an insight into the depth of anger and concern and to explore options for reform.

The Nepal Mountaineering Association held one such interaction on 1 July 2019. Its panel comprised the president of the Trekking Agencies' Association of Nepal (TAAN), the former government minister for environment and technology, the president of the Nepal Mountaineering Association (NMA), the director-general of tourism and the chair of the NMA Environment Conservation Committee. It was stated from the outset that this was an information sharing assembly and that the NMA would not comment on any suggestions that might be made at the meeting. Sadly many of those in positions of influence in Nepal are very often looking for financial or personal gain and not enough are there for the benefit of the people they are supposedly representing, although there are rare and wonderful exceptions. The majority attending this particular meeting all felt the exercise was simply a PR job for Everest and an opportunity for those with political aspirations to further their cause. Few believed these consultations would actually achieve any positive outcomes.

In 1990, as Nepal moved towards a return to democracy, the NMA broadened its membership not only to those people directly involved in mountaineering but also to commercial organisations that 'supported' mountaineering. There was a dramatic increase in the number of 'commercial members' operating outlets, food stores, equipment stores, manufacturing industries and agents as opposed to mountaineers. Imagine the BMC run by commercial interests. This commercial bias continues today and manifested itself at the meeting. Many of those commenting avoided the issue at hand, the problems on Everest, instead promoting their specific commercial enterprises. Suggestions were made concerning the improvement of the EBC trail, lodge hygiene, lodge costs, waste disposal along the trail and so forth. These are valid concerns, but not much to do with mountaineering as it is practised on Everest and an absence of relevant mountain experience among those attendees who spoke up. There was from many quarters a complete denial of the traffic jam that sparked international concern and other well-documented issues from the 2019 season. The meeting was a bust, and nothing will come of it.

So why is it so hard to fix Everest? You can see why at a glance from two images. One is a photograph from 1988 taken by Ed Webster of Robert Anderson heading up from the South Col towards the summit having climbed a new line on the east face. There are no fixed ropes, meaning no Sherpas to fix them, no support climbers carrying oxygen, because he is climbing without, no collection of tents at the South Col because this is the cusp of the great change that saw Everest developed as a commercial peak.

Compare this image to that taken by Nirmal 'Nims' Purja in May 2019 that was published around the world showing hordes of people approaching the South Summit standing in the now infamous 'traffic jam'. ('Yes,' ran the headline for *Outside Online*, 'this image is real.') Now put a price tag of $50,000 on the head of every climber seen in each of these two images and the numbers soon stack up. The typical cost for climbing Everest with a foreign agency is $45,000 and up. With a local Nepali operator it ranges between $25,000 and $40,000. No one in Nepal wants to reduce the contribution Everest makes not only to government officials but also to every level of the Everest support mechanism within the tourism sector. This is why the suggestion to double the permit fee and so halve the numbers on Everest won't happen. It works for the government but operators won't want to take that course of action for fear of losing money.

Nepali law states that only Nepali agents can operate on Everest. So every climber and every foreign expedition outfitter has to work through a Nepali agent. It's a system that acts like a cartel and like most cartels lacks transparency. Every step towards the summit of Everest is managed for profit. Many responsible local agents and guides will tell you privately there are unscrupulous operators offering Everest at a price that doesn't stretch to providing properly qualified staff and infrastructure. The consequence of this is that clients are not necessarily provided appropriate support, especially in challenging weather conditions. It's no coincidence that the fatality rate on other 8,000m peaks was much higher this spring that it was on Everest: there isn't the same infrastructure to help out cheap outfitters who cut corners.

Lack of client experience featured highly in the NMA session. It was felt that many operators turn a blind eye for financial gain. Technical training sessions and the level of luxury provided at EBC contribute to the impression among inexperienced clients that the agent or guide will look after them, whatever happens. It was felt there should be a mandatory clause in all permit applications that require a potential client to have spent several nights camping above 7,500m, and be able to prove it.

Another concern is how Indian authorities offer financial incentives to climbers in government service for summiting Everest, encouraging false summit claims. This also plays into the hands of the low-cost operators, since many Indian clients use them. In June 2019 the Indian Mountaineering Foundation concluded its 2020 Everest Expedition selection and training program by stating it was the best-attended course the IMF had ever run. The numbers of Indian mountaineers on Everest will surely increase next season.

Of course the issue of helicopters came up. Today there are many companies offering sightseeing flights to EBC and these numbers are dramatically boosted with rescue and logistical flights. The fact you can no longer be in Khumbu's main valley without hearing a helicopter raised concern. Anger was also expressed concerning the lack of government reaction to the insurance scam that has also been highlighted in the world's media. Again, because of the immense investment in helicopters and the hidden links between operators and politicians, it's unlikely that anything will change soon. (See 'Nepal 2018-19' in Area Notes for more on this.)

The perennial questions of where and how the government uses peak fees raised the blood pressure of many participants. The total for Everest alone in 2019 was $4.39m, not much in a European context but a meaningful sum in Kathmandu. It's a good question that never gets answered. Following rumours that Everest might be closed next season, the government has issued a strong denial, together with documents showing that discussions have taken place about Everest at the highest of ministerial levels.

Why is it so hard to fix Everest? The simple answer is that those with the power to implement solutions are the very people making the most from the greed and chaos that currently exists there. Some climbers on the mountain are dedicated amateurs, mountain lovers; some others see the opportunity for fame and financial gain, to the exclusion of all moral or environmental concerns. Some clients, once they have summited, return home set themselves up as 'motivational speakers' and cash in: greed isn't restricted to Nepalis. Many foreign guides working on the mountain, who return to Everest year after year and actually experience these problems, know exactly what needs to be done to resolve the situation. Yet they are largely powerless against vested interests, including a small group of powerful Sherpas who have political connections that stretch to the very top. Until these powerful chains of greed and corruption are broken, little will change.

*

Treating the Dead with Respect

Climbing Mount Everest, *writes Jonathan Westaway*, has long been a metaphor for extreme achievement: something that is both hard and hazardous. And, over the years, the bodies of those seasoned Sherpas who perished in accidents or climbers who succumbed to the cold and altitude have testified to just how dangerous it is to attempt. But recent overcrowding has led to snaking queues of climbers above 8,000m have been forcing climbers to spend dangerously long periods at altitude, leading to a spate of 'blue sky' deaths.

The adventure filmmaker Elia Saikaly described his recent experience on Everest, where at least 11 people died descending from the summit this season:

I cannot believe what I saw up there. Death. Carnage. Chaos. Lineups. Dead bodies on the route and in tents at camp four. People who I tried to turn back who ended up dying. People being dragged down. Walking over bodies. Everything you read in the sensational headlines all played out on our summit night.

What, if anything, can be done to ensure that these and past human remains on Everest are treated with dignity and respect, in ways that reflect the wishes of the deceased and their families? And how can we prevent a new wave of deaths during the next summit season?

Recovering bodies from Everest is extremely difficult and hugely expensive. High altitudes, strong winds and sub-zero temperatures make climbing Everest enough of a challenge, let alone freeing and carrying down a newly frozen body. Recovery expeditions risk the lives of Sherpas and other high-altitude workers. Some corpses have remained in limbo for decades, becoming landmark features in the landscape. Their images circulate on social media and have been given nicknames by mountaineers, something that has caused significant distress to families and loved ones.

Sometimes religious sensitivities lead to action. After lobbying by families, in 2016 the government of West Bengal paid $90,000 to recover the bodies of two Bengali climbers, enabling them to be returned for cremation according to Hindu rites. Western states offer no such support. Expensive insurance plans that cover recovery are rarely purchased. Some grieving families request that their loved ones be left united with the mountain that they loved. For decades, climbers have made improvised disposals of their teammates' bodies down the steepest faces of Everest into the glacial basins below. Now, as climate change and melting glaciers reveal more and more bodies, new approaches are required.

The Chinese and Nepali authorities have different ways of managing the mountain. On the Tibetan side, the Chinese mountaineering authorities only allow experienced climbers to ascend. They have also been known to clear bodies from the north-east ridge in an effort to clean up the image of commercial mountaineering in Chinese-occupied Tibet.

Nepal is less tightly regulated, leading to cut-price expeditions and overcrowding. In the absence of proficiency checks, the country attracts inexperienced climbers seduced by the social status of reaching the summit of Everest. They risk not only their own lives, but those of others too. Inevitably, more people are currently dying on the Nepali side of Everest.

The Nepali authorities have begun to coordinate annual clean up expeditions to remove litter from the mountain, which frequently bring down human remains in the process. However, they often lack the means to identify them and there is no clear indication that they are disposed of in culturally appropriate ways.

The governing body of the world's mountaineering associations, the International Climbing and Mountaineering Federation (UIAA), urgently needs to bring together all stakeholders in Everest's future. Engaging in dialogue with Chinese state agencies on activities in occupied Tibet is complicated, but the UIAA could assist the Nepali state in tightening regulation and implementing proficiency tests for prospective climbers to tackle the overcrowding that will otherwise risk further deaths next season.

Agencies such as the International Committee of the Red Cross and the International Commission on Missing Persons should also be invited to share their experience with local NGOs and state agencies to improve methods of locating and identifying human remains as well as the recording of their removal and disposal, and the notification of next of kin.

Finally, the UIAA needs to develop a values-based code of ethics for the mountain that would bring together not only the above parties, but also the insurance industry, adventure travel companies and, most importantly, the Sherpa community. The aim must be to develop a shared understanding of how to look after the mountain and its climbers.

As the labour force on the front line of dealing with human remains on the mountain, the Sherpa community should be central to this process. Here, the UIAA should look to existing successful models that prioritise indigenous rights, such as the San Code of Ethics. After decades of invasive and exploitative research into their genes and culture, the hunter-gatherer San people of southern Africa developed this ethical framework with an NGO to ensure that research is mutually beneficial and conducted in line with San values.

There are no easy solutions to the bodies on Everest, nor the deaths that precede them. But anything other than urgent change will disfigure the mountain and seriously damage commercial mountaineering's reputation for good stewardship. Indifference is not an option.

JACQUES MOUREY, MÉLANIE MARCUZZI,
LUDOVIC RAVANEL & FRANÇOIS PALLANDRE

Effects of Climate Change on High Alpine Mountain Environments

Evolution of Mountaineering Routes in the Mont Blanc Massif over 50 Years

In high Alpine environments, glacial shrinkage and permafrost warming due to climate change are having significant consequences on mountaineering routes. Few research projects have studied the relationship between climate change and mountaineering; this study attempts to characterise and explain this evolution over the past 40 years of routes described in *The Mont Blanc Massif: The 100 Finest Routes*, Gaston Rébuffat's emblematic selected guidebook, first published in 1973. The main elements studied were geomorphic and cryospheric changes and their impacts, determining the manner and possibility for each route to be climbed. Thirty-one interviews and comparison with other guidebooks led to the identification of 25 distinctive geomorphic and cryospheric changes related to climate change affecting mountaineering itineraries. On average, each itinerary has been affected by nine changes. Among the 95 itineraries studied, 93 have been affected by the effects of climate change; 26 of them have been greatly affected; and three no longer exist. Moreover, periods during which these itineraries can be climbed in good conditions in summer have tended to become less predictable and periods of optimal conditions have shifted toward spring and autumn, because the itineraries have become more dangerous and technically more challenging.

Introduction

Climate change led to a temperature increase of 2°C in the Alps between the end of the 19th century and the beginning of the 21st with a strong acceleration in warming since the 1990s. In this context, and being very sensitive to climate variations, high Alpine environments have undergone major change. The total surface area of Alpine glaciers decreased by half between 1900 and 2012 while rock faces experienced an increase in the frequency and volume of rock fall. These changes raise the question of what the effects might be on recreational mountain activities, and especially on mountaineering. Mountaineers climbing during the summer months are undeniably noticing important changes to the environment to which they must adapt by modifying their techniques. Although awareness of this issue dates back to the 2000s, only a few studies have been conducted to confirm it. As such, the evolution of mountaineering itineraries due to climate change remains poorly documented.

This article aims to describe and explain the evolution over nearly half a century of mountaineering itineraries in the Mont Blanc massif (MBM), the birthplace of mountaineering and still a major mountaineering destination. It is impossible to document all mountaineering itineraries as several thousand have been climbed in the MBM. The 1975 Vallot guidebook alone includes 747 itineraries. Thus, our study focuses on itineraries in Gaston Rébuffat's famous guidebook, *The Mont Blanc Massif: The 100 Finest Routes*. Using recent guidebooks and interviews, the itineraries described by Rébuffat in 1973 were compared with their current state. First, the geomorphic and cryospheric changes that have affected the area were identified. Then, for each itinerary, the specific changes that have affected it were established and also the degree to which these changes have changed the route's technical level and danger. The evolution of the manner in which mountaineers tackle these routes due to the effects of climate change is then be discussed, along with the consequences for the popularity of mountaineering.

Mont Blanc Massif

Mountaineering originally developed in the western Alps, and especially in the MBM, at the end of the 18th century. Since then, it has evolved considerably through technical, cultural and ideological changes. The Golden Age of mountaineering was marked by a series of important first ascents, notably those made by Edward Whymper and his guides in the MBM, as well as the Matterhorn. In 2018 Chamonix and Courmayeur applied for mountaineering to be included on UNESCO's Intangible Cultural Heritage Lists. Over the past 200 years, the evolution of mountaineering has been mainly due to socio-cultural reasons. However, current changes to the high mountain environment due to climate change are challenging accepted mountaineering practices. The MBM (*Figure 1, overleaf*) is located in the north-west Alps between Switzerland, Italy and France, and covers 550km². About 30% of its surface is covered with ice with some 100 glaciers, including the Mer de Glace, the largest glacier in the French Alps with an area of 30km². A dozen peaks exceed the altitude of 4,000m, including Mont Blanc, the highest summit of the Alps (4809m).

The MBM presents a cross-range asymmetry. Six of the largest glaciers of the massif are located on its north-west aspect, where slopes are gentler than on its very steep south-east aspect, which is characterised by small glaciers bounded by high near-vertical rock walls. This asymmetry implies different climatic contexts. In Chamonix (1044m), the mean annual air temperature (MAAT) is 7.2°C, while in Courmayeur (1223m), it is 10.4°C. At the Aiguille du Midi (3842m), the MAAT is -8.2°C (reference period: 2008-10, Météo-France data). In Chamonix, MAAT increased by 1.7°C between 1934 and 2009. It is important to note this warming mainly affects winter temperatures; these increased by 2.8°C compared to summer temperatures, which increased by 1.5°C (Météo-France data). Moreover, MAAT

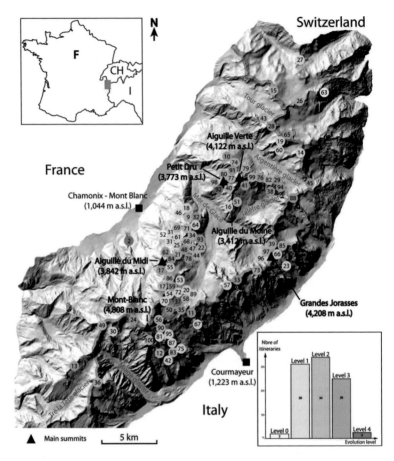

Figure 1 Location of the Mont Blanc massif, the itineraries studied and their level of evolution.

increased four times faster over the period 1970-2009 than during the period 1934-70. MAAT also increased at high elevations: above 4,000m, it increased by 1.4°C between 1990 and 2014. Since 1990, the MBM has experienced seven summer heat waves, four of them in the last decade. In France, summer 2018 was the second hottest summer since 1900. Only summer 2003 was hotter. In Chamonix, average annual precipitation is 1,288mm. In Courmayeur, it is 854 mm. At 3,500m, precipitation is three times higher than in the town of Chamonix. Since the end of the Little Ice Age (LIA), precipitation levels have experienced little change; however, there has been a clear decrease in snowfall days relative to total precipitation days and there is more frequent and intense melting. Consequently, in the Swiss Alps between 1,139m and 2,540m, snow-cover duration shortened by 8.9 days/decades[-1] during the period 1970-2015, with a snow season starting 12 days later and ending 26 days earlier than in 1970. While these changes in snow cover are elevation dependent and less pronounced at higher altitudes, snow quantity at high altitude is also decreasing. With higher and faster warming at high altitudes than the global average, climate change is causing substantial change to high mountain environments. In the MBM, the glacial surface area decreased by 24% between the end of the LIA and 2008 with a considerable increase in the acceleration of melting since the 1990s. Mean glacier mass balance in the European Alps was -0.31m ± 0.04m wea^{-1} [Editor's note: wea^{-1} means 'water equivalent per year'] during the period 1900-2011 and -1m wea^{-1} during the first decade of the 2000s, which illustrates the acceleration of glacial shrinkage. In the MBM, the region-wide mean mass balance was -1.04 ± 0.23m wea^{-1} between 2003 and 2012; the Argentière glacier mean mass balance over the same period was -1.46 ± 0.4m wea^{-1}. The loss of ice thickness is also significant. At 1,900m, between 1994 and 2013, the Argentière glacier lost 80m of ice depth. On the Mer de Glace, the rate of glacial thickness loss increased from 1m per year (1979-1994) to more than 4m. The Mer de Glace loss in thickness was up to 60m at its front (1500m) during the period 1979-2003. At the same time, glacier fronts retreated dramatically: 366m between 1994 and 2007 for the Mer de Glace, with a particularly rapid period of shrinkage of 40m/y between 1998 and 2005. Glacial shrinkage affects high elevations, above the glacier equilibrium line altitude (ELA) that separates the accumulation and ablation zones. Between the 1960s and 2008, the glacier surface areas on the French side of the MBM decreased by 16% between 2,200m and 2,600 m, 11% at 2,600 to 3,000 m, 6% at 3,000, to 3,500 m and 3% at 3,500m to 4,000m. For example, the surface of the Talèfre glacier lowered by 5m to 10 m between 3,000m and 3,500m over the period 1979-2003. At 3,613m, the Géant glacier surface lowered by 20m between 1992 and 2012.

Glacial shrinkage coincides with a rise of the ELA of 170m between 1984 and 2010 in the western Alps. Also, combined with a decrease in winter snow accumulation, the snow cover on the glacier surfaces tends to decrease both in area and thickness. As a result, crevasses appear earlier in spring and areas of bare ice increase in summer. The decrease in snow cover on glaciers also results in an increase in the number of open crevasses, while snow bridges may be getting more fragile. The fragility of snow bridges is probably increasing as the average altitude of the 0°C isotherm has risen by 400m since 1980 and frost frequency has decreased. The snowpack does not refreeze and consolidate, especially during the night. As such, snow bridges are probably weakening earlier in spring and during heat waves.

In some cases, glacier retreat leads to more frequent serac fall from the hanging fronts of warm and cold-based glaciers. [Editor's note: Cold-based glaciers are at freezing where they meet the ground, warm-based glaciers are not.] In the MBM, serac fall mainly occurs during the warmest periods of the year and, at the secular scale, during or at the end of the warmest periods.

Due to glacial shrinkage, para-glacial processes – meaning non-glacial earth-surface processes, sediment accumulations, landforms, land-systems and landscapes that are directly conditioned by glaciation and de-glaciation – are intensifying. A para-glacial period starts as a direct reaction to de-glaciation and ends when all glacial sediments have been removed or stabilized. In this study, para-glacial processes refer mainly to the erosion of moraines through rock fall and landslides, illustrated by the gullying of the inner flank of lateral moraines due to steep slopes up to 80°.

At the same time, permafrost – ground that remains permanently at or below 0°C for at least two consecutive years – tends to warm and degrade. Even if all rock falls cannot be attributed to permafrost warming, as it is a natural erosion process in high mountain environments, its degradation results in more frequent and voluminous slope instabilities. In the MBM, more than 850 rock falls greater than 100m³ occurred between 2007 and 2018. Permafrost is continuously present above 3,000m on average on north faces and above 3,600m on south faces.

The change in the high mountain environment raises the question of how mountaineering itineraries have been affected and what effect this has had on their popularity.

Rébuffat as Reference Sample

Rébuffat's selected guidebook has for several decades been a major source of information for alpinists. It was the first guidebook to offer a selection of routes based on their quality, unlike guidebooks of the same period, such as the Vallot series, that drew up more exhaustive lists of all the routes of a region. It also arranges routes by increasing difficulty, from *Facile* to *Extrêmement Difficile* as well as commitment, so can be used as a reference for progression. All types of routes are covered – rock, snow, ice and mixed – and they have been chosen from throughout the massif (*Figure 1*), making it this selection both relevant and representative of all mountaineering itineraries in the MBM.

Not all the itineraries in Rébuffat were included in this study: itineraries one and three to eight were ruled out because they are located outside the MBM. On the other hand, several itineraries are presented together in the book, as they can by climbed the same day or on the same trip into the mountains, but these have been treated separately for this study. Itinerary 17 is an example: Rébuffat recommends combining the normal route on Mont Blanc du Tacul (4248m) with the Cosmiques ridge on the Aiguille du Midi (3842 m) in a single day. Altogether, 95 itineraries were analysed. In some cases, several descents are possible; only the most classic were chosen.

Methodology

Our study is structured according to two main data collection methodologies. First, semi-structured interviews were carried out with alpine guides, including instructors at the National School of Skiing and Mountaineering (ENSA), hut-keepers, employees in charge of trail management, first ascentionists and guidebook editors. In total, 31 people were interviewed. These people all have a good knowledge of mountaineering itineraries and 19 of

Main effects of climate change on high alpine environments	Geomorphic changes affecting and modifying mountaineering itineraries	Number of itineraries affected (XX/95 - YY %)	Part(s) of the itinerary affected the most	Effects on the climbing parameters	References
Permafrost degradation	1. Rockfalls	55 - 52	Route	danger	Matsuoka and Sakai, 1999; Matsuoka, 2001
	2. Rock collapse	30 - 31	Route	danger	Gruber and Haeberli, 2007; Ravanel et al., 2017
Melting of ice/snow covers and evolution of snow ridges	3. Surface of ice/snow covers in bare ice earlier in the season (or almost permanently)	58 - 55	Route	difficulty	
	4. Slope angle increase	53 - 50	Route	difficulty	Galibert, 1960
	5. Retreat of ice/snow covers; apparition of the bedrock in general very fractured	53 - 50	Route	danger	Delaloye, 2008
	6. Snow ridges becoming narrower	25 - 24	Route	difficulty	
Glacial shrinkage	Paraglacial processes — 7. Appearance of moraines and increase of their height	47 - 45	Approach, Descent	danger, lengthening	Mortara and Chiarle, 2005
	Paraglacial processes — 8. Increase of the moraines slope angle	47 - 45	Approach, Descent	danger	Luckas et al., 2012; Ravanel and Lambiel, 2013
	Paraglacial processes — 9. Destabilization of rocks (rockfalls, landslides) in the moraines	47 - 45	Approach, Descent	danger	Deline, 2008; McColl, 2012; Eichel et al., 2018
	Paraglacial processes — 10. Development of torrent on proglacial zones	3 - 3	Approach, Descent	danger	Collins, 2008
	11. Appearance of smooth slabs of bedrock	77 - 73	Route	difficulty	Berthier et al., 2014
	12. Appearance of destructured bedrock	30 - 28	Route	danger, difficulty	Ravanel et al., 2013
	13. Appearance of new crevassed area	47 - 45	Approach, Descent	danger, difficulty	
	14. Wider crevasses and bergschrunds	78 - 74	Approach, Route, Descent	danger, difficulty	Ogier et al., 2017
	15. Weakening of snow bridges			danger	
	16. Collapse of the front of cold-based glaciers	4 - 4	Descent	danger	Margreth et al., 2011; Faillettaz et al., 2015
	17. Serac falls from the front of cold-based glaciers	12 - 11	Route	danger	
	18. Serac falls from glaciers surfaces	23 - 22	Descent	danger	Le Meur and Vincent, 2006; Vincent et al., 2015
	19. Collapse of the front of warm-based glaciers	7 - 7	Descent	danger	
	20. Modification of the supraglacial hydrology (drainage channels more frequent, wider and deeper)	4 - 4	Approach, Descent	lengthening, danger	Miller et al., 2012
	21. Glacier slope angle increase	73 - 70	Descent	difficulty	Berthier et al., 2014
	22. Glaciers surfaces more often in bare ice	49 - 47	Approach, Route, Descent	difficulty	Rabatel et al., 2013
	23. Development of supraglacial debris covers	24 - 23	Approach, Descent	lengthening	Deline, 2005
	24. Rocks falling and sliding from the glaciers surfaces	11 - 10	Approach, Descent	danger	Purdie et al., 2015
	25. Less frequent night freezing			danger	Böhm et al., 2010; Pohl et al., 2019

Legend:
- Approach
- Route
- Descent
- ● Increase in danger
- ● Increase in technical difficulty
- ▲ Lengthening and greater drudgery of the way

Table 1 Climate-related geomorphic and cryospheric changes affecting mountaineering itineraries and their climbing parameters.

them have been active in the MBM since the 1980s, but only four senior Alpine guides who have frequented the range since the 1970s were interviewed. The two main questions were: 'What are the ongoing long-term changes on these itineraries since the 1970s?'; and 'How have these itineraries changed with regards to technical difficulty, objective dangers, and optimal periods for making an ascent?' The interviewees were only asked to report long-term changes. Attribution of climate-related changes was carried out by two researchers both familiar with the MBM and their results were compared afterwards. In some cases, to confirm the information collected during the interviews, descriptions of itineraries from Rébuffat's guidebook were compared with those from recent guidebooks.

Two sets of interviews were conducted in fall 2017. The first set led to the identification of the climate-related changes that have affected the itineraries (*Table 1*). Some of these have been the subject of scientific research, which has enabled us to confirm their existence and describe them more accurately. A second set of interviews was conducted in order to list the geomorphic and cryospheric changes affecting each of the 95 itineraries studied. At least 10 itineraries were considered per interview, which thus tended to be relatively long: up to three hours. The studied itineraries varied from one interview to another, depending on the memories of the interviewees. In the end, each of the 95 itineraries was studied during at least two different interviews. The database was formalised as a table, cross-referencing each of the 95 itineraries with the 25 geomorphic and cryospheric changes. This was completed during the interviews. The results are presented in *Table 1*. However, one of the limits of this method of data formalisation is that the location and the intensity of each of the changes identified were not recorded. Each itinerary was divided into three parts: the approach, which begins in the valley or at the top of a cable car and ends either at the foot of the rock wall to be climbed or at the bergschrund; the route and its continuation to the summit; and the descent, which begins at the summit and ends in the valley or at the top of a lift.

During this second set of interviews, a five-level scale was developed to evaluate the evolution of the climbing parameters of each itinerary. The climbing parameters considered are: itinerary type (ice, snow, mixed or rock), technical difficulty, level of exposure to objective dangers, and any changes to the optimal period for making an ascent, i.e. when the number or intensity of changes affecting it are lowest.

- *Level 0* The itinerary and the parameters determining the way the route is climbed have not changed.
- *Level 1* The itinerary and its climbing parameters have slightly evolved. Only a short section of the itinerary is affected by geomorphic and cryospheric changes, and this does not result in a significant increase in objective dangers and/or in technical difficulty.
- *Level 2* The itinerary and its climbing parameters have moderately evolved. The optimal periods for making an ascent have become rare or unpredictable in summer and shifted toward spring and sometimes autumn. Objective dangers and technical difficulty are increasing and mountaineers have to adapt their technique.
- *Level 3* The itinerary and its climbing parameters have greatly evolved. Generally, the itinerary can no longer be climbed in summer. Objective dangers and technical difficulty have greatly increased due to the number and intensity of the geomorphic changes affecting it. Mountaineers have had to fundamentally change the manner in which they climb the route.
- *Level 4* The itinerary has completely disappeared: it can no longer be climbed.

The identification of the changes affecting a mountaineering itinerary varied greatly from one person to another depending on the climbing circumstances encountered during the ascent (i.e. the occurrence or absence and the intensity of the changes previously identified), the technical level and number of clients and their personal perception. Changes identified were not always the same, nor assessed to the same degree. As an example, at the end of the summer season when the glacier surface is icy, any increase in steepness is more significant and easier to identify compared to the beginning of the season when the glacier surface is still covered with snow. Moreover, interviewees tended to underestimate the number of changes affecting an itinerary. Indeed, it seems individuals usually noticed only the changes that are relevant when making an ascent, without necessarily taking into account the season and high-mountain climate-related evolution. It was the interviewers' role to encourage interviewees to identify only long-term changes rather than focusing on their last ascent. For this reason, a great number of interviews were conducted in order to validate data collected.

Results

Twenty-five geomorphic and cryospheric changes were identified (*Table 1*). They result from glacial shrinkage, a reduction of ice-snow cover, changes in the structure of snow ridges, and permafrost warming. For each geomorphic change, its impact on climbing parameters was identified (*Table 1*): increase in objective dangers, technical difficulty and commitment, lengthening of the itinerary and any increase in the effort required to climb it.

All the types of changes that have affected each route between the 1970s and today were listed. On average, an itinerary has been affected by nine geomorphic changes. The appearance of bedrock (85 itineraries affected), wider crevasses and bergschrunds (78) and steeper glaciers (73) are the three most commonly observed changes. They cause an increase in the level of danger and technical difficulty. Alpine guides interviewed all had to deal with thinner and weaker snow bridges, while crevasses that were never or rarely observed now appear more often.

Finally, regarding the scale used to evaluate changes to the itineraries studied from a mountaineering point of view (*Figure 1*), two had not evolved (level 0), 30 had slightly evolved (level 1), 34 had moderately evolved (level 2), 26 had greatly evolved (level 3), and three had disappeared (level 4). Four examples are described here to better illustrate those evolutions and the implications for mountaineering. Moreover, there is a direct correlation between the number of geomorphic changes affecting an itinerary and its level of evolution. On average, for level 1, 7.4 changes were affecting the itineraries, 10 for level 2, 11.5 for level 3 and 12.5 for level 4. It is also important to note that during the summer of 2018, the evolution levels of three itineraries changed: from 1 to 3 (Cosmiques ridge: itinerary 17), 1 to 4 (Lépiney route: itinerary 37) and 1 to 2 (Rébuffat-Bacquet route: itinerary 55). The geomorphic changes responsible for those three evolutions have been identified thanks to a network of observers, mainly guides and hut-keepers, developed to study geomorphic changes in the MBM.

Patterns of Change

The first example is the disappearance of a rock route because of massive rock fall: the Petit Dru (3733m) west face. The *Bonatti* route, itinerary 92 in Rébuffat, was Walter Bonatti's emblematic rock climb first climbed in 1955. However, most of the route disappeared after a 700m pillar collapsed in 2005. This route has a level 4 evolution: see *Figure 2*.

Petit Dru (3733 m a.s.l.)

700 m

—— Bonatti route (1955)
☐ 2005 rockfall scar

Figure 2 The Petit Dru west face,
October 2017. A major part of the
Bonatti route has disappeared because
of a rock collapse in 2005 and a further
rock fall in 2011 (292,000m³).

An example of a snow and mixed route that can no longer be climbed in summer because of ice-snow cover melting early is the *Whymper* couloir on the Aiguille Verte (4122m), itinerary 41 and the line of the Verte's first ascent in 1865.

In 1973, Rébuffat classified this classic itinerary as a snow climb. Today, the ice-snow cover necessary for an ascent of the couloir has been significantly reduced (*Figure 3*). Indeed, it completely melts out early in summer and fractured bedrock is exposed. Rock fall is consequently frequent. In addition, the berg-schrund at the bottom of the couloir becomes very wide and difficult to cross. Rock fall is observed frequently and a 22,000m³ rock fall occurred on the right bank of the couloir in August 2015. These environmental changes have led to an increase in technical difficulty and inherent danger of the route and it is now possible to climb it only very early in summer. The change applied to this itinerary is Level 3.

Two instances of a rock route whose approach has been affected are the south face of the Aiguille du Midi (3842m) and the east face of the Aiguille du Moine (3412m). The *Rébuffat-Bacquet* route (itinerary 55), climbed in 1956 on the south face of the Aiguille du Midi, is a classic rock climb that sees a lot of traffic in summer. Apart from a small rock fall, it has not yet been directly affected by climate change, but the approach to the original starting point of the route has become more difficult because of two factors. First, the east ridge of the Aiguille du Midi that leads to the bottom of the face is becoming narrower. It is oriented west-east, meaning melting is much more significant on its south side than on its north. This makes it steeper, and it tends to become icy earlier in summer. Crevasses also now appear. Second, because the Géant glacier at the foot of the face has lost over 25m in depth over the past 30 years, the route's historic starting point is now difficult to reach (*Figure 4*). Climbers now have to follow the start of the *Contamine* route, which is technically more difficult, graded F6b instead of F6a, than any pitches on the Rébuffat-Bacquet. These environmental changes have led to an increase in the technical difficulty and commitment needed to reach the start of the route. The level of evolution applied to

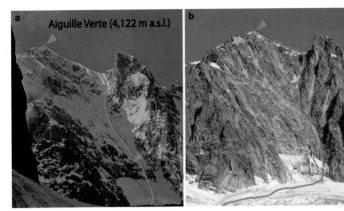

Figure 3 The *Whymper* couloir on the south face of the Aiguille Verte (4122m). The route is marked in red. A: situation at the end of the 1960s (picture from the guidebook). B: situation at the end of August 2017 (C Lelièvre). The ice-snow cover in the couloir has undergone a significant reduction, exposing fractured bedrock, leading to frequent rock falls (orange arrows). The orange star indicates the point where a 22,000m³ rock fall released in 2015. The red triangles indicate similar features.

Right: *Figure 4* Aiguille du Midi south face, September 2018. The original start to the Rébuffat-Bacquet route (1956) is no longer accessible directly. The lower part of another route must be climbed to join it.

this itinerary is 2. Because the surface of the Géant glacier lowered greatly during the 2018 heat wave, the route was not accessible at the end of the summer period. A very difficult climbing section has appeared. This situation is identical for the majority of rock routes but the increase in difficulty varies depending on the extent of ice-thickness loss and the nature of the terrain exposed. In some cases, the route may lose its intrinsic logic and aesthetic if sections of climbing appear that are much more difficult than the rest of the route. This is the case for the *Labrunie-Contamine* route (itinerary 51) on the Aiguille du Moine (3412m) east face. A 15m section of F6c climbing is now exposed at the

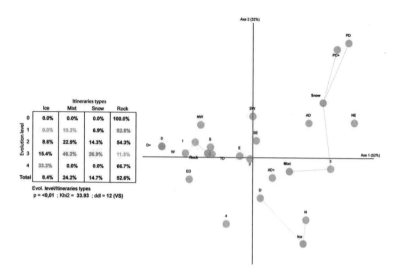

Figure 5 Cross-tabulation and graphical representation of the relationships between the level of evolution of a route for mountaineering purposes and its nature (rock, snow, ice and mixed), difficulty and aspect. The closer the circles are, the more meaningful their relations are. The statistically strongest relationships are underlined.

start of the route because of the lowered surface of the Talèfre glacier. The rest of the route is graded F6a maximum. This short, difficult section has made the route less attractive, and it is now climbed less frequently than before. The level of evolution applied to this itinerary is 2.

Another category is a rock route whose descent is more difficult and dangerous because of glacial shrinkage, an example being the Aiguille de l'M (2844m). The mountain's north ridge (itinerary 18) is a very popular rock route. The approach and route are not affected by geomorphic or cryospheric changes, notably because of its lower altitude. However, the way down follows a south-facing couloir to reach the Nantillons glacier at 2,500m. Because of the lowering of the glacier surface, the couloir is becoming steeper and exposed to rock fall coming from the lateral moraine of the glacier. In order to reduce the danger and technical difficulty, abseils and ladders have been installed in the couloir. Therefore, the itinerary can be climbed all summer and the descent is now less technically difficult. The level of evolution applied to this itinerary is 1.

Discussion

In general, snow, ice and mixed itineraries have been more affected by climate change, with a 2.4 average level of evolution, compared to rock routes with a 1.6 average level of evolution. This finding is confirmed by a correspondence factor analysis (CFA) linking the level of evolution of the itineraries with their type (rocky, snow, ice and mixed), difficulty, and orientation: see *Figure 5*. Itineraries undergoing level 3 evolution are mainly mixed and snow routes (46.2% and 26.9%, respectively) graded *Assez Difficile* or *Peu Difficile* and facing north-east. On the other hand, rock routes are statistically underrepresented (11.5%) in this evolutionary scale. The routes undergoing level 0, 1 and 2 changes are mostly rock routes (100%, 82.8% and 54.3%, respectively) for the highest level of difficulty *Extrêmement Difficile* and *Très Difficile*. Variable aspects are represented. In the 0 level of evolution, ice routes are statistically underrepresented (0%). We can conclude that climate change affects rock routes less than snow, ice and mixed routes.

Not all the geomorphic changes identified in this work affect the itineraries in the same way. Approaches are mainly affected by: wider crevasses and bergschrunds (53 of 95), para-glacial processes (41) and the appearance of new crevassed areas (27). The changes most affecting rock routes are: the appearance of smooth slabs or unstable bedrock (77) and all changes related to the disappearance of ice-snow cover and the evolution of snow ridges (52). Finally, the changes predominantly affecting descents are a steepening of glaciated slopes (63), wider crevasses and bergschrunds (59), and para-glacial processes (41). There is also a correlation between some changes and the orientation of the routes. For 39 routes located on southern slopes 23 are affected by processes due to permafrost degradation and 22 by the appearance of smooth slabs or fractured bedrock. On the other hand, changes in serac fall and the appearance of bare ice mainly affect north-facing routes. Other changes, such as the reduction in ice-snow cover, equally affect routes on southern and northern aspects.

Seasonal Changes

It is difficult to measure the effects of one or several changes on the climbing parameters of a route. In general, changes identified imply an increase in technical difficulty, danger and commitment of these itineraries in summer but seasonality must also be addressed.

The evolution of mountaineering itineraries is conditioned on two different timescales. The main timescale addressed in this study is climate-related and covers the period from the 1970s to 2018. However, deterioration of climbing parameters can be reduced or increased by seasonal factors. Changes are usually less impactful at the beginning of the summer season, when the winter snowpack has not yet melted out, even if snowpack in general is decreasing both in quantity and duration, and they increase at the end of the summer season or during heat waves, which are becoming more frequent and intense due to climate change. Itineraries in an optimal period for making an ascent – more and more commonly outside the summer period – are not necessarily any more difficult or dangerous than before. For this reason, windows for mountaineering tend to be more variable in summer and are shifting toward spring, autumn, as temperatures start to drop and new snowfalls occur and even winter, especially for snow, ice and mixed routes. Depending on the nature of the itinerary, much more attention must be paid to changing climbing conditions. According to the interviewees, the summer mountaineering season has shifted by three weeks toward spring compared with the 1980s. This confirms work done in the Écrins massif.

There isn't necessarily a direct link between the level of change of an itinerary and its popularity. A notable example is the classic route to the summit of Mont Blanc (itinerary 24). It has been greatly affected by climate change, with an increase in technical difficulty and especially in its level of danger. Rock fall is increasingly frequent in the Grand Couloir du Goûter and causes a significant number of accidents. Between 1990 and 2017, there were an average of 3.7 deaths and 8.5 injuries per summer on the crossing of the couloir and the climb to the Goûter ridge, mainly due to human error and rock fall. In addition, large crevasses, which are difficult to cross, are appearing even at high altitude above 4,000m, while the summit ridge is becoming narrower. The descent described by Rébuffat is no longer used in summer, as it has become too crevassed. Even though the level of change applied to this itinerary is 3, it is still one of the busiest mountaineering itineraries in the world because of the prestige of climbing the highest summit in the Alps.

On the other hand, some itineraries that have only been slightly affected by climate change are much less popular than in the past. To explain this, other socio-economic factors and the evolution of mountaineering itself must be considered. Today, mountaineers tend to limit their risk-taking and exposure to objective dangers such as rock and serac fall. Other itineraries are no longer popular because the approach is long or the in situ equipment is old. As an example, according to the guides interviewed, the north face of the Aiguille de Bionnassay (4052m), itinerary 49, was a classic ascent during the 1980s. Today, it is no longer climbed in summer despite a relatively low level of change (2) because of the danger of serac fall. This danger was also present 40 years ago.

In some cases, the evolution of mountaineering itineraries due to the effects of climate change leads to an increase in popularity. This is the case for the traverse of the Dômes de Miage (3673m), itinerary 13, a famous and beautiful snow climb. During the summer of 2015, a crevasse opened on the summit ridge, which itself had become narrower and icier. In addition, a rock fall occurred on the route, making it more technically difficult and exposing it to further rock fall. The ridgeline was no longer being traversed, with climbers choosing to descend by the ascent route. This made the itinerary less aesthetically pleasing and the number of people staying at the Conscrits hut (2602m), which gives access to the route, fell by 25% that summer. The same situation occurred in 2016 and 2017, with significant economic consequences for the hut-keeper. The Couvercle hut (2679m) is facing the same situation, with climbing parameters on most routes deteriorating earlier in the summer season. According to the former two hut-keepers, the steady decline in the number of overnight stays, 35% over the last 15 years, has been accentuated by the evolution of mountain itineraries, perhaps concurrently with socio-economic factors.

Is the aesthetic quality of high mountain areas deteriorating? Geomorphic and cryospheric changes result in significant changes to the landscape. The general drying of high mountain environments leads to the appearance of more and more rocky terrain as glacial surfaces decrease. With snow cover on glacier surfaces melting out faster and at higher altitudes, more bare ice appears, and debris cover is increasing as rock falls form more continuous deposits. All the interviews carried out indicate that high mountain landscapes no longer conform to the classic representation of blue ice and 'eternal snow'. The motivation of some mountaineers to go into the high mountains is thus reduced. 'I note there is less interest to go on glaciers [...] that are dirty, with a dull colour; they are less attractive in a certain way,' the guide B Pelissier said in October 2017.

The Limits of Rébuffat
Because Rébuffat's guidebook dates from the 1970s, it does not feature any steep, narrow ice climbs, like the *Supercouloir* on Mont Blanc du Tacul, which appeared after Rébuffat's book thanks to improving equipment. According to the guides interviewed, the formation of ice gullies is becoming increasingly less frequent and the quality of ice is often lower. During the winters of 2016 and 2017, almost no such ice gullies formed in the MBM. It seems the main factors explaining the disappearance of these routes are the lack of winter and spring snowfall and the more rapid melting of the ice-snow cover. This phenomenon seems to be very recent and is due largely to an increase in the frequency of winter warm spells since the beginning of the 2000s.

Another factor limiting our methodology must also be highlighted. Because some itineraries have the same approach and descent, some changes have been overrepresented. This is particularly the case for para-glacial processes affecting approaches and descents in the Mer de Glace basin. One way of limiting this bias would have been to consider only the routes themselves, and not the approaches and descents but this method would not have given an accurate representation of the difficulties mountaineers are facing throughout the whole itinerary.

Moreover, it is not possible to objectively compare the grade of itineraries between the 1970s and today, as the grading system, equipment and technical level have changed considerably. Finally, because rock slope instabilities resulting from post-glacial decompression are relatively uncommon in the MBM and difficult to differentiate from the many rock falls resulting from permafrost degradation, they have not been considered in this study.

Conclusion
The impact of climate change on high mountain environments has altered mountaineering itineraries. This study presents an exhaustive list of 25 geomorphic and cryospheric changes related to climate change affecting a typical mountaineering itinerary. On average, an itinerary in the MBM is affected by nine of these changes. Moreover, the impacts of each of these

changes have been documented and quantified for the first time. The exposure of bedrock, the widening of crevasses and bergschrunds, and steepening of glaciated slopes are the main changes.

The impact of these changes on mountaineering has been quantified for 95 itineraries. Only two routes have not changed, 30 have slightly, 34 moderately, 26 strongly and three have disappeared altogether. As a result, mountaineering itineraries tend to be more technically difficult and more dangerous. Optimal periods during summer months have become rarer and more unpredictable, resulting in progressive reduction in terrain available for mountaineers as the summer season progresses and good periods are now more likely to occur in spring, autumn and even winter on some itineraries. Changes in a mountaineering itinerary due to the effects of climate change may lead to a significant decrease in its popularity, but socio-economic factors must also be considered.

Climate change is expected to accelerate during the coming decades and this will lead to ever-increasing changes to the highly sensitive high-mountain environment. Changes to mountaineering itineraries described in this article are expected to continue and increase. This perspective may have significant consequences for mountaineering and the ability of mountain professionals, such as guides and hut-keepers, to adapt.

Acknowledgments
The authors thank the personnel of the ENSA library for making the library and all its resources available to us and Neil Brodie, instructor at ENSA, for the English language editing. This study was funded by the EU ALOCTRA project AdaPT Mont Blanc. Finally, we gratefully thank the anonymous reviewers and the editor for their constructive comments on the manuscript.

References
For reasons of length, the extensive referencing for this article has been omitted. All references are available with the full paper online at *https://www.tandfonline.com/doi/full/10.1080/15230430.2019.1612216?scroll=top&needAccess=true*

ED DOUGLAS

Climbing and Flying

In 1867, a month before he turned 17, the future editor of the *Alpine Journal* W A B Coolidge stood where I am now, on the summit of Piz Badile, celebrating the first ascent. His write-up in the *Journal*, then edited by Leslie Stephen, was perfunctory: he refers to the Badile, 'the Shovel', as Cima di Tschingel, really the Cengalo, and offers a sequence of timings that show Coolidge to be a fit young man, leaving the thermal baths at Masino at 5.22am and returning at 1.52pm, having spent 42 minutes on the summit. It took me a shade under three hours just to reach the Gianetti hut. He left no impression of the summit and my own is rather fragmentary: the rolled-up lid of a sardine can at my feet, which I pocket as a souvenir; the Cengalo's summit, a pile of rubble looking like a mortally dangerous version of Jenga; and at the foot of the peak evidence of the gigantic rock fall, some four million cubic metres, that sheared off Piz Cengalo's north face in August 2017, 150 years after Coolidge, killing eight hikers. This followed a similar if smaller collapse in 2011. Footage taken of the 2017 rock fall from above by climbers on the north face of the Badile is well worth seeking out, but best watched from behind the sofa. You don't need to tell alpinists that mountains have a strong desire to lie down, but something more is at work here: the climate emergency is in town.

My climbing partner notices the absence of snow and ice on our horizon. 'Pretty dark out there,' he says, or something to that effect. I look at the black peaks around us and can only agree. The vagaries of glaciation was a subject that fascinated Coolidge and his contemporaries, particularly Douglas Freshfield, who had made the first ascent of Cengalo the year before Coolidge climbed the Badile, and Francis Fox Tuckett, whose uncle was Robert Were Fox, geologist and fellow of the Royal Society. During Coolidge's period as editor, famous for its hatchet-wielding, Tuckett wrote an extended, two-part review of Albert Heim's 1885 work *Handbuch der Gletscherkunde*, the Swiss geologist's 560-page treatise on the emerging science of glaciology. (Heim's contribution was acknowledged with the naming of the Heim glacier in Antarctica. He also had a side-interest in near-death experiences, having experienced one himself and knowing lots of alpinists.)

While Heim's immense book has obviously been superseded, it contains much data of interest to modern glaciologists and also possibly to François Devouassoud, Coolidge's guide on the Badile and Freshfield's on the Cengalo. Devouassoud was born in 1831 in the village of Les Barrats, now a suburb of Chamonix and when he went to school in Sallanches the glaciers flowing north from Mont Blanc had only just passed their greatest extent. In 1825, the village of Les Bois had even been evacuated as the glacier,

The Swiss artist Samuel Birmann (1793-1847) drew the Lower Grindelwald glacier (above left) in September 1826 (pencil, pen, watercolour, bodycolour, 39.2cm × 49.7cm), and the Mer de Glace in August 1823 (above right) (pencil, pen, watercolour, bodycolour, 44.3cm × 58.9cm). *(Kunstmuseum Basel)*

then known as the Glacier des Bois, extended down to the valley floor. As Devouassoud started his working life in 1849 the process went into reverse. According to Heim, building on the work of François-Alphonse Florel and others, between 1850 and 1878 the glacier retreated a total of 1.05km. Tuckett, writing in the mid 1880s, explained how this process was now going into reverse as a new cycle of increasing glaciation got underway; this was part of the natural rhythm of the planet, a cycle of warming and cooling reflected in the growth and retreat of glaciers.

Only this time, it didn't. As *Figure 1* illustrates[1], the period of glacial retreat Heim describes merely stalled until the Second World War before the process of retreat resumed until the end of this particular period of study in 2003. Since then the process has only accelerated. Ten of the hottest summers on record have occurred in the last 20 years. Last summer, 2018, was the joint-hottest on record, with an unprecedented series of wild fires across northern Eurasia. Since the extraordinary summer of 1976, which many will recall from their halcyon days, global temperatures have risen by -0.5°C. In 1988 the small gondola at the top of the Montenvers railway opened, to ferry passengers from the terminus to the ice grotto tunnelled into the glacier. Thirty years ago, there was a staircase of three steps leading down to its entrance. Now, thanks to glacial retreat, there are several fights totalling 350 steps. Before too long the entire operation will have to move upstream: there simply won't be a glacier left at the current site at all. '*Il n'y a dans les Alpes rien de constant que leur variété*,' Horace-Bénédict de Saussure wrote in *Voyages dans les Alpes*, but not even he could have believed what a changing climate could do to the mountains.

The pattern of abrupt change everywhere visible in the Alps is repeated in mountains around the world. In the summer of 2019, Josh Maurer and

1. S Nussbaumer, H Umbühl & D Teiner, 'Fluctuations of the "Mer de Glace" AD 1500 – 2050', *Zeitschrift für Gletscherkunder und Glazial Geologie*, Innsbruck, Universitätsverlag Wagner, 2007.

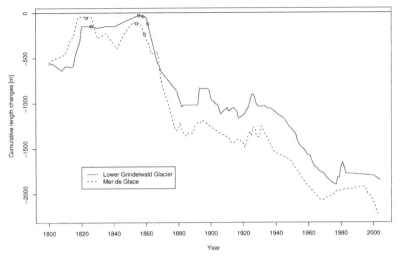

Figure 1 Cumulative length variations of the Lower Grindelwald glacier (solid line) and the Mer de Glace (dashed line) from 1800 onwards, relative to the 1600s maximum extent.

colleagues from Columbia University published a paper[2] on Himalayan glacial retreat that was staggering both in its scope and its implications. From the 1970s, US spy satellites have been looking down on central Asia and that data has now been declassified. Maurer and his colleagues were able to track the changes affecting 650 Himalayan glaciers. Not only had they shrunk, Maurer and his team discovered the rate of melting was twice as fast between 2000 and 2016 as it was between 1975 and 2000. They were also able to assess the volume of glaciers being lost, not just the surface area. This study followed an assessment from the Kathmandu-based International Centre for Integrated Mountain Development (ICIMOD) earlier in the year predicting that in a best-case scenario Himalayan glaciers will lose more than one third of their mass by the end of the century and in the worst case, which with the US withdrawal from the Paris Agreement has become more likely, two thirds will be lost, impacting Himalayan communities that rely on glaciers for irrigation or replenishing natural sources. Add in changes to monsoon patterns and population growth, and the region as a whole is facing unprecedented environmental challenges affecting hundreds of millions.

Mountain glaciers are of course only a small part of our warming world, at least when viewed in the context of the melting Greenland ice sheet and changes in Antarctica. Even a small rise in sea levels has devastating impacts on the coast where many of us live. Most of the world's mega-cities are at or very near sea level and the coastal population continues to increase both as a proportion and in absolute terms. Suddenly, looking down the north face of the Badile at the rock fall from the Cengalo, the immensity of

2. J Maurer, J Schaefer, S Rupper & A Corley, 'Acceleration of Ice Loss across the Himalaya over the Past 40 Years', *Science Advances* 5 (6), 2019, DOI: 10.112/sciadv.aav7266.

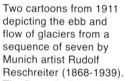

Two cartoons from 1911 depicting the ebb and flow of glaciers from a sequence of seven by Munich artist Rudolf Reschreiter (1868-1939).
The figure in the cartoons is the mountaineer, glaciologist and mathematician Sebastien Finsterwalder (1862-1951) who in June 1911 was studying the Vernagtferner glacier in the Ötztal Alps in Austria. Finsterwalder pioneered the use of repeat photography and photogrammetry, the use of photography to measure in three dimensions. His work has proved a valuable resource in illustrating climate change. The Vernagtferner was one of the first Alpine glaciers to be depicted in art and has proved particularly vulnerable to climate change.

this event shrinks into obscurity, a perspective far more dizzying that being perched on the summit of a mountain, even one as steep as the Badile. Following in Coolidge's footsteps, both as climber and editor, is a sobering task. His angle of attack was born from a sense of exploration, of getting to grips with a range of mountains hardly known in the capitals of Europe, where the notion that man could upset the balance of nature was laughable. Now the Alps are threaded with infrastructure, the arteries through which we metabolise the earth's resources. As places of recreation they are equally transformed. I was able to fly into Milan and drive to the mountains in a matter of hours, one more tourist among hundreds of thousands.

There, I mentioned it: the 'F' word. Peter Foster records in his new book, reviewed on p330, how T Graham Brown flew Imperial Airways from Croydon via Paris to Basel to resume his Alpine season in 1926, among the first alpinists to go climbing by air. It cost him £8, roughly the price of a flight to Kathmandu now. The airline flew little more than 10,000 people that year; easyJet alone now flies almost a quarter of a million *each day*. Cheap flying is a hallmark of our age, allowing quick trips to the mountains where our immediate forebears were restricted to long visits by car. This has bred a superficial attitude to the mountains; they have become playgrounds in a way that would see Coolidge, a man steeped in Alpine culture and dedicated to its study, reaching for a hatchet. Many current Alpine Club members share the sense that popular mountain regions are to be avoided and happily there are lots of corners of the Alps that are still delightful, if you know where to look. But what moral responsibility do we have to change our behaviour? We are, after all, the ultimate canaries in the coal-mine, scrambling over peaks that are rotting from the inside as the climate warms, adapting our behaviour just as insects head north and the tree line rises. In the scheme of things, what the world's mountaineers get up to is neither here nor there, but should we not talk about it? Set an example? Faced with my circumstances in the overheating 21st century, what would my eminent predecessor Coolidge do?

As arch-individualists, alpinists generally don't appreciate a moralistic lecture, and that's not my intention. Some young people are starting to turn their backs on the thoughtless indulgence of cheap aviation, as the impact of the industry becomes apparent. Many more are carrying on regardless, blithely trusting on someone else to sort out the problem, arguing they are entitled to what previous generations took for granted. Flying's contribution to emissions only accounts for 2.4% of the global carbon budget from around a hundred thousand flights a day, but flying is set to triple on current forecasts. On an individual basis, the impact of flying is immense: one trans-Atlantic return flight emits more carbon dioxide than a citizen of Nepal does in a year. Even my flight to Milan exceeded the annual carbon budget for those living in several sub-Saharan African countries.

Should I simply stop flying? I've thought long and hard about this. I've certainly adapted my behaviour in other areas. I've vastly reduced the amount of meat I eat, to the extent that I'm borderline vegetarian, with half the carbon impact of being an omnivore. I've cut the amount I use my car, easy for me since I live in a city and can cycle most places. Both these lifestyle changes, if I'm honest, have as much to do with improving my health and saving me money as they do about reducing my carbon footprint, even though I can't pretend it doesn't make me feel a bit better about my flying habit: a return flight to Kathmandu is roughly the same as giving up meat for a year.

Of course, there's a strong argument that I should give up both, although the law of unintended consequences applies here. Tourism is one of the few industries Nepal has successfully developed, creating jobs and securing the viability of protected areas: in 2017, 67% of tourists, around 630,000 people, visited one of Nepal's national parks or nature reserves. In 2014, 1.38m Nepalis[3] were working in the tourism sector; there were 790,000 visitors that year, so that's almost two jobs per visitor and within the mountaineering and trekking sector, the ratio of jobs to tourists is even higher. This is despite the rather pitiful low-value nature of Nepali tourism: tourist spending remains low, around $54 per day in 2017, compared to a regional average of more than $100. So while tourism as a proportion of Nepal's GDP is surprisingly low, given the country's reputation as a destination, its significance as an employer is crucial. If tourists stopped flying there, what would those workers do? Most probably join the exodus of Nepali youth, averaging 1,600 men and women each day, burning jet fuel to fly abroad in search of work in the Gulf or Malaysia. Taking the train to the Alps is a no-brainer, but not flying to the Himalaya is more equivocal than it seems.

---

3. The World Bank, 'Nepal Sustainable Tourism Value Creation', May 2018.

Should I offset? Pay a little extra into a scheme that draws down the carbon dioxide I've chosen to put out there? Many environmentalists are justifiably sceptical when it comes to aviation offsetting schemes; where does that £1 Ryanair offers to charge you to ease your conscience really go? The International Civil Aviation Organisation (ICAO), a UN body, has committed itself through offsets and emission reduction to stabilise emissions from 2020 onwards, although many analysts are sceptical about the value of this far more comprehensive project: the Carbon Offsetting and Reduction Scheme for International Aviation, or CORSIA. China has still to decide if it wants to join, and there is a danger airlines will use biofuels as offsets, essentially creating a new market for hugely destructive palm oil. (If you run a private jet, don't panic: they are exempt.) Academic studies have however shown that properly managed offsetting schemes can make a difference: the Swiss-based NGO myclimate.org is a good option.

Perhaps, though, I should look closer to home. Moorland and bog restoration near my home in the Peak District is a viable approach to locking in and even sequestering carbon, as well as an opportunity to improve biodiversity in a country – my country – that is one of the most nature-degraded in the world. There are similar efforts in Scotland to re-establish the Caledonian forest, like the Trees for Life project (treesforlife.org.uk). Wouldn't it be magical if I could ameliorate some of the damage done in a lifetime of flying by improving my own backyard? It's a simple matter to calculate the carbon offset cost of a flight: the myclimate website has a handy carbon cost calculator. Others are thinking along the same lines: the British Mountaineering Council is just one outdoor body working on policies around the climate emergency and considering linking with conservation NGOs to create a scheme the outdoor community can pay into to support viable carbon-offsetting and improved bio-diversity.

One final thought: alpinism at its best is about self-reliance. Over the years the definition of what that means has evolved and been refined. It wasn't so long ago that climbers would toss garbage and extraneous supplies into the void if it was slowing them down and not think twice about it: like whoever left the sardine tin I collected from the Badile. Most of us, I think, now frown on that sort of thing. Eventually, I expect the same will apply to environmental responsibility around travelling to base camp. It's about taking responsibility for your own actions, the antithesis of the heavy helicopter usage and careless use of resources on Everest. Already there is discussion about including such behaviour, taking responsibility for your carbon footprint, as part of the qualification process for mountaineering grants. What's obvious is that we cannot go on as we are. The jury's back and the verdict is in. It's time to face the consequences of our actions.

Art

Cascade de la Folie
John Ruskin, 1849?
Watercolour over pencil and ink, with bodycolour. 46.1cm x 37.3cm.
Courtesy of Birmingham Museums Trust.

ANGELO RECALCATI

'And This May Be Seen'

Leonardo da Vinci and the Alps

Giuseppe Bossi's portrait of Leonardo da Vinci:
an engraving published in 1810.

'And this may be seen, as I saw it, by anyone going up Mon Boso, a peak of the Alps ...'

Thus begins Leonardo da Vinci's account of his climb on Monte Rosa, among the very first such descriptions of the Alps. Mountains, like more or less everything else in the world, fascinated Leonardo, whose death five hundred years ago has sparked so much celebration of his life and work. Interest in the Alps from one of history's greatest artists and polymaths has long drawn the attention of cultural historians hunting for the roots of western Europe's fascination with mountain landscapes. The notes he left behind on what he thought about the Alps and what he experienced there also intrigued mountain historians: where exactly is 'Mon Boso'?

Leonardo da Vinci's 'mon boso': Monte Rosa as seen from the Lombard plain.

In 1885, Douglas Freshfield, the recent editor of the *Alpine Journal*, published 'The Alpine Notes of Leonardo da Vinci'[1], the first attempt to tackle this subject. There was at that time no modern philological study of Leonardo's manuscripts and no proper chronology either, so Freshfield can be forgiven if his conclusions were wrong. He relied on a recently published translation of Leonardo's manuscripts edited by the German art historian Jean Paul Richter, who knew little about mountain geography. He theorised that the peak 'Mon Boso' was not Monte Rosa as Richter guessed but Monte Viso, a theory later scholarship has discounted.

Italian scholar and veteran of the Risorgimento Gustavo Uzielli published another long study about Leonardo and the Alps in 1889[2], correctly identifying the peak as Monte Rosa but writing, erroneously, that Leonardo made his visit there around 1511. W A B Coolidge followed Uzielli in his 1904 annotated edition of Josias Simler's 1574 work *De Alpibus Commentarius*. The author Francis Gribble gave Leonardo and the story of Mon Boso a whole chapter in his 1904 book *The Early Mountaineers*, and more by luck than judgement suggested the end of the fifteenth century for Leonardo's Alpine climb. The first proper chronology of the *Codex Leicester*, Leonardo's startling collection of notes on the natural world that includes the Mon Boso passage, was published in 1909, confirming Gribble's hunch. That didn't end the wayward theorising: the art historian Kenneth Clark, who catalogued and then edited a book of the royal collection of Leonardo's drawings at Windsor Castle, claimed Leonardo had made drawings of Monte Rosa,

1. Proceedings of the Royal Geographical Society.
2. Bollettino del Club Alpino Italiano.

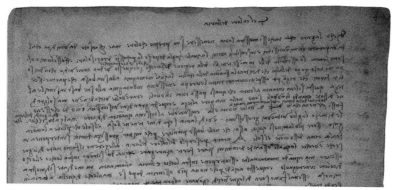

The page of the Codex Leicester that includes Leonardo's description of his journey to 'mon boso'.

when in fact his Alpine drawings depicted the mountains above Lecco; Clark also repeated the error of 1511 as the date of Leonardo's climb.

Reading the phrase quoted above from the *Codex Leicester*, the reader is left in no doubt: in concise but clear and detailed terms, Leonardo emphasises the truth of his experience on the slopes of Mon Boso, the name by which Monte Rosa, especially its southern side, had been known since the 14th century. Considering attitudes at that time towards Alpine landscapes, Leonardo's journey to Mon Boso was extraordinary. It was only in the 18th century, with a combination of Enlightenment scientific enquiry and the new aesthetic of the sublime, that the Alps was recognised as somewhere appealing and worthy of enquiry. Leonardo, the precursor *par excellence*, showed from his writings and art that he understood the value of experiencing and participating in the natural world: the Alps was no exception.

This, then, is the first known testimony of a climb in the high Alpine regions, one that was motivated both by the aesthetic and the scientific, written in the pages of the *Codex Leicester* under the title 'The Colour of Air':

I say the blueness we see in the atmosphere is not intrinsic colour, but is caused by warm vapour, evaporated in minute and insensible atoms, on which the solar rays fall making them luminous against the infinite darkness of the fiery sphere which lies beyond and includes it. And this may be seen, as I saw it, by anyone going up Mon Boso a peak of the Alps ... And no mountain has its base at so great a height as this; it rises above almost all the clouds and snow seldom falls there, only hail when the clouds are at their greatest height, and this hail is preserved in such a way, that if it were not the rarity of the fall and of mounting clouds which happens only twice a season, there would be a very high quantity of ice raised there by layers of hail, which I found very considerable in the middle of July; and I saw the air above me dark and the sun shining on the mountain was far brighter there than in the low plains, because lesser thickness of air lays between the top of the mountain and the sun.

The mountains in this drawing, RL 12410, are sometimes identified as Monte Viso and more frequently as Monte Rosa but actually depict the Lombard Prealps. Easily recognisable in the central panorama, with sunlight coming from the left, after the slightly drawn Pizzo Stella, are the Cornizzolo, Monte Croce, the top pyramid of Legnone, the two Grigne, Pizzo Rotondo, and Monte Melaccio; towards the foreground is Monte due Mani and to the extreme right the Pizzo dei Tre Signori. At the centre bottom of the sheet Leonardo drew the peaks between Legnone and the northern Grigna, illuminated by the setting sun that picks out the walls of Sasso Cavallo and Sasso dei Carbonari, well known to him. At the top right of the sheet is the pyramid of Pizzo Arera.

The Lombard Prealps in winter from the roof of Milan Cathedral with the central detail of RL 12410 for comparison.

With extraordinary intuition Leonardo attributes the cause of the blue of the sky to the phenomenon of the selective scattering of light by the atmosphere, a phenomenon only explained by physicists in the 19th century. Later in the codex, Leonardo illustrates his experiment using wood smoke against a black screen with the aim of 'confirming the experience of Mon Boso.' His observations led him to conclude correctly that beyond the atmosphere space is also black and by implication that the density of the atmosphere decreases with altitude. The fact he found 'ice raised by layers of hail' suggests he encountered a glacier revealing the typical stratification made from layers of snow that have turned into ice over a period of years, taking on a grainy appearance similar to hail.

Where and when did Leonardo make this Alpine excursion? The topographical features he describes suggest some way up a high mountain. Alongside Freshfield's theory about Monte Viso, we can also exclude the hypothesis of W A B Coolidge, more recently argued by Philippe Joutard, that Mon Boso is Monte Bo (2556m) in the Alpi Biellesi; Monte Bo's modest height doesn't allow Leonardo's description of the phenomena he encountered. Monte Rosa remains the most plausible location and we can assume Leonardo climbed to altitudes of about 3,000m, most probably from the upper Valsesia or possibly the upper Anzasca valley, with access to Monte Rosa's impressive east face, both at that time part of the Duchy of Milan.

The only indication of date Leonardo offers is 'mid July'; the year can only be estimated, mainly from dating of the codex, which was compiled in fine copy in the very first years of the 16th century, a transcription of notes from various notebooks now no longer available and done while Leonardo was in Florence, having left Milan in 1499 with the fall of Lodovico il Moro. It is

The Lombard Prealps from the west bank of the river Adda, 2km upstream of Trezzo, are the main subject of sheet RL 12414. From the right it's possible to identify Albenza, Monte Tesoro, Resegone, Grignone with its smooth south-east aspect and the rough Grignetta with the profile of the serrated Segantini ridge.

therefore most plausible that Leonardo's visit to Mon Boso took place when he lived in the Duchy of Milan between 1482 and 1499. The year 1511, which Uzielli offered and was taken up by Coolidge and others, is without justification. By then the *Codex Leicester* had been in existence for several years.

The 'experience of Mon Boso' was perhaps the most significant Leonardo had in the Alpine world, but his interest later turned to the Prealps and Alpine valleys of Lombardy. We know about this from the numerous annotations in his codices and from several of his drawings, themselves hugely important because they are absolutely the first true portraits of Alpine mountains.

In the *Codex Atlantic*, so called because of its large size, are numerous annotations referring to the Prealps and Lombard Alps. He writes of 'trips to do in May', and among the fruit he gathers are descriptions of the main characteristics of the territory of Valtellina and Valchiavenna. These journeys were certainly not just for pleasure: he inspected mines, quarries and forests and checked aquifers, paying close attention to the economic

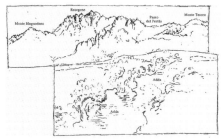

Reconstructed from two fragments RL 12413 and RL 12414 this drawing depicts the Resegone: in the lower part we can see the course of the river Adda.

production of the duchy. The Grigne in particular, often clearly visible from Milan, attracted his attention on several occasions. From his descriptions we learn that he climbed the Val Meria from above Mandello del Lario into the heart of the Grigne, visiting the cave of Ferrera, noting its correct size, and describing the great walls of Sasso Cavallo and Sasso dei Carbonari. Even Leonardo could not imagine these cliffs, 'the greatest exposed rocky walls found in this country,' would become the arduous playground of Riccardo Cassin, Nino Oppio and so many young climbers from the current generation.

Another view of Resegone and the river Adda valley from the Sanctuary of Rocchetta above Airuno, for comparison with the previous illustrations.

The Grigne and the Prealpi of Lecco are the subjects of four drawings, three preserved at Windsor and one at the Biblioteca Ambrosiana in Milan. Among his many landscape drawings, these are real views of real mountains and not just preparatory studies for the mountainous backgrounds of his greatest paintings. They are four small rectangular sheets slightly larger than a postcard, made of paper with a red tempera primer on which Leonardo has outlined with a firm and precise mark ridges, walls, valleys and spires with an eye to mountain structure never before encountered.

In these drawings, we can see the hand of Leonardo the artist and Leonardo the investigator of nature, an illustration of his unprecedented sensibility towards the reality of the natural world. Shapes, lights and shadows are so faithful that they allow accurate identification not only of the mountains, but also of the place from which they were drawn and even the time of day. The reason Leonardo's mountains appear so real is that he is the

View of the Sasso Cavallo and the Sasso dei Carbonari leaning against Grignone from the entrance of Val Meria. Leonardo called them 'the greatest exposed rocky walls in this country', so impressed that he recognised them, observing and drawing them from Milan.

first painter who studied their geology and morphology in depth, in the same way that it would not be possible to portray realistically a human body without knowing anatomy.

He did these drawings in the last years of his second stay in Milan, which he left in 1513. Two were drawn from the centre of Milan or a few miles from it and from the Adda valley, not far from the residence of Vaprio d'Adda, where he was often a guest of his student and heir Francesco Melzi. It is the Prealps of Lombardy that are the Alpine subject painted by Leonardo and not Monte Rosa as has been affirmed, and reaffirmed quite recently, without justification. The relative closeness of these mountains to his residences in Milan and Vaprio, his walks among them, the valleys, the woods, the mines and the natural curiosities surely left in his soul a sweet feeling of familiarity, a feeling renewed in all those who love the mountains when they see them from afar. So we can imagine it was for Leonardo, now in old age, seeing these peaks from Milan on a clear sunny day or during a trip along the Adda. And in portraying them he drew on memories of distant experiences, perhaps even adventures.

Leonardo defined himself as 'a man without letters' because he hadn't followed the Classical scholastic path, entering instead the workshop of Verrocchio as his pupil; his training and knowledge developed addressing the theoretical and practical problems of a typical Renaissance studio.

'Wisdom is the child of experience' is one of the mottos that occurs often in his writings and is one of the most distinctive features of Leonardo's mental habit, which is free of the cultural conditioning of his time, habits that might have limited him. Instead, his original intellect was left unencumbered to reach a form of total creative understanding using essential elements from both science and art.

This synthesis is a feature of Leonardo's *Book of Painting*, better known as the *Treatise on Painting*, the only one of his theoretical works that was widely known, and even then mostly from the middle of the seventeenth century. In this work we find the fruit of his experience in the Alpine world, not only with regard to his vision of landscape and the relevant pictorial techniques to better represent it, but also descriptions, affirmations and intuitions that demonstrate Leonardo's acute perception and analysis of its natural history: flora, geology, fossils, the shaping of the mountain landscape through rain and snow, glaciers and rivers. In short, we see his attempt to penetrate the same evolutionary mysteries of nature that he offers in the background of the 'Gioconda': his figurative manifesto. Perhaps it is superficial and a little vain for scholars to look for a precise location. Leonardo's intentions were much deeper. Behind the Gioconda's enigmatic expression lies Leonardo's dynamic conception of nature: a truly cosmic vision.

DONALD M ORR

Thomas Moran and the American Mountain Vision

'The Grand Canyon of the Yellowstone', 1872. *(Smithsonian Institution)*

During a period of some 50 years from 1825 to 1875 an artistic movement grew in America that had its foundations in European Romanticism but was inspired by the wilderness in the locality of New York State's Hudson river. Throughout the 1840s and 1850s there occurred 'a period of expansion and consolidation for the native school named for the Hudson River'[1] whereby a generation of artist-adventurers would travel and record mountain scenery from the White Mountains to the Rockies and to the Andes of South America. While Albert Bierstadt (1830-1902) ventured west to record sunlit scenes in Yosemite, it was Thomas Moran who entered the heart of the continent, taking his 'Hudson River' aesthetics first into Wyoming, then across Colorado, to create the definitive images of the mythic 'West' that would influence both photographers and filmmakers in years to come.

The American painter Thomas Moran (1837-1926) arrived in the United States in 1844 at the age of seven from Bolton, Lancashire to settle in Philadelphia where his father was a textile weaver. Later, as an art student of James Hamilton (1819-78) and greatly influenced by him, Moran developed a style that reflected the Romantic landscape tradition that flourished in

1. B D Yaeger, *The Hudson River School*, Smithmark, New York, 1996, p37.

Europe, dominated by the paintings of Turner and the writings of Ruskin both of whom he admired and respected.

He became one of the many artists to be linked with the great surveys of the United States interior organised by the American government but he, above all others, became the most associated with and closely related to his subject matter, to the extent that by the end of the 19th century 'his landscape views, especially those of Yellowstone and the Grand Canyon, were recognized as the definitive treatments of those wonders.'[2]

In 1864 an Act of Congress had established Yosemite Valley as a place of special significance for the nation, but the wilderness could not venerate itself; 'it needed hallowing visitations from … painters in oil like Bierstadt and Thomas Moran, and painters in prose like John Muir to represent it as a holy park of the West.'[3]

In the period after the American Civil War it was recognised that the nation required some form of stylised unification, some logo, badge or emblem to bond the people and provoke a sense of forward momentum, even destiny. It may be argued that the Revolutionary War of 1776-83 created the United States but the American Civil War of 1861-5 determined the kind of nation it would become. The destruction of towns, property and economic infrastructure linked with the loss of 625,000 lives resulted in a long and painful process of rebuilding a united nation. The quest to establish some kind of image had, in a sense, been symbolised in the past by the movement westward of settlers and the discovery of new lands, forests, plains and mountains. That mountains could 'act as barriers that constitute the natural limits of the nations they encircle; and as an environment that gives birth to specific peoples'[4] were the aspects that fired the expeditions of the 1870s and gave rise to the emblematizing of the West as a continuing American challenge, the reinvigoration of a national identity, and a powerful incentive for commerce and industry to seize the opportunities for new investment.

From 1867 to 1879 the United States government organised four expeditions in the West that have become known as the Great Surveys due to their wide geographical range, their long duration, and the comprehensive nature of their research. They were funded by the Department of War, the Department of the Interior, the Smithsonian Institution and private industry that had a vested interest in aspects of the projects. Soil types, rock structures, ores and mineral deposits, and fossil remains were all sought, noted and classified alongside the charting of the landscape, while aspects of climate, water resources and transport routes through remote areas were also recorded.

The United States recognised that 'the ability of mountain landscapes to emblematize the national imaginary encouraged protection measures that designated them as national parks'[5] and reawakened the spirit of adventure

2. J Kinsey, *Thomas Moran and the Surveying of the American West*, Washington, Smithsonian Institution, 1992, p6.
3. S Schama, *Landscape and Memory*, Fontana, London, 1996, p7.
4. B Debarbieux and G Rudaz, *The Mountain*, Chicago University Press, 2015, p76.
5. Ibid, p104.

that would make these suggested national parks permanent national treasures. From the outset the governing feature was 'an attempt to find nobility in an uncivilised region'[6] and the establishment of national parks and the formation of federal forests created a people's wilderness, both psychologically and physically, which, at the same time, fostered the growth of commercialism and tourism in those wild places.

Moran was 34 when he joined the United States Geological and Geographical Survey of the Territories and travelled west to Wyoming and the Yellowstone region. Two years later he joined a government survey to the Grand Canyon led by John Wesley Powell and the following year, in 1874, he was again involved in survey work in Colorado. The artwork developed from these expeditions became the basis for the rest of his career to the point that he adopted the nickname 'Yellowstone' and established a monogrammed symbol on his canvases indicating the work of Tom 'Yellowstone' Moran. His prolific output of western mountain landscape paintings and related drawings and prints secured him fame and a considerable fortune. This allowed him to travel to Europe, Mexico and the eastern United States where he also produced many fine paintings but those of the American West and its mountains embody his most substantial influence on American art.

The Hayden Geological and Geographical Survey of the Territories was not the first expedition to enter the Yellowstone region. Known by mountaineers, in the original sense, trappers, traders and soldiers as well as indigenous peoples, it was first explored by John Colter of the Lewis and Clark Expedition who returned to the area in 1807-8 and sent back descriptions that augmented the district's already mythic qualities. More serious expeditions returned annually from 1869-71, fired by the traveller's tales that arrived back east. Ferdinand Hayden's survey was in its fifth year when Moran joined it on its way to Yellowstone. All manner of information was required covering all aspects of geological science alongside different forms of visual record: sketches and prints, drawings, paintings and photographs.

'The Grand Canōn of the Yellowstone'[7] brought Moran to public prominence in 1872 when his large canvas, 7ft x 12ft, became the first American landscape by an American painter to be purchased by the United States government. The painting is a formidable image depicting both the range of the country before him and its inherent power centred on the falls pouring into the vast defile and sending up a cloud of spray into the valley. The viewer is channelled towards the off-centre falls, the massive walls of the valley and the succession of pillar-like rock towers and tall trees directing the eye towards the cascade. The colour structure enhances this movement, leading us from the darker foreground into the yellow and cream light of the rock scenery in the central valley to be held at the heart of the gorge by a shadowed area whose light core is the waterfall itself. Distance and verticality are the keynotes, but the scale of the image is greatly enhanced by the

6. Kinsey, p23.
7. 'The Grand Canōn of the Yellowstone', 1872, oil on canvas, 213cm x 266cm, National Museum of American Art, Smithsonian Institution.

'The Chasm of the Colorado', 1873-4. *(Smithsonian Institution)*

inclusion of diminutive figures in the foreground: some recording the scene and others looking out over the vastness of the rock landscape. Thanks to Moran's painting, the Yellowstone ceased to be a sulphurous place of infernal mystery but was transformed into a haven of natural wonder, stirring the American imagination. Well beyond the geographical and geological importance of the area, the minds of Americans were opened to the interior of their own country as an area of thrilling danger and challenge, of inspiration and fulfilment, an image promised a more positive view of the future.

The expedition of 1873 led by John Wesley Powell, a one-armed Civil War veteran who had been exploring the Colorado river and its tributaries since 1867, furnished the production of 'The Chasm of the Colorado'[8] unveiled in 1874. Powell's 'sympathetic studies of native Americans and his scientific and practical theory of arid land management'[9] contributed a vast amount to America's understanding of the West and the visual impact of Moran's canvas animated the government and inspired further exploration. This painting was also purchased by Congress to hang in the Capitol opposite the Yellowstone canvas where its similar size allows a dramatic counterpoint to the earlier picture. Where the Yellowstone revealed a spectacular vast valley, the Colorado displays the immense panorama of fold after fold of stunning rock scenery, rendered with a strong natural accuracy, as it stretches off into the distance where cloud and rainstorms stop the eye from being lost in the huge expanse of stone structures that disclose the enormity of the landscape. The immediate foreground is painted in a mid-tone, followed directly in the middle distance by deeper, darker tones backed by sunlit rock faces. This creates a tonal structure similar to the Yellowstone canvas where the land unfolds into the distance, leading the eye and the imagination beyond the

8. 'The Chasm of the Colorado'. 1873-4, oil on canvas, 214cm x 267cm, National Museum of American Art, Smithsonian Institution.
9. Kinsey, p99.

'Mountain of the Holy Cross', 1875.

Napoleon Sarony's portrait of Thomas Moran, from Bolton to the American West.

limits of the image. Like the Yellowstone canvas this too displays a surety of handling and a rendering of illusionistic spatial depth that is almost breath-taking. The Grand Canyon's arid characteristics, the dearth of vegetation, are brought to the fore, but his juxtaposition of storm, rainbow, river and canyon convey the land's latent power, its harshness and tension, and also offer an invitation to explore, to see for oneself the grandeur that was part of the frontier. In America, it seems to say, anything is possible.

In 1874 Moran joined a further Hayden expedition in Colorado where they had succeeded the previous year, after considerable difficulties, in sur-veying the Mountain of the Holy Cross. This almost legendary mountain with its unique central gully crossed two thirds of the way up by a broad horizontal ledge creating a perfect cruciform feature, was hidden deep in the Colorado Rockies. The painting Moran fashioned, the 'Mountain of the Holy Cross',[10] was different in several respects. The canvas is vertical as opposed to the two previous large horizontal paintings. Scale and vast gran-deur were again related but this time the remoteness of the location and the arduous nature of travel in the area were implied: he reveals a trackless waste that can only be accessed by following a boulder-strewn, timber-choked river high in the mountains. Above this, beyond source and tributaries, rises the Mountain of the Holy Cross dominating the surrounding peaks and dwarfing the river landscape. The composition is centred on the river

10. 'Mountain of the Holy Cross'. 1875, Oil on canvas, 210.2cm X 164.5cm. The Gene Autry Western Heritage Museum, Los Angeles.

where strong, skilful rendering of rock, wood and water textures fill the valley with a naturalistic execution that leads the eye to the head of the valley where, cradled in mist, sits the mysterious mountain dominated by its uniquely Christian symbol. Overshadowing the canvas are allusions to suffering and salvation. The painting's composition suggests the journey to the mountain will not be easy: the foot of the cross will only be attained by effort, confrontation and personal transition. This was certainly true for those involved in the survey but it also stands not only as a metaphor for those seeking release or liberation in their own lives but also as a vital directional image for a nation searching for reconciliation with its recent past.

The tradition of the sublime in nature had been established in Europe as far back as the 17th century and Moran made great use of dramatic examples of landscapes, just as his predecessors had, 'where objects and scenes are noted not only for what they are but also for what they are like.'[11] The dynamic storms and atmospheric effects, the gorges and precipitous rock scenery, the majestic waterfalls and luminous rainbows all stood as metaphors for a land at once magnificent and splendid but also blessed and charged with a cosmic association. Where Bierstadt had flooded his Yosemite canvases with these qualities he had done so with a series of atmospheric impressions and powerful sunlit effects that all too often said more about Bierstadt and his attitude to painting than the vertical rock walls of Yosemite. Moran's approach was more considered and realistic while still bound within the Romantic tradition. Features could be enhanced, lone pines introduced, thunder clouds rearranged and tonal shifts in colour accommodated, but the actual structure of the land was allowed to remain, and to reflect its own power and grandeur. Beyond all else Moran sought to convey a sense of place from scenes far from the frontiers of common experience, to relate an encounter with a wilderness that did not rely on accentuation or pictorial effects but boldly displayed the splendour and dignity of the American West; a land of sparse vegetation, desert scenery, strange geological features, dramatic colours and seemingly measureless open spaces that bound the depicted landscape but still promised further discoveries.

Thomas Moran, perhaps more than any other painter, 'played a decisive role in awakening sensitivity to scenic views and in exerting pressure on political and administrative institutions'[12] to protect singular areas of outstanding beauty throughout America. The United States government recognised the need for symbolic status and 'readily made the mountains an emblematic place, a remarkable scenic landscape, a wild aspect of their territory, an ecological asset, even a reserve for unusual species.'[13]

Moran's images of the West were utilised by many companies seeking to advertise their locale or the beauties of their area; the Union Pacific Railway, the Denver and Rio Grande Railway, the Rocky Mountain Herald, and the US Postal Service all employed images of his work, the latter in the

11. Kinsey, p20.
12. Debarbieux & Rudaz, p104.
13. Debarbieux & Rudaz, p112.

commemorative stamp marking the 75th anniversary of Colorado's state-hood. His influence on photographers and cinematographers who worked in the Western genre can be seen especially in the film work of John Houston, while the photography of Ansel Adams followed in this tradition, where he 'did his best to translate his reverence into spectacular nature-icons.'[14]

The popularity of Moran's western images reveals both the sympathies of the artist and a great deal about the society they were produced for. His art is not pure fabrication, but neither is it mere documentation. Moran's success was not solely based on his artistic abilities or his opportunities to witness such sights through his connection with the survey; his work does not reveal an American Eden nor is it ever a sentimentalised view of natural grandeur under sunny skies but somehow his large canvases display the personal and cultural battle for a new definition in the West and in America that helped the recreation of the national identity and disclosed its direction into the new century. Moran understood the consequence of the West as a microcosm of American culture and made the West an enduring aspect of the American consciousness.

While Moran's large landscapes of the Yellowstone and the Grand Canyon can still inspire awe in those viewing them today, it is perhaps his greater legacy to us that our sense of place in the world can be heightened and our sense of spirituality enhanced by 'observing nature or landscape paintings ... and to the ways that civilisations have experienced and cultivated that keen awareness of nature and the landscape.'[15] It may be assumed in some quarters that humanities interaction with the mountain environment is a modern phenomenon and based solely on contemporary mountaineering or mountain sports and skiing developments but the thrill of exploration and the lure of travelling into the unknown, the search, consideration and assessment of an expedition into new territories still exerts a powerful spell; a spark, if not ignited then certainly fanned, by Moran and the National Surveys of America of the 1870s.

14. Schama, p9.
15. Debarbieux & Rudaz, p32.

ROBIN N CAMPBELL

John Ruskin's Alpine Watercolours

By the time he was 16, Ruskin was already a capable water-colourist,
illustrated in this painting of the north side of the Stelvio.

This year's section frontispieces celebrate the bicentenary of John Ruskin's birth. Ruskin was elected to the Club in 1869 in recognition of
his contribution to mountain literature, *Of Mountain Beauty*, which formed
Volume IV of his massive work *Modern Painters* (Works 6).[1] He fell in love
with the Alps on a family tour in 1833 and although he had no strong aspi-
ration to climb them, he was familiar with many Alpine ranges long before
the Club was founded in 1857. He was as much an artist as a writer, and like
many artists he drew every day. Even in 1833 aged 14, he was producing
passable Alpine drawings. By the time of the family Alpine holiday in 1835,
aged 16, following instruction from A V Copley Fielding, he was capable of
outstanding watercolour work, such as the drawing of the north side of the
Stelvio shown above, and the fine drawing of Castle Rock of Triermain at
the Ruskin Library.

1. This notation indicates the 6th volume of E T Cook & A Wedderburn, *The Library Edition of the Complete
   Works of John Ruskin*, 39 volumes, London, George Allen, 1903-12. In later references I give only volume
   number and page. These volumes are available online at the Ruskin Library and elsewhere.

He became particularly fond of Chamonix and its Aiguilles and spent much time there, gathering material for *Of Mountain Beauty*. His father complained in 1837 that his son 'knows the shape of every needle round Mont Blanc, and could not tell you now where Threadneedle Street is.' (2, xxxiv, footnote 1)

Ruskin's skills as a mountain artist were second to none. Indeed, there is a case for putting him amongst the greatest artists in the British watercolour tradition. Stephen Wildman, the present director of the Ruskin Library, made such a claim 20 years ago, 'Ruskin was modest about the drawings of Alpine rocks and peaks made between 1844 and 1849 ... yet they represent his first individual achievement. The intervening continental tour of 1845 was in many ways a turning point in his confidence, not least in the realisation that his own ambitious brown ink drawings, though stylistically old-fashioned, were no less successful than those of Harding, who had accompanied him. The development of a more confident handling of colour in the later 1840s brought him to a point where his work as a watercolourist stands comparison with any of his peers.'[2] Ruskin's modesty was partly due to his fervent admiration for Joseph Turner's watercolour work, which he celebrated in *Modern Painters* and in many other publications. As a result of his perfect knowledge of Alpine topography, he saw immediately that Turner's Alpine watercolours were imaginative works based on the elements of the scene but not at all concerned with reproducing its appearance. Ruskin lamented the absence of the imaginative element in his own work: 'I can only draw what is before me,' was his frequent complaint. But what he did better than any other (including his hero Turner) was to select what was important in the scene before him, and to render it with great accuracy and beauty.

Ruskin's art has been fêted in the *Alpine Journal* many times, most recently by Cynthia Gamble in *AJ* 1999, pp185-96. Gamble's contribution included useful discussions of items 8, 12 and 13 below. For this year's frontispieces I have added five Ruskins to the seven owned by the Club or Library, hoping to demonstrate his all-round excellence in Alpine drawing. Our pages only allow small images. Readers wishing for more detail of these images and others may consult several sources: *Sublime Inspiration* (Abbott Hall Gallery, 1997); the exhibition catalogue in footnote 2; Peter Mallalieu's *The Artists of the Alpine Club* (AC, 2007); Christopher Newall et al, *John Ruskin: Artist and Observer* (Paul Holberton, 2014); and many public collections with online images. I comment below on the 13 images used. Ruskin was not concerned to sell or exhibit his drawings, so they are almost never titled and rarely signed or dated. I have used Charles Warren's titles for those exhibited at the Club in 1982, museum titles where they make sense, and invented titles where necessary. Undated drawings can sometimes be dated by inferences drawn from Ruskin's diaries[3] or other accounts of his travels, but these inferences are often dubious since the diaries have many gaps.

2. *Ruskin, Turner and the Pre-Raphaelites*, Tate Gallery, 2000, p147.
3. J Evans & J H Whitehouse, *The Diaries of John Ruskin*. 3 vols, Clarendon Press, 1956-9.

Charles Warren photographed in 1938 before going to Everest. The Club benefitted from Warren's extraordinarily generous gifts of seven Ruskin drawings, the only Ruskins in its Collection. Four were given during his lifetime and three were bequeathed. For those wishing to know more about Warren, there are two excellent obituaries: in *AJ* 2000, pp278-83, and *The Independent*, 14 May 1999. The drawings have been exhibited here and overseas on many occasions. *(Alpine Club)*

'The Lyskamm from the Gornergrat'

Gifted to the Club by Charles Warren. The drawing shows Lyskamm, Castor and Pollux. It can be dated to 1844 or 1849, since these were the only years in which Ruskin visited Zermatt. The 1844 visit is sometimes overlooked since the single diary entry for 19 July suggests an early departure the following day. However, according to his autobiography *Praeterita*, the Ruskins were there for three days, and on 20 July they visited the Riffelberg (35, p335). In 1849, he went again to the Riffelberg on 7 August (inscribed date on *Diaries*, plate 36). So either date is possible for this picture.

It is not at all typical of Ruskin's work. Like his hero Turner, he mainly avoided drawing snowy peaks, and when he did he sometimes used white body-colour, as here, rather than leaving the white of the paper. A comparable work would be Abbott Hall Gallery's 'View from my Window at Mornex' in which body-colour is used to paint the peaks of Mont Blanc on the left of the drawing, so the Lyskamm drawing is not so isolated as to raise doubts of authorship. However, when he employed the pure watercolour method of leaving the paper he achieved much finer results: *cf* his 'Mont Blanc, St Gervais', also Abbott Hall Gallery. Excellent images of both Abbott Hall Ruskins can be viewed at *www.watercolourworld.org*.

'Dom and Täschhorn from Zermatt'

Inscribed 'Zermatt'. Victoria & Albert Museum. As with the previous drawing this may date from 1844 or 1849. In 1844 the Ruskins were obliged to stay in a chalet, so perhaps that provided the frame for this lovely drawing of the Mischabel giants.

'The Mountains opposite Vevey'

Inscribed 'Vevay. Aug 26?' Gifted to the Club by Charles Warren. This is a view not of Vevey, but from off Vevey looking south across Lake Geneva to the St Gingolph shore opposite. The impressive mountains shown are in the ranges of Les Cornettes de Bise-Dent d'Oche. I am indebted to Prof David Hill for making this clear from his analysis of a similar Ruskin drawing in King's College, Cambridge (see his blog site *https://sublimesites.co*). David Hill suggested that the date of the drawing may be 1851, and that it is an evening rather than a morning view: the shadowing supports this. However, Ruskin was in Vevey almost every year and his diary has many gaps in it, so other dates are possible, for example 1846 where his diary puts him in Vevey on 15 August, the next entry being Chamonix on 23 August. He was in Chamonix for only four days,[4] encountering bad weather, and might well have returned to Vevey to make this drawing on 26 August, a day of excellent weather according to James D Forbes, who was nearby. The drawing owes perhaps more to Turner's approach to watercolour than others in the Club's Collection. It is certainly a magnificent work.

'The Mouth of the Rhône from Lake Geneva'

Inscribed 'Vevey. Aug 26?' Birmingham Museums. Birmingham has read Ruskin's inscription as 'May' rather than 'Aug', but once you have seen 'Aug' it is hard to see 'May'. The drawing was surely made on the same evening boat outing as the previous drawing. In my judgment this is one of Ruskin's most beautiful watercolours. Again, I thank David Hill for identifying the location.

'Lake of Lucerne and Uri Rotstock'

Inscribed 'Grütli'. Bequeathed to the Club Library by Charles Warren. A large and fully finished watercolour exploiting the full range of blues and purples and done by Ruskin at the height of his powers. It shows the cliffs on the west side of the Bay of Uri, the most southerly arm of Lake Lucerne, with the meadow below them known as Grütli (now Rütli) which is the traditional site of the first Swiss Confederacy of the cantons Schwyz, Uri and Unterwalden. In the background is the Uri Rotstock, the highest of the peaks around Lake Lucerne at 2,928m. The Bay of Uri was the subject of a late watercolour by Turner, which exists in several versions. Ruskin sketched a watercolour version of Turner's view, which shows the whole bay from Brunnen at the entrance; this is in the David Thomson Collection (Paul H, Walton. *Master Drawings by John Ruskin*, Pilkington Press, 2000). The bay is also the subject of a superb drawing by John Robert Cozens in the British Museum (BM 1900, 0411.27). Our picture is drawn from a closer viewpoint facing south-west and shows only the west shore, perhaps taken from a boat. When it was exhibited in the Tate Gallery (see footnote 2), Stephen Wildman suggested a date of 1858 for it. There are three other drawings of these

---

4. Letter to George Richmond 30 August 1846, **36**, p63.

cliffs in the Ruskin Library, and again for one of these (1996P1576) a date of 1858 is suggested. However, Ruskin visited Lake Lucerne on many occasions, and the date of these drawings is very uncertain. Two drawings of the Bay (29.R and 29.R.b) were exhibited by Ruskin in 1878, but it is not clear which two and as usual he gave no clue regarding date. His discussion of the two pictures exhibited should be read in full (13, 509-11) to understand the context of his negative remarks about them, which relate only to his success in capturing the beauty of pine trees. Since there are no carefully drawn trees in our drawing, it seems unlikely that ours was one of those exhibited.

'Cascade de la Folie'

Birmingham Museums. A large and celebrated watercolour, frequently exhibited and illustrated. There is a magnificent illustration in the Tate exhibition catalogue (footnote 2) p160. Originally it was given the title 'Cascade de la Folie, and its Uplands' and these uplands are of course (L to R) the Aiguilles de l'M, Grands Charmoz-Grépon, and Blaitière-Fou. The low tones used suggest that it was sketched in twilight or moonlight, giving the scene a spectral quality heightened by the grey and ghostly Aiguilles.

'Montagne de la Côté, Chamonix'

Gifted to the Club by Charles Warren. Often referred to as the Crête de la Côté, the route taken by the Mont Blanc pioneers followed this crest between the Bossons glacier and the Taconnaz glacier on its far side. The peaks of the Taconnaz can be seen thrusting through the boiling and swirling clouds. Despite its small size, it succeeds on all levels as a compelling study of glacier, mountain and cloud forms. According to Ruskin's 1854 list of Chamonix drawings (5, xxi-xxii) he made four drawings of the Montagne de la Côté in 1849, and this is probably one of these. A photogravure after it was used to illustrate *Modern Painters* IV (6, 261, Plate 36)

'View of the Aiguille du Plan'

Victoria & Albert Museum. This beautiful drawing shows the NW aspect of the Aiguille du Peigne, a satellite peak of the Plan. To the left is sketched in outline part of the Dent du Caïman, the Aiguille des Ciseaux, and the Aiguille du Blaitière. It is very likely that this is No. 38 'Aiguille du Plan, from its base' from Ruskin's 1854 List of Chamonix drawings (5, xxii), dated by him to 1849. Ruskin derived a small sketch from it (6, 233, Fig. 38) to illustrate the similarity of structure between this aspect of the (lower) Plan and the Blaitière, and drawing attention to the 'hollow in the heart of the aiguille .. as smooth and sweeping in curve as the cavity of a vast bivalve shell' (6, 231). This huge sweep of slabs was eventually climbed by Pierre Mazeaud's party in 1960.

'Cloud on the Aiguille du Goûter from Chamonix, Moonlight'

Inscribed 'Moonlight Chamouni/J Ruskin (186?)'. Bequeathed to the Library by Charles Warren. This watercolour was sold at Sotheby's 14 July

1988 (Lot 171) for £16,500. Presumably it was bought there by Warren or by a dealer who then sold it on to him. The 4th digit of the inscribed date is obscure and might be 0,5,6 or 8. Ruskin was not in Chamonix in 1866 or 1868, according to the *Diaries*. The date is enclosed in brackets, so it may be the date that Ruskin signed it rather than the date that he drew it. At any rate, it is a most unusual and arresting drawing, with Ruskin's attention plainly concentrated on the moonlit cloud pouring off the Dôme du Goûter to settle in a curled formation on the Aiguille. In Ruskin's diary entry for 4 July 1844 he comments on a similar cloud 'it rose from the Aiguille de Goûter exactly like an Indian's plume of feathers on his forehead . . curving round in the contrary direction under the Dôme', and added the tiny drawing in the margin shown below. It is possible that our drawing is related to this one.

'Valley of Lauterbrunnen'

Undated. Metropolitan Museum of Art. The viewpoint of the drawing is Unspunnen Castle in Wildersil, which overlooks the valley. The peak obscured by cloud in the distance is perhaps the Mönch. The Met suggests a date c1866 for this drawing. Certainly, Ruskin spent three weeks in Interlaken and the Lauterbrunnen in May and June 1866 (*Diaries*, 589-90), but he was there on other tours too, so the date might well be earlier. One indication of an early date is his attempt to draw every tree. In the Notes about his own drawings in an exhibition of 1878, he remarks that, 'Even the lower Swiss hills were a good deal more than his [Turner's] match, and that he well knew. Elsewhere, I have noticed his prudence in "counting their pines," or at least estimating their uncountableness! I did not understand his warning, and went insanely at them at first, thinking to give some notion of them by sheer labour.' (13, 510). A photogravure after this drawing appears in the *Works* (5, lviii): see above illustration.

'The Aiguilles du Dru and Mer de Glace, Moonlight'

Inscribed 'Mer de Glace – moonlight'. Gifted to the Club by Charles Warren. Cynthia Gamble's discussion notes Charles Warren's suggested date of 1863. Ruskin's diary entry for 24 September 1863 reports, 'Yesterday up the Montanvert in fresh snow and across the glacier: loveliest serrated edge of Bouchard-Dru – just fresh sprinkled. Sketched moonlight.'

'Glacier des Bossons'

1874. Gifted to the Club by Charles Warren. A photogravure after this drawing appears in the *Works* (2, 240). Ruskin made a brief visit to Chamonix in 1874. His diary for 16 October records that he, 'Sketched Bossons glacier from window.'

Two Editors

Montagne de la Côte, Chamonix
John Ruskin, 1849?
Watercolour over pencil. 12.4cm x 21cm.
Gifted to the Alpine Club by Charles Warren.

PETER FOSTER

Edward Lisle Strutt

A Portrait

Lt Col Edward Lisle Strutt's portrait
as president of the Alpine Club.

'Inflexible in opinion, outspoken and totally unmoved by the changing times through which he lived'[1], 'a complex and difficult man, certain of his own opinions... pompous and arrogant;'[2] 'he is remembered not for his climbing or his absorbing journals but for his virulent antipathies.'[3] This is a short selection from numerous similar epithets applied to Lt Col Edward Lisle Strutt (1874-1948), 'Bill' to his friends, editor of the *Alpine Journal* from 1927 to 1937 and president of the Club from 1935 to 1937.

1. W Unsworth, *Everest*, 3rd ed, London, Bâton Wicks, 2000, p72.
2. W Davis, *Into the Silence*, London, Bodley Head, 2011, p379.
3. S Goodwin, 'The Alpine Journal: A Century and a Half of Mountaineering History', *Himalayan Journal* 60, 1.

Strutt on Everest in 1922, sitting on Charles Bruce's left. 'It may possibly be,'
Bruce said of Strutt, 'that we are a little too young for him.'

Strutt's mother made sure he was
raised a Catholic, despite his father,
who died in an industrial accident
when Strutt was three, insisting
on him being raised an Anglican.

At St Moritz in 1904. 'Life for a
member of the leisured upper class
in Edwardian England remained
most agreeable.'

In the years between the wars the Alpine Club lost the leadership of the
alpine world and Strutt's reactionary views, expressed intemperately in the
pages of the *Journal*, contributed to the decline in the Club's prestige. He
railed against the new techniques and attitudes being adopted, especially
by continental climbers: the 'foolish variation' that was Welzenbach's direct

route up the north face of the Dent d'Hérens, the 'mechanisation' involved in Comici's ascent of the north face of the Cima Grande – 'a repulsive farce' – and the 'suicidal follies' of those attempting the Eigerwand. As Jack Longland, a leading British mountaineer of the period and future president of the Alpine Club, observed:

> *The Alpine Journal still spoke with enormous authority, but the trouble was not only that it spoke with dislike of much that was happening, but that many people simply stopped listening!*[4]

Who was this man, under whose editorship the *Journal* 'too often appeared in the role of a shocked and censorious maiden aunt, appalled by the immoral goings-on of the younger generation'?[5] From the outset Strutt enjoyed every advantage that resulted from wealth and rank in late Victorian England. During his birth in 1874, at Milford House in Derbyshire, his mother, like the Queen some years earlier, was given chloroform to ease the pain of childbirth; 'one bottle was used and a second begun which had the most marvellous effect' with the result that 'she was wonderfully well and the baby too.'[6] His father, the Hon Arthur Strutt, was the second son of the 1st Baron Belper, local magnate and Liberal politician. The Strutt fortune, on which the family's position was based, had been made from cotton by Lord Belper's grandfather, Jedediah: inventor, business partner of Arkwright and mill-owner. The early generations of Strutts had been nonconformists though later generations had moved towards the established Church of England. Strutt's mother Alice[7] was Roman Catholic; her father, Ambrose Phillipps, had converted to Catholicism and devoted his energy and wealth to the cause of reconciling the Anglican church with Rome. Lord Belper was adamant that any sons of Arthur and Alice be brought up as Anglicans and Strutt was duly baptised an Anglican but when he was aged three, his father died in a gruesome accident at the family mill, crushed between the large wheel and a smaller one. After that his mother raised him a Catholic.

In 1887, aged 13, he was sent to Beaumont College, a Society of Jesus boarding school in Windsor, founded 15 years earlier to provide a gentler alternative to the rigours of the society's Lancashire fortress of Stonyhurst. His time at the school coincided with its 'glittering period of fashionable success'[8], when it was considered the Catholic alternative to Eton. During this period the school roll included a sprinkling of sons of peers and important squires, dispossessed claimants to the thrones of France and Spain and

4. J Longland, 'Between the Wars 1919-39', *Alpine Journal* vol 62, p88.
5. Ibid.
6. L Phillipps de Lisle, Strutt's maternal grandmother, quoted in M Pawley, *Faith & Family: the life and circle of Ambrose Phillipps de Lisle*, Norwich, Canterbury Press, 1993, p358.
7. Alice was one of 16 siblings. Strutt's uncles included Everard, who had been killed in the Indian Mutiny and was awarded a posthumous VC, Rudolph, killed in 1885 in the 15m battle of Abu Klea in the Sudan, which also did for the adventurer Fred Burnaby and was immortalised by Henry Newbolt, and Edwin who became an MP. Three aunts became nuns.
8. P Levi, *Beaumont*, London, Deutsch, 1961, p25.

three or four Spanish dukes. Throughout his life, Strutt would enjoy 'the freemasonry of titled and Catholic families abroad, especially in Austria.'[9]

From Beaumont he went to the University of Innsbruck, enrolling as a student in 1892, and it was here, presumably, he developed his facility for languages, becoming fluent in German and French and well versed in Italian. Although now 18, he was placed in the charge of Beatrice Tomasson[10], an English governess living in Innsbruck. Fifteen years his senior, she had established her credentials as a private tutor and companion in the households of Prussian generals. She was also a mountaineer and they climbed together with guides during two seasons in the Austrian Alps; their relationship gave rise to the quip, 'the student eloped with his governess.'[11]

In 1893 Strutt went up to Oxford. His college, Christ Church, was favoured by the nobility and the wealthy, and his Oxford was that of *Sinister Street* and *Zuleika Dobson*, when academic ambitions were not great and undergraduates devoted themselves to the art of living. The welcoming speech given by Compton Mackenzie's fictional head of college is barely parody:

> You have come to Oxford,' he concluded, 'some of you to hunt foxes, some
> of you to wear very large and very unusual overcoats, some of you to row for
> your college and a few of you to work. But all of you have come to Oxford
> to remain English gentlemen.[12]

Undergraduates were generally rowdy and frequently boorish; while Strutt was in residence, members of the notorious Bullingdon Club smashed all the windows in Christ Church's Peckwater Quad. Amongst his contemporaries were two other future presidents of the Alpine Club: Tom Longstaff, also at Christ Church, who took a third in physiology, and Leo Amery, at Balliol, who with the excuse of his recent first in Classical Mods, 'gave over the summer term of 1894 to idling on the Cherwell in punt or canoe and to all the innumerable diversions which can make Oxford so delightful to those who wish to study life rather than books.'[13] But Strutt was not seduced by Oxford's charms; perhaps they seemed too juvenile and frivolous. Commenting some years later on Strutt's aloofness, Gen Charles Bruce, whose sense of fun could be distinctly childish, observed, 'It may possibly be that we are a little too young for him'[14]. Strutt did not return to Oxford after completing his first year and thus took no degree.

Possessing independent means, Strutt had no need of employment but in 1898, aged 24, he took up part-time soldiering and this remained his principal occupation until he was compulsorily retired in 1921. He was commissioned into the 3rd Battalion (Militia) of the Royal Scots, the oldest and senior infantry regiment of the line of the British Army. Although pur-

9. T Blakeney, 'The Alpine Journal and its Editors III', *Alpine Journal*, vol 81, p153.
10. Beatrice Tomasson (1859-1947). In 1901 she made the first ascent of the south face of the Marmolada with the guides Bettega and Zagonel.
11. H Reisach, 'Beatrice Tomasson and the South Face of the Marmolada', *Alpine Journal* vol 106, p107.
12. E M Compton Mackenzie, *Sinister Street*, London, Macdonald and Jane's, 1978, p421.
13. L Amery, *Days of Fresh Air*, London, Jarrolds, 1939, p31.
14. C Bruce, quoted in Unsworth, *op cit*, p72.

chase of commissions had been abolished, the high cost of living for officers ensured the social exclusivity of the officer corps and Strutt's fellow officers in the battalion included a marquis and three sons of the Duke of Buccleuch. On the eve of the Boer War, it is inconceivable that a young officer with Strutt's upbringing felt anything but confidence in his place and the position of Great Britain in the world.

In March 1900, Strutt, newly promoted captain, embarked for South Africa. Being a militia battalion, the 3rd was not obliged to serve abroad. Nevertheless, all but four men had volunteered. By August the war seemed to the British won, but it had merely entered a new phase of guerrilla fighting, which continued for almost two years. Strutt's battalion formed part of a mobile column, its duties mainly connected with protecting lines of communication but it also took part in the 'Great de Wet Hunt', during which the elusive Boer commander and his two thousand men evaded the attentions of 15,000 British troops. Strutt was mentioned in dispatches. The battalion returned to England at the end of July 1902 and within 10 days the regimental cricket XI, of which Strutt was a member, had, in a surprising display of ingenuousness or insouciance – Strutt considered it sportsmanship – proceeded to Holland, largely pro-Boer and anti-British, to play matches against Haarlem and the Gentlemen of Holland, winning the first and narrowly losing the second. The team was promptly ordered home to avert a diplomatic row.

Reflecting on the war 30 years later and exhibiting a by then well-developed chauvinism, Strutt wrote in an exculpatory obituary of Lord Methuen[15], whose generalship had been disastrous, that in contrast to the 'imbecilities' of France and Germany in their small colonial wars in Africa, 'it remains a solid fact that the South African war ... was a well-conducted affair. Moreover it was fought against a well-armed, gallant and *white* [his italics] enemy.'[16] But Britain's prestige had undeniably been dented and the nation's self-confidence, celebrated five years earlier at Queen Victoria's Diamond Jubilee, that festival of Empire, wobbled. Nevertheless, in the decade leading up to the First World War life for a member of the leisured upper class in Edwardian England remained most agreeable. Strutt, tall, good-looking, immaculately dressed, down to the tassels on his socks, appeared to the Italian Count Aldo Bonacossa 'altogether ... the typical English gentleman.'[17] And 'the virtue' of such an Englishman, was 'that he never doubts. That is what the system does for him.'[18]

From 1902 Strutt visited the Alps regularly, in summer and winter. His usual base was St Moritz: fashionable, expensive and frequented by royalty. It was here that he became acquainted with the Austro-Hungarian imperial family, to whom he would later render loyal service. Amongst Swiss mountain resorts, St Moritz had led the way in developing winter sports to

15. Field-Marshal, Lord Methuen (1845-1932) was elected to the AC in 1870 and made honorary member in 1927.
16. E Strutt, 'Field-Marshal Lord Methuen', *Alpine Journal*, vol 45, p146.
17. A Bonacossa, 'Reminiscences', *Alpine Journal*, vol 70, p219.
18. G Dickinson, quoted in J Morris, *Farewell the Trumpets*, London, Penguin, 1979, p306.

Strutt was 'a typical English gentleman,' according to Count Aldo Bonacossa. And 'the virtue' of such an Englishman, was 'that he never doubts. That is what the system does for him.'

amuse its visitors: skating, tobogganing – the Cresta run opened in 1884 – bobsleighing[19] and skiing. During the winter of 1897-8, a friend had sent Strutt a pair of Norwegian skis to try, 'only the second appearance of these weapons at St Moritz, the first having been worn by Sir Arthur Conan Doyle.'[20] Strutt was unimpressed, concluding their role was limited to facilitating the approach to a climb. He certainly had no time for the later development of downhill racing, which he condemned as 'pot-hunting'. He objected to the introduction of a vulgar spirit of competition in the mountains and one senses he deprecated the loss of exclusivity resulting from the package tours of Cook and Lunn[21], which accompanied the popularization of skiing. Strutt climbed extensively in the Bregaglia and Bernina. He described many of these expeditions in an article published in the *Alpine Journal* of 1910, which already shows glimpses of a querulous temperament, quick to criticize: bad roads, rapacious innkeepers, a guide dropping an ice axe, an antipathy to Germans in contrast to the charming Austrians, a keen interest in Alpine history and topography and a concern for its accuracy, traits that would find fuller expression in later articles and as editor of the *Alpine Journal*.

St Moritz also provided the back-drop to his courtship of Frances Holland whom he married in October 1905. Strutt recalled his wedding day in a letter to Charles Meade[22] who was to be married imminently, and offered some advice:

> … *the great thing to do is to have just the right amount of drink at lunch. Not too much as you begin to yawn and sweat – as did a fellow I was best man to! Not too little because you feel (and look) frightened. I lunched with three other fellows and drank: ½ bottle of champagne (I never touch it), two glasses of port (never take it at lunch) and one large old brandy. I was at all events sober … and did not break down and weep bitterly. Don't buy a new hat, your best man carries it and if the inside is dirty, people blame the said best man*

19. '[T]hat most futile of *all* sports,' remarked Strutt bitterly, following an accident. *Alpine Journal*, vol 25, p5.
20. E Strutt, 'Between the Inn and the Adda', *Alpine Journal*, vol 25, p5.
21. Sir Arnold Lunn (1888-1974) was blackballed from membership of the AC because of his association with his father's travel company. Yet, according to Lunn, it was Strutt who, during his presidency, encouraged him to re-apply, hinting that he was not above rigging the ballot.
22. C F Meade (1881-1975). In 1913, on his third attempt to climb Kamet (7756m) in the Garhwal, he reached the col at 7,100m that now bears his name. He was vice-president of the Club 1934-5.

Emperor Charles and his wife Zita, whom Strutt was sent to Austria to protect in 1919. Zita remained grateful to Strutt for the rest of her life. He was captivated by her. 'Determination was written in the lines of her square little chin, intelligence in the vivacious brown eyes, intellect in the broad forehead half hidden by masses of dark hair.' A freelance effort to return Charles to power earned Strutt a mild rebuke from Lord Curzon and resigned his commission.

for his disgusting turn-out. See your boots [hotel servant] does not forget to black the <u>soles</u> of your boots, otherwise 'price 12/6' is visible and is not appreciated on the bride's side of the church.[23]

An example of his sense of humour, perhaps, although more likely he was being serious.

On 28 June 1914, Strutt was, as usual, in the Engadine, climbing with his favourite guide Josef Pollinger. That day, in Sarajevo, Archduke Franz Ferdinand of Austria and his wife Sophie, in whose company Strutt had been photographed at St Moritz a few years before, were assassinated. War followed. On 14 October, 40-year-old Captain Strutt was in France with the British Expeditionary Force and found himself in temporary command[24] of the 2nd Battalion Royal Scots, then in action in the vicinity of Neuve Chapelle. On leaving his trench to report to his divisional commander, he was blown up by a 'bouquet of six shells', which burst low in quick succession. Thrown several yards, Strutt was wounded and temporarily paralysed. Six months later he returned to active duty on the staff and in October 1916 was ordered to Gen George Milne's headquarters in Salonika to act as principal liaison officer with the French commander of the allied forces in the Balkans, Gen Maurice Sarrail. This was no easy task. Disagreements about strategy between London and Paris led inevitably to tension between the respective headquarters. Sarrail was 'a political general down to his

---

23. E Strutt, letter to C F Meade 19 September 1913.
24. By the end of the day, the only officers fit for duty were subalterns, the battalion having lost nine commanding officers, killed or wounded, in three days.

Strutt married Frances Holland in 1905. She captioned these photos of the happy couple as 'Bill trying to back out,' and 'Bill quite beaten.'

infantryman's boots'[25] and his radical politics and anti-Catholic sentiment would have been repugnant to Strutt who, opinionated and habitually outspoken, must have had to cultivate reserves of tact and diplomacy to maintain smooth relations. That, improbably, he did so, and to the satisfaction of his superiors, is illustrated by four mentions in dispatches, the award of the DSO and numerous foreign decorations, including the *Légion d'honneur*.

Defeat in 1918 led to political upheaval in Germany and Austria. The kaiser immediately went into exile in Holland. In Vienna the imperial government gave way to a republic but the Hapsburg emperor Karl, or Charles[26] remained in Austria, powerless and isolated at Eckartsau, a royal shooting-lodge, and under increasing pressure to abdicate or accept exile. Concerns for his safety and that of his family reached George V. Fearing they might suffer the fate of the Russian imperial family, for which he reproached himself, the king required something be done, and on 22 February 1919, Strutt, who was staying at the luxurious Hotel Danieli in Venice, received new orders: 'You will proceed at once to Eckartsau and give Emperor and Empress moral support of British Government. They are stated to be in danger of their lives, to be suffering great hardships and to lack medical attendance. Endeavour by every possible means to ameliorate their condition.'[27]

Commenting on these orders, Strutt wrote in his diary: 'We all concluded that the Emperor must mean the Emperor of Austria but disagreed as to interpretation of "moral support". None of us had any idea where Eckartsau was.'[28] Next day, the British military mission to secure the safety of the imperial family – Lt Col Strutt and his batman – set out for Vienna and arrived three days later having left in its wake a host of grovelling petty officials:

25. A Palmer, *The Gardeners of Salonika*, London, Simon & Schuster, 1965, p30.
26. Emperor Charles I (1887-1922) had become heir to the imperial crown following the assassination of his uncle, Archduke Franz Ferdinand, and succeeded Emperor Franz Josef I in 1916.
27. G Brook-Shepherd, *The Last Habsburg*, London, Weidenfeld & Nicholson, 1968, p229.
28. E Strutt, quoted in G Brook-Shepherd, *op cit*, p230.

*Guard asks us for tickets but quails at my retort and retires backwards mur-
muring the inevitable 'Küss die Hand, Excellenz...' At Graz a prolonged halt
is made and everyone has to descend and be searched. We naturally refuse to
dismount and the officials retire bowing.*[29]

A haughty demeanour, bluster and bluff would characterise his dealings
with Austrian officialdom at every level, from railway guard to chancellor.
On meeting the emperor and empress, Strutt recorded his acutely observed
first impressions in his diary. The 31-year-old emperor was 'an eminently
loveable if weak man, by no means a fool, and ready to face his end as
bravely as his ancestress, Marie Antoinette. It was impossible to avoid liking
him.' The Empress Zita captivated him. 'About medium height with a slim
figure she looked younger than her age, twenty-six. The first impression
I had was one of extraordinary strength of character softened by her own
remarkable charm. Determination was written in the lines of her square
little chin, intelligence in the vivacious brown eyes, intellect in the broad
forehead half hidden by masses of dark hair. Without extraordinary claims
to beauty, the Empress would always attract attention in a crowd.'[30] During
the next few weeks Strutt's sympathy for their cause[31], his practical help in
improving supplies and his commitment to their safety – he slept with his
revolver beneath his pillow – gained the trust of the imperial couple.

On 17 March, Strutt received a telegram from the War Office advising
him to get the emperor out of Austria and into Switzerland at once, adding
ominously that the British government could not guarantee the journey. In
other words, Strutt was on his own. Strutt offered the emperor his spare
uniform and Glengarry bonnet as a disguise but the emperor refused to slink
across the border so Strutt determined on a more brazen tactic. He ordered
that the imperial train be reassembled in all its splendour and positioned
just a few miles from Eckartsau. These preparations inevitably attracted
the attention of the Austrian government, which saw an opportunity to exchange an unhindered passage for the emperor's abdication. Strutt, who had
promised Charles that he would leave as emperor, went to see Chancellor
Renner. Taken aback by Strutt's bawling in his 'best Boche style' and threatened with a draft telegram in which, without any authority, Strutt advised
blockading Austria – an enormous bluff – the chancellor caved in and the
emperor travelled to Switzerland without interference. Strutt's parting from
the imperial couple was 'like a dream'. He could remember little of what
was said except the empress' last words: 'Only an Englishman could have
accomplished what you have done for us.'[32] Strutt knelt and kissed her hand.

29. Idem.
30. Ibid p232.
31. His heart got the better of his head. To the British military attaché in Vienna he declared, absurdly: 'the
only thing for England to do was to occupy Austria and Hungary in force and to rule both through the person
of the Emperor.' T Montgomery-Cuninghame , ibid, p231.
32. Ibid, p246. Her gratitude was long lasting. On the occasion of the AC's centenary dinner in 1957, Empress
Zita sent a message of congratulations, adding, 'my thoughts and my prayers go towards your former President,
gallant Colonel Strutt, whose magnificent support to my family and myself I shall always remember.' *Alpine
Journal*, vol 63, p73.

But this was not to be the end of his involvement in the emperor's affairs.

The emperor did not abandon hope of a restoration and two years later, in February 1921, was determined to return to Hungary and reclaim the crown. He sent a secret summons to Strutt who travelled from St Moritz to the emperor's villa on the shore of Lake Geneva. Charles I planned to enter Austria secretly and asked him to reconnoitre a route across the frontier that would avoid the need for a passport. Strutt duly embarked on an escapade worthy of an episode from John Buchan's *John MacNab*, in which three wealthy English gentlemen relieve their ennui in a daring enterprise for a wager. 'With a "letter from a friend" in my pocket betting me 5000frs that I could not cross the frontier without showing my passport,' Strutt climbed steep rocks above the left bank of the river Inn by night to enter Austria and return without detection, but the 'journey was most unpleasant in the dark and suited only for a practised mountaineer.'[33]

News of Strutt's freelancing on behalf of the emperor reached the foreign secretary, Lord Curzon, who 'was doubtful of the propriety', which is to say convinced of the impropriety, 'of a British subject ... on the Special Reserve of officers, continuing to associate ... with an ex-enemy sovereign and discussing with him political plans which must gravely affect the interests of this country.'[34] Strutt escaped severe censure but, in his own words, he 'compulsorily joined the great majority of unemployables,'[35] code perhaps for a prudent resignation of his commission.

In 1922 Strutt went to Everest as Bruce's second-in-command but, now aged 48, his heart may not have been in it. Everest expeditions strip bare a man's character. His querulous nature emerged unfettered, as George Mallory described:

> *A usual and by now a welcome sound in each new place is Strutt's voice cursing Tibet – this march for being more dreary and repulsive than even the one before, and this village for being more filthy than any other. Not that Strutt is precisely a grouser; but he likes to ease his feelings with maledictions and, I hope feels better for it.*[36]

The expedition's transport officer, Capt John Morris, thought Strutt the greatest snob he had ever met and as an officer in the Indian army of the Raj, he had encountered a few. Strutt took against George Finch – 'I always knew the fellow was a shit'[37] – but, for all his execrations, there was no malice in Strutt, who later would draft and second Finch's application for membership of the Alpine Club. On the mountain, Strutt skilfully fulfilled his brief to locate the sites of the intermediary camps up the east Rongbuk glacier, dragged himself up to camp four on the North Col, and was on hand at camp three

33. Ibid p260.
34. G Curzon, quoted in G Brook-Shepherd, *op cit*, p261.
35. E Strutt, 'Post-war Frivolities: Graians and Ortler', *Alpine Journal* vol 37, p18.
36. G Mallory, quoted in D Robertson, *George Mallory*, London, Orchid Press, 1999, p185.
37. The unconventional Finch polarised opinion and Strutt's view was not unique. Quoted in J Morris, *Hired to Kill*, London, Hart-Davis, 1960, p145.

to provide succour to the exhausted and frost-bitten party returning from the first bid for the summit. Edward Norton, whose diaries are notable for the paucity of comment on his companions, singled out Strutt for his kindness. But when an early opportunity to return home arose, Strutt took it and according to Longstaff the expedition was not sorry to see him go.

Strutt assumed the editorship of the *Alpine Journal* in 1927 and over the following ten years members of the Club accustomed themselves to his imperious manner, 'his long, hissing in-drawings of breath after he had removed a cigarette in a Dunhill holder from his lips, before laying down the Law as He saw It.'[38] His editorial commentary is a litany of attacks on the use of crampons and pitons, guideless climbing, competition and nationalism, and, importantly, the resultant acceptance of 'unjustifiable' risk. It was these outpourings that won him his reputation as an inveterate reactionary, especially amongst the younger members.

His strictures may simply have been the product of a lack of imagination and a choleric temperament but, though unsympathetic to the quasi-mystical views of Geoffrey Young and Frank Smythe – 'psychological bilge'[39] – he saw in mountaineering a nobility that was being tarnished by competition, and believed that no man's death in pursuit of a pastime was justified. And who would gainsay that? Indeed, although as editor of the *Journal* his voice was often prominent, it was not a lone voice: he spoke for many in the Club.

'In the *Alpine Journal* that I now relinquish[40] I have said hard things at times of better men, of better mountaineers, than myself ... I can but say that it was 'all zeal' – zeal for the future of True Mountaineering, zeal for the old traditions of Journal and Club.' He added: 'Let this be my apology – if such be needed.'[41]

Acknowledgement

I am grateful to Jasper Meade for permission to reproduce the extract from Strutt's letter to C F Meade.

38. D Busk, 'The Young Shavers', *Mountain* 54, p40.
39. E Strutt, postcard to T Graham Brown, 26 October 1935, National Library of Scotland, acc 4338/5.
40. Worn out, he wrote, privately: 'it is the continuous grind ... letter after letter begging people to send their papers in – all in vain – that has killed me!' Letter to T Graham Brown 11 October 1937; National Library of Scotland acc 4338/7.
41. E Strutt, 'Valedictory Address', *Alpine Journal*, vol 50, p11.

LINDSAY ELMS

The First Editor

The Legacy of Hereford Brooke George

Hereford Brooke George, first editor of the *Alpine Journal*, with his niece: date unknown. *(George Family)*

*George, more than most of the climbers, 'looked the part'. With a red beard and
great height, he was massive and confident both of mind and of body, with a record
both on the mountains and in the sphere of Alpine organisation quite equal to the
reputation he later acquired as an historian.*[1]

Hereford Brooke George was born at Bath in Somerset on 1 January
1838, the eldest of three children born to Richard Francis George,
surgeon, and his wife Elizabeth Brooke. He entered Winchester College as
a scholar in 1849, and in 1856 became a fellow at New College, Oxford,
which remained an exclusive Wykehamist enclave. He did well in his 'mods',
with first classes in Classics and maths, but took seconds in his finals. He
graduated in 1860, proceeding to his MA in 1862 and was called to the
bar at the Inner Temple on 6 June 1864, following the western circuit until
1867 when he returned to New College as tutor in the combined school
of law and history. He was ordained in 1868, but undertook no parochial
work. After the separation of the law and history schools in 1872 he became
history tutor at New College, filling that office until 1891. In this period
New College was transformed from one of the smallest Oxford colleges to
one of the largest, opening itself to fellows beyond Winchester, a process
George helped drive and then described in his *New College 1850-1906* (1906).
He played a prominent part in the establishment of the inter-collegiate
system of lecturing at Oxford and was one of the first members of the
Oxford University volunteer corps.

His historical writings and teaching were chiefly concerned with military
history and the relationship between history and geography: *Genealogical
Tables illustrative of Modern History* (1874), *Battles of English History* (1895),
Napoleon's Invasion of Russia (1899), *Relations of Geography and History* (1901),
Historical Geography of the British Empire (1904), and *Historical Evidence* (1909).
The AC member and assistant editor T S Blakeney, always a delicately shrewd
observer, described him as 'a solid rather than a light-hearted writer.'

Hereford George took up mountaineering during that familiar period
W A B Coolidge called the 'Golden Age', between the ascent of the Wetter-
horn in 1854 by Alfred Wills, although not of course the *first* ascent, and
Edward Whymper's triumph and tragedy on the Matterhorn in 1865. It was
the decade during which almost all the major peaks in the Alps were first
climbed, culminating in the particularly successful years of 1864 and 1865.
On George's first visit to Switzerland in 1860, he met Leslie Stephen, who
would follow him as editor of the *Alpine Journal*, at Zermatt and accompanied him up to the Riffel by the Gorner glacier. In 1862, George accompanied Stephen on the first passage by the Jungfraujoch, and made the
first ascent of the Gross Fiescherhorn on 23 July 1862 with Adolphus War-
burton Moore and guides Christian Almer and Ulrich Kaufmann. In 1863,
he made a passage of the Col du Tour Noir with Christian Almer as guide,
and investigated the relative positions of the heads of the Argentine, Tour,

1. R Clark, *The Victorian Mountaineers*, Batsford, 1953.

and Saline glaciers. His interest in climbing was chiefly geographical and scientific and he was one of the first Alpine climbers to use photography.

In 1861, George joined the Alpine Club. That year the establishment of the *Alpine Journal* was suggested at a meeting in his rooms at New College and George went on to edit its first three volumes (1863 to 1867). In his very first 'Introductory Address', he explained that it had been thought worth making more widely known 'the amount of geographical and other information' that Alpine Club members acquired each year that had hitherto only been available to those able to attend the Club's meetings. Narratives would be written by members of the Alpine Club, but it was hoped that with 'Alpine Notes and Queries', a very useful portion of the *Alpine Journal* would be open to anyone filling in gaps in climbing knowledge. Any fears that the Journal had arrived too late and that all the great ascents had been done could be easily dispelled. George directed readers to less frequented areas of the Alps. 'Moreover,' he wrote, 'the Himalayas, which are daily becoming more accessible to enterprise, offer an unlimited field for adventure,' as well as all the other ranges where 'the Englishman's foot is some day destined to scale.'

Also important to George was the inclusion of scientific objectives: there were nine such papers on subjects as diverse as the structure of névé, minimum thermometers, phosphorescent snow, electricity in the Pyrenees, and on. Of more immediately pragmatic use was the 'Report of the Special Committee of the Alpine Club on Ropes, Axes and Alpenstocks' reports on Ropes and Ice Axes, discussions on glacial theories, camping out (tents, sleeping bags, cooking apparatus) and 'Accidents and their Causes'. In volumes two and three, George went well outside the Alps, dealing with the Caucasus and outlying Alpine areas.

He forged a style the *Alpine Journal*, according to Blakeney: 'was long to lose, if indeed it ever completely did so.' He had the advantage that his tenure began as the Golden Age reached its climax: 1864 and 1865. He reprinted Whymper's letter to *The Times* with the dramatic account of the first ascent of the Matterhorn and the disaster that followed, and happier stories, like Moore's ascent of the Brenva. Some of his successors seemed to relish controversy. Coolidge could famously do anything with a hatchet except bury it. George avoided such heat, as Blakeney recorded: 'he was not involved in any particular quarrels or disputes, such as enlivened some later editorships. Nor had the day arrived when mountain masses were to become increasingly sub-divided until every point or declivity had its name as a peak or a pass.'

In 1866, Hereford George published *The Oberland and Its Glaciers: Explored and Illustrated with Ice-Axe and Camera*, which included 28 photographic illustrations by Ernest Edwards. In its review, *The Gentleman's Magazine* said:

> … *two tools [ice-axe and camera] that have not much in common, yet have conspired to produce one of the best books we have yet seen illustrated by photograph. … Mr. George is admirably adapted to the character of the work. The narrative portions are smart and racy; the descriptive clear and concatenated.*

On the Unter Grindelwald Glacier, circa 1862. The image appears in George's well received *The Oberland and its Glaciers: Explored and Illustrated with Ice-Axe and Camera*. *(George Family)*

The southern aspect of Mount Victoria, third-highest peak on Vancouver Island, where George's great-grandson perished in 2006. *(Lindsay Elms)*

Hereford Brooke George in his academic gown, New College, Oxford. *(George Family)*

George had written the book to popularise the glacier theories of John Tyndall. In his introduction he wrote:

The writer has often found that people who have never seen a glacier, however keenly they may be interested in glacier theory for its own sake, and in mountain adventure on behalf of their friends, are unable to obtain any clear idea of what a glacier really is, except from elaborate viva voce explanation of Alpine pictures. Professor Tyndall's 'Glaciers of the Alps', the most lucid in style of all works on glacier theory, was written mainly to enunciate an entirely new doctrine, and therefore contains much of argument and controversy, which are necessary for a sufficient understanding of subject by those who are content to take one set of opinions on trust, without entering deeply into the controversy.

Tyndall, the prominent 19th century Irish physicist, must have seemed the ideal mountaineer to George, having made his first visit to the Alps in 1856 for scientific reasons and becoming one of the great pioneering climbers in the process. He visited the Alps almost every summer from 1856 onward. In the Alps, Tyndall studied glaciers, especially glacier motion and in 1860 he wrote his *Glaciers of the Alps*. His explanation of glacial flow brought him into dispute with others, particularly James David Forbes, who had done much of the early scientific work on glacier motion. But Forbes at that time didn't know the phenomenon of 'regelation', the theory of ice melting under pressure and freezing again when pressure is reduced, a process Michael Faraday discovered a little later.

In 1876, members of the Alpine Club who were resident at Oxford University and shared an interest in Alpine pursuits formed the Oxford Alpine Club. George was one of the prime movers. A year after the club was officially founded they produced the first printed list of members. The original rules from 1876 stated that the club was to consist of 'not more than Thirty Resident Members of the University interested in the objects of the Alpine Club.' Candidates who were members of the Alpine Club were admitted automatically, for others admission was by ballot, with one adverse vote in six resulting in exclusion. The club would dine once a year, early in Trinity term, and would have one meeting each year in October. The subscription was set at 15 shillings, later reduced to 12s 6d, and included dinner. The only reference to the management of the club in the original rules was rule six: 'A Secretary, who shall also be Treasurer, shall be elected annually at the meeting in Michaelmas Term.' There was no provision for a president, nor any kind of committee. Hereford George was elected the first secretary, fulfilling this role from 1876 to 1901, when he was elected the club's first president. He had been running the club for 25 years; presumably the position of president was created as a tribute.

Very few records survive of the ordinary meetings held each year. However, a few notices show that the meetings generally consisted of someone, often Hereford George, reading a paper, sometimes accompanied by photos. There was probably very little club business to be dealt with at these meetings, since George had already dealt with most of it. He used to send around circulars to the members, asking for them to inform him if they disagreed with one of his proposals. It seems nobody ever did. For example, in 1879 members were more or less told that the secretary was sending £5 of the club's money 'to the relief of the sufferers by the great fire, which recently almost destroyed Meyringen [Switzerland].' In 1901, when Hereford George relinquished the job of secretary, the members' list failed to record who took over the role. In 1909, the Oxford mountaineering community divided into the Oxford University Mountaineering Club for undergraduate members, and the Oxford Alpine Club for alumni.

In 1870, George married Alice Bourdillon Cole, with whom he had two sons. A decade later, George, who inherited a moderate fortune from his father, found himself in financial dire straits. His wealth came from his interest in the West of England and South Wales Bank at Bristol, and although he took no active part in the management of its affairs he was a director. The failure of the bank in 1880 not only injured George financially but involved him with his fellow directors in an aborted trial for irregularities in keeping the accounts. Hereford Brooke George died at Holywell Lodge, Oxford on 15 December 1910.

During his editorship of the *Alpine Journal*, and after Edward Whymper's accident on the Matterhorn in 1865, Queen Victoria had written in her diary how 'four poor Englishmen including a brother of Lord Queensberry have lost their lives in Switzerland, descending over a dangerous place from the Matterhorn and falling over a precipice.' The dangers of alpinism clearly vexed her because almost two decades later, during another deadly season in the Alps, she asked her private secretary Sir Henry Ponsonby to write to the prime minister William Gladstone seeking to make public her disapproval. Gladstone's measured reply settled things. 'It may be questionable whether, upon the whole, mountain-climbing (and be it remembered that Snowdon has its victims as well as the Matterhorn) is more destructive than various other pursuits in the way of recreation.' George was no longer the *Alpine Journal* editor, but even at the time he had felt it necessary to comment. He was not given to editorialising.

In an odd twist of fate, in 2006, Hereford Brooke George's great-grandson Brooke George died aged 61 in a mountaineering accident on a mountain named after Her Majesty: Victoria Peak, the third-highest mountain on Vancouver Island, Canada.

History

View of the Aiguille du Plan
John Ruskin, 1849?
Watercolour over pencil. 37.9cm x 50.3cm.
Victoria and Albert Museum.

ERIC VOLA

Shipwrecked on Mont Blanc

How the Vincendon and Henry
Tragedy Changed Alpinism

'Shipwrecked on Mont Blanc': The cover of *Paris Match* from January 1957.
An Alouette stands beside the Vallot refuge at the grim conclusion of
attempts to rescue François Henry and Jean Vincendon, preparing
to evacuate eight rescuers who have been trapped there.

Christmas, 1956: all of France and Belgium are following the protracted agonies of two young climbers marooned on Mont Blanc. Two hundred journalists crowd Chamonix. The tragedy fills the airwaves of Radio Télévision France and the pages of *Paris Match* creating as great an impact on the French public as the Matterhorn disaster did on the British in 1865. It will lead to major reform in French mountain rescue with the founding of the Pelotons de Gendarmerie de Haute Montagne, France's police mountain rescue units. It sees the public arrival of helicopters in mountain rescue. It will also mark French alpinists, professionals and amateurs alike, for generations

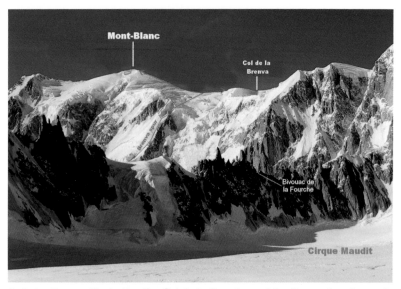

A photo-diagram illustrating the Col de la Fourche and the Brenva face beyond. The young Vincendon and Henry planned a winter ascent of the Brenva, inspired by recent successes on the route.

to come, as questions are asked about what went so badly wrong. Forty years after the tragedy, French author Yves Ballu publishes a history of this harrowing event: *Naufrage au Mont Blanc* (Glénat, 1997): Shipwreck on Mont Blanc. Twenty years later the story's importance warrants another edition (Guérin, 2017), with a new foreword from my old friend Claude Dufourmantelle, who tried more than most to save the lives of his fellow alpinists. 'Le Duf' is one of the last survivors of the tragedy; his foreword sets the scene.

May 1956, Algeria: the ambush at Palestro[1]. Guy Mollet [then prime minister] pushes France into the sort of peacekeeping mission that quickly becomes a fully-fledged war. Khrushchev crushes Hungary as a distracted Eisenhower looks on, too busy defending Aramco's interests in Saudi Arabia at the expense of the French and British then entangled in their Suez affair. Morocco becomes independent; pan-Arabism and political Islam establish themselves in the world of geo-politics with the objective of telling us what the price of oil will be.

Kids and teenagers from the war are now young adults; for them, war with its wounds has drifted into the past and in its place America, enriched by the conflict, spreads over a convalescent Europe the image of James Dean and his rage to live. Those young men, those kids take up mountaineering as part of this revival. The new generation's mantra is to do better than its elders, tearing up alpinism like it was rock'n'roll and they were Elvis.

1. Fighters from the Armée de Libération Nationale killed 21 men from a French army platoon, several being murdered after their capture.

So 1956 was, in Le Duf's words, 'a pivotal year', and it ended with what became known as the Vincendon and Henry affair: two young men, city boys, setting out in winter to climb a route on the Italian side of Mont Blanc. This was a serious enterprise. Winter climbing was not then accepted among the majority of climbers and was taboo for guides. What these young men planned was a transgression, or to use today's term, a disruption. Like Le Duf, Jean Vincendon was 23 years old. Born and educated in Paris, he started climbing on the Fontainebleau sandstone boulders. Just 5ft 6in and slim in build, he had not yet done any big routes apart from the south ridge of Aiguille Noire de Peuterey in 1955, or any serious ice climbs. Even so, that year he was admitted to the aspirant guide course at the École Nationale de Ski et d'Alpinisme (ENSA). His teachers were Armand Charlet, André Contamine and Louis Lachenal, who impressed him the most. Like his heroes, he dreams of the Himalaya and climbing major Alpine routes that will open the doors of the Groupe de Haute Montagne (GHM), French alpinism's most exclusive club.

Vincendon met François Henry climbing at Freyr in the Ardennes. Born in Brussels, he was just 21 but had been climbing for four years. Unlike Henry, he was tall: 6ft 3in. His father Louis was a chemist but during the war had been active in the Zéro resistance network with Henry's mother Jeanne. Arrested by the Gestapo they were sent to Dachau, Ravensbrück and Mauthausen but miraculously survived, although Jeanne died in 1950 from the aftereffects.

Like their heroes Terray and Lachenal, the two young men wanted to climb major routes: the Croz and Walker spurs – and why not the Eiger's north face? Except Vincendon has to work that July as a UNCM[2] instructor in the Pyrenees and by early August has his leg in a cast from a fall, putting an end to that summer's climbing ambitions. They set themselves another goal: the Brenva in winter. It is the easiest of the big routes on the Italian side of Mont Blanc but remains a serious ice route even for seasoned ice climbers, let alone in winter. Winter ascents were then so uncommon the Chamonix guides office is closed. As Claude Deck put it, climbing in winter was only for 'those strong enough to rely on themselves.' That opinion was largely shared by Chamonix mountain guides and would only change with a new generation in the 1960s.

Vincendon got the idea for the Brenva in Chamonix, listening to Dufourmantelle describe his first winter attempt in 1955 with partners François-Xavier Caseneuve, nicknamed 'the Yeti', and André Brun. All three were students at the École Centrale in Paris. They had given up at the start of the spur itself in the face of heavy snowfalls, deciding to make another attempt the following December. Several weeks later, on 26 February 1956, the well-known Paris alpinists Jean Couzy and André Vialatte made the first winter ascent. They took the brand new Aiguille du Midi cable car, opened in the summer of 1955, skied down the first part of the

2. The Union Nationale des Centres de Montagne was born in 1944 from the Jeunesse et Montagne movement and in 1965 itself became part of the UCPA under French sports minister Maurice Herzog.

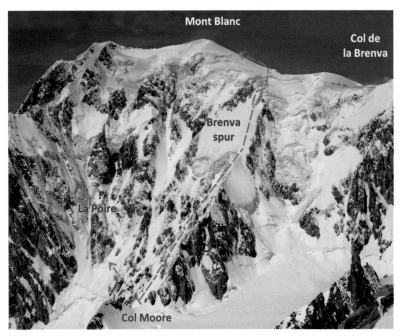

The Brenva face, illustrating the spur and the Pear, the objective of Walter Bonatti and Silvano Gheser who abandoned the first winter ascent in the face of heavy snow and traversed into the Brenva above the slower-moving Franco-Belgian team.

Vallée Blanche and climbed up to La Fourche bivouac hut. Starting from there at 4.45am, they reached the Mur de la Côte at 7.30pm and descended directly by the Corridor, pausing on the Grand Plateau to wait for the moon to reach the Grands Mulets hut at midnight. Next day Vialatte was in time for the train back to Paris. Speed climbing is not so new.

Vincendon would like to have joined Dufourmantelle and Caseneuve, who were the same age but already seasoned alpinists. Le Duf had started climbing at the age of 15 and the pair had serious ice routes under their belts. Both were students at the École Centrale, had climbed together for several years and were technically on a par. They made a very strong team: Lionel Terray certainly rated them. Late in the morning of 17 December Le Duf and the Yeti took the Aiguille du Midi cable car, a special dispensation since it was closed, and like Couzy and Vialatte skied the first part of the Vallée Blanche before climbing the steep 150m couloir to La Fourche. Unlike the first pair, they didn't set out until 7am but still reached the top of the Brenva at 6pm, using their headlamps for the last hour as darkness fell. Like Jean Couzy and Vialatte, they ignored the summit and headed straight down to Chamonix, benefitting from their decision to climb fast and light during the full moon and so avoid a bivouac. Things had gone like clockwork but next day, below the hut at Jonction, Le Duf fell 20m down a crevasse, losing his ice axe and a crampon in the process. The Yeti was able to help him to safety after much effort using loops in the rope.

Back in Chamonix, on 21 December, the pair meet Vincendon and Henry at Le Choucas[3], giving them details of their ascent and advising them in case of bad weather to descend the Brenva or if at the top to go over the summit to the Vallot bivouac hut. The snow going down directly to the Grands Mulets is deep and they should look out for crevasses. Another friend, Bob Xueref tells them: 'whatever, go to the summit for safety. If we have to come and fetch you, it will be by the Aiguille du Goûter.'[4]

Vincendon and Henry leave Chamonix on 22 December carrying huge rucksacks. Unlike Le Duf and the Yeti, or Couzy and Vialatte, they have decided on a more heavyweight approach. They have even packed a tent. Like the others, they take the cable car and plan to ski but their loads are heavy and they dump the skis at the bottom of the first slope. Soon after they meet Walter Bonatti. Bonatti has been planning the first winter ascent of the Pear: a much more difficult route than the Brenva but also starting from La Fourche. His rope mate is Silvano Gheser, a lieutenant and instructor in the Alpini. Four days earlier these two had made a reconnaissance to La Fourche and found ideal conditions. Coming down they had seen two dots high on the Brenva: Le Duf and the Yeti, moving swiftly. Now Bonatti is ski touring in the same area. He does not tell the French and Belgian climbers that in two days he will attempt the Pear: he believes that by then they will be in Chamonix.

At 4.30pm, at the Torino refuge, before descending, Bonatti sees two dots on the Géant glacier coming towards him, presumably Vincendon and Henry who have decided to give up. Two days later, on 24 December, Bonatti and Gheser take the cable car back up to the Torino and are told about two French who have spent the previous night at the refuge. Approaching the slope up to La Fourche, they see two figures coming down. Vincendon and Henry have given up after waking that morning to a veil of clouds. Bonatti can't see a cloud anywhere. When Bonatti tells them who he is and that he is going to make the first winter ascent of the Pear, Vincendon and Henry change their minds, following the other rope back to the La Fourche hut. Days later, Bonatti tells *Nuova Stampa* that conditions that day 'were ideal, better than in summer.'

From the refuge, Bonatti and Gheser cross the Brenva glacier to the Col Moore to assess conditions; part of the route is shared with the Brenva and their tracks will benefit Vincendon and Henry. The snow is good but while cutting steps Bonatti's axe suffers a thin but lengthy crack down its shaft. Back at La Fourche, Bonatti makes a makeshift repair to the axe, 'wrapping it in a tight corset of strong twine, which made it perfectly serviceable.'[5] Henry, second on the French-Belgian rope and so not required to cut steps, offers Bonatti his own axe, which the Italian accepts. 'La Poire needs perfect equipment,' Henry tells him, downplaying his act of generosity. Bonatti notes the

3. Le Choucas, the 'Jackdaw', was for French climbers what the 'Bar Nash' was for the British.
4. Quoted in Ballu.
5. Bonatti *My Mountains – Christmas on Mont-Blanc*.

Having finished the Brenva spur after a bivouac and a storm, with Vincendon and Henry on his rope, Bonatti and Gheser split again to summit Mont Blanc and descend to the Vallot on the evening of 26 December. The Franco-Belgian team never arrived, bivouacking and then descending towards the Grands Mulets, bivouacking again and then missing the exit to become marooned above the Combe Maudite.

superiority of their equipment, 'particularly their long down sleeping bags capable of dealing with low temperatures.'[6] In return Bonatti suggests they join him on the Pear, knowing Vincendon and Henry will likely not accept since their training and acclimatisation are insufficient for such a difficult climb. Vincendon know this and decides to stick with the Brenva.

The climbers wake at 2.30am on Christmas Day, a Tuesday. They leave the hut at 4am. The first minutes in the winter cold are painful. At the Col Moore, the two parties separate, the Italians traversing left to the foot of the Pear while the French and Belgian start on the Brenva. Bonatti soon realises they have started too late: the sun rises as they reach a steep couloir below the Pear itself that is full of loose snow. The route is prone to avalanche. At 8:30am they give up on the Pear and make a long diagonal traverse to the Brenva. Just as they get there, an avalanche falls a thousand metres filling the Brenva cirque below. Bonatti is astonished to find the Franco-Belgian party is still below them. Heavily laden, they have been slow, but they do not seem in difficulty.

Bonatti and Gheser start up the tracks left by Dufourmantelle and Caseneuve and at 2pm stop for an hour to eat. Vincendon and Henry still do not catch them. Bonatti starts again, knowing the last part of the route is steeper and may require step cutting. At 3.30pm he and Gheser are 100m below the last seracs near the steep section that ends the spur. In normal

6. Bonatti *My Mountains – Christmas on Mont-Blanc*.

conditions, it would take an hour or two to reach the summit of Mont Blanc and another half hour or so to reach the Vallot bivouac hut below the Bosses ridge. But it is winter, and as they climb the last steep slope of the spur night falls and the wind strengthens. 'A little altimeter-barometer would have been enough to warn us the previous night,' Bonatti wrote in *Mountains of my Life*. 'But in those days no one made much use of them. (I used one constantly from then on precisely because of this experience.) Nor were there any reliable weather forecasts. At that time everyone trusted his own empirical observation and relied on vague premonitory signs.' This hasn't been enough. A storm has broken; the wind speed reaches more than 40mph. 'In those circumstances, it would have been normal to lose our life.'

Claude Dufourmantelle on the summit of the Breithorn. His rapid ascent of the Brenva was an inspiration for Vincendon and Henry, and who raised the alarm when he thought they were in trouble.

He looks for shelter and finds a hole he enlarges with his borrowed axe. Gheser's feet are freezing: he's made the mistake of wearing cotton socks. Bonatti gives him his *pied d'éléphant* half sleeping bag. A hundred metres below, Vincendon and Henry shelter in a snow-hole. There is no chance of sleep. By morning 40cm of fresh snow has fallen and the storm continues. Thick cloud blankets the mountain. Vincendon and Henry aren't well but don't want to go down as Dufourmantelle and Caseneuve advised. As Bonatti says later, they were already too high, near the top of the spur, and the fresh snow meant descending would be dangerous. In the morning, Bonatti goes down to fetch them using his two ropes tied together for the first 80m. They all join Gheser. Henry's left foot is frozen but with Bonatti's apperance their spirits are high.

Bonatti senses that without his help the other pair won't make it. He puts them on his rope, Gheser, then Henry and Vincendon. Blinded by the storm he finds a way through the snowy maze. Missing the easy exit on the right leading to the Brenva Col, he takes the middle exit of the three, heading straight up to tackle the final seracs with technical difficulties that Dufourmantelle and Caseneuve didn't encounter. Suddenly, at around 3pm, the sky clears: they can see the summit. The climbers are some 150m above the Brenva Col (4303m), at the top of the ridge of the Mur de la Côte, 350m below the summit between the Lower and Upper Red Rocks.[7]

7. W Bonatti's estimates in *To My Mountains: – Christmas on Mont-Blanc*.

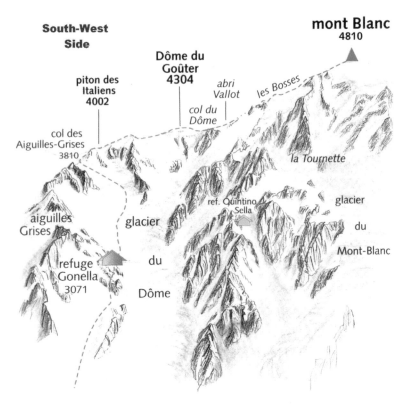

A diagram illustrating the route taken by Bonatti and Gheser to the Gonella hut, which they reached from the Vallot on 28 December after another bivouac. Rescuers reached them there on 30 December.

Bonatti's instinct and experience seems to have saved them. But they are not yet out of danger. Bonatti starts for the Grands Mulets via the old lower route, the *Passage Balmat*[8], but after 100m with snow up to his waist he discovers the fresh snow is unstable and dangerous. They return to their starting point at around 4,450m. One solution is to cross diagonally to the Vallot hut (4362m) but the snow looks deep and avalanche prone. The easiest and safest solution is to climb to the summit of Mont Blanc and descend the Bosses ridge to the Vallot. The bitter northerly has blown it clear of loose snow; the slope is firm and straightforward. Yet climbing in a fierce wind is exhausting, particularly after the ordeal of their bivouac. Bonatti is worried. Night will be on them in an hour and he knows a second night out in the open could mean death. With a wind of 40mph and a temperature dropping to -30°C, the wind chill will be ferocious: -70°C. He has to reach the Vallot before sunset and Gheser is weakening. As Bonatti recalls afterwards, 'there

8. *The Passage Balmat*, also called the 'Old Route' or the 'Forbidden Route' was forbidden by the Chamonix guides after the famous Arkwright accident on 13 October 1866.

was no difficulty, we only had to walk.' Visibility was 'now good' and the two parties split again in order to 'go as fast as possible.'[9]

Having set off together, after half an hour or so Vincendon and Henry slow down. A hundred metres below the summit, above the Petits Mulets, Bonatti sees them lagging behind some 60m to 90m.[10] He shouts into the wind to go faster. They respond, 'No problem.' Bonatti then concentrates on the task in hand, thinking that on such straightforward ground and with their tracks Vincendon and Henry will soon join him. As night falls he reaches the summit, blasted by the freezing wind. Without stopping, Bonatti and Gheser go down the Bosses ridge. By the time they reach the Vallot it's pitch-dark.

The sheet-metal refuge is in an appalling state. Everything is frozen and it's impossible to light a fire. There's no food or medicine, nothing but frozen blankets. The temperature inside that night is -18°C. Realising how bad Gheser's feet are, he uses methylated spirits from their stove to rub his feet. He also lights a candle on the windowsill for Vincendon and Henry, but they don't arrive. Bonatti keeps looking out of the door. Why haven't they arrived? He suggests going to look for them but Gheser tells him that will be suicide. Day breaks, the morning of Thursday 27 December. The storm still rages and there is no sign of the others. 'I could not imagine,' Bonatti wrote later, 'that so high up Vincendon and Henry, only a little distance behind us, were going to take, without us knowing, the most absurd of decisions: turn back down (but this is what they did!) and then go for the couloir of the Old [Balmat] Passage, which we had avoided as being extremely dangerous. Why would Vincendon and Henry do such a folly?'[11] He decides against going down to Chamonix, although it's much shorter, preferring to descend the Bionassay ridge to the Gonella. He thinks the snow on that side will be less avalanche-prone. Friends coming up from Courmayeur should be at the Gonella waiting for them.

Gheser's feet are so swollen he can't put his boots on. With blankets from the Vallot and bits of a sleeping bag Bonatti fashions some makeshift shoes, fixing Gheser's crampons to them with lanyards, belts and wire. They finally leave the Vallot at 10am, descending through a maze of seracs, crevasses and mounds of snow. A snow bridge breaks and Bonatti falls 20m into the crevasse beneath before being stopped by the mass of snow forming between his legs. Gheser holds the rope and Bonatti climbs up it to where the crevasse narrows. Then he continues with his crampons but the final part is overhanging. He asks Gheser to make loops on one of the rope's ends, lower it to him and fix it securely. Using this, he swings his body until he can reach the crevasse's lip and then with Gheser's help escapes its clutches. This manoeuvre has taken 2h 30m. The time is 5pm and the Gonella is still 700m below them. They must bivouac again and take shelter against a serac.

9. W Bonatti, *La Rivista Mensile*, CAI, 1957 and 'Christmas on Mont Blanc', *To My Mountains*, 1961.
10. W Bonatti, *Una Vita Cosi*, Milan, RCS Libri, 2014. Published three years after Bonatti's death.
11. W Bonatti, *Montagnes d'Une Vie*, Arthaud, 1997.

The cold is intense. Bonatti gives Gheser his thicker mittens and the hood of his anorak. Like on K2 during his terrible bivouac at 8,100m he keeps beating his boots with his ice axe until the pain returns and he's confident blood is flowing again. At 5am the moon emerges. The weather is now perfect and the sun rises brightly. They know they will survive. It will take them a full day, advancing slowly, sometimes on all fours, to reach Gonella where they find good blankets and wood to make a fire but no food. Bonatti's Italian friends have organised a rescue party from Courmayeur and reach them two days later on 30 December.

Two Castaways on Mont Blanc

When Bonatti last presses Vincendon and Henry to keep following him, they stopped two or three rope lengths below the Petits Mulets, the last rocks some 110m below the summit of Mont Blanc. Unlike Bonatti and Gheser, Vincendon and Henry aren't acclimatised, which may be a factor in their subsequent decision to descend. It's likely they bivouack near the Petits Rochers Rouges but we can't be sure. Nor is there any way of knowing whether they attempt to reach the summit the following morning of 27 December.[12] At some point they clearly begin descending the slopes between the Petits Rochers Rouges and the lower Rochers Rouges, the old Passage Balmat, aiming for the Grand Plateau and the Grands Mulets refuge.

The Chamonix guide Joseph Maffioli is at the Brévent with a telescope and reports that Vincendon is falling frequently, held by Henry. At some point, not witnessed, Vincendon takes Henry with him and they tumble 60m down a steep couloir, losing their glacier glasses, rucksacks and gloves. François Henry also loses his crampons and over-boots. They bivouac again at the bottom of the Rochers Rouges at around 4,200m, having descended just 400m in a full day.[13] The following morning, Friday 28 December, as Bonatti and Gheser begin their final descent to the Gonella, Henry manages to get Vincendon down to the Grand Plateau. But perhaps partially blind due to the loss of their sunglasses, they lose their way and instead of going left towards the Grands Mulets they go straight down and find themselves on the brink of the 300m icefall that hangs above the Combe Maudite at around 3,900m, perched on an unstable cornice. Exhausted and frostbitten, they cannot turn around and climb back up. They are essentially trapped. Only a rescue can save them now.

Until the end of the war there was no national rescue system in France. Rescues were local volunteer efforts. Lucien Devies, the powerful president of the Fédération Française de la Montagne (FFM),[14] instituted the first national system based on the established Austrian mountain rescue organisation, coordinating some 20 different organisations by 1948. He was

12. Testimony of Blanc who spoke with François Henry after the crash of his helicopter three days later.
13. According to the observers from Planpraz and the Brévent, Simond, Pellin and Maffioli.
14. Fédération Française de la Montagne, created in 1945 by the sports minister with the delegation to organise mountain rescues in France. Its president Lucien Devies was also in charge of its rescue committee.

particularly active in Chamonix, where the larger number of rescues required the task be shared between different bodes and coordinated through the Société Chamoniarde de Secours en Montagne (SCSM). Although the SCSM reports to the FFM rescue committee, its role is simply to delegate rescues to one of the three organisations in Chamonix with the necessary men and equipment. These are the powerful Compagnie des Guides de Chamonix, jealous of its privileges; the École de Haute Montagne (EHM), whose guides train French mountain troops; and ENSA, which is fairly new and attached to the sports department of the French education ministry. However, in winter ENSA runs only skiing instructor courses, and so many of the instructors are not available.

The head of the SCSM is Pierre Dartigue, a well-regarded doctor, but he can't simply order a rescue. Each of these organisations has their own rules and chains of command. And apart from the EHM, it's up to each guide to make his own decision. Rescues in winter are exceptional and there is a real gulf between local professionals and city-dwelling amateurs. After the tragedy, the *France Observateur* quotes the president of the guides: 'The Chamonix … company refuses to risk the life of Chamonix fathers to save two reckless individuals who are not from here.' Even the more sober Claude Deck, in the first 'official' account of the tragedy for *La Montagne et Alpinisme* published in 1983, will write: 'in 1956, the brotherly pre-war emulation between amateurs and professionals had given way to somewhat bitter competition and rivalries.'

There are other players in the rescue: the Compagnie des Guides de Saint-Gervais Mont-Blanc, which is not part of the SCSM, much smaller than its Chamonix equivalent and more easy-going. The Saint Gervais guides had participated in the famous 1950 Malabar Princess rescue and their leader Louis Piraly will now prove sympathetic and helpful. Apart from these official structures, alpinists from outside the valley, amateurs from the cities, mostly Paris and Geneva such as Claude Dufourmantelle, Marcel Bron and their friends, will also get involved.

On 26 December, while both ropes are struggling to reach the summit of Mont Blanc, Le Duf, unaware that Vincendon and Henry have waited two days before starting their ascent, assumes something has gone wrong. He contacts Dartigue who tells him there is no rescue in winter but suggests he contact Joseph Burnet of the Chamonix guides. Two rescue parties could be sent up, one from St Gervais and the Goûter hut, the other from Chamonix and the Grands Mulets. This is what had happened after the Malabar Princess crash.[15] Burnet refuses, telling Le Duf: 'Go yourself if you want.'[16] The night's heavy snowfall, Burnet adds, has made a rescue too dangerous. Most guides then had little experience of winter climbing, fearing avalanches, like the one that took the life of René Payot during the Malabar Princess rescue.

---

15. Air India Flight 245, a Lockheed L-749 Constellation named *Malabar Princess* on the Bombay-Istanbul-Geneva-London route with 40 passengers and eight crew crashed into Mont Blanc on the morning of 3 November 1950 at the Rochers de la Tournette (4677m) on the Italian side, killing all on board.
16. C Deck, *La Montagne et Alpinisme*, 1983.

Bonatti and the Italian rescuers descend in heavy snow with Gheser on a sledge.

And as Le Duf points out, 60 years later, it is peak skiing season and the guides are busy. Burnet having refused, Dartigue calls Louis Piraly, president of the St Gervais guides. Le Duf speaks with him but Piraly has no guides available to organise a rescue. Both Piraly and Burnet agree the avalanche risk is too high and they must first locate the missing climbers. Pierre Dartigue is like a general without soldiers.

Le Duf and his friend Rémy de Vivie now ask Rébuffat for help but he tells them he has no spare equipment to lend them and is not interested in a private rescue. Jean Franco, of Makalu fame, is the manager of UNCM and will soon be director of ENSA. He also declines but as a gesture of goodwill gives Le Duf his own ice axe to replace the one Dufourmantelle lost when he fell in the crevasse at the Jonction. The EHM seems more promising. They are guides but being military have no clients and no insurance issues. They can also count on the French army's greater resources. An Auster 5 pilot is available at Le Fayet's tiny airstrip but he cannot take off until the runway is cleared of snow. No flight is possible that day. Le Duf's partner Caseneuve has gone back to Paris and since he can't do anything on his own tries to find friends to form a rescue party. He also calls Vincendon's parents to alert them that their son may be in trouble. That same afternoon, Le Duf finds two friends, François Aubert and Noel Blotti, also planning a winter ascent and consequently well equipped. They agree to go up to Tête Rousse from Les Houches the next day, 27 December.

While Le Duf and his friends are slogging through deep snow towards the Nid d'Aigle, Dartigue has an idea: why not use a helicopter? The notion of helicopter rescue in the mountains is still new. Lucien Devies had initiated some experimental flights two years earlier: a Bell 47 flew 11 sorties, reaching an altitude of 4,500m. The pilot even made two rescues, one on the Mer de Glace and another on the Argentière glacier, the first helicopter rescues in the Mont Blanc range. There were still stringent technical limits but testing continued and won approval from well-known alpinists and guides like Roger Frison-Roche, Maurice Herzog, Gaston Rébuffat and Louis Lachenal who all accompanied flights. Armand Charlet estimated that a helicopter could do as much work in half an hour as three rescue parties over two days.

Dartigue asks the Haute-Savoie prefect for two search helicopters, preferably the new Alouettes powered by revolutionary gas-turbine engines. Dartigue knows all about the altitude record Sud-Aviation's test pilot Jean Boulet set in 1955, reaching an altitude of 8,209m. During the summer of 1956 Boulet had rescued an alpinist at the Vallot refuge in his Alouette II. The machine was superbly adapted to mountain flight. Apart from its turbine, the Alouette's low cockpit offered easy access and its two long skates ensured stability on snow. The Alouette could hover easily. It was also light, weighing 900kg, far less than the alternative: heavy-wheeled, piston-engine Sikorskys.

The army agrees to Dartigue's request, but rather than Alouettes sends two much heavier machines from Le Bourget-du-Lac airbase. The first is a Sikorsky S-55, a stalwart of the Indochina War. The pilot is Jacques Petetin, a 25-year-old flying instructor who has climbed Mont Blanc – aged 14 – and knows mountaineering and the area well. His co-pilot is Raymond Dupret. Petetin's S-55, which he calls the 'Happy Elephant', has an official ceiling of 10,900ft, around 3,300m, but the pilot knows how to push that by over-revving the engine, something he has done before to land a glaciologist on the Col du Dôme (4260m). With them is a new model, the Sikorsky S-58, forerunner of the Westland Sea King, with its more powerful engine. Its ceiling is even lower, the aircraft being designed for submarine warfare. Pilot André Blanc, born in Algeria, has never set foot on a mountain.

At 1.15pm on 27 December, Petetin lands the Happy Elephant on Le Fayet's tiny airstrip to pick up Piraly, president of the St Gervais guides. They take off but the Grand Plateau is covered in clouds. Fifty minutes later they are back having seen nothing but they know almost for certain that Vincendon and Henry are not at Tête Rousse, the Goûter or Vallot huts. They have also seen Le Duf and his two companions near the Nid d' Aigle, stopped by heavy snow. Then news arrives that Joseph Maffioli, guide and head of the ski patrol at Le Brévent, has spotted one, perhaps two alpinists above and to the right of the Rochers Rouges and approaching the Passage Balmat. Petetin puts more fuel in the Happy Elephant and takes off again, but even guided from Le Brévent where the climbers are clearly visible, cloud prevents Petetin and Piraly from seeing anything and they turn back. Petetin reaches Le Bourget that evening in falling snow with just 150m of visibility, flying just above the main road so he can find his way by the lights of trucks. It has been a miserable day, not least because the parents of Vincendon arrive to face the gathering flock of journalists from Paris, Lyon, Grenoble. News reaches Chamonix that Bonatti and Gheser are on their way to Gonella. Everyone is now certain that the Mont Blanc castaways are Jean Vincendon and François Henry.

At noon next day, 28 December, the day Bonatti and Gheser reach the Gonella, the Auster 5 pilot takes Piraly up to locate the missing climbers. Through binoculars he sees their tracks and guiding the pilot, Vincendon and Henry come into view. On their return they have a meeting with Petetin who has flown back to Le Fayet in the Happy Elephant. They know now that the two alpinists have not moved since the previous day. The weather is perfect and Petetin proposes landing the Happy Elephant near the two climbers. Piraly takes a 20m rope and takes off with him. Yet after passing within yards of the two castaways, Petetin realises he cannot land: the snow on the glacier is too deep, there are crevasses and the slope is not flat enough. The helicopter would simply sink in and topple over. He could stop much higher on the Dôme du Goûter (4304m) but who will bring the stricken climbers up there? Piraly alone cannot do it. And how will he get down? There's no chance of being lowered from the chopper. At this altitude an S-55 can't manage a stationary hover. Like a bicycle, it has to move forward to stay upright. Petetin has come so close that he sees clearly the smiling faces of Vincendon and Henry. 'How sad to know, feel, listen in my head and my heart, those two boys the same age as mine, dying there, and unable to do more.'[17]

Piraly, the only guide so far to get involved, has already called the press to explain his plan for the morning. He will try to get Vincendon and Henry to move further up towards the Dôme du Gouter where he can get out of the helicopter on a rope ladder and then clip them to a rope to help them get in the helicopter. If landing on the Grand Plateau is impossible then he could be dropped on the Dôme du Gouter itself with several other guides to prepare a landing ground. If the weather is fine, the two climbers, for the first time in a week, could be sleeping in a bed. But Piraly has no one to go with him. Joseph Burnet categorically refuses to ask any of his guides to take what he considers too high a risk. He suggests instead Piraly contacts Lionel Terray but he is not in Chamonix. Piraly actually needs at least six guides and with no volunteers his rescue is stillborn.

In the meantime, Claude Dufourmantelle and his friends François Aubert and Noel Blotti have abandoned their attempt to reach the Dôme du Gouter because of deep snow. Blotti has also twisted an ankle and is no longer fit enough to participate. Le Duf now wants to go up to the Grands Mulets. He finds more friends besides François Aubert: Rémy de Vivie, Marcel Bize and the Swiss Marcel Bron, Roger Habersaat, Claudi Asper and Mario Grossi, all experienced alpinists from the Androsace, although they only have their skiing gear. He asks the SCSM president Dartigue to lend him some equipment. Dartigue calls the FFM in Paris, but gear from there will take too long to arrive.

At 3.30pm Petetin and Piraly take off again to drop backpacks with blankets, food, drugs and five identical messages attached to smoke grenades: 'Go up immediately 200m to the Grand Plateau. It is the only place where the helicopter will be able to land and collect you.' Piraly takes a photo with one castaway standing and the second in a coiled position. This appears in the newspapers. Vincendon and Henry cannot open the rucksacks: their hands are frozen hard. But they read one of the messages and at 4pm start moving up, extremely slowly. By 5.20pm they have climbed up only 50m. It is too late for the S-55 to take off again.

---

17. Ballu, ibid.

The Military Moves In

Gilbert Chappaz is one of the EHM ski and climbing instructors and also a member of the Chamonix guides. Hearing about Piraly's rescue plan he goes to Le Fayet to meet him but must first get approval from his commanding officer Yves Le Gall. Le Gall is 44 and recently returned from the Indochina War. A military man, he has no experience of mountaineering. Dartigue is only too happy to give all the rescue authority and responsibilities to Yves Le Gall, who now takes charge of all operations. The helicopter operation Piraly has proposed is accepted but Le Gall prohibits any rescue party on foot. With the agreement of Nollet, commanding officer at Le Bourget, and Lacroix, commanding officer of the helicopter squadron, he decides to fly 12 EHM guides in two parties to land on the Dôme du Goûter. That will allow seven hours to reach the castaways and bring them up to the Col du Dôme. For this he needs a second helicopter. Nollet and Lacroix allocate the new Sikorsky S-58 under the command of Alexis Santini, a Corsican veteran of the Indochina War. Santini hesitates. His S-58 has never been tested in the mountains or on snow but he has little choice: his commanding officers insist.

Le Gall's operation needs seven hours and he will only give the green light with a whole day of good weather and acceptable flight conditions, despite being told the Vallot hut can be used as a base for the rescuers. He follows tactics learned in the Indochina War for retrieving wounded soldiers from the field. In the morning, 29 December, the airstrip is covered in clouds and the helicopters are grounded. Only in the early afternoon does the weather clear. Piraly is waiting to take off with Petetin in the Happy Elephant when a large amount of equipment is loaded on board and he is told Le Gall is taking his place. His mountaineering and rescue experience is brushed aside. From the helicopter Petetin sees Vincendon and Henry still moving towards the Grand Plateau. They see the hole in which they have bivouacked the night before. The rucksacks they dropped are no longer where they fell so it's assumed they have taken them. The helicopter drops more food, clothes and stoves six yards from Vincendon, and a second load is dropped 12 yards from Henry. They see them seize the loads and wave their arms.

Hopes that Vincendon and Henry can still be saved are high that night. Journalist Philippe Gaussot writes in *Le Dauphiné Libéré* how the fresh supplies 'should allow them to hold on another 24 hours and even without being over optimistic, three or four days.' Santini, arriving at Le Fayet in his S-58, is confident that if the weather is fine tomorrow he will get them to safety. Dufourmantelle asks Le Gall if he can be dropped with two or three of his friends near Vincendon and Henry with the aim of bringing them down to the Grands Mulets. Le Gall refuses. As a military commander he won't tolerate 'amateurs' or be responsible for their safety. Only EHM guides will work on this rescue: no civilians.

Le Duf then meets Lionel Terray, who has been at a conference in Val d'Isère. On his way home he has picked up a hitchhiker, Bob Xueref, a climbing pal of Jean Vincendon who is on the way from Lyon having heard the news. Terray is indignant the Chamonix guides have refused to organise a rescue. The hero of Annapurna, one of the few 'outsiders' in the Chamonix guides, has already fallen out with the company's leadership over a rescue the year before on Les Droites. He meets Vincendon's parents and then several of the EHM. It's a heated exchange. Terray asks them why they haven't organised a rescue party on foot. He is told he is not required. Le Gall wouldn't change his plan for Le Duf and he won't do it for Terray either. Terray tells him he will organise a ground rescue on his own.

Later that same day Terray is asked if he wouldn't mind showing the EHM team how to use the oxygen systems they want to take with them. So at 7.30am on Sunday 30 December, Terray runs an impromptu seminar using Gilbert Chappaz as guinea pig. Then, at 9am, Santini, André Blanc and a member of the EHM take off in the S-58 for a reconnaissance flight. It's the first time the chopper has flow in the mountains and at altitude. During a test hover, the S-58 stalls. Weather conditions are not good and the wind is strong. Above 1,800m visibility is nil, says Santini. As the weather worsens, it's clear the whole day will be lost.

Furious, Terray is convinced too much time has been lost relying on helicopters that can't operate in poor weather when a traditional ground rescue is still possible. He organises a party with Claude Dufourmantelle, Rémy de Vivie, François Aubert and his friend Hubert Josserand, an ENSA teacher, the only one who will volunteer. The SCSM refuses to cover their insurance, at least until Lucien Devies gets wind of this and reverses the decision. A second team is also available, the Swiss Marcel Bron and his friends from the Androsace, and Terray asks Bob Xueref to stay behind in order to sort out equipment arriving from the FFM in Paris. They will aim to catch up the following day at the Grands Mulets, following the first party's tracks.

Terray and the others set off, taking the Aiguille du Midi cable car to the Plan de l'Aiguille. The company refuses to let them use cableway to the service platform at the Aiguille des Glaciers, which would save them three hours and allow them to reach the Grands Mulets that evening. Instead they have to bivouac in the remains of the top station of the defunct Glaciers cable car. The same thing happens to the second party, which sets out when the EHM finally agree to lend it equipment.

On the morning of Monday 31 December, Le Gall's EHM teams are ready at Le Fayet airstrip, but the two Sikorskys need more preparation. Finally, at 9am, Santini and Blanc take off in their S-58 taking with them the guide Honoré Bonnet.[18] But the wind is too strong and half an hour later they are back to Le Fayet. Night will fall at 5pm so if Le Gall sticks to his seven-hour window, then by 10am another day will be lost. At noon, the weather turns fine but the EHM guides will not now be in situ before 1pm and won't finish their mission before 7pm, too late for the helicopters to fly. Terray's team is now leaving Jonction and at best they will sleep at the Grands Mulets. Vincendon and Henry seem doomed.

18. Future coach of a highly successful French skiing team that won more than 32 Olympic medals in 10 years.

A badly frostbitten Gheser arrives at Courmayeur on a sledge.

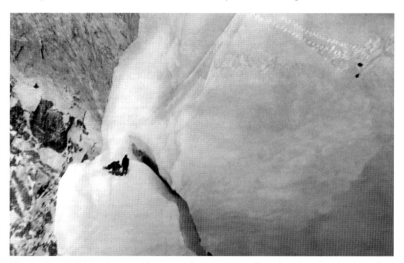

Vincendon and Henri spotted on top of a serac overhanging the Combe Maudite. The two black dots above right are the tent and food dropped which they didn't have the strength to use.

Then news arrives from Le Brévent: one of the castaways is moving. He's still alive. The Corsican Alexis Santini, has become increasingly irritated at the presence of his commanding officers. The air minister is also on the strip. He decides to have a go anyway, despite the low chances of success. He says he will attempt to pick up Vincendon and Henry direct from the Grand Plateau. With Blanc as pilot and himself as co-pilot they will try

Above: EHM guides Honoré Bonnet and Charles Germain in the Sikorsky S-58 shortly before the crash. In the cockpit are André Blanc and Alexis Santini. The S-58 was the forerunner of the Sea King but ill-suited to flying at altitude or hovering. Neither Blanc nor Santini had mountain experience and had to be persuaded to wear mountain clothes.

Above: The crashed S-58 and a contemporary newspaper illustration showing the EHM guides putting Vincendon and Henry in the wreckage. It would become their resting place until the spring.

to stabilise the helicopter long enough for the guides to get Vincendon and Henry into the cabin. Petetin advises him to get properly equipped. The Corsican replies he has no intention of staying up there. But Petetin insists and eventually Santini and Blanc put on mountain boots, fur flying-suits and gloves. As well as Bonnet, they take a second guide, Charles Germain.

Petetin and Le Gall take off first in the Happy Elephant to mark the landing zone for Santini. They see the castaways have not moved for the last two days and they haven't put up the tent, but they are alive and wave their hands to them. He also sees that the snow is powdery and deep and his helicopter is caught in the downwash of a strong southerly. The S-58's manoeuvre will be difficult. Petetin radios the information to Santini who tells him to stand by. At 12.45pm, the S-58 takes off. At the Grand Plateau they see the two climbers. Blanc starts the landing approach, trying to stabilize his heavy aircraft: to no avail. The rotor blades whip up a maelstrom of powdery snow, which floods the helicopter's cockpit, blinding the pilot and unbalancing the S-58. Its rotor blades hit the snow and the aircraft crashes onto its side,

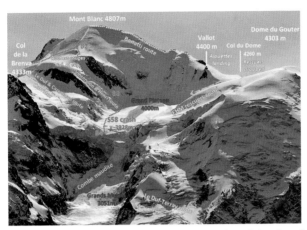

A photo-diagram showing the location of the S-58 crash and the directions of approach by the two rescue parties, the EHM from above and Terray and Le Duf from below.

its tail broken. All the occupants get out safely and no one is seriously wounded, although Germain is badly bruised by Bonnet falling on him. Now six men are shipwrecked above the Combe Maudite.

Nollet, base commander at Le Bourget, asks Petetin to get the men out in three or four flights. Petetin refuses. He knows the only place he can land safely is the Dôme du Gouter, which he has done before. Visibility is always better there and the winds more predictable. The decision is taken to drop four guides on the Dôme du Gouter to rescue the two pilots first, then Vincendon and Henry. Petetin lands safely and drops Gilbert Chappaz. On the next flight he drops Jean Minster and some equipment. Two more flights and there are now four on the Dôme du Gouter. The last flight had been quite risky: Petetin needed three attempts to take off and he says that's it for the day. His engine filter has frozen and he says it's like flying a fixed wing, not a helicopter.[19] Yet the mission is accomplished. The guides agree that Chappaz and Minster will go to the Grand Plateau while the other two head for the Vallot where they will regroup later.

Meanwhile, on the Grand Plateau, Honoré Bonnet has decided to get the two pilots, neither with mountaineering experience, up to the Vallot and then come back for Vincendon and Henry who are terribly frostbitten. Their hands and feet are blocks of wood but they don't comprehend how badly they are injured. They have been incapable of using any of the equipment and food dropped in previous days but they are able to converse with Bonnet. Learning Bonnet is a member of the GHM, which they dream of joining, they mention climbs they could do together in the future. Years later, the memory of that conversation will leave Bonnet in tears. He gives the pair a shot of Benzedrine. François Henry looks in a better condition

19. J Belliard & R Romet, *Secours Extrême*, Flammarion, 1986.

Vincendon, left, and Henry half buried in the snow, unable to move, hands, feet and faces frozen but still semi-lucid. Charles Germain faces the camera.

than Jean who says that without François he would not be alive.

Bonnet and the others are with them for two hours and then at 3pm the two guides leave with the two pilots. Once again Vincendon and Henry are alone. The party of four hasn't gone 30m before André Blanc falls into a crevasse, stopping his 90kg at the surface on his arms. Blanc is already in shock from the crash and feels a growing sense of guilt. He slips two metres into the crevasse but Bonnet holds him, and is then able to crawl on his belly to the edge of the slot. He tells Blanc he will drop him a loop of rope to put his foot in to get up and out. But Blanc doesn't understand or react. He's gone berserk, believing he's going to die in the crevasse.

So Germain and Bonnet set up a rope system to haul him up and Bonnet finally manages to grab the pilot and pull him out. Blanc is unable to move so Bonnet drags him to the crashed helicopter and puts him beside Vincendon and Henry, who tries to raise his spirits and warm his hands with his own, even though they are as hard as rocks. The sight leaves Bonnet in tears. Later, in hospital, Blanc will tell François' father what his son told him about their ordeal. Having untied from Bonatti's rope, Vincendon had become more and more tired. Henry tried to make him follow Bonatti's tracks but night fell and they were forced to bivouac for the second time. The following day, they turned downhill, trying to reach the Grands Mulets. He told Blanc about Vincendon's fall and the equipment they lost, the bivouac at the base of the Rochers Rouges and losing their way next day. On the Saturday or Sunday François had managed to drag Vincendon back onto the Grand Plateau. Blanc said that all the time Henry was talking to him, the young man didn't stop trying to warm Blanc with his frozen hands.

Now Minster and Chappaz arrive and evaluate the situation. Vincendon and Henry are in a desperate state. Their feet and lower legs are blocks of ice; their hands are useless, their arms frozen to the elbow. They don't seem to comprehend the dreadful state they're in. They seem happy, dreamy even, apologising for the trouble they are causing and telling the EHM guides they will help out on future rescues. Bruised badly during the crash, Germain is not in good shape and Blanc is still shocked, his hands and arms not functioning. Minster gives him some Coramine to get him moving. The four EHM guides then consider their options: stay put and wait for reinforcements; split into two teams, one taking the pilots to the Vallot and the second staying with Vincendon and Henry; stick together, get the pilots to the Vallot and come back the following day with reinforcements for the two stricken climbers.

The first option is judged pointless; they will just sit there and freeze. The second is possible but with threatening weather and the state of the pilot Blanc, the third is chosen. A lamp is lit in the helicopter and with an aching heart Chappaz tells the two castaways: 'We will come back.' Once again the two are alone.

Bonnet and Germain leave first with Santini, Minster and Chappaz follow with Blanc. Night is on them and a north-west wind brings snow. Blanc is suffering and it takes eight hours of painful toil on the part of the two guides to reach the Vallot at 1.30am. Germain, Bonnet and Santini aren't there. Deteriorating weather and a malfunctioning compass force them to bivouac in the bergschrund below the Vallot at 11.30pm.

Lionel Terray is now at the Grands Mulets hut after a confusing day. Soon after the S-58 crash, Terray and Dufourmantelle are approaching the Grands Mulets when they see the Auster 5 flying over several times. The pilot then shouts through his open window: 'The helicopter fell!' They think he's said, 'They fell!' meaning the climbers. They turn back and then meet the second party, which has bivouacked 200m below. They discover from Marcel Bron, who has a radio link with Le Gall, that it's the S-58 that has crashed. Le Duf now decides to return to the valley but Terray and other volunteers go back up to the Grands Mulets for the night even though he is now convinced that Vincendon and Henry are dead.

For the last few days, the weather has not been bad: misty and cloudy enough to stop helicopters flying but with negligible snowfall. Any rescue party leaving before 28 December would have reached and likely saved the two castaways. This explains Terray's fury at the Chamonix guides and the EHM commander Le Gall, who all refused to organise a ground rescue. For the last two days they have been following the trail Le Duf and the Yeti made as they descended before Christmas. Now, on New Year's Day, the weather is awful and it snows hard, making the slopes above avalanche prone. Terray decides to descend, which is difficult with this heavy snowfall. Back in Chamonix, Terray is sharply critical of the whole rescue organisation. *Le Dauphiné* publishes the reaction to this from the Chamonix guides, who accuse Terray of organising an amateur rescue, that the dangers were too great and he was after publicity. Terray was defiant, telling journalists that guides who had judged conditions too dangerous had stayed put in the valley, 'their arms crossed', without testing the premise.

Years later, Le Duf still argues that a ground party, moving on foot, should have been agreed at once, which would 'in all instances' have reached Vincendon and Henry. 'That Le Gall decided against this was probably to limit the risks, but in difficult conditions there is no rescue possible without

Jean Boulet landing his Alouette near the Vallot to evacuate the EHM rescue party. Had the helicopters been used from the start, Vincendon and Henry would have survived.

the commitment of the rescuers and a risk that they accept.' He sees Terray, 'one of the greatest French guides as well as one of the greatest French amateur climbers', as 'an ideal link between the two worlds.' Le Duf also acknowledges that as a famous man, Terray didn't need to give skiing lessons and didn't have a family to support, so his position was more comfortable than 'his comrades in the Chamonix guides who were just doing their job.'

At the Vallot hut, the EHM guides have organised themselves and take care of Blanc who is in a poor state. Bad weather hampers flying for the next two days. Petetin tries to land the Happy Elephant near the Vallot, flying up alone to save weight. Having watched from the hut, Santini radios Nollet to stop Petetin from trying again: 'He's going to break his neck!'[20]

The decision is finally taken to use the Alouettes. The air force has a dozen brand new machines based at Mont-de-Marsan north of Pau in the Pyrenees. The boss of Sud-Aviation offers the services of his two test pilots Jean Boulet and Gérard Henry, the only Alouette pilots with mountain flying experience. During the afternoon of 2 January the Alouettes land in Chamonix, where the skies are clear, because of cloud at Le Fayet.

Next morning, 3 January, the Auster 5 pilot flies over the wreckage of the S-58: it's almost buried in snow and there's no sign of life. The first Alouette takes off at 9am and picks up Santini from a landing pad the EHM guides have prepared outside the Vallot. He's flown to Chamonix hospital and is soon joined by Blanc, arriving in the second Alouette. Everyone at the Vallot is brought down in an hour and a half. Jean Boulet proposes flying a rescuer to the site of the S-58 crash, now buried in fresh snow, and then hovering as he climbs down a rope ladder to assess the situation.

20. J Belliard & R Romet, *Secours Extrême*, Flammarion, 1986.

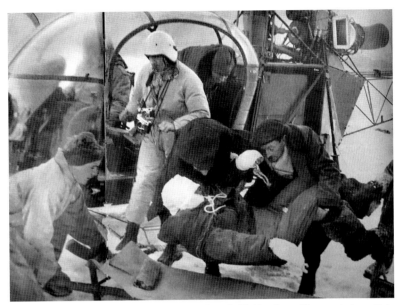

The pilot Blanc taken out of the Alouette in a field 40m from Chamonix hospital.

Le Gall decides to fly up there with him to assess the situation, with the second Alouette following behind. There are no signs of life. Le Gall concludes 'without,' as Terray puts it, 'leaving his seat,' that Vincendon and Henry are dead. He announces an end to operations. There is one final flight over the crash site. The Swiss glacier pilot Hermann Geiger, the 'Eagle of Sion', who has flown scores of mountain rescue missions in his Piper Super Cub, also flies over the wreckage and also fails to spot any signs of life. He proposes landing on the Grand Plateau and Piraly volunteers to go with him, but it's too late: no one believes the two young men are still alive.

The media storm falls away although the backlash continues for a while. The FFM president Lucien Devies tries to calm the situation, proposing all parties join forces to bring down the bodies. The attempt brings a bitter response from the parents of Jean Vincendon. 'Rémy de Vivie, a friend of my son, tells me the French Alpine Club has taken the initiative to organise a party to bring down the bodies of my son and François Henry. This party of alpinists from Paris would include several Chamonix guides. During the agony the two boys suffered, they refused to help: it was their right. Now they must stay with their feet in their slippers.'[21] The guides are unrepentant. 'Those who through vanity attempt climbs beyond their capabilities … dismiss too easily the risks taken by their rescuers.' The French army are no more sympathetic, calculating the financial cost of the rescue at €3m in today's money and complaining that the loss of the helicopter would impact the training of pilots heading to the conflict in Algeria.

21. Ballu.

The crashed Sikorsky half buried in snow with Vincendon and Henry inside.

It's an opinion shared by many, but not the FFM and Lucien Devies, whose committee states that 'rescuing our fellow human beings in distress is a human duty, even if risks have to be taken'. Among the well-known personalities questioned by the press for their view is Georges Carpentier, the ageing French boxing champion who in 1921 fought Jack Dempsey for the world heavyweight crown: 'Everything had to be attempted, even beyond reason, even if it was folly. Two men have risked their life for something difficult and noble. Taking risks to save them was paying tribute to their courage and guts.'[22]

The SCSM and the military high command ask Lucien Devies to review the controversy and soon after the end of rescue operations, on 10 January 1957, Devies announces the FFM will explore what lessons can be learned from the 'first major rescue failure since the end of the war' in the place with the most personnel and equipment. The enquiry concluded that co-operation had failed, with the guides refusing to participate. Not only that, as Terray claimed volunteers were actively discouraged. Established proto-

22. Ballu.

cols were ignored in favour of helicopters whose use was unproven. The helicopters used lacked the required capabilities and not all the pilots were sufficiently experienced. The SCSM, the co-ordinating body, was impotent, shut out by the EHM command, which closed itself off from outside influence. Delays and serious confusions appeared in the decisions. The failure to mount a rescue effort on foot was particulalry criticised, since it most likely resulted in the death of Vincendon and Henry.

Several months later Devies and his FFM committee publish an outline of a new national organisation for mountain rescue. In August 1958, new regulations are passed making the rescue system a national service reporting to the interior ministry. Most significantly, new rescue units are formed by the Compagnies Républicaines de Sécurité (CRS), the gendarmerie and the army. In 1961, a special unit of the Gendarmerie Nationale is created which will eventually become the highly efficient PGHM mountain rescue unit. They will train highly effective rescuers and progressively take over all mountain rescues from the volunteer associations. Helicopters dramatically change things, but it is not until 1972, when the PGHM takes over all mountain rescue that controversies with the Chamonix guides ceases.[23] Lucien Devies does what he can to dampen the controversy that follows this tragic drama, refusing to publish anything in the CAF magazine *La Montagne et Alpinisme*. Only in 1983, three years after Devies' death, is my old friend Claude Deck allowed to publish the first detailed article. Fifteen years later Yves Ballu publishes his book.

The guides who feel most guilt about the fate of Vincendon and Henry are those who have done most, particularly Gilbert Chappaz and Jean Minster. Just after the end of the rescue operation, Chappaz tells a journalist: 'In leaving them there, I had the feeling of committing a crime.' For 50 years Gilbert Chappaz is haunted by the fact that he did not fulfil his promise and that François Henry died despising him.

In June 2007, Yves Ballu organises a meeting at the Chamonix cemetery between them and Jean Henry, older brother and climbing companion of François Henry.[24] Gilbert Chappaz tells Jean: 'If you knew all the miseries we suffered ... I went last and I told him [François Henry] I will come back to get you.' Jean tells him gently that he doesn't have to excuse himself. 'By going there you showed them that they had not been abandoned.' As one of Chappaz' sons recalled later: 'It was as if suddenly my father had taken off a rucksack filled with a huge rock. All at once he stood straighter.' Gilbert Chappaz dies five months later, relieved and at peace.

23. E Vola, 'The 1966 Drus Rescue', Summitpost.
24. Epilogue written by Jean Henry in January 2017 on Yves Ballu's blog.

J G R HARDING

The Other Anne Lister

The portrait of Anne Lister by the Halifax artist Joshua Horner
painted around 1830. *(Alamy)*

L ast year marked the centenary of the end of the First World War. It was
also the year British women, at least those over the age of 30, won the
right to vote. This prompted me to reflect on the mountaineering careers of
remarkable women whose paths I have crossed but whose climbing achievements are scarcely remembered. First among them is Anne Lister, the Halifax landowner and adventurer now familiar to millions thanks to Sunday
night television. The BBC 'discovered' Anne Lister (1791-1840) with its

2010 documentary *The Secret Diaries of Anne Lister* and made her famous with Sally Wainwright's 2019 corset-busting drama *Gentleman Jack*, turning this swashbuckling, unabashed Regency lesbian and pioneer of women's liberation into a celebrity. Less familiar to a BBC audience is her astonishing role as one of the pioneers of alpinism.

Anne Lister's tumultuous life would have remained obscure had she not committed it to her immense diary, comprising four million words and filling 24 leather-bound diaries. These preserve an invaluable social, cultural and economic record of Regency Halifax where, as chatelaine of Shibden Hall, the Lister family's ancestral home, Anne played a leading role as landowner, estate manager, landscape designer, scientist and writer. They also record in a secret code intimate details of her sexual conquests.

From childhood, Anne displayed exceptional intelligence, independence, self-confidence, courage and an insatiable curiosity. As a girl, she insisted on studying 'masculine' subjects; she fenced and played chess. At 12, she read Homer, Xenophon and Sophocles in the original Greek and studied Demosthenes' rhetoric. At 15 she became fascinated by erotic Classical poetry, embarked on her first serious lesbian affair and invented her secret diary code, combining classical Greek lettering with numerical and invented symbols. Aged 24, she took over the management of the Shibden estate, its mines and cloth manufacturing business from her ex-soldier father and directed her formidable energies to local affairs.

These activities and other incidents in her adventurous life might have remained folk memory had not her kinsman John Lister discovered her hitherto hidden diaries when he inherited Shibden Hall in 1867. The scholarly Lister was quick to appreciate their historic value and between 1887 and 1892 drew on them to publish 121 articles in the *Halifax Chronicle* depicting life in the town during the early 19th century. Yet he was stumped by the diaries' extensive encrypted passages and only cracked the code with the help of local antiquarian Arthur Burrell. On discovering that they described in explicit detail Anne's lesbian affairs, Burrell urged Lister to burn them. Lister, secretly gay himself and with an eye to posterity, simply walled them up. There they mouldered until his death in 1933 when he left them to the Halifax Corporation. Although the general public were denied access, the municipal librarian divulged the secret code to his daughter Muriel Green who, in 1938, deposited a typescript about Anne's life entitled *A Spirited Yorkshire Woman* with the British Museum. In the early 1950s, the code was revealed to scholars Vivien Ingham and Phyllis Ramsden on their assurance that 'unsuitable material should not be published.' It took them 11 years to decipher the diaries in full after which pressure from the women's liberation movement persuaded the corporation to give other researchers freedom to publish.

Serendipity determined that around the same time the first account in English of Anne's role as a pioneer mountaineer was published in the *Alpine Journal*. I came across Vivien Ingham's 1968 article *Anne Lister's Ascent of the Vignemale* (*AJ*, vol 73), written shortly before Ingham's death,

Mont Perdu, or Monte Perdido (right) from the upper reaches of the Ordesa valley, climbed by Anne Lister on her first Pyrenean adventure in 1830. *(Kev Reynolds)*

while researching material for my book *Pyrenean High Route*. I was puzzled that although the FFM's *Pyrénées Centrales* guidebook (Pau, 1965) credited Anne with the second ascent of the Vignemale in 1838 by a new route, no British mountaineering literature referred either to this or to an earlier ascent of Mont Perdu in 1830. Yet Anne's Mont Perdu climb preceded by 12 years the ascent in 1842 of the Stockhorn by the 'Father of British Mountaineering', Prof J D Forbes, generally regarded as the first British pioneer ascent of any recognisable Alpine peak, and by five years the birth of Lucy Walker, the 'first British woman alpinist'. It also anticipated by 23 years the trumpeted Pyrenean climbs of the British pioneers Packe and Russell. Ingham gently skirted around Anne's sexual orientation, describing her as 'a forceful woman of great energy and masculine tendencies'.

Anne's early adulthood was devoted to running Shibden leavened by an active social life with travels both at home and abroad. In 1827, a cultural tour of Italy preceded her first essay into the Alps when she crossed both the Splugen and Simplon passes, trekked up the Mer de Glace, though with her intention of climbing Mont Blanc left unfulfilled, and finishing that season with a fortnight's hike through the Bernese Oberland sleeping rough in simple cabins. Treating her ascents of Snowdon and Ben Nevis as mere jaunts, she was smitten with mountain fever by the time she went to Paris in 1830 to study anatomy under Georges Cuvier, staying there as a guest of Lady Stuart de Rothesay, wife of the British ambassador. When the glamour of Paris' glittering diplomatic social life palled, Anne persuaded her hostess to visit the Pyrenees, a venture not lightly undertaken since in July of that year France had been gripped by the revolution Victor Hugo portrayed in his *Les Miserables*. Furthermore, the Pyrenees were regarded as a particularly sensitive region: to prevent Gallic revolutionary contagion spreading south, Spanish authorities had closed the frontier.

Undeterred, Lady de Rothesay's 12-strong entourage established itself that August in the fashionable resort of Luz Saint Sauveur in the upper Gave valley. Quickly bored with local sightseeing, Anne engaged a local guide Jean-Pierre Charles to accompany her on a four-day mountain trek. After marvelling at the stupendous cirque of Gavarnie, she decided to climb Mont Perdu, at 3,355m the third highest mountain in the Pyrenees, invisible from the

Suranne Jones as Anne Lister in the recent BBC television series *Gentleman Jack. (BBC)*

village of Gavarnie but accessible from the head of Spain's Ordesa valley. Political complications apart, this trip posed additional security risks as robbery and brigandage were then endemic in the Spanish Pyrenees. Anne summarily dismissed such considerations and after hiring a smuggler as an additional guide, the three of them crossed the frontier via the then heavily glaciated Brèche de Roland equipped with crampons and *bâtons ferrés*. They spent the night of 25 August in a shepherd's hovel at Gauriz and the following day climbed Mont Perdu, Anne making the first female ascent. Returning to Luz on their fifth day, Anne described it as 'not quite a lady's expedition'.

Four days later she was off again, this time hiking alone the 45km from Luz to Luchon and thence, after another 25km trek, to Viella in Spain. Here she was arrested by the Spanish police and escorted to the frontier village of Benasque. Before being deported, she threw herself into the resort's traditional summer festival with typical abandon, dancing the wild fandango and sinking draughts of 'rich, strong wine', thereby preceding by many years Hilaire Belloc who immortalised his own Benasque visit in his Pyrenean paeon *Tarantella*. Back at Luz several days later, she was greeted by an apoplectic but greatly relieved Lady de Rothesay.

In 1834, Anne formally 'married' Ann Walker, a seriously rich neighbouring Yorkshire heiress 10 years her junior, motivated in part by Ann's wealth as well as emotional attachment. Their three-month honeymoon in France, Switzerland and Italy included a 17-day circuit of Mont Blanc dossing down in barns and haylofts, followed-up with a month-long trek through the Dauphiné, Rhone valley and Auverge. Four years later, in 1838, Anne, now aged 47, returned to Luz Saint Sauveur with an ailing Ann Walker in tow, ostensibly to give Ann a six-week health cure. Once again engaging Charles, she set her sights on Vignemale (3298m), the finest and highest peak in the French Pyrenees whose reputation for inaccessibility had only been shattered the previous year when a local guide Henri Cazaux had climbed it via the Ossoue glacier. While undertaking a training climb on the nearby peak of Pimene, Anne bumped into Cazaux, promptly engaged him as second guide and then belatedly discovered he had already agreed to climb the Vignemale with Joseph Ney, prince of Moscow and son of Napoleon's Marshal Ney. Anne decided to forestall the prince by attacking the mountain by a new approach from the head of the upper Ara valley. On 6 August, Anne, Cazaux and Charles left Luz Saint Sauveur on horseback to spend a flea-bitten night at the Saoussats Dabats cabane sleeping head to toe with five shepherds. At 2.45am the following morning, they quit the cabane and after a seven-hour climb over rock, snow and ice reached the Vignemale's summit at exactly 1pm. Resting for a few hours, they descended to Gavarnie to complete their 22-hour round-trip. A month later, Henriette d'Angeville, aged 44, became the second woman to climb Mont Blanc. The modern FFM guidebook rates Anne's route as *Assez Difficile*.

Still not content, Anne persuaded a barely fit Ann Walker to join her for a five-day, unguided trek into Spain. They got as far south as Jaca and on re-crossing the range into France, Anne shinned up the Pic du Midi d'Ossau before finishing their 200-mile trek at Cauterets. Back at Luz on 14 August, Anne was furious to learn that the prince of Moscow was now claiming to have made the first amateur ascent of the Vignemale. Promptly instructing a lawyer in Lourdes to draft a certificate confirming the facts, she confronted Cazaux at his home where he meekly signed the certificate as correct and shamefacedly shook hands with this *femme superbe*. Their *affaire d'honneur* was concluded by their sinking several bottles of wine together. The local newspaper inserted a correction to the prince's earlier claim, but Anne declared that she cared nothing for mountaineering triumphs because she climbed only 'for my pleasure, not for *éclat*'.

The Pyrenees had whetted Anne's appetite for more exotic adventures. Fascinated from youth by Achemenian Persia's wars against Greece and Xenophon's 1,500-mile march from Mesopotamia to the Black Sea, she persuaded Ann Walker to fund a joint venture to Scandinavia and Russia, but without revealing that her real aims were to reach Tehran and Baghdad via Georgia. After commissioning two specially designed carriages equipped to meet all foreseeable contingencies, Anne, now aged 48 and Ann, 10 years younger, left England in July 1839. Intensive cultural tours of Norway, Sweden, Helsinki and St Petersburg preceded five months in Moscow, which 'exceeded all expectations', as guests of Anne's aristocratic friends where they indulged in a dizzy social whirl. Ann wanted to stay put but Anne, despite falling madly for the beautiful Princess Radziwill,

The north face of the Vignemale, photographed in 1974, from the upper Vallée de Gaube. *(John Harding)*

was determined to press on. After substituting their original carriage for one adapted to run on sledges in winter with interchangeable wheels for the summer, they left Moscow for Tbilisi in Georgia on 3 February 1840.

Their 1,500-mile, two-month overland journey in the middle of the Russian winter initially involved a madcap sleigh down the frozen Volga river as the temperature plunged to -37°C with the additional hazard of their carriage falling through the ice. Daytime travel became an endless misery as a biting east wind and driving snow coursed freely through the carriage's irreparably broken window. At night they slept either in primitive villages or in towns such as Kazan where they stayed with Prince Cerbedjab, a descendent of Genghis Khan who had led his Kalmyks into battle at Leipzig in 1813. Anne was disgusted with the degradation of the women in his harem, but delighted to explore its exotic market thronged with Cossacks, Tartars, Kalmyks and Mongols. During one passage through treacherous marsh country with their small Cossack escort, they were surrounded by a band of 20 Chechens. Preparing for a fate worse than death, both ladies drew their pistols. 'I thought we could make a tolerable fight. I felt not the least afraid, nor was Ann,' wrote Anne later. At the last moment, the Chechens thought better of it.

For Anne, the highlight of their perilous journey was the passage across the 'magnificent' Caucasus by the recently built Russian military road, which snaked through the 12km, 1,000m-deep Daryal gorge, a 'chaos, sublimely wild and desolate', ever threatened by avalanches. Sixty-nine days after leaving Moscow, the intrepid pair reached Tbilisi on 12 April 1839, triumphant but utterly exhausted. Restored by lavish hospitality offered by Russian and Georgian aristocracy, Ann was aghast at the prospect of going any further and also deeply concerned about the expedition's mounting costs. But Anne, ever-curious and impatient to explore lands afar, left her partner to recover in Tbilisi and picked up an escort of Cossacks and Tartars to embark on another dangerous journey, menaced by hostile tribes and swollen rivers, to Baku and the Caspian. Back at Tbilisi, Anne resisted Ann's pleadings to call a halt and persuaded her to undertake a horseback journey along the wilder fringes of the Caucasus escorted by Cossacks. They visited churches, cathedrals and monasteries, covered ground previously untrammelled by Europeans, and stayed at primitive mountain villages. Exhausted by five weeks of rough travel, they descending to Zugdidi to stay as guests of the hereditary ruler Prince Bijan Daidani. Set in the low-lying, mosquito-ridden Migrelian plain, the town's dank, unhealthy climate proved the worst possible place in which to recuperate so they retreated to the mountains. The weather was dreadful and by now Anne had contracted malaria and typhus. She made her last diary entry on 11 August 1840 having pushed her body beyond its limits and died at Kutaisi on 22 September aged 49.

A grief-stricken Ann Walker was now confronted with the task of getting both herself and Anne's embalmed body sealed in a coffin back to Halifax. After a nightmare journey to Moscow, she resumed her homeward journey to Halifax the following spring and on 23 April 1841 had her lover's coffin interned at her local parish church. Broken in mind and body, Ann Walker lived at Shibden for two years before being committed to the asylum from which she was only released shortly before her death in 1854.

My tenuous bond with Anne Lister stems from 14 separate visits to the Pyrenees, including a 68-stage east to west ski traverse of the range. In 1974, Mont Perdu became my wife Georgina's first Pyrenean summit and in 1980, a descent of its north-east face was a rare venture into ski extreme. Also in 1974, an unintended variant of the Vignemale's Arête de Gaube with John Blacker almost came to grief and five years later, a massive avalanche peeled off the Petit Vignemale and buried all but one of our party, killing my cousin Alain and leaving me with everlasting remorse. In June 2016, Georgina and I spent two days at Kutaisi on a painting holiday, unaware at the time that the inimitable Anne Lister had died in this wildly romantic place 176 years before.

Bibliography

J Harding, *Pyrenean High Route*, Tiercel Publishing, 2008.

V Ingham, 'Anne Lister's Ascent of the Vignemale', *Alpine Journal*, 1968, vol 73.

A Steidele, *Gentleman Jack*, Serpents Tail, 2018.

C A RUSSELL

One Hundred Years Ago

Lt Col Edward Strutt. *(Reproduced from The Last Habsburg by Gordon Brook-Shepherd, published by Weidenfeld and Nicolson, now part of Orion, which is unable to trace a copyright holder.)*

In the aftermath of the First World War many Alpine resorts, severely affected by the global influenza epidemic, which had raged for several months, were still often almost deserted during the opening weeks of 1919. With the exception of local parties few skiers were in a position to return to the principal regions. Aldo Bonacossa and Adriano Revel made the first ski ascents of the Helsenhorn and other peaks to the east of Monte Leone; and Arnold Lunn, while assisting former prisoners of war who had been interned in Switzerland, completed a number of ski tours in the Bernese Alps with Josef Knubel.

With the restoration of normal communications in Europe several members of the Alpine Club returned to the Alps and were able to complete a series of outstanding climbs in August during a long period of perfect weather. In the Mont Blanc range S L Courtauld and E G Oliver made the first ascent of the Innominata ridge on the south-east face of Mont Blanc. After undertaking various training climbs and examining the route from

Punta Innominata Courtauld and Oliver bivouacked above the Col de Frêney with their guides Adolf Aufdenblatten and Adolphe and Henri Rey. On the following day they completed the climb and continued up the Brouillard ridge to the summit where they met and were congratulated by Francesco Ravelli who with the brothers Giuseppe and Battista Gugliermina had attempted the route on several occasions.

Elsewhere in the range George Mallory and Harold Porter climbed the Aiguille des Grands Charmoz and opened a new route on the north-west face of the Aiguille du Midi. A few days later R L G Irving, climbing alone, made the first ascent of the Aiguilles Grises ridge, joining the frontier ridge above the Col de Bionnassay. Later in August the first traverse of this col was completed by R W Lloyd with Josef and Adolf Pollinger after climbing the steep north face. Lloyd and his guides then moved to Zermatt where they followed an unusual route on the Matterhorn, climbing the north-east, Hörnli ridge, traversing the *Galerie Carrel* on the west face and descending by the north-west, Zmutt ridge. The fine weather enabled guideless Italian parties to complete two new routes on the Liskamm: the Gugliermina brothers reached the east, higher summit after climbing the south-west face; and Ravelli's party ascended directly to the west summit by a line on the south face.

In September Harold Raeburn, another Alpine Club member, undertook a daring expedition in the Dauphiné. Climbing on his own he completed an east-west traverse of the Meije with a diversion to examine the west ridge before descending to the Promontoire hut.

In South Africa the Mountain Club had been seriously affected by the conflict with many members absent on active service. Although the club was greatly reduced in size exploration of Table Mountain (1087m) was continued by a few enthusiasts including J W Fraser and F Humphries who completed *Spring Ridge*, another severe route for the period.

In the Southern Alps of New Zealand heavy snowfalls during the winter months were followed by a long period of bad weather and it was only in March that settled conditions allowed Samuel Turner to pursue his ambition to make a solo ascent of the High Peak of Mount Cook (3724m). After being forced to retreat by strong winds during a first attempt Turner retraced his steps two days later and finally reached the summit where his flag was seen by Alfred Cowling, a guide at the Hermitage hotel, and another witness. Although as Turner acknowledged he was fortunate to negotiate the Linda glacier and north-east ridge alone, his success – the first solo ascent by an amateur – was an outstanding achievement by a determined climber.

In Bolivia Rudolf Dienst, one of several German climbers resident in La Paz, completed a number of notable climbs in the Cordillera Real. In May he made the first ascent of the imposing ice peak Huayna Potosi or Caca Aca (6095m) accompanied by O Lohse, the manager of a local tin mine. In the following month Dienst with Adolf Schulze of Ushba fame made the first ascents of Ancohuma (6430m), the highest peak in the Sorata group, and the neighbouring Haukaña (6206m).

In the Canadian Rockies V A Fynn and the guide Rudolph Aemmer explored a large area south of Banff where they made the first ascent of Mount King George (3422m), the highest peak in the Royal group. After attempting to ascend the unclimbed Mount Sir Douglas (3406m) near Palliser Pass, Fynn and Aemmer were disappointed to learn that J W A Hickson with Edward Feuz Jr had reached the summit of this peak on the previous day. Hickson and Feuz also made the first ascent of Mount Joffre (3450m), another high peak in the region. Further north Howard Palmer's party made the first ascents of McDonnell Peak (3270m) in the Fraser group and Paragon Peak (3030m) in the Rampart massif while visiting the Jasper district.

At home the revival of mountaineering after the war was led by a group of outstanding climbers in the Lake District including G S Bower, C F Holland, H M Kelly and J I Roper. With *D Route* on Gimmer Crag, *Great Central Route* on Dow Crag, *Kern Knotts Buttress* on Great Gable and numerous other severe or very severe routes the standard of climbing was raised considerably during the year.

In March the death occurred of Frederick Gardiner who had climbed in the Caucasus with F C Grove, A W Moore and Horace Walker and is remembered as an early exponent of guideless climbing. He completed many notable expeditions with the brothers Charles and Lawrence Pilkington including the first guideless ascents of the Meije and Finsteraarhorn during a long and successful climbing career.

This account is concluded by recalling a remarkable achievement by a member and future president of the Alpine Club. During the chaotic period following the collapse of the Austro-Hungarian Empire, Karl, the last Habsburg emperor, who had refused to abdicate, had taken refuge with his wife the Empress Zita and their family at Eckartsau, a hunting-lodge near the Danube north-east of Vienna, where they were suffering from lack of supplies and medical attention. In February, following an appeal to King George V, Lt Col Edward Strutt, an officer serving with the Royal Scots in Salonika and a linguist fluent in French and German, was instructed to proceed to Eckartsau to assist the family by all possible means. In March, after arranging for the delivery of food and fuel Lt Col Strutt on his own initiative and with a small detachment of British soldiers succeeded in escorting the emperor and his family by train to safety in Switzerland.

The emperor, who died at an early age and his family never forgot this chivalrous action and many years later the empress recalled their rescue in a message to the Alpine Club to mark the Club's centenary.

> *... Once more on this occasion my thoughts and my prayers go towards your former President, gallant Colonel Strutt, whose magnificent support to my family and to myself in the crucial times of the beginning of 1919 I shall always remember in deepest gratitude. ...*

A fitting tribute to a brave and resourceful soldier.

• For a fuller portrait of E L Strutt, see Peter Foster's article on p189.

Area Notes

Cloud on the Aiguille du Gouter from Chamonix, Moonlight
John Ruskin, 186?
Watercolour over pencil. 22cm x 28.5cm.
Bequeathed to the Alpine Club Library by Charles Warren.

LINDSAY GRIFFIN

Alps & Dolomites 2018

Micha Rinn starting up the upper schist prow of *Perfect Storm*.
(Simon Richardson)

As the years pass and climate change takes an increasing toll on the mountains of the Alps, there are fewer truly significant new routes to report outside the winter season. Are the Alps worked out when it comes to major lines? Certainly not: in the summary below we find the first ascent

247

of a completely virgin face on a major 4,000m peak. We also find new routes on some of the most popular (and famous) peaks in the chain. This report attempts to give a snapshot of achievements in 2018, representative of the current activity in modern Alpine climbing. We start with the Mecca, the Mont Blanc range, and then progress eastward.

Looking for aesthetic new lines in the Mont Blanc massif? Go remote. There can be fewer places more remote in this range than the Miage face of **Mont Blanc** (4808m), high above the Mont Blanc glacier and approached from the Quintino Sella hut. Arguably the most prominent feature is the Red Pillar leading to the Brouillard ridge a little distance below Picco Luigi Amedeo (4460m). This was climbed by the legendary Giancarlo Grassi, with Jean-Noel Roche, in July 1983 (650m to the ridge, D+/TD-, V-). During this ascent Grassi noticed a narrow hidden ice couloir to the left (north) of the pillar, and returned in April 1984 to climb it with Enrico Tessera (650m, TD+, 90°). However, it is not clear if either climb continued to the summit of Luigi Amedeo. Immediately left of this couloir another pillar rises to the Brouillard ridge. This remained untouched until August, when over two days Micha Rinn (Germany) and Simon Richardson (UK) climbed a zigzag line up ramps and corners on the right side of the pillar (pitch grades from 4 to 6a+) to the point at around two-thirds height where the rock on the face transitions to black schist. The pair climbed this surprisingly solid and steep schist for six pitches to a tower, where they bivouacked. Next day they made a rappel and climbed an overhanging corner (5c) to easier ground, which led in 100m to the top of Picco Luigi Amedeo. It had now begun to snow, and the pair continued up the Brouillard ridge and over the summit in a ferocious storm, navigating in a white out to the Vallot hut amidst avalanching slopes. Both climbers felt this was the worst weather they had ever experienced in the Alps. They spent two nights in the hut, then in less than perfect weather traversed over the Aiguille de Bionnassay to the Durier hut, passed the night there, and continued next day over the Domes de Miage to the Tré-la-Tête hut. On the final day they descended to Les Contamines and returned through the tunnel to collect their car left in the Val Veni. The 700m new route to Picco Luigi Amedeo has been named *Perfect Storm* (ED1, 6a+) and is probably the first new route on this part of the Miage face since 1989.

Although there were no outstanding first ascents by female alpinists, the young Italian Federica Mingolla continues to establish hard routes in the high mountains. The 24-year old from Torino paired with Gabriele Carrara to put up a new line, *L'Isola Che Non C'è* (Neverland) on the east face of the **Aiguille Croux** (3256m), on the Italian side of Mont Blanc not far from the Monzino hut. The pair spent five days in early September working the route, ground up, in as clean a style as they felt possible: bolted belays, very few protection bolts, a handful of pegs, and the majority of the protection from small Friends. At first they returned to the Monzino hut each night, until they reached the top of pitch seven, where a quasi-horizontal 6a+ traverse leads right for 40m to a corner. From this point retreat down the route

Pointe Louis Amédée
(4460m)

Himalamiage
(1989)

Lune de Miage   Gugliermina/Gugliermina/Brocherel   Perfect Storm   Fanta Couloir   Red Pillar
(1986)   (1901)   (2018)   (1984)   (1983)

A photodiagram of *Perfect Storm*. *(Simon Richardson)*

becomes highly problematic, if not impossible, and the two spent a night on the wall before reaching the summit. They came back on 12 September climbing the route all free at 7b+, 7a obl. Repeat ascensionists will need to be confident at the grade, as the climbing is often run out. While pitch seven provides the technical crux, the twelfth and last pitch follows a 7b crack through an exposed overhanging headwall high above the chaotic Frêney glacier. This ascent provides a good example of accomplished sport climbers transitioning their skills to the high mountains, and Mingolla seems to be at the forefront of female activity.

On 12 June, Max Bonniot, Pierre Labbre, and Manu Romain (France) solved a longstanding problem: the first free ascent of *Groucho Marx* (700m, ED3, 6b, A3, now 7b) on the east face of the **Grandes Jorasses** (4208m). The three climbed the 400m central section, which is a more or less vertical rock wall where the major difficulties are located, in nine pitches.

Groucho Marx follows the prominent central dièdre slanting left to a large roof, and until 2006 and the birth of *Little Big Men* (Batoux-Daudet, 2006: 700m, ED4, A3, 6a, M6) was the only route to breach the central rock wall. The line was certainly on the radar of French icon Jean-Marc Boivin in 1981, when he and François Diaferia climbed to the Great Terrace below the steep section of the face, whereupon they realized the dièdre was a much bigger undertaking than they had anticipated. They traversed right and climbed a new line close to the right edge of the wall. Two young guides and brothers from Rome, Cristiano and Fabio Delisi finally climbed the route on 13-15 August 1983. Above the Great Terrace they climbed 11 pitches up to 6b and A3 (copperheads) on excellent granite to reach the mixed ground leading to the upper Tronchey, which they followed to the top. This was by far their most significant route in the Alps. Fabio gave up climbing and became a travel agent in Kuala Lumpur, while Cristiano, who had led most of the hard pitches on the route, continued his guiding career and was the founder of a principal Italian trekking agency. He sadly died of cancer in 2005. In March 2012 Sébastien Bohin, Dimitry Munoz and Sébastien Ratel, made the first winter ascent, and later Ratel, noting that it might go free, returned with Max Bonniot. The dièdre was wet, so instead the two created a new route to the right at 7b. Not surprisingly, on *Groucho Marx* it was pitch three, the A3 roof that provided the 7b free crux, but there is a pitch of 7a high on the route.

Whilst it might have been climbed before, until 2018 the south-west ridge of the popular **Tour Noir** (3837m) in the Argentière glacier basin did not appear to have a recorded ascent. A more detailed inspection reveals a possible reason: the rock on the lower section of the ridge is steep and unstable. This section can be avoided on the left by a ramp on the south-west face, but until recently this ramp has been threatened by a large serac barrier. Climate change has largely eliminated the serac and the entry pitches are now safe. On August 5, Micha Rinn (Germany) and Simon Richardson (UK) made the 400m ascent, joining the route up the south-east flank at 3,760m, and finishing up the exposed but excellent rock of the south ridge integral. The route was graded AD (IV+), is objectively safe, but best climbed early in the season when snow and ice bind the loose terrain together.

In 1983 the Valtournenche guides Marco Barmasse and Walter Cazzanelli climbed the *South Face Direttissima* (ED1) on the **Matterhorn**. The first solo ascent was made in 2007 by Hervé Barmasse, Marco's son and also a Valtournenche guide. Seven years before his solo ascent, Hervé had put up *Per Nio* with Patrick Poletto, a difficult rock route that climbs the 'Scudo', the shield of rock below Pic Tyndall and one of the steepest sections of the south face of the mountain. In September it was the turn of 28-year-old François Cazzanelli, a Cervinia guide and son of Walter, to make his own mark on the Matterhorn. With Marco Farina, Emrik Favre, Roberto Ferraris and Francesco Ratti, he completed *Diretta allo Scudo*, a 350m climb that finishes at the top of the shield, passing through the steepest and most difficult section via complex route finding. This had been a prolonged effort: Cazzanelli had made an initial attempt in 2012, and a further five before completing the route in 2018. Well, not quite completing. Several of the top pitches used aid and the team want to return to free climb the route, which they estimate will be 7a/7a+, 6b+ obl. Bolts were placed for protection and belays, though trad gear used where possible.

In the Bernese Oberland Dani Arnold and Stephen Ruoss (Switzerland) made the first ascent of the north-east face of the **Gross Grünhorn** (4044m). This face, which rises from the upper Fiescher glacier, features in Dumler and Burkhardt's classic coffee-table book, *The High Mountains of the Alps*. Yet it may be the only face on a major 4,000m peak to have remained

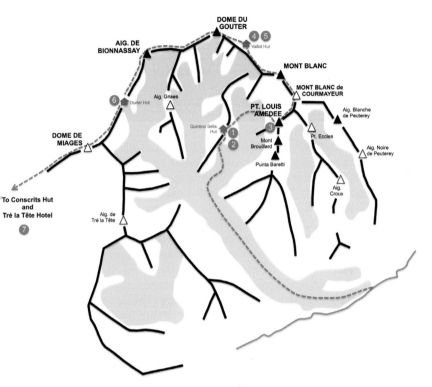

Topo of west face of Pointe Louis Amédée showing line of *Perfect Storm*. (Micha Rinn)

completely unclimbed until 2018. In 1967 Swiss guidebook writer and pioneer Christoph Blum climbed the left bounding ridge, the *East Pillar*, at D/TD, a classic outing on sound granite at V-); it was Blum that pointed Arnold towards a potential first ascent. The two Swiss climbed the 600m face on 12 May from the Finsteraarhorn hut, negotiating steep snowy mixed ground up to M7 and steeper pure rock (in rock shoes) at 6b+. They used trad gear, leaving three pitons in place, on the individual pitches, but bolted all the belays for a convenient rappel descent.

On 11 January, Luka Lindič (Slovenia) and Ines Papert (Germany) completed what is thought to be the first winter traverse of the **Watzmann Group** (2173m). This famous peak of the Berchtesgaden lies close to their house, and while seeing much traffic in summer has little to no activity in winter. During early season ski touring in the region the two realized the most logical line would be to follow the skyline from east to west, ending on the highest summit. The pair started with the north-east ridge of the Kleine Watzmann, then traversed over all five Watzmann 'children', before climbing direct up the east face of the highest summit at M5 80°. The *Watzmann Family Traverse* had 3,450m of ascent and was completed in 19½ hours car to car.

Arguably the most significant if non-calendar winter ascent in the Dolomites during 2018 took place on the east face of **Cima Brenta** (3,150m) over two days in mid December. The protagonists were two great local activists and mountain guides, Alexander Beber and Matteo Faletti. Beber had made an attempt on this ephemeral line in 2014 and then returned at least once a year to see if it was in condition. In late 2018, while on a family holiday in southern Arizona, Beber noticed that a friend had published a photo on social media, a selfie of herself on top Croz dell' Altissimo, and in the background the east face of Cima Brenta, plastered and gleaming in white snow and ice. On returning home he enlisted Faletti and after a six-hour approach the two started up the line with full bivouac equipment. The face proved drier, and hence harder, than anticipated and the pair needed their warm equipment at the top of pitch seven. Next day, after a night of -20°C, the two climbed another seven pitches to a ledge at the end of the difficulties, where with impending darkness, they decided to walk off. The 550m route has been named *CRAM* (Circolo Recreativo Aziendale Mountime), and above the entry slopes (150m, 65°) gives relatively sustained climbing up to AI5, M6, 90°. The east face is complex formation characterised in part by a sheer orange wall set above a long scree-snow slope. *CRAM* follows a series of very steep grooves on the more broken face immediately right of this wall, and was repeated in a single day on 23 December.

The 550m south-west face of the **Cima Scotoni** (2874m) has been the scene of several milestone ascents in the history of Dolomite climbing. Indeed, the first ascent, by K2 summiteer Lino Lacedelli, was for years considered by many to be the hardest route in the Dolomites. Much later, in 1990 Christoph Hainz created the 23-pitch *Zauberlehring*. Considered a masterpiece of modern climbing at the time, Hainz used no bolts and overcame difficulties up to 7c. The rejection of bolts, combined with the friable rock for which the Scotoni is infamous, led to obligatory difficulties of 7b.

Two events of note took place on this face during 2018. In June, after eight days work spread over two years, the Italian Simon Gietl, who in 2006 achieved the third ascent of *Zauberlehring* and returned in 2009 to make the first winter ascent, completed *Can You Hear Me?* (VIII+, A2). Gietl climbed roped solo, and in keeping with Hainz's ethic used no bolts on any of the 27 pitches. The route was dedicated to Gerhard Fiegl who died in 2015 on the descent from Nilgiri South (6839m) after making the first ascent of the south face. Fiegl, a regular climbing partner of Gietl, had scoped the line of *Can You Hear Me?*, and asked Gietl if they could attempt it together in traditional style. Gielt promised that he wouldn't climb it with anyone else, and with Fiegl now gone the only option was to climb it solo.

The Scotoni also saw one of the most significant ascents in the Dolomites during 2018. Over two days in September, climbing with fellow Italian Lorenzo d'Addario, Nicola Tondini made the first single push free ascent of his own route *Non Abbiate Paura di Sognare* (700m, 8b, 7b+ obl). Tondini had established the 24-pitch line over seven years, always climbing ground up and not using aid for progress: he used skyhook rests only to place protection pitons. Bolts were limited to nine belay stations. In 2017 he eventually freed every pitch but was missing the continuous free ascent. *Non Abbiate Paura di Sognare*, meaning 'don't be afraid to dream', is very much a 'direttissima' up the steepest (meaning 'overhanging') part of the south-west face, to the right of *Zauberlehring*. There are three pitches of 7c+/8a and above, and four pitches of around 7b+ that are quite run out.

Over on Austria's highest mountain, the **Grossglockner** (3798m), Austrians Ulrich Muhlburger and Hans Zlobl, climbed a new route on the rocky south-south-east face to give the 750m *Power of Love* (VII, A1). They describe it as the 'first modern alpine sport climb' on the mountain, and in order to meet 'modern safety standards' bolted all the belays. However, most protection is from trad gear, with only a few bolts and pegs placed on the 11 pitches. The climb is also serious: stone fall is ever present and the rock somewhat friable. The route tops out on the *Stuedlgrat* (AD+) at 3,600m, some distance from the summit, and was climbed over two non-consecutive days in September. This was one of three new routes climbed by Zlobl on the Grossglockner during 2018.

Less well known is the Austrian Valsertal in the Zillertal Alps, home to the **Sagwand** (3227m). This area had been something of a playground for the late David Lama over the last five years. On 15 February, Lama and fellow Austrian Peter Muhlburger made the first ascent of the *Sagzahn Verschneidung* (800m, M6 A2), a prominent dihedral between the Sagwand and Schrammacher. Lama had attempted this line in winter on three occasions previously, realizing that he had severely underestimated the difficulties. The route has around half a dozen difficult mixed pitches before less taxing snow gullies in a big corner system lead to the top.

Scottish Winter 2018-19

Andy Inglis climbing the first pitch of *The Chancel* (VIII,8) on Beinn a'Bhuird.
(Guy Robertson)

Last winter was a long one: good routes were climbed as early as October and as late as May. Even so, major thaws in the key months of November, December and February meant little opportunity for reliable conditions to form. The weather cooled down in March, but by then many climbers had lost patience; on Ben Nevis there wasn't enough base snow for even the most reliable gullies to form ice.

The most difficult new route was *The Forge* (X,10) on An Teallach by Guy Robertson and Greg Boswell. This discontinuous crack-line up the middle of the awe-inspiring vertical wall above *Hayfork Gully* was one of the most sought after winter objectives in the country. The route was climbed in two pitches with Boswell leading the long first pitch, which proved to be the crux. Boswell described the climbing as 'very technical, super physical with multiple boulder-problem-style cruxy sections along the way'. Often there were only 'minuscule hooks and no foot placements'. The pitch was likened in style to *The Hurting* (XI,11) in Coire an t- Sneachda.

There were three impressive additions to Beinn Eighe. On 30 January, Murdoch Jamieson and Guy Robertson added an excellent winter-only line to the Far East Wall of Beinn Eighe. *One Man's Mountain* (VII/VIII,8) takes the prominent left-facing corner right of *Vishnu*. Two days later, Jamieson returned with Uisdean Hawthorn to make the first winter ascent of *Heavy Flak* (VIII,8), a summer E1 on the Eastern Ramparts. The third addition was equally challenging but in a more adventurous location. Martin Moran and Robin Thomas made the first ascent of *Scarred for Life* (VIII,9), a line loosely based on the summer line of *Scarface* (E1), on the rarely visited north face of Sgurr Ban.

In March, Guy Robertson and Andy Inglis pulled off one of the finest new routes of the season when they made a first winter ascent based on *The Chancel* on Beinn a'Bhuird. This five-pitch E1 on the west face of Mitre Ridge was first climbed in summer 1978 and graded E1 5b. Robertson and Inglis made a reconnaissance trip the week before, and the eventual ascent required many hours of trail breaking through deep snow.

It would be a mistake to judge the winter purely by new routes. In many ways the most significant event was the third ascent of *Anubis* (XII,12) on Ben Nevis by Greg Boswell. The first winter ascent of this overhanging summer E8 on The Comb was made by Dave MacLeod in February 2010 and is widely regarded as the most difficult winter route on Ben Nevis. Together with Boswell's route *Banana Wall* in the Northern Corries, it is the only route in Scotland that merits a Grade XII rating. The heavy snowfall at the end of January turned Ben Nevis as white as a Christmas cake, and Boswell was quick to take the rare opportunity to attempt this severely over-hanging line when it was completely frosted. Boswell first tried the route with Helen Rennard on 30 January and returned three days later to make a successful ascent with Robbie Phillips. Boswell's ascent of *Anubis* makes him the only climber to have climbed two Scottish Grade XIIs.

Perhaps the most pleasing aspect of the winter was the emerging gener-ation of younger Scottish winter climbers eager to tackle the more testing routes. Jamie Skelton and Matt Glenn hit the headlines when they made the second winter ascent of *Feast of The East* (VIII,9) on the Eastern Ramparts on Beinn Eighe in March. It transpired that despite the poor winter the pair had enjoyed a very successful season with ascents of *Ventricle* (VII,8), *Darth Vader* (VII,7), *Sioux Wall* (VIII,8) and the second ascent of *Shape-shifter* (VIII,8) on Lurcher's Crag. In addition, Skelton made ascents of

Murdoch Jamieson climbing the third pitch of *Heavy Flak* (VIII,8) on Beinn Eighe's Eastern Ramparts during the first winter ascent. *(Uisdean Hawthorn)*

Daddy Longlegs (VIII,9) with Jack Morris, and the hard test-pieces of *The Needle* (VIII,8) and *Centurion* (VIII,8) with Tim Miller. With enthusiasm, energy and talent like this, the future of Scottish winter climbing looks bright.

The season was overshadowed by a terrible accident on Ben Hope on 5 February that took the lives of Steve Perry and Andy Nisbet. The exact details will never be known but it seems likely that they fell from the upper section of a new route they were climbing on the west face. This tragedy took the wind out of everyone's sails. Andy Nisbet had such a positive impact on Scottish winter climbing, continuously innovating and taking a great interest in everyone else's activities, that it seemed the game would never feel the same again.

Nisbet's winter record is without comparison. By the mid 1990s he had made first ascents of over a quarter of the 600 or so Scottish routes graded V or over, with a distinct bias towards the higher grades. In total, he is thought to have climbed over one thousand new winter routes. One has to look to the records of Fred Beckey in North America, or Patrick Gabarrou in the Alps to find climbers whose influence has been as long lasting and profound.

Murdoch Jamieson on the first ascent of *One Man's Mountain* on the Far East Wall of Beinn Eighe. *(Guy Robertson)*

Andy Nisbet was born in 1953 in Aberdeen. His parents had a keen interest in the hills and took him hillwalking from an early age and by the age of 19 he had complete all the Munros. He studied biochemistry at Aberdeen University where he began regular rock climbing on the local sea cliffs. The following year he attended rock and winter climbing courses at Glenmore Lodge and was soon regularly climbing Grade IVs on Lochnagar.

In 1977 Nisbet made the first winter ascent of *Dagger* on Creagan a'Choire Etchachan, his first grade V new route. Breakthrough into the big time came the following December when he made the first winter ascent of *Vertigo Wall* (VII,7) on Creag an Dubh Loch with Alfie Robertson. Although their ascent was flawed, relying on several points of aid, this intimidating and very steep Tom Patey VS, high on Central Gully Wall, was regarded as one of the last great problems of the time.

The winter of 1980 saw a race between rival Edinburgh and Aberdeen teams to pick the major Cairngorm plums. In January, conditions on Creag an Dubh Loch were exceptionally icy. The Edinburgh team of Rab Anderson and Rob Milne were there first, climbing the long-sought after *White*

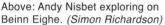

Above: Andy Nisbet exploring on
Beinn Eighe. *(Simon Richardson)*

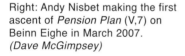

Right: Andy Nisbet making the first
ascent of *Pension Plan* (V,7) on
Beinn Eighe in March 2007.
(Dave McGimpsey)

Elephant (VII,6) on the Central Slabs. They were later overheard in a pub
talking about the exceptional amount of ice on *Goliath*. Word got back to
Andy who climbed the steep grade VII route four days later with Neil Morrison. It didn't go all Nisbet's way that winter however, as later in the season
he was beaten to the prestigious first ascent of *The Citadel* (VII,8) on the
Shelter Stone by Murray Hamilton and Kenny Spence, when he crashed his
car leaving Aberdeen.

Hard mixed climbing in the early 1980s was a rather different game
to now. The crux pitches on the big Shelter Stone routes were originally
ascended on powder-covered rock wearing thin gloves. In 1981, Nisbet
began to experiment with mixed climbing techniques on Carn Etchachan
above Loch Avon. It was a poor winter with little snow and ice, but the deep
cracks of the Northern Cairngorm granite proved ideal for jamming ice axe
picks. It was another three years before the term 'torquing' was coined for
this technique when Colin MacLean nearly succeeded on the very steep
layback crack of *The Outlands* on Lochnagar.

Nisbet and MacLean formed a formidable partnership during the winter

of 1985. That January they visited Glen Coe and came away with one of the great problems of the day: a winter ascent of *Unicorn* (VIII,8), the striking summer E1 corner-line in Stob Coire nan Lochan. As west coast climbers gnashed their teeth at Aberdonians poaching one of their best winter lines, Nisbet and MacLean were already working on their next project: a winter ascent of *The Needle* (VIII,8) on the Shelter Stone. After two weeks of continuous effort, the route was eventually climbed with a bivouac. Even though it was climbed nearly thirty-five years ago, *The Needle* is still one of the most sought after high-standard winter routes in Scotland and has only seen a dozen or so repeats. Back in the mid 1980s it was probably the most difficult mixed climb in the world. *No Siesta* on the Grandes Jorasses, a similar breakthrough for the Alps at the time, was not climbed until 1986.

Later that year, Nisbet started working at Glenmore Lodge where he met Andy Cunningham. Although Cunningham was new to high-standard mixed climbing, he was quick to learn and the two Andys formed one of the most effective partnerships in the history of Scottish mountaineering. Over the next three winters they added over 25 outstanding grade V routes all over the Cairngorms and Northern Highlands. Their additions in the Northern Corries had a profound influence on the shape of Scottish mixed climbing. *Fallout Corner* (VI,7) and *The Migrant* (VI,7) helped popularise mixed climbing in the Northern Corries. Today, both routes are recognised as modern classics, and receive many ascents each winter.

Andy moved on to become the most prolific explorer of the Northern and Western Highlands. Working with Martin Moran, who sadly lost his life in the Garhwal last summer, from a base in Loch Carron in the 1990s, Andy had a superb opportunity for investigating some of the less well-known corners of the Highlands. The transition from chasing the hardest ascents to pure exploration was a natural progression and resulted in hundreds of new routes with strong partners such as Jonathan Preston, Dave McGimpsey, Sandy Allan and latterly Steve Perry.

Nisbet's knowledge of the Scottish mountains became unparalleled. He was new routes editor of the *Scottish Mountaineering Journal* for 30 years, authored three editions of the Cairngorms guide, two volumes for the Northern Highlands, compiled the popular *Scottish Rock Climbs* and *Scottish Winter Climbs* volumes, and wrote major sections in several other Scottish guidebooks. His quiet manner, bushy red beard, unbounded enthusiasm and unfailing optimism became synonymous with Scottish mountaineering. Despite being a well-known figure, Andy was warm, humorous, humble and always intensely interested in what others were up to. He was president of the SMC from 2010 to 2012 and was awarded the Scottish Award for Excellence in Mountain Culture in 2014.

Although Nisbet will be forever associated with winter climbing, he was also an accomplished rock climber. During the summer, he would explore the hills looking for new winter lines, adding many rock climbs in the process. The exact number is unknown, but it is likely to exceed his winter tally, and he was almost certainly the most prolific explorer of mountain rock climbs in the Highlands. Overseas he made ascents of alpine classics such as the north faces of the Matterhorn and Eiger and added a difficult new winter ED2 on the Col du Peigne. Further afield he made the first ascent of north-west ridge of Rooster Comb in Alaska, and in 1985 attempted the north-east ridge of Everest which was unclimbed at the time. His greatest achievements in the Himalaya were the first ascents of Nanda Kot's south face in 1995 and Nilkanth's west ridge in 2000.

The loss of Andy Nisbet leaves a gaping hole that will be impossible to fill. Undoubtedly, his greatest legacy was inventing the Scottish mixed climbing game that we play today. As climbing historian Greg Strange put it: 'Above all else, Andy should be remembered for his continued pushing for the recognition of technical mixed climbing. In 1981 when he did his first Carn Etchachan routes, people were concerned that they weren't really winter ascents at all, as they just had a dusting of snow and were climbed on frozen turf. Now, of course, it is recognised that these are the ideal conditions to climb this terrain. Through the development of modern mixed, Andy opened up an entirely new form of climbing.'

TIMOTHY ELSON

India 2018

Flat Top (6100m) in the Brammah area. The north spur is centre right
and the east ridge is on the left. *(Timothy Elson)*

The 2018 season in India was quieter than normal in terms of successes, due to unseasonably bad weather in the post-monsoon season. However, there were two outstanding ascents and one major repeat. The highlight of the pre-monsoon season was the first ascent of Janhukot (6805m) by the British team of Malcolm Bass, Paul Figg and Guy Buckingham; they climbed the south-west buttress to the south ridge over four days. It was Malcolm Bass' third attempt at climbing Janhukot and Paul Figg's second attempt. The highlight of the post-monsoon season was the fifth ascent of Cerro Kishtwar (6173m) by a Japanese team made up of Genki Narumi, Yusuke Sato and Hiroki Yamamoto by a new route on the north-east face in mid September. They were caught in a terrible storm on the descent that washed away roads and Manali's petrol station, causing havoc across the northern Indian Himalaya, and so had a real battle to make it down. The major repeat was of the 1997 British route (Murphy, Cave, Fowler and Sustad) on the north face of Changabang (6864m) in May by the French team of Léo Billon, Sébastien Moatti and Sébastien Ratel, part of the Groupe Militaire de Haute Montagne (GMHM). It is rare for routes of this calibre to be repeated.

There were 117 Indian expeditions and 34 foreign expeditions registered with the Indian Mountaineering Foundation in 2018. Most were to popular mountains such as Kun (7077m), Nun (7135m), Deo Tibba (6001m) etc. There were numerous teams in Kashmir climbing in both the pre- and post-monsoon period, and there seemed to be few access issues. However in November 2018 there was a political assassination in Kishtwar and in 2019 there have been several terrorist incidents within Kashmir, which led to an escalation with Pakistan: this is expected make access to Kashmir's mountains more difficult for the 2019 season. It should be noted that the current FCO advice is not to travel to Jammu & Kashmir with the exception of Ladakh.

The weather in the post-monsoon season was the worst for a generation according to residents in Manali and Padum. The Rohtang pass tunnel is due to open in 2019, which will provide quicker access north of Manali: to Lahul, Pangi and Spiti. There is also a plan to link Manali to Leh with a railway, which would be one of the highest in the world and will connect Delhi to Leh in 20 hours. In Kashmir, there is a plan to create an all-weather tunnel on the Srinagar to Kargil road to bypass the Zoji La. The state of Uttarakhand, which includes Garhwal, is due to get air ambulances in 2019. These are not mountain rescue helicopters but may be used to evacuate causalities in remote locations. In 2018 there was a semi-permanent high-altitude medical and research centre at Stok Kangri (6154m) base camp for the season, where 500 patients were treated and 14 evacuations were conducted. Stok Kangri is the most popular trekking peak in India, located near Leh.

In August 2018, Uttarakhand's high court banned overnight camping in *bugyals*, alpine meadows, which led to a ban on trekking. However, latest information suggests this ban has been overturned after the government of Uttarakhand challenged the order on the grounds that many people's livelihoods are dependent on income from trekking groups.

Janhukot
In the pre-monsoon season the British team of Malcolm Bass, Paul Figg and Guy Buckingham made the first ascent of Janhukot (6805m) via the south-west buttress to the south ridge. They were accompanied by Hamish Frost who made a film about the trip, available online. Janhukot had been attempted seven times previously, including a 2004 attempt by Malcom Bass and Paul Figg, and a 2014 attempt by Malcom Bass and Simon Yearsley. After climbing the lower buttress, the 2014 expedition reached the top of a feature known as 'The Castle' on the south ridge, at 6,600m only a couple of hundred metres from the summit but strong wind and impending darkness forced retreat. Janhukot is 18km up the Gangotri glacier adjacent to Chaukhamba (7138m), which sits at the head of the Gangotri glacier. The team reached base camp (4400m) below Kedar Dome (6940m) on 22 May. They acclimatised on Kedar Dome between 25 and 27 May. After a rest it took two days to get from base camp to the base of Janhukot on 1 June. At 1.30am next day, the team headed up the funnel and ramp on the

The line of the first ascent of Janhukot: south-west buttress to south ridge.
(Hamish Frost)

south-west buttress, reaching a safe bivy spot at 9am in the morning where
they rested for the remainder of the day. The second day they reached a
bivy spot 100m below the junction with the south ridge and on the third day
reached the ridge and continued along knife-edge terrain. In the afternoon
the weather deteriorated and after trying to dig into the ridge, thought better
of it and moved up to below the Castle, where they made a 50m abseil to a
perfect bivy spot in a wind scoop. Next morning was very Scottish, i.e. mist
and drizzle, but at 7am they set out anyway for the summit, which they
reached in the afternoon; they were back at the tent by 9pm. Next day they
made a long descent down the ridge and then the east side of the mountain,
the same descent Malcolm Bass and Simon Yearsley had used in 2014. They
graded the route ED1, Scottish IV with 1,700m of vertical height gain.

Cerro Kishtwar
In September the Japanese team of Genki Narumi, Yusuke Sato and Hiroki
Yamamoto climbed a new route over six days on the north-east face of
Cerro Kishtwar (6173m), the fifth ascent of the mountain. Cerro Kishtwar
is the stunning Patagonian-type mountain – hence the name – situated in

Cerro Kishtwar's east face with Chomochior on the right. The Japanese route climbs the bottom left of the east face then goes around the buttress and out of the photo. *(Mick Fowler)*

the centre of the Kishtwar Himalaya. It was first climbed in 1993 by Mick Fowler and Steve Sustad, although the previous year Brendan Murphy and Andy Perkins had got to within 100m of the summit over 17 days up a futuristic line on the north face. The second ascent had to wait until 2011 when restrictions on mountaineering in the Kishtwar were lifted and Stephan Siegrist, Denis Burdet and David Lama climbed the north-west face. In 2015 Hayden Kennedy, Marco Prezelj, Manu Pellisier, and Urban Novak climbed the east face and last year Siegrist returned with Thomas Huber and Julian Zankar to climb the north face direct. The Japanese team set up basecamp on 3 September in the Chomochior valley, the same side of the mountain that Marko Prezelj et al made the third ascent of Cerro Kishtwar via the east face in autumn 2015. In fact the Japanese team were inspired to attempt their line from a photo provided by this team.

After acclimatising they set off up the north-east face on 20 September from their advance base below the face, climbing a 1,000m snow gully with a steep ice section at the top on the first day. On day two they had 500m of technical climbing to get to the summit: they went without bivy kit as they had a short weather window. The second day started with a skinny ice pillar and some tricky mixed pitches to reach the upper wall where they climbed bold mixed pitches. The team reached the summit at 11pm and started rappelling into the night, stopping for two hours to brew and reaching their tent at midday on 22 September. By this time a storm had moved in; this was the season's major storm that caused havoc throughout the northern Himalaya region. They continued to make a further 20 abseils down the face whilst being hit by avalanches. They were in a serious situation but luckily at midnight found a safe place to stop for the night. On their fourth day out they reached the glacier to be met with three feet of fresh snow to wade through to reach advance base, which had been destroyed by snow. Having rebuilt their camp, it was rocked by an avalanche and so they moved it 200m down the glacier under a boulder to sit out the storm. They finally returned to base camp on 25 September. They named the route *All Izz Well* (VI, WI5, M6, 1500m) after the Bollywood film *3 Idiots*.

Changabang

From 11 to 13 May the French team of Léo Billon, Sébastien Moatti and Sébastien Ratel of the Groupe Militaire de Haute Montagne (GMHM) made the second ascent of the 1997 route on the north face of Changabang (6864m). The north face was climbed over 10 days by Andy Cave, Brendan Murphy, Mick Fowler and Steve Sustad; tragically, Murphy died in an avalanche on the descent. It is rare for routes of this calibre to be repeated in the Himalaya, however a direct route on the north face was climbed in 1998 by a US-Russian team. The French team made a remarkable three-day ascent of the route using a combination of the line attempted in 1996 by Roger Payne, Julie-Ann Clyma, Andy Perkins and Murphy and the 1997 route. The route is 1,200m and climbed in 40 pitches. The team stopped short of the main summit to make the long and difficult descent down and around the mountain.

Kashmir & East Karakoram

With the removal in 2016 of foreign nationals requiring a protected area permit to visit the Nubra valley, the popularity of the Indian east Karakoram has increased with foreign expeditions. There were Indian expeditions to Saser Kangri I (7672m), Plateau (7287m) and Saser Kangri IV (7416m); sadly the well-known climber Pemba Sherpa died in a crevasse fall descending from a successful ascent of Saser Kangri IV.

To the south of the Saser Kangri group an Estonian expedition visited the Kunzang range in July, making a long approach from Rongdo and crossing a high pass (5981m) to the Phurdupka glacier. From the North Phurdupka glacier, they took four days to make the first ascent of peak 6801m via the south-west ridge and west face; the peak has various different names on different maps so the Estonians named it Rangston Gyathok, which means '100 years of independence' in Ladakhi and celebrates the hundredth anniversary of the Republic of Estonia.

In July a German expedition also started from Rongdo and set up base camp in the Rongdo valley. Initially their aim was to climb peak 6064m but regular rock fall on their intended route put them off and they switchd to peak 6235m. On 22 July they climbed the south face of Phokto Scheyok (Black Pyramid) (6235m); the expedition noted that the valley had numerous 500m unclimbed granite walls, as well as several unclimbed 6,000m peaks.

The north face of Chiling II (6253). *(Alex Mathie)*

Ladakh

In August, Pawel Sharma, Passang Tenzing and Girish Singh from the Himalayan Mountaineering Institute (HMI), Darjeeling, made the first successful traverse from Kang Yatse I (6401m) to Kang Yatse II (6250m). These are both popular peaks situated close to Leh.

Zanskar

Missing from 2018's India summary was the first confirmed ascent of Chiling II (6253m) and the first ascent of the east ridge of Chiling I (6349m). Jon Griffin and Tad McCrea (USA) made the first ascent of the east ridge of Chiling I (6349m) in August 2017 and named the route *Wantonly Tarnished* (600m, 70°). On 29 July 2017, a Spanish team of Oriol Baró and Lluc Pellissa made the first confirmed ascent of Chiling II (6253m) via the east ridge in a 23-hour push, rating the 900m route ED, 6b, M4+ 80°. In 2015 an American team got to within 80m of the summit via the same route before retreating; there has been some confusion on the naming of Chiling I and II in the past with both being referred to as Z2, which, on the Indian Mountaineering Foundation classification, is a mountain further south above the Durung Drung glacier. Chiling I seems to have first been ascended from the south by an Italian expedition in 1977 and had a further ascent in 1982. The 2017 Spanish team had started their trip climbing in the Shafat valley climbing various routes on the Shafat Fortress and its surrounding peaks; they made the first ascent of the east buttress of Shafat Fortress (c5900m, 700m, 6b, A0 and snow). They then climbed the west summit of Shafat

The Mulung Tokpo team heading to their high camp. *(Derek Buckle)*

Fortress (5700m) via a route named *Estética Goulotte* (900m, V/5+, M5).

In 2018 some of the Spanish team returned to the Shafat valley, the team was made up of Iker Madoz, Oriol Baró, Edu Espanyol, Edu Sanchez, Anna Gimeno, Ferran Rodriguez, Luis Alfonso Sanz and Santi Gracia. They spent three weeks in June in the valley and had almost consistently good weather, allowing them to make 30 new routes from V to 7b on routes from 150m long to alpine undertakings. The rock is reported to be excellent granite and good climbing was reached within half an hour's walk from base. Ferrán, Oriol and Iker climbed two alpine routes on peaks 5600m and 5950m. Chiling II (6253m) saw two attempts in 2018, the first in June by a British team of Alex Mathie and Matt Harle and the second in the autumn by Alan Rousseau and Tino Villanueva (USA). In June the British team first attempted the east buttress of Lalung III (6126m) for acclimatisation, which is situated at the head of Lalung valley where the Lalung and Chiling peaks form its eastern boundary. They reached a shoulder at 5,600m but were then snowed off the peak. After that they attempted the north face of Chiling II (6253m) on 21 June but were turned around by heavy spindrift avalanches. The American team had the same objective in the autumn, the north face of Chiling II (6253m). However the storm of 22 and 23 of September scuppered their trip. Police came to rescue them and they evacuated base camp. The same thing happened to the British Kishtwar expedition made up of Tom Livingstone, Uisdean Hawthorn and Will Sim. Their main aim was the first ascent of Barnaj II (c6300m). The team were 'rescued' after the storm of 22 September, but after negotiation was allowed

Above: Open bivy site looking over the Hagshu valley. *(Beth Goralski)*

Left: Tower 1 in the Kange valley. Tower 7 is to the right. *(Beth Goralski)*

to continue. After that they went to attempt Chiring (c6300m) but only got as far as its base, after which they made the decision to abandon.

In September an Alpine Club team including Derek Buckle, Drew Cook, Mike Fletcher, Adele Long, Gus Morton and Tony Westcott explored the Mulung Tokpo. They approached from Leh via the Kargil road to Padum where they started the two-day walk in to base camp at the head of the Mulung glacier. They established a high camp at 5,085m in the south branch of the Mulung glacier and on 19 September Derek, Drew, Mike and Adele made an attempt on peak 5631m via its north face, retreating 300m from the summit due to cold and unconsolidated snow. The same day Gus and Tony gained the Aari Dont col (5480m) and Gus continued onto the summit of Aari Dont (5557m) to make the first ascent via the north-west ridge. The rest of the team repeated the ascent of Aari Dont the following day with Derek and Mike continuing on to climb the adjacent peak Chilh Point (5537m). When they returned to base camp they were also hit by the big storm of 22 September. Their base camp was buried and they abandoned everything other than essential gear and waded down Padum.

Kishtwar Eiger (6000m) with base camp in the foreground. *(Timothy Elson)*

An American team, Beth Goralski and Lindsey Hamm, visited the Kange valley north of the Hagshu valley in September where they attempted peak 19,000ft. They attempted a ridge with seven spires that would lead to the summit, but after initial exploration of the north face could not find a safe line. They set off on the ridge on the 20th of September and climbed the first spire with climbing up to 5.9 to a bivy. The next day they decided to retreat due to the complex looking ground ahead and a deteriorating forecast. While retreating they were hit by the major storm of 22 and 23 September, they made it back to base camp on 22 September and their base camp was quickly buried. After they storm they went down to the nearest village and decided to abandon their expedition.

Kishtwar

Expeditions to the Kishtwar side of the Himalayan watershed in the autumn of 2018 were also affected by the storm of 22 and 23 September and the following continually bad weather, resulting in no expeditions being successful, apart from fram the Japanese ascent of Cerro Kishtwar described above. The Anglo-New Zealand Kishtwar expedition made up of Timothy Elson and Richard Measures attempted Flat Top (6100m) and Kishtwar Eiger (6000m) from the Brammah glacier. They approached via Kishtwar itself up the Marau valley and the Nanth Nullah but arriving at base camp

At the base of the north spur. *(Timothy Elson)*

Day one on Kishtwar Eiger with Brammah II, Flat Top & Brammah I.
(Richard Measures)

Ice climbing on Kishtwar Eiger during day two. *(Timothy Elson)*

were caught in the storm and after this the mountains were buried under snow for the rest of the expedition. The pair made a three-day attempt on the north spur of Flat Top (6100m) and retreated due to bad weather. Up to their highpoint the climbing had been technically interesting, mixed climbing up to Scottish VI. They went up for a second attempt but received a new, worse weather forecast and attempted the easier east ridge in a single push, retreating from 5,400m when they realised they were not going to made the summit in a day. Following that they reached 5,700m on the south face of the Kishtwar Eiger (6000m): enjoyable climbing similar to Scottish gully climbs with several bold ice pitches. However they retreated in a storm on the second day of their attempt. The mountains surrounding the Brammah glacier were once very popular, due to their short approaches, modest altitude and striking lines. However, this was this was thought to be the first expedition to the area in almost 30 years.

Above: Route attempted by US team on 6,000m peak adjacent to Arjuna. *(Whitney Clarke)*

Left: Airy climbing above the Kijai Nala. *(Josie McKee)*

In September Whitney Clarke, Josie McKee and Caro North (USA) visited the Kijai Nala where they initially intended to attempt the west face of Arjuna (6230m). Arjuna's west face currently has four routes on it: two from Polish climbers in the early 1980s, which must have been among the hardest technical routes in the Himalaya at the time, and two from 2017 as reported in last year's *Alpine Journal*. The rock on Arjuna is reported to be granite of exceptional quality covered in chicken-heads. As with other teams in the post-monsoon period the Americans had poor weather, which impeded their acclimatisation and scoping of their routes. On 17 September they received a favourable forecast and set out for Arjuna. It took them a full day to navigate the maze of glacier to the mountain and upon reaching Arjuna the west face was caked in snow, so they switched objectives for a 6,000m peak just to the north. The next day they set off up the south-west face, climbing from 4,900m to 5,500m on the first day, encountering difficulties up to 5.10. Next day they climbed six pitches before the weather closed in and they retreated back to their 5,500m camp. On 20 September they descended the lower section of their route and returned to basecamp just missing the big storm of 22 and 23 September.

Himachal Pradesh

In September the Swiss Stephan Siegrist and Jonas Schild aimed to attempt the north face of Shiva (6142m) in Himachal Pradesh along with photographer Dominic Fischer. The expedition did not get off to the best start with base camp being put on the wrong side of the mountain. The storm of 22 September hit as they were moving base. They then scoped out the line on the north face of Shiva and decided that after the heavy snow it was unfeasible and moved to the west ridge only to meet similar conditions. They did put up an 8a+ crack-line in the Jobri-Nala valley: this is thought to be the hardest crack in India at the moment. Shiva was first climbed in 1973 by a Japanese team via the south ridge; the south-west ridge was climbed in 1975 by another Japanese team. In 1988 the west ridge was climbed again by a Japanese team and in 2012 Mick Fowler and Paul Rams-den climbed the 'prow' of Shiva, the

The 'Unknown Mountain', Baspa valley. *(Hansjörg Auer)*

north-west buttress that involved sustained hard mixed climbing and won them the Piolet d'Or.

In October Hansjörg Auer, Max Berger, Much Mayr and Guido Unter-wurzacher made the first ascent of 6050m above Sangla in the Baspa valley. The team climbed the route in alpine style over three days, 3 to 5 October, climbing the south-east face and finding beautiful mixed climbed that was never extreme. Each afternoon on the route they had snow showers and during their stay they did not experience stable weather.

In June Damien Gildea attempted a solo ascent of the south face of Chau Kang Nilda (6303m), meaning the 'Blue Moon in the Sky' in Spiti; he reached around 6,150m before being stopped by a large crevasse.

From 5 to 15 January 2019 the inaugural Piti-Dharr International Ice Climbing Festival was held in Spiti, where both novice and experts climbed and several first ascents were made. The potential for ice climbing in the region of the Himalaya is only just beginning to be explored.

Uttarakhand

In the Garhwal, the major ascents were the first ascent of Janhukot and the repeat of the original route on the north face of Changabang, already

Chombu (6362m) seen from the slopes of Pheling. *(Nicholas Hurndall Smith)*

described above. As with other areas in the Himalaya the post-monsoon weather was not stable. In the autumn Alex Gammeter and Philipp Bührer from Switzerland made the first ascent of Sri Kailas West (6803m) via the south face. After arriving at the start of October and acclimatising, they set off from a high camp on 20 October and climbed the south face with descent via peak 6617m's south face. In October the British team of John Crook and Dave Sharpe attempted the massive north-east ridge of Nanda Devi East (7434m) but were shut down at 6,300m by the large amount of snow that had fallen earlier in the month.

Sikkim

In 2018 there seemed to be very few expeditions to Sikkim, other than a British expedition made up of Derek Buckle, Nick Hurndall Smith and Nick Berry, who went to attempt the first ascent of Brumkhangshe (5635m). The team encountered deep snow, which hindered mountain activity. After establishing base camp the team went exploring, after being turned around by deep snow on an acclimatisation foray on Brumkhangshe (5635m), they then made an ascent of the trekking peak known as Pheling (5500m). Nick and Nick also came close to summiting Eagle Peak (5540m) and then made a determined attempt on Brumkhangshe in a single push reaching a col at 5370m.

Thanks to Alex Mathie, Hansjörg Auer, Tom Livingstone, Kaushal Desai, Beth Goralski, Anindya Mukherjee, Nick Berry, Nick Hurndall Smith, Derek Buckle, Malcolm Bass, Whitney Clark and Nigel Buckley for providing extra information.

IAN WALL

Nepal 2018-19

On the first ascent of Lapse of Reason on Kyajo Ri (6186m). *(Marek Holeček)*

In order to make the Nepal report more timely and logical, its time-frame will in future run from June of the previous year and so include the post-monsoon, winter and pre-monsoon season. In order to make that change, this year includes the pre-monsoon for 2019.

Everest 2018
In an indifferent winter season, Spanish climber Alex Txikon and Pakistan's Muhammad Ali Sadpara made an attempt to climb from the Nepal side without supplementary oxygen. The team was poised for a summit bid before being beaten by low temperatures and strong winds. As part of their acclimatisation cycle they summited Pumori (7161m) on the 20 January 2018.

As Nepal prepared to celebrate the 65th anniversary of the first ascent of Everest, officials at the tourism ministry were expecting a bumper year.

It was also the 40th anniversary of the first ascent without bottled oxygen. In early April, the surviving members of the 1978 Everest Expedition, including Peter Habeler and Reinhold Messner, assembled in Kathmandu and later went on to visit Everest Base Camp (EBC). Members of the expedition also scattered the ashes of Norman Dyhrenfurth, who died in 2017.

The route-fixing team, known as the Icefall Doctors, had left Namche Bazar in mid March to start work on the fixed lines. For this work each member of the team received a minimum wage of $3,000, paid from the $600 levied for the purpose on each foreign climber attempting Everest, Nuptse or Lhotse via this route. This team of fixers – Pasang Tenjing Sherpa, Pasdawa Sherpa, Lakpa Dendi Sherpa, Jen Jen Lama, Siddi Bahadur Tamang, Pemba Chhiri Sherpa, Tenzing Gyaljen Sherpa and Datuk Bhote – became the first to reach the summit in 2018. A serac collapsed in the icefall on 25 April injuring two Sherpas. One was treated at EBC's 'Everest ER' while the other was flown to Kathmandu for treatment for a back injury. The first commercial summit came on 29 April: four Sherpas with two Chinese clients.

Soon after, one of those dramatic but short-lived controversies so familiar on Everest burst into life when Willie Benegas and Matt Moniz skied down from 7,200m to 6,400m on 2 May without obtaining a the necessary ski permit from government authorities. All sorts of threats were issued by the Department of Tourism, but these were counter-balanced by a letter of support being sent to the DoT by more than 150 climbing Sherpa stating that the incident had 'not posed any threat to the mountaineering sector'. However the question, 'Where was the LO in all of this?,' still remains unanswered. In the end the case was dropped and the pair was allowed to continue with their summit plans.

More than 500 climbers including 247 foreign mountaineers and the Sherpa Women Everest Expedition 2018 were well acclimatised and ready to make their summit push. Kenton Cool succeeded in summiting the peak for the 13th time, the most number of ascents by any British mountaineer, along with his client, television celebrity Ben Fogle. There was the usual crop of records set over the season. Kami Rita Sherpa, 48, from Thame made his 22nd ascent of Everest; Lhakpa Sherpa, 45, made her ninth, this time from the Tibetan side. Another 'record' set in 2018 was that Furtenbach Adventures only took 21 days on the mountain for their team to reach the summit, via the North Col, thanks to pre-acclimatisation in altitude chambers before reaching Nepal. A similar practice was used by Alpenglow, resulting in their guides and professional skiers summiting both Cho Oyu and Everest in 23 days. This comes with a high price. These expeditions were charging $80,000 to $110,000 per member, while Seven Summits expedition members paying $130,000 had a mid-expedition break in Kathmandu. It's reported two members actually flew home during this period before flying back in to resume their expedition.

During the winter season of 2017-18 the Nepal government announced new guidelines for climbing and mountaineering activities, which included a ban on double amputees and visually impaired climbers from attempting Everest. However just before the 2018 season these rules were relaxed after pressure from Nepal's supreme court, the public and the mountaineering fraternity. This caught Harti Budha Magar, an ex-British Gurkha and double amputee off guard and he was unable to activate his Everest plan for 2018 but 70-year-old double amputee Xia Boyu from China did accomplish his Everest ambition, standing on the summit on 13 May, the culmination of a 40-year struggle and his fifth attempt.

Highlighting the strength of Nepali female climbers, Nima Jangmu Sherpa summit Lhotse on 29 April and Everest on 14 May and then went on to summit Kangchenjunga on 23 May. Nima Jangmu has now set the world record of summiting all three of the highest Himalayan peaks of Nepal not only within one season but within 25 days. Nima is also the first Nepali woman to summit Kangchenjunga, a prize several other Nepali women had their sights on.

As with all mountain environments there are constant changes in Everest's topography; this season saw an unusual number of crevasses open up just above camp one on Everest together with an ice cliff several metres high whose verticality some expedition members couldn't manage. Some changes are advantageous. The Hillary Step has also now become the Hillary Ramp, following 2015's earthquake, further reducing the threat of delays through congested sections. But the 2018 spring season was blessed with an extraordinary period of 11 days of fine weather with little jet-stream activity and a high-pressure system sitting over the region.

These conditions boosted those heading for the summit, but some were caught out at 8,000m when a potentially lethal situation suddenly developed on both sides of Everest. Without warning several teams experienced oxygen equipment failure. All the systems were produced by the same manufacturer and without warning began releasing oxygen from regulators straight into the atmosphere. All bar one expedition had sufficient regulators and oxygen bottles in reserve to allow the summit push to continue and the CEO of the British company flew out to Kathmandu to oversee the handling of the situation, to the satisfaction of the majority.

Among the summit climbers this year was Steve Plain, 36, who set the world record for climbing the Seven Summits in the shortest time: 117 days. He took just seven hours to reach the summit on Everest from camp four on the South Col. The weather on Everest was so good, outfitters in Kathmandu complained the season had ended too soon as expedition members returned early after a successful expedition and then immediately left Nepal. The high success rate also exposed a scam: two summit climbers on a Seven Summits expedition were found to be without permits. After investigation it turned out that junior office personnel in the ministry and the agency had conspired to pocket the peak fees, amounting to $22,000, anticipating that some of the expedition would fail and names could be swapped out. Thanks to the good weather, everybody made it and the fraud was exposed. Seven Summits was fined and the personnel involved fired.

There were on average two or three rescues a day on Everest and its neighbours: Global Rescue alone reported 66 operations. There were also five deaths: Lama Babu Sherpa went missing near the south summit on 14 May and presumed dead; the Russian climber Rustem Amirov died at camp two on Lhotse on 17 May; Tshering Dorji Sherpa was seriously injured after he was struck by falling rocks and snow near camp two and airlifted to hospital in Kathmandu; Pasang Norbu Sherpa, 41, from Solukhumbu district died from a stroke at high camp while heading for the summit on the Tibet side on 18 May; Gjeorgi Petkov, from the Republic of Macedonia, died above camp three after suffering a cardiac arrest while heading for the Yellow Band on 20 May; Japanese climber Nobukazu Kuriki radioed for help suffering from a persistent cough and chest pain but it proved impossible to locate him during the night of 20 May and his body was found above camp two on 22 May; finally, IFMGA guide Damai Sarki Sherpa fell into a crevasse near camp two while accompanying a foreign climber to a waiting helicopter.

By the end of the season when the Sagarmatha Pollution Control Committee (SPCC) had finished its clean-up operations 32,241kg of garbage generated by climbers at EBC and camp two had been collected. Combustible garbage was taken to the waste management facility in Namche Bazar. Non-combustible garbage, around 4,000kg of it, was taken to Kathmandu for recycling. At least 12,995kg of human waste and 4,010 kg of kitchen waste was collected from EBC. Sadly these figures showed an increase on previous seasons. The SPCC has partnered with the Everest Biogas Project to convert human waste into biogas through an anaerobic digester. Tara Air flew out at least 100 tonnes of waste from the Mount Everest region in 2018 as part of its commitment to sustainable development goals.

The SPCC has been working for more than 25 years to keep Everest and its foothills clean, building appropriate waste management infrastructure, setting up a system for waste segregation and disposal, strengthening community participation in waste management, disseminating public education and formulating policies for proper waste management in coordination with the government.

As usual there were issues with liaison officers who were reported absent from expeditions despite being paid handsomely to be on site from the outset right through to the end of an expedition. This happened despite a new government rule that a guide or liaison officer must accompany expeditions. LOs are still failing to show up despite expeditions having to pay for them. Guides on lower mountains often come to an arrangement to remain at 'high camp', allowing expeditions to continue under their own steam, or else don't set foot on the mountain at all.

A more welcome change involves Everest certificates. While I have difficulty in accepting the certificate scheme for those summiting Everest post 1992, when commercial expeditions got underway, I am pleased the government has finally awarded them to over 500 Nepali guides who made it to the summit of different mountains in recent years. For these guys it is a great addition to their CVs when it comes to securing additional employment, not only in Nepal but around the world.

Nowadays, **Lhotse** is commonly included as part of the Everest itinerary with a dozen climbers summiting before going home. There were an estimated 50 members reaching the top including 79-year-old Matsumoto Tatsuo who became the oldest person to summit the mountain. Two Americans made a successful ski descent of the world's fourth highest mountain, a 7000m vertical ski line initially descending the Lhotse couloir before entering the steep open lower part of the face of the mountain.

The weather on Nepal's other 8,000ers was more difficult with **Dhaulagiri** seemingly getting hit the hardest. Carlos Soria, seeking his 12th 8,000m peak, had to abandoned his ninth attempt on Dhaulagiri due to bad weather. Ryan Kushner got to 7,620m before weather stopped his independent team. Italian Simone La Terra was sadly blown off the mountain to his death when a gust of wind hit his tent in an unprotected flat location. Also in the Dhaulagiri Himal, nine climbers including five Koreans died in a freak accident on **Gurja West** (7193m). Initially it was assumed a large landslide had killed them but further investigation revealed a large serac barrier high above base camp collapsed and the consequent displacement of air blasted base camp, sending expedition members into a deep ravine nearby where they died as a result of the fall.

Widely regarded as the most deadly of the 8,000ers, **Annapurna** was climbed by Hong-bin Kim with four Sherpas. The South Korean climber, 53, who lost all of his fingers to frostbite while climbing Denali in North America in 1991, reached the summit on 13 May. On **Manaslu**, a Swiss team abandoned their effort due to dangerous avalanche conditions. Yet Manaslu had a good autumn season with over 200 successful ascents although there was a strange incident reported that allegedly involved two Chinese climbers on separate expeditions who had a mega fallout resulting in crampons being used as weapons. One climber was airlifted to a hospital in Kathmandu for treatment while the other is said to have fled the scene. Many of those climbers who eventually reached the summit were initially stranded at lower altitude because of a dispute between the government and the ministry of tourism resulting in a lack of helicopters and a breakdown in the logistical supply chain. Needless to say the situation ended up with all sides blaming the other.

On **Cho Oyu**, Rolfe Oostra and Bulgarian Atanas Skatov summited without supplementary oxygen or Sherpa assistance. On **Makalu** Thomas Lämmle summited without supplementary oxygen. The mountain was also summited by a team consisting of the female climber Gao Xiao-Dan, along with Nima Gyalzen Sherpa, Jit Bahadur Sherpa and Ang Dawa Sherpa who later died from altitude-related problems. Swedish mountaineer Carina Ahlqvist was evacuated from Makalu after she suffered snow-blindness.

On **Kangchenjunga** there were multiple summits in difficult conditions. Israeli climber Nadav Ben Yehuda narrowly escaped after being injured in a fall and left for dead. When fellow climbers later saw him move, a complicated rescue ensued. He suffered spinal and rib injuries as well as severe frostbite. The Israeli was briefly famous in 2012 for helping a stricken Turkish climber on Everest. Chris Burke summited on 20 May and Asian Trekking managed to get 11 Indian clients to the summit.

Simone Moro arrived in Kathmandu in late December 2018 to attempt a winter ascent of Manaslu, without gas, along with Pemba Gyalje Sherpa but abandoned his expedition in January due to heavy snowfall and avalanche danger.

Away from the 8,000m peaks, **Ama Dablam** (6812m), technically a more challenging peak, saw a number of accidents during the 2018 season. Sherpa rescuers recovered the body of Malaysian climber Raman Nair Hachoodan, 41, from a gorge at around 5,300m after he went missing at 6,300m on 15 May. According to rescuers, the climber fell from high camp as he descended with two other climbers due to bad weather. In late November an American died as a result of altitude sickness, this followed the earlier death of an Australian climber who died as a result of rock fall cutting his abseil rope.

In October 1988 two Icelandic mountaineers, Kristinn Rúnarsson and Þorsteinn Guðjónsson who were 27-years-old at the time disappeared on **Khangri Shar (Pumori West).** Both men set off leaving their British companion at base camp to monitor their progress. Unfortunately they disappeared into cloud above 6,600mand were not seen again. It has now been confirmed that the climbers reached the summit on 18 October 1988 but met with disaster on 19 October during their descent. The discovery of their bodies was made by American climber Luke Smithwick on 12 November. Smithwick abandoned his expedition as a result. Earlier he had completed a route on the north face of **Nirekha** but as yet there are no details.

Zsolt Torok, Teofil Vlad and Romeo 'Romica' Popa from Romania completed a new route on the south-east face of **Pumori** (7161m) in alpine style. They called their route *Le Voyage du Petit Prince*. Mixed climbing between the foot of the south-east face at 5,600m and the exit to the summit ridge at 6,700m was compared to the Eiger's north face, says Torok, 'with similar elements like The Ramp, the White Spider' and the Waterfall Chimney.' The Romanian trio spent five nights on this extremely steep wall where there was a lack of bivouac sites.

Two guided teams lead by Garrett Madison (USA) made the first and second ascent of **Tharke Kang** (6710m), a newly opened peak to the north of Gokyo in the Khumbu region. A helicopter was used to avoid its dangerous icefall near the Nup La and ropes were then fixed on steeper sections of the north-west ridge. The summit was reached on 3 and 4 November. On 25 October David Lama succeeded in completing the project that he and Conrad Anker had started on **Lunag Ri** (6895m). In 2016 Conrad suffered a heart attack and had to be evacuated off the mountain, ending the expedition. Lama reached the summit via the west ridge. Wolfgang Drexler Thallmair, Yokachi Tamang and Lawang Tamang made the first ascent of **Dhechyan Khan** (6019m) situated in the Damdor Himal via the south ridge.

The team went on to make the first ascent of **Nguru Far East** via the south couloir and west ridge.

In far western Nepal, a British expedition led by Julian Freeman-Attwood and comprising Nick Colton, Ed Douglas, Christoph Nettekoven and Bruce Normand made a number of first ascents in the Takphu Himal, including **Takphu** itself, **Til Kang** (6369m) and four other peaks. After resting in Kathmandu, Normand returned to the west to make three more first ascents of 6,000m peaks in Mugu district: his tally of 6,000er first ascents for the season was eight. See Attwood & Normand's article on page 281. A six-man Japanese expedition reported reaching the summit of a peak called **Pankar Hatani** in the Manaslu region but so far no details have emerged or, despite research, the exact location of their peak.

Disputes over Fees and Camping Charges
When Nepal adopted its new constitution in 2015, a federal system of government was put in place, prompting a struggle between central government and local communities over the distribution of funds collected from tourists: 'TIMS' trekking fees, national park fees, conservation area fees, camping fees and so forth.

In October 2017, Khumbu authorities imposed a $20 fee for entering the region, collected in Lukla, and in the spring season of 2018 a community charge was levied on all tourists and Nepali staff staying in higher-altitude villages: a 'community room tax'. In October 2018 authorities in the Makalu region imposed a $20 per night camping charge, a major hike in costs since you can't trek in the Makalu region without spending most nights camping.

In many cases and with a full understanding of the reasons behind these charges, they seem reasonable. However, these new taxes were imposed without notice and were seen as duplicated fees, resulting in continuing disagreements between all levels of administration, total confusion for agents and many angry trekkers who were faced with last-minute price increases. Discussions were continuing to resolve the situation this spring.

It's a similar story in the Annapurna region, where local municipalities want to manage their own finances, causing a three-way tug-of-war between local, provincial and federal governments. Despite the Annapurna Conservation Area Project (ACAP) successfully balancing a local economy based on agro-forestry with the need to protect the environment, there has been growing resentment against restrictions on harvesting fodder and grass, grazing and the use of natural resources. There are also complaints that ACAP, and other centrally administered organisations, do not share tourist revenue with local governments for the benefit of local communities.

Areas affected within the Annapurna region include Manang, Mustang and Lamjung. Deputations from rural communities have presented their case to district offices in Pokhara requesting ACAP lifts its restrictions on developing local infrastructure, to allocate proportional tourist income to the most popular tourist districts. This situation can only escalate in the future with the local communities demanding access to funds generated from trekking-peak fees. As yet the outcomes of these discussions have not been made public. In the meantime local communities will continue to implement ill-conceived schemes that will have an immediate but hopefully short-term negative impact on tourism.

2019

On 16 April, the tourism ministry issued a press release detailing permits to 824 expedition members belonging to 100 individual expeditions to climb 27 peaks. Of these, 377 climbers from 39 expeditions were seeking permission to climb Everest, not far off half. This number includes 364 foreign climbers from 34 expeditions and 13 Nepalis from five. As in 2018, many teams now include Lhotse as part of their Everest itinerary: 92 climbers from 10 expeditions had permission to climb Lhotse. Forty-nine climbers belonging to five different expeditions had acquired permission to climb Ama Dablam, 32 mountaineers from five teams had permission to climb Kangchenjunga and 53 climbers from three teams had permission to attempt Makalu. Three teams had permission to climb Annapurna and Dhaulagiri.

On 23 April a party including former Gurkha Nirmal 'Nims' Purja became the first team to reach the top of a Nepali 8,000m peak in 2019: **Annapurna**. His project of climbing all 14 of the 8,000ers in seven months was on a roll. It's worth noting that the three officials appointed as liaison officers to the three Annapurna expeditions were unable to provide any information on their respective expeditions since they never left Kathmandu. The rescue of a 49-year-old Malaysian anaesthesiologist Chin Wui Kin on Annapurna created a storm when it revealed his rescue could have been more efficiently handled had the supposed insurance company acted more swiftly. Sadly Chin Wui Kin succumbed to his injuries in hospital having been repatriated to Singapore. On the other side of Annapurna, Felix Berg and Adam Bielecki planned to attempt a new and technically difficult route on the north-west face but due to bad weather and the consequent lack of acclimatisation, the pair returned home without setting foot on the mountain.

Everest got more than its fair share of media exposure during the 2019 spring season but unfortunately for all the wrong reasons. Nepal issued a record number of permits and the route was eventually fixed on 14 May after a delay due to Cyclone Fani. With the ropes in, 150 expedition members rushed to the summit close on the heels of the rope-fixing Sherpa team. The jet stream returned causing more delays but during the next weather window almost 800 people were heading for the summit. The 'Mad Dash', which wasn't so much of a dash but more of a traffic jam was captured by Nirmal 'Nims' Purja in his now infamous summit-ridge image. The consequence was some people spending 20 hours above the South Col with many beginning to run out of oxygen causing stress and anxiety. By the time this photo was taken the death toll had already risen to 11 and would climb later to 12. There was a range of reasons for this: budget expedition packages unable to afford qualified and experienced guides; inexperienced expedition members moving too slowly; and to a certain extent a falsely secure environment created by agents going over the top in providing luxurious base camp amenities. In a worsening trend, expeditions on Everest this year had a total of 73 oxygen bottles disappear, although Nepali operators denied these had been stolen.

There was some useful science done. On 13 June the National Geographic Society installed the world's highest weather stations on Everest to provide researchers, climbers and the public with real-time information about mountain conditions. The EverDrill Project is a joint venture between the universities of Leeds, Aberystwyth, Sheffield and Kathmandu and the Himalayan Research Centre. Working at 5,200m on the Khumbu glacier, the team used a pressurised jet of hot water to drill boreholes deep into the glacial ice. Strings of temperature sensors were installed into the boreholes and left to collect data for several months. Researchers found that there was evidence to suggest the ice was warming at a rate of around 0.5°C per decade suggesting floods and droughts were likely to become more common along with glacial lake growth.

An expedition consisting of two government surveyors along with Sherpa climbers summited Everest collecting data for the measurement of the exact height of the highest point on earth. There's been discussion that the height of Everest might have changed as a result of the 2015 earthquake. Begs the question, why mount an expensive expedition when there are satellites that can do the job more efficiently?

Two foreign expedition companies, Alpenglow and Furtebnbach, continued with their use of altitude tents at home countries for pre-acclimatisation before reaching Nepal. Both companies recorded good results using this method. Everest ER, the temporary health post situated at EBC during the expedition season, reported a big increase in the number of inexperienced climbers they were seeing, registering their total number of patients as 582, 58% of them Nepali. It was the fourth-busiest season since they began operations in 2003.

Four of the 12 deaths were Indians: 78 permits were issued to Indian climbers, the largest group of permit holders. Indian mountaineering media expect 2020 to see an even larger number of Indians attempting Everest. Of the 21 deaths across the Nepal Himalaya eight were Indians. There were also fake summit claims by Indian climbers. With Indian climbers being offered government incentives for reaching the summit of Everest the question of motivation must be raised.

The Nepali government commissioned a huge clean-up operation, following China's decision to implement new rules for climbing Everest. Three tons of rubbish were removed from the mountain and four bodies. (See Jonathan Westaway, page 129.) From 1 April Nepal decided diverted all flights from Kathmandu to Lukla to ease maintenance work being done at Tribhuvan International Airport. Flights were moved to a rural airstrip four hours' drive away, although the option of an expensive helicopter flight was still possible from Kathmandu. This not only caused confusion but the alternative lacked the necessary infrastructure to cope with the high numbers of tourists. At the time of writing there is a plan to keep this as the normal access route into the Khumbu region to ease flight congestion in Kathmandu.

On **Dhaulagiri**, Romanians Horia Colibasanu and Marius Gane and Slovak Peter Hamor were all set for their summit bid via a new line on the north-west ridge, but although they were above the crux of the route they had to retreat in the face of bad weather. Korean climber Hong Sung-Taek made his sixth attempt on the south face of **Lhotse**, and for the first time in spring, as opposed to the post-monsoon season. Over a period of two months he and his team set up five camps on the south face before striking for the summit. Strong wind, snow, and then an avalanche that almost swept the climbers away near camp three forced the team to retreat from around 7,700m, between camps two and three. After this close call, almost all members decided to descend. Only Hong and five Sherpa remained. The six braved deteriorating weather conditions as they continued toward the summit, before ultimately deciding to abandon the expedition.

Nirmal 'Nims' Purja, the former UK Special Forces member who opened the season with his ascent of Annapurna as part of his Project Possible had completed 11 of the 14 8,000m peaks as the *Alpine Journal* went to press. Those summits were: Annapurna on 23 April; Dhaulagiri on 12 May; Kangchenjunga on 15 May; Everest on 22 May; Lhotse, also on 22 May; Makalu on 24 May; Nanga Parbat on 3 July; Gasherbrum I on 15 July; Gasherbrum II on 18 July; K2 on 24 July; Broad Peak on 26 July. Purja has relied on helicopter transfers and bottled oxygen but the stamina required for this attempt is still exceptional.

Insurance Fraud

Over the last 15 years or so, many of us in the Nepal-based trekking and climbing world have been aware of insurance scams affecting our industry. Although the Nepali government has long fought shy of admitting the problem, media attention has gradually been building alongside insurance premiums. In 2013 the British Mountaineering Council published an investigation of the issue and last year the former AFP reporter Annabel Symington published the results of a nine-month investigation that showed how deep and extensive the problem is.

In an effort to generate business helicopter companies began years ago offering 'commission' to guides or agents calling for helicopter assistance in rescuing trekkers in the mountains. This practice has now developed to such an extent that by 2018 many organisations – hospitals, agencies, helicopter companies and others – were illegally profiting from inappropriate invoicing, raking in millions of dollars. Kaji Sherpa, known as Mr Speed, described the people responsible for the fraud as 'mafia'. Krishna Prasad Devkota, secretary of the Ministry of Culture, Tourism and Civil Aviation was quoted as saying, 'High profile people are involved in the scam and they are now being investigated by the police and the tax authorities.'

In a frank admission, Devkota acknowledged that his own job was on the line for investigating irregularities within the government. An article published in the *Nepali Times* quoted a tourism ministry official admitting that some of the owners of unscrupulous companies involved in the scam enjoyed high-level political protection because they are party donors and offer politicians free helicopter rides during elections or complimentary hospital treatment.

Medical and security assistance company Traveller Assist released a dossier on ten high-profile persons and 23 companies that Traveller Assist believes orchestrated and controlled over 90% of insurance fraud in Nepal, with evidence including company registration documents, copies of shareholder agreements, details of offshore bank accounts, lists of assets purchased in part from fraudulently obtained funds, copies of emails discussing commission payments and written statements from key witnesses. Traveller Assist itself has faced questions after issuing strongly worded threats about insurance boycotts and demands to individual companies.

Some of the hospitals accused of irregularities include some of the best-known names in Nepali healthcare, including CIWEC, SWACON hospital and ERA hospital. Evidence was found of misdiagnosis and overtreatment, as well as exorbitant rates. These revelations about systematic fraud prompted more of them. TV producer Anthony Gordon, who had filmed the six-part series 'Everest Air' for the Travel Channel, used his first-hand knowledge to add to the evidence, 'out of frustration at the government's lack of action'. He described organising the rescue of a sick climber on the Lhotse face of Everest through Alpine Rescue Services, expecting a bill for around $4,000. Instead, managing director Ram Nepal charged $8,000, sending a second helicopter to collect the fee. Additional invoices were then presented for a flight from Lukla to Kathmandu and hospital admission and treatment there, even though the climber was treated in Lukla and made their own way back.

Gordon revealed witnessing instances of double billing and implicated both SWACON and CIWEC hospitals, as well as the well-known Nepali agency Seven Summits Treks. He also reported the shocking story of how the body of a dead Sherpa was recovered at a cost of $20,000 after being commissioned by another film crew. The recovery was filmed but the Sherpa's body was then dropped in a crevasse because, Gordon claimed, the family were unable to meet the $250 excess and told Ram Nepal of Alpine Rescue Services to leave the body on the mountain.

In May 2018, after facing the most expensive season on record for insurance claims in Nepal, international insurers joined forces to put pressure on the Nepal government to address the fraud issue. After a 90-day investigation, a committee appointed by the tourism ministry confirmed that fraud was happening. A spokesman told AFP: 'When we began our investigation we did not realise the magnitude of the problem.'

Despite promises to bring those responsible to justice, no charges have yet been brought. None of the changes to rescue procedures the ministry promised to stop the fraud have been implemented. The struggles within government seem to be as blurry as the details of the investigation itself. Comments by government officials seem to contradict each other and relevant ministries blame each other. However, at the beginning of 2019, tourism minister Rabindra Adhikari told AFP: 'We are deeply committed to taking action against them. The government will make no compromises in this regard.'

In February, officials at three government agencies, the health ministry, the central bank and the Central Investigation Bureau (CIB) of Nepal police told the Kathmandu Post that the prime minister's office had ordered them to complete their investigation as soon as possible. On 27 February, tourism minister Rabindra Adhikari was killed in a helicopter crash in the Kangchenjunga region of eastern Nepal, along with the pilot Capt Prabhakar KC, tourism entrepreneur Ang Tsering Sherpa, owner of Yeti Airlines, security personnel Arjun Ghimire, Yubaraj Dahal, an official in the prime minister's officer, the deputy director-general of Civil Aviation Authority of Nepal (CAAN) Birendra Shrestha, and CAAN engineer Dhruba Das Bhochhibhaya.

The tourism minister's untimely death put the brakes on urgently needed reform and it seems likely that it's business as usual for Nepal's rescue fraudsters. Apart from the obvious criminality, these prominent individuals and companies are doing Nepal and its adventure tourism industry an incredible disservice. Most clients never ask why a trek is so cheap, only why it's so expensive. But unless the Nepali government takes strong action to solve this problem, in a few years' time the industry will run on corruption and decent businesses will close down. That will be a great shame for Nepal.

TIMOTHY ELSON

Pakistan 2018

Adam Bielecki after left traverse on the upper part of the west face of
Gasherbrum II (8035m), reaching the final summit ridge. *(Felix Berg)*

The biggest news from the Pakistan Karakoram in 2018 was undoubtedly the first ascent of Latok I (7145m) from the north side by the
Slovenian-British team of Aleš Česen, Luka Stražar, and Tom Livingstone
in August. However the dramatic helicopter rescue of the Russian alpinist Alexander Gukov from 6,200m on the mountain's north ridge prior to
this dominated the international news media: Gukov and Sergey Glazunov
reached the junction at the top of the north ridge over 11 days but did not
summit. Glazunov disappeared on the descent leaving Gukov alone on the
mountain for six days before a dramatic static-line rescue by the Pakistani
military saved him. In fact rescues and recoveries were a big part of the story
of the Karakoram in 2018, with rescues on Nanga Parbat in winter, Latok
I, Ultar Sar, and Broad Peak; the pilots who carried out many of the rescues
cannot be praised enough. Other major ascents were a new route on the
west face of Gasherbrum II (8035m) by the Pole Adam Bielecki and Felix
Berg from Germany in alpine style and a new route solo by the well-known
Austrian Hansjörg Auer on the west face of Lupghar Sar West (7157m).
Finally, K2 got its first ski descent from Andrzej Bargiel, who skied from
summit to base camp in eight hours, a remarkable achievement.

Latok I with the north ridge right of centre of the picture. *(Tom Livingstone)*

Latok I

The major ascent of the season in the Karakoram was the first ascent of Latok I (7145m) from the north side by the Slovenian-British team of Aleš Česen, Luka Stražar and Tom Livingstone over seven days in August 2018. It was initially and erroneously reported that they had climbed the north ridge direct, but in fact they climbed three-quarters of the ridge before taking a traverse line rightwards to the col between Latok I and II, then completed their ascent up the south side. This was the second ascent of Latok I, the first ascent being from the south by a Japanese team in 1979. Česen, Stražar and Livingstone climbed the most logical line on the face, starting out up snow gullies on the right-hand side of the ridge in order to miss out the difficult lower rock section. They climbed this at night and in the early morning before stopping at safe places to bivy. They then linked snow features until a traverse hard right at three-quarters height on the north ridge led them to the col (c6700m) between Latok I and II. Overnight on their fourth night on the face the weather deteriorated, and on 9 August they left their bivy late at 11am, summited that day and descended back to their high camp. It took them two days to descend, which they mostly did down their ascent route except for the base where they descended the rock rib rather than the exposed snow gullies. The vertical height of the route was 2,400m and the team gave it an alpine rating of ED+.

The north ridge of Latok I has seen attempts by a veritable who's who of the climbing world over the last 40 years. In 1978 a US team comprising George Lowe, Jeff Lowe, Michael Kennedy and Jim Donini reached c7,000m on the north ridge in capsule style, spending 26 days on the route and only retreating when Jeff Lowe became critically ill. Over the ensuing

Tom Livingstone soloing on the first part of the face.

40 years over 20 teams have attempted the ridge with none getting as high as the US team's first attempt. In 2017 the Russian team of Anton Kashevnik, Valery Shamalo and Alexander Gukov reached 6,700m in an epic 14-day round-trip: see *AJ* 2018. Kashevnik and Shamalo suffered serious frostbite and both lost fingers and toes. Last summer Alexander Gukov returned with Sergey Glazunov and launched on 12 July, slowly making their way up the north ridge. On 23 July they made a summit push and Glazunov reached a point that he thought was the summit: Gukov was a rope length below and did not go up. They then started their descent but sadly on 25 July Glazunov disappeared while rigging an abseil.

Gukov sent an SOS signal but was unable to move and so sat out bad weather with no food or water for six days before being rescued by a long line. This almost ended in disaster: Gukov was not unclipped from his belay and only his anchor ripping allowed a happy outcome. Gukov, once recovered, reported he thought they had reached the top of the north ridge but not the summit of Latok I and the consensus seems to be that this is the case.

This was the second rescue from Latok in 2018. On 21 July an avalanche hit a Korean team led by Eun Soo Koo on the north face; two of the team sustained serious injuries before they were rescued by helicopter on 22 July. Thomas Huber led a German-French team to the north face of Latok I in August and September but after reconnoitring the face thought it unjustifiably dangerous. There was also a second Russian team on the mountain in July who attempted the north ridge and north face. Latok I was a popular destination in 2018.

Rescues

These were not the only dramatic rescues and searches in 2018 and into the 2019 winter season in Pakistan. There were 44 expeditions registered with the Pakistan Alpine Club and it has been reported that 17 called for helicopter rescue or evacuation in the 2018 season: that is 38%. In Pakistan, helicopter rescues are commissioned through a company called Askari Aviation and performed by the 5th Pakistan Army Aviation Squadron. Any climbers wishing to be rescued must have paid a rescue bond, currently $10,000, with Askari. (Two helicopters are required under Pakistani military aviation regulations to fly over glaciated terrain.) There is also a plan offered through the Pakistan Association of Tour Operators (PATO) promising an expedition organised or facilitated through one of their members need not pay the rescue bond with Askari but will cover it for them.

There has been universal praise for the skill of Pakistani military pilots who have carried out these high-altitude rescues; this has been acknowledged with the Alpine Club's Spirit of Mountaineering Commendation as well as medals from the Russian ambassador for the rescue of Alexander Gukov from Latok I. In last year's *Alpine Journal* the rescue of Elisabeth Revol from high on Nanga Parbat was described. Since then it has been reported in the French media that Revol has unfairly criticised the rescues for not trying to rescue her climbing partner who was stranded at 7,200m in winter on an 8,000m peak. It is not often possible for a helicopter to rescue someone from that altitude, and her rescue in itself was pretty miraculous, combining the expertise of the Polish K2 winter expedition and the Pakistani military pilots.

In the summer there was a helicopter recovery of the body of Austrian climber Christian Huber from Ultar Sar (7388m). A team comprising Huber and British alpinists Tim Miller and Bruce Normand were attempting the south-east pillar when, on 29 June, while sitting out a storm at 5,900m on the route, their tent was hit by an avalanche. Miller managed to dig Normand out but by the time they had uncovered Huber he had perished. On Sunday 1 July two helicopters came to recover Huber's body from a very small landing platform prepared by Miller and Normand. Huber's body was recovered, and Miller and Normand were rescued. Key to this rescue was the close contact maintained between the climbers and the rescuers via an In Reach device. The climbers were able to tell the helicopters not to come when the weather was not suitable for landing and so forth.

The most highly publicised rescue of the summer was that of Alexander Gukov from Latok I, already described. This faced some criticism, as it hadn't been confirmed whether the team had paid the rescue bond, with the Russian government putting pressure on the Pakistani government to rescue its national. This highlights another issue: who pays for these rescues. In Gukov's case, the helicopters were out for six days in poor weather attempting to rescue him and it has been reported that Askari has not yet been reimbursed. On the other hand, Bruce Normand is reported to have paid outright for the recovery of Huber's body when he returned to Islamabad.

Left: Hansjörg Auer on the summit of Lupghar Sar West. *(Hansjörg Auer)*
Right: Hansjörg Auer with Lupghar Sar West in the background. Auer, widely regarded as among the very best all-round climbers of his generation, died aged 35 in the Canadian Rockies on 16 April 2019 in an avalanche that also killed his fellow Austrian David Lama and the American Jess Roskelley. *(Hansjörg Auer)*

We can only hope the Pakistani military continues to offer helicopter rescue but payment for rescues must be forthcoming.

A further remarkable rescue in the summer was of the well-known British climber Rick Allen on Broad Peak (8047m). Allen went missing on 9 July while descending from a solo summit attempt. On 10 July a drone piloted by Polish brothers Andrzej and Bartek Bargiel (see K2 ski descent) was used to find Allen. After identifying where he was, fellow climbers were then able to help him down to base camp; he had reportedly fallen around 400m and had frost-nip and only minor injuries. He was then airlifted out from the Baltoro glacier.

Sadly in the winter season of 2018-19 there were the widely reported deaths of Tom Ballard from the UK and the Italian Daniele Nardi on the Mummery Rib of Nanga Parbat (8126m). They were reported missing on 24 February 2019 and on 28 February Pakistani climbers, including Muhammad Ali Sadpara, Imtiaz Hussain and Dilawar Hussain, were helicoptered to Nanga Parbat's base camp to initiate a search for them. On 4 March more climbers were dropped at base camp, this time members of the K2 winter expeditions including Alex Txikon of Spain. They ascended to camp two on the rib and had a near miss with an avalanche before searching higher on the mountain with a drone and discovering the bodies of the climbers on 9 March. The search for the climbers was played out in public with daily updates in a way that a few years ago would have been unimaginable.

Lupghar Sar West

On 7 July Austrian climber Hansjörg Auer soloed the first ascent of the west face of Lupghar Sar West (7157m). The mountain had its first and only other ascent by a German team via the south-west ridge in 1979. Auer approached Lupghar Sar West from the Baltbar glacier, acclimatising in the

Lupghar Sar West (7157m), west face first ascent route. *(Hansjörg Auer)*

area for several weeks before setting out from base camp on 6 July for his attempt. He bivvied at the base of the face, c6,200m, and set off early in the morning up the left-hand side of the west face, joining the north-west ridge at 6,900m. Here he left his rope and bivy kit and continued to the summit. At one point on the ridge he very much regretted leaving the rope as the hardest climbing was on this section. Auer summited at 11.30am and then returned via his ascent route, which he reports was more difficult than the ascent, reaching his bivy at 8pm that evening. The difficulties were in the 55°/M4 range and he reported that soloing made dealing with the altitude easier as he was more focused and had fewer emotions.

K2

On 22 July Polish alpinist Andrzej Bargiel made the coveted first ski descent of K2 (8611m). He skied from the summit down the Bottleneck, onto the Česen spur and then out onto the lower section of the south face. Bargiel climbed the Česen spur over three days, summiting at 11.30am, before making his ski descent. This involved one abseil above the Bottleneck, the prominent narrowing gully high on K2 below the high serac band, and a forced wait for clouds to clear at camp four (7700m) before he was able to continue with the rest of his descent. He arrived at base camp at 7.30pm, giving a height loss of around 3,600m in only eight hours. This was Bargiel's second attempt at skiing K2, the first being in 2016, and there had been several prior attempts including two fatal accidents. Hans Kammerlander abandoned his attempt to help rescue another climber in 2001. Bargiel's brother Bartłomiej has made a film of the descent available online, including dramatic drone footage. Bartłomiej and his drone were also instrumental in the rescue of Rick Allen on Broad Peak: see above.

Gasherbrum II

Adam Bielecki (Poland) and Felix Berg (Germany) climbed a new route on the west face of Gasherbrum II (8035m) on 16 July. Their line goes between the 1975 Polish route on the face and the 1995 Mexican route. Bielecki and Berg, along with Jacek Czech and Borys Dedeszko, set off from their high camp at c6,900m and climbed to the summit and back in a day. Czech and Dedeszko turned around at around 7000m.

Pakistan's 8,000ers

The 8,000ers in Pakistan had a short weather window in the summer of 2018 with almost all ascents occurring in a 10-day period towards the end of July. On K2 (8611m) there were a record 60 people who reached the summit, all by the Abruzzi ridge or Česen spur, the majority of these ascents were by commercial expeditions using large amounts of fixed ropes, oxygen, high-altitude porters and guides. As noted above the highlight on K2 was its first ski descent by Andrzej Bargiel. On the other 8,000m peaks, Nanga Parbat (8125m), Gasherbrum I (8080m), Gasherbrum II (8035m) and Broad Peak (8051m), there was less commercial activity and more smaller independent teams. Each of the peaks had ascents in the summer, including a new route on Gasherbrum II (see above) and a spirited attempt on the Rupal flank of Nanga Parbat, the biggest face anywhere in the world, by Czech duo Marek Holeček and Tomas Petrecek, who reached 300m from the summit but turned around in high winds. They spent 10 days up and down the wall in what sounds like an epic attempt. There was also an attempt to traverse Gasherbrum I and II by Masha Gordon, Helias Millerioux and Yannick Graziani, although bad weather curtailed their attempt. The feat of linking two 8,000ers in a single push was done for the first time by Reinhold Messner and Hans Kammerlander in 1984 and repeated in 2008 by the Polish-Slovak team of Piotr Morawski and Peter Hamor. The winter attempts on K2 and Nanga Parbat in 2018 were covered in last year's journal. In the winter of 2018-19 there were winter attempts on these peaks once again. There were two teams attempting the first winter ascent of K2, the last 8,000m peak without a winter ascent: a Spanish team led by Alex Txikon and a Kazakh team led by Vassiliy Pivtsov. Neither of these teams reached high on the mountain and both supported the search for Ballard and Nardi when they went missing on Nanga Parbat, effectively ending their attempts.

Baltoro

There were three teams attempting Gasherbrum IV (7932m) in 2018. David Göttler (Germany) and Hervé Barmasse (Italy) attempted the south-west face but were driven back by heavy snow. A Spanish team comprising Oriol Baró, Roger Cararach, Iker Madoz and Marc Toralle attempted the first ascent of the south pillar but retreated from 6,200m because of the same bad weather and heavy snowfall. The third expedition trying Gasherbrum IV was an Italian military expedition attempting to repeat the original route on the mountain 60 years after its first ascent. Tragically Maurizio Giordano died in a serac avalanche while descending from camp three at c7,000m, which led to the expedition being abandoned.

On 11 May Laila Peak (6096m) had its first ski descent down the north-west face by the French team of Carole Chambaret, Boris Langenstein and Tiphaine Duperier. On 25 May the Swiss-Italian team of Cala Cimenti, Julian Danzer and Matthias Koenig made the second ski descent.

In August Andres Marin (Columbia), Anna Pfaff and David Allfrey (both US) climbed in the Great Trango Tower group repeating the American route on Great Trango Tower (6286m) and then climbing *Eternal Flame* (5.13a) on Nameless Tower (6239m), first climbed in 1989 by Kurt Albert, Wolfgang Güllich, Milan Sykora and Christoph Stiegler, and free climbed by the Huber brothers in 2009. Following this Marin made what is most likely the first solo ascent of Great Trango Tower in a 12-hour push on 22 August.

Biafo and Choktoi

The Swiss duo of Damian Göldi and Marcel Jaun attempted the unclimbed Baintha Brakk West I (6660m), aka Ogre IV, via the south face, a route one rib further west than the original route on Baintha Brakk (7236m), or

The Ogre. They reached 5,800m on the route before Jaun became ill, then sat out a day of bad weather before descending to base camp. On the other side of this mountain range a Kazakh team comprising Kirill Belotserkovskiy and Max Ten attempted the north-east buttress of Baintha Brakk West II (6540m). They set off on 4 August and reached 5,800m after two days of very difficult climbing. However, at this point they decided they were insufficiently acclimatised and moving too slowly to make the summit. They descended next day and had a close call falling into the bergschrund when their anchor failed. The German-Italian-French team of Thomas Huber, Simon Gietl, Rainer Treppte and Yannick Boissenot, mentioned in the Latok section, having investigated the north face of Latok I and decided it looked too dangerous, switched plans to the south pillar of Latok III (6946m). They set up camp at the base of the pillar but bad weather came in curtailing further attempts. Earlier in the summer Alex Huber and Fabian Buhl made the first ascent of a stunning ridge on Choktoi Ri (6166m), which they called the *Big Easy* (2200m, 5.10+, A1).

Kondus Valley
In July and August, Jess Roskelley, Kurt Ross (both US) and Nelson Neirinck (Belgium) made the first ascent of two 6,000m peaks in the Kondus valley. The first peak climbed was Chhota Bhai (6321m) in a three-day round-trip from base camp: *Naps & Noms* (AI4). Following this they made the first ascent of Changi Tower II (6250m) in a four-day round-trip, calling their route *Hard Tellin' Not Knowin'* (M6, A14). On descent their ropes were chopped by rock fall but they made it down safely.

Thagas Valley
Nicolas Favresse, Mathieu Maynadier, Carlitos Molina and Jean-Louis Wertz made the first ascent of two 6,000m peaks in the Thagas valley before Maynadier was injured from rock fall, evacuated from the mountain by the team and then airlifted to safety. The first climb was the first ascent of Pathan Peak (c6000m) via *The Pathan Pillar* (900m, 6b, A1). The team fixed the lower section over three days and then made the summit push over two. While setting up the last abseil to their portaledge, the ledge Molina was standing on collapsed onto Maynadier knocking him out. He recovered consciousness and the others got him to camp and next day descended off the wall before a helicopter evacuated Maynadier from base camp. Molina and Favresse then made the first ascent of Pathani Peak (c6000m) via a route they called *Pathani* (600m, 6a, M6) in a 17-hour round-trip.

Ghoro Valley
In July an Italian expedition led by Maurizio Giordani made the first ascent of the west-south-west face of Kris Peak (5428m). This was mostly a big-wall climb, which they called *Water World* due to the melt water that came down the route during the day. They spent two days fixing the route then three days on their summit push, grading the line VIII, A2.

Shimshal

Pete Thompson and Philip de-Beger (UK) visited the East Shuwert valley situated close to the Shimshal pass in September and made the first ascent of 6040m on 22 September. North of the Shimshal, a Slovenian team of Tomaž Goslar, Mojca Švajger and Irena Mrak visited the Koksil valley where they made the first ascent of various 5,000m peaks and noted a lot of potential for further exploration. They had originally intended to climb in the Hindu Kush but were denied permits due to security issues; it seems as if no expeditions visited the Hindu Kush in 2018.

Hispar

In the Hispar region, other than Hansjörg Auer's ascent of Lupghar Sar West, there was an expedition by Canadian Raphael Slawinski and Alik Berg to the unclimbed Pumari Chhish East (6850m). After acclimatising they attempted the south face of Pumari Chhish East but returned due to dangerous conditions. After that they investigated the east face but this was threatened by seracs. They then switched their attention to Gus Zrakun Sar (5980m). Climbing over Emily Peak (5936m), they bivvied, then next day made a 16-hour return trip to the summit of Gus Zrakun Sar. This was the first ascent of this peak.

Hindu Raj

In June a Dutch expedition made up of Ruud Rotte, Danny Schoch, Menno Schokker and Bas Visscher visited the Thui and Ghamobar groups in the Hindu Raj. After acclimatising they attempted the north-east ridge of Kachqiant (5990m) but retreated from 5,450m after heavy snow. Schokker and Rotte then attempted the south-east ridge of Ghaintar Chhish (6273m) but retreated from 5,800m after experiencing avalanches and very poor rock. Schoch and Visscher then made a second attempt on the north-east ridge of Kachqiant and summited on 1 July, climbing the route in three very long days from base camp.

Thanks to Tom Livingstone and Hansjörg Auer.

JIM GREGSON

Greenland 2013-18

Mark Robson climbing *Silence is Golden* (TD), Tower of Silence (730m).
(Simon Richardson)

For alpinists with an interest in the Arctic, the 40-year archive of Area
Notes for Greenland, so assiduously compiled for us all by Derek Ford-
ham, has been essential reading and research. Since Derek laid aside his
pen in 2009, sources of information available to devotees of the north have
changed. We can still look to the records of the Mount Everest Foundation
and the Gino Watkins Memorial Fund (GWMF) for where they bestow
their valuable grant assistance, and in a similar vein the Arctic Club and the
Scottish Arctic Club. The Alpine Club has also supported members ven-
turing to Greenland locations, myself included and the *Alpine Journal* has
carried articles and reports from Greenland expeditions: so far so good for
teams originating in the UK.

Above: Mark Robson climbing the north spur (D) Dwarf One (870m). *(Simon Richardson)*

Right: Mark Robson descending the east ridge of Castle Peak (780m). *(Simon Richardson)*

For information on expeditions from other nations, fuller coverage has become available in the pages of, in particular, the *American Alpine Journal* and its excellent online adjunct, the searchable *http://publications.american-alpineclub.org*, perhaps the most reliable source of Greenland mountaineering information in the age of the internet, and especially valuable since the Danish Polar Centre records and functions were devolved to the Greenland authorities in Nuuk from 2010.

As a sometime beneficiary of MEF and GWMF grant support for some of my own Greenland trips I have been looking back over the years since the *AJ* carried the last of Derek's Area Notes. Since 2009 there seems to have been a falling-off with fewer than ten British groups receiving grant aid for Greenland and just a few more being supported by the GWMF. My own most recent expedition in early 2018 got support from both the MEF and GWMF, as well as the Austrian Alpine Club. I recall receiving news of the award from GWMF with an accompanying comment that 'the panel recognised the strength of your team but regretted that it did not include younger mountaineers who might have benefitted from the opportunity to learn from such experienced expeditioners.' I had tried hard to recruit such but none applied.

My expedition article in *AJ* 2016 commented on the increasing costs of mounting a Greenland expedition. A comparison between my first trip in 1991 and 2018 shows per capita costs doubled. Even though it was possible in 2018 to fly the first leg of the journey, from the UK to Iceland, for less than £30 courtesy of easyJet, after that the zeros kept coming, until a six-person group had to meet total expenditure exceeding £46,000. For young people finding a full share of this sort of sum is in itself a mountain to climb. However, while not discounting the escalating costs of insurance, if you really want to go, a way can be found.

Keeping a watchful eye on Greenland adventuring, it seems there is less interest now in heading for the many Greenland areas where hundreds if not thousands of striking alpine peaks can be found, and as the number of expeditions diminishes, the sort of areas I prefer, with high and wide glaciers and exciting alpine peaks, preferably with the opportunity for first ascents, are being overlooked in favour of different sorts of objectives.

Since 2009 there has been a definite swing of interest towards areas in Greenland with high-standard rock climbing. At the same time there has also been an increase in the number of trips where access has been by sailing boat or sea kayak, or both, as there are many places where impressive and impos-

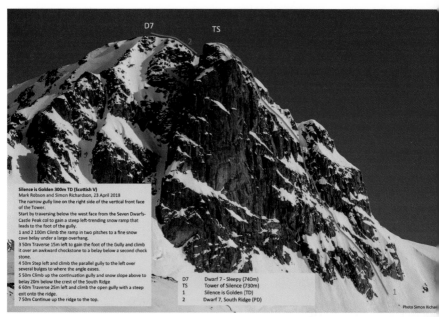

Silence is Golden 300m TD (Scottish V)
Mark Robson and Simon Richardson, 23 April 2018
The narrow gully line on the right side of the vertical front face
of the Tower.
Start by traversing below the west face from the Seven Dwarfs-
Castle Peak col to gain a steep left-trending snow ramp that
leads to the foot of the gully.
1 and 2 100m Climb the ramp in two pitches to a fine snow
cave belay under a large overhang.
3 50m Traverse 15m left to gain the foot of the Gully and climb
it over an awkward chockstone to a belay below a second chock
stone.
4 50m Step left and climb the parallel gully to the left over
several bulges to where the angle eases.
5 50m Climb up the continuation gully and snow slope above to
belay 20m below the crest of the South Ridge
6 60m Traverse 25m left and climb the open gully with a steep
exit onto the ridge.
7 50m Continue up the ridge to the top.

D7	Dwarf 7 - Sleepy (740m)
TS	Tower of Silence (730m)
1	Silence is Golden (TD)
2	Dwarf 7, South Ridge (PD)

Photo Simon Richar

Tower of Silence. *(Simon Richardson)*

ing sea cliffs abound, particularly in the south and along parts of the west coast. Chartering ski-equipped aircraft for glacier and icecap landing has become very expensive and consequently been avoided; this will likely mean many areas will not get the same levels of attention as was once the case.

Among the sailors, the Rev Bob Shepton has continued to gather crews of climbers to push this exciting and demanding branch of mountaineering. Under Bob's pilotage the exploits of the Belgian-US 'Wild Bunch' in 2014, and again in 2015, with a deviation across to Baffin Island, a group of lap-top-using South Africans dubbed the 'Nerdy Bunch', and the British 'Mild Bunch' all benefitted from Bob's keen eye for promising cliff terrain, mostly along the west coast of Greenland.

Other sailing-and-climbing groups have been active in the south. Renowned French ocean-going skipper Isabelle Autissier took a Franco-Belgian team to the Cape Farewell region in 2016, where significant first ascents were made on the Thumbnail and Igdlorssuit Tower. Earlier, in 2014, the two-man team of Ralph Villiger from Switzerland and the Austrian Harald Fichtinger sailed to the east coast of Liverpool Land where they made a difficult first ascent of Kirken, a twin-topped spire first noticed by the whaler William Scoresby Jr in the 1820s. The west coast areas of Uummannaq and Upernavik fjords also provided good rock sport for Polish climbers in 2017 after an earlier trip by an Oxford University group who found some big walls there.

Mountaineers who turned themselves into sea kayakers and then worked very hard for their climbs have included in 2014 Olly Sanders (UK) in the

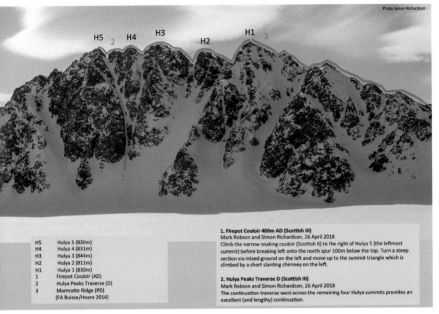

H5   Hulya 5 (830m)
H4   Hulya 4 (831m)
H3   Hulya 3 (844m)
H2   Hulya 2 (811m)
H1   Hulya 1 (830m)
1   Firepot Couloir (AD)
2   Hulya Peaks Traverse (D)
3   Marmotte Ridge (PD)
      (FA Buisse/Hoare 2014)

1. Firepot Couloir 400m AD (Scottish III)
Mark Robson and Simon Richardson, 26 April 2018
Climb the narrow snaking couloir (Scottish II) to the right of Hulya 5 (the leftmost summit) before breaking left onto the north spur 100m below the top. Turn a steep section via mixed ground on the left and move up to the summit triangle which is climbed by a short slanting chimney on the left.

2. Hulya Peaks Traverse D (Scottish III)
Mark Robson and Simon Richardson, 26 April 2018
The continuation traverse west across the remaining four Hulya summits provides an excellent (and lengthy) continuation.

Hulya Peaks. *(Simon Richardson)*

Cape Farewell region, and also in 2014 the Swiss Silvan Schupbach and friends, who paddled to Renland and the stupendous Mirror Wall with a polar bear encounter on the return journey. Undeterred, Schupbach and other friends went in 2016 to paddle even further round Cape Farewell from Nanortalik to get to Apostolen Tommelfinger.

Renland's fabled walls and towers, first brought to the world's attention by Dick Griffiths' West Lancashire Scouts expedition some years ago have gained more suitors of late. Philippe Batoux (F) and friends sailed there in 2015, to attempt a new line on the spire of Griundtvigskirken but then had more success on walls at the head of Skillebugt a short way to the east. Also in 2015, Leo Houlding's UK group climbed and filmed the ascent of *Reflections* on the huge Mirror Wall. The following year, Geoff Hornby and friends made their way to Renland for more new routeing; sadly, Geoff suffered an injury, preventing him from joining the actual climbing.

The better-known and more-visited rock climbing areas in the far south have also continued to attract climbers. During the last five years there have been groups from the USA, Poland, the Basque region, Britain, Slovakia and Argentina. Some of these teams were content trying to free climb existing routes but there were also new climbs made on the Torssuqatoq Spires and the Tasermiut fjord walls.

The intrepid American Mike Libecki, either solo or with friends, has continued his regular visits to Greenland's east coast. He has pioneered new climbs in the Kangertitivatsiaq fjord, north from Tasiilaq; British climbers and an international team that arrived by yacht in 2016 have also been at

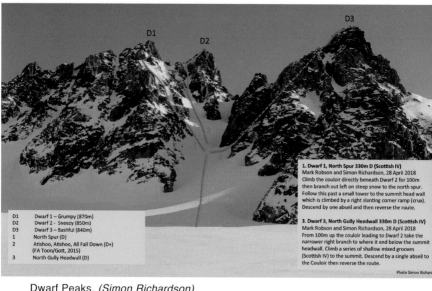

D1
D2
D3

1. **Dwarf 1, North Spur 330m D (Scottish IV)**
Mark Robson and Simon Richardson, 28 April 2018
Climb the couloir directly beneath Dwarf 2 for 100m
then branch out left on steep snow to the north spur.
Follow this past a small tower to the summit head wall
which is climbed by a right slanting corner ramp (crux).
Descend by one abseil and then reverse the route.

3. **Dwarf 3, North Gully Headwall 330m D (Scottish IV)**
Mark Robson and Simon Richardson, 28 April 2018
From 100m up the couloir leading to Dwarf 2 take the
narrower right branch to where it end below the summit
headwall. Climb a series of shallow mixed grooves
(Scottish IV) to the summit. Descend by a single abseil to
the Couloir then reverse the route.

D1	Dwarf 1 – Grumpy (870m)	
D2	Dwarf 2 - Sneezy (850m)	
D3	Dwarf 3 – Bashful (840m)	
1	North Spur (D)	
2	Atishoo, Atishoo, All Fall Down (D+)	
	(FA Toon/Gott, 2015)	
3	North Gully Headwall (D)	

Photo Simon Richardson

Dwarf Peaks. *(Simon Richardson)*

work here. The Fox Jaw cirque, close to Kummiut, also had visitors in 2014, following Libecki's initial forays there many years ago.

Libecki himself has been busy, shifting his attention much further south on Greenland's east coast, which has required a number of long seaborne approaches of up to 500km from Tasiilaq to access very impressive rock walls and towers, particularly in Inugsuarmiut fjord. Thus far he has had these areas to himself.

Recently, in 2017 and 2018, one or two small British groups have accessed the Roslin and Bjørnbo glaciers in the Stauning Alper, making a few new climbs. Once very popular, the Staunings summertime access is complex and unreliable due to changes wrought by climate change. In wintertime and spring, avalanche conditions can be severe in this region. This far north in Greenland, assistance with logistics can benefit from the services of the very experienced and well-established Tangent Expeditions International, a company owned and operated by Paul Walker (UK) which has a growing base at the airstrip of Constable Pynt (Nerlerit Inaat), the most usual point of entry to east Greenland now.

Tangent's client base has diversified in recent years, and it's a good choice for independent groups needing logistical support. My own privately organised expedition groups operating in North Liverpool Land (2014, 2015 and 2018) have used Tangent's snowmobile and advance freighting services to reach the northern icecap and glaciers for further exploration and numerous first ascents.

The team of experienced mountaineers who accompanied me in 2018 was successful, making a number of first ascents despite experiencing some severe and testing storm conditions during April and early May. The full report for this expedition, holding maps, photographs and topos can be found at *https://www.arcticclub.org.uk/assets/documents/mef-final-report*. Although our group had experience from spectacular locations around the world, their reactions and impressions of the High Arctic and its weather, climbing conditions, and the presence of polar bears provided me with some amusement, but their companionship made the trip memorable.

Despite the ever-increasing costs of going there, Greenland still exerts a magnetic pull for the adventurous mountaineer and explorer. It remains one of the largest reservoirs of unexplored and unclimbed peaks on the planet. Despite climate change galloping apace throughout the Arctic it is still a fantastic region to visit so long as it is treated with respect and care. To date I have been fortunate to make 18 expeditions to Greenland and dream of trying to get to 20 at least.

Further reading
More information on the areas and expeditions mentioned can be found in recent issues of the Alpine Journal and the American Alpine Journal. See also the websites *www.climbgreenland.com* and *www.arcticclub.org.uk*.

J Gregson, *Exploring Greenland: Twenty years of Adventure Mountaineering in the Great Arctic Wilderness*, Vertebrate Publishing, 2012.

B Shepton, *Addicted to Adventure: Between Rocks and Cold Places*, Adlard Coles Nautical, 2014.

Argentina & Peru

On the lower slopes of Cerro Overo on the epic traverse
of the Famatina Range.

Once again, Argentina experienced a high devaluation of its currency, in the order of a hundred per cent, so it's become much cheaper for foreigners. There are also new low-cost flights and better access to the mountains, most of them awaiting a first ascent or a new route. Unusually, many of these flights do not require travellers to go through the capital Buenos Aires. These direct routes between Argentine cities are consequently less expensive and quicker. The weather has been good and on Aconcagua, Argentina's most visited mountain, there was a very good season with no deaths: this was the first season with no fatalities for 29 years. All ascents are from the 2018 season except where stated.

Chañi Massif, Jujuy

An Argentine-French team hiked to the old military refuge at 4,700m at the base of Chañi Chico during the first half of November with help from locals with donkeys, trekking through ancient abandoned villages on sections of the Inca trail. They climbed a number of walls. The Argentines Martin Molina and Martin López Abad and Maud Vanpoulle of France climbed a distinct needle south-east of Mount Von Rosen, which they thought virgin

On the Cuesta del Tocino on the first part of the Famatina traverse.

but afterwards appeared to have been climbed already by Martín Altamirano and Martín Castillo. The group made a variation on the upper section. The route was 500m, 6c on the last section and named *Bebé Cóndor Vuela* for the condors that live there.

Maud reported that, 'Our next objective was the south pillar of the Chañi Chico (5571m) itself, which we had came for and appears to be the most sustained wall in the area in terms of steepness and length. The cracks and sections unfold perfectly to let us gain height and headache, pitch after pitch. The rock is splendid and we did not even need a piton, all of it mostly very solid, apart from the top section. The summit lets us a see an infinite view of the desert to the north and the way down could not be easier with a walk off and one abseil.'

The route turned out to be 600m, 7a and was named *Coca, Hypoxia y Carnavalito* (coca leaves, hypoxia and northern carnival) for the culture of the north of Argentina. The next day another party of our group comprising Argentines Carlos Torino, Ignacio Karlen and Pepe de la Cuesta also opened a route, slightly to the left of their line up to 6c. Before the bad weather, Maud teamed with Martin López Abad and opened two short lines of aprox 130 meters next to the refuge grading both up to 6b. The place appears to have a lot of potential for route opening of medium length, on good granite, mostly on traditional gear, and also for more technical lines with mixed equipment.

Chaschuil-Pillahuasi, Catamarca

During 2019 Marcelo Scanu explored the ranges of the Río Pillahuasi near Chaschuil. There are many summits and entire ranges without ascents.

Chicho Francia nearing the top of the first pitch on the east face of Vallecitos. *(Matías Hidalgo Nicosia)*

Chicho leading the start of the steep second pitch. *(Chicho Fracchia)*

The line of Divina Providencia on Vallecitos (5435m).

On 24 February, Scanu made the first ascent of Bayo (4274m) after a long walk in with Andrés Zapata via the east face. They saw a lot of wildlife, especially guanacos, vicuñas and condors and during his climb Scanu was attacked by a bad tempered hawk. On 19 April Maxi Ortigoza and Scanu teamed up to climb Bayo's range south summit called Cumbre Carrizo (4160m) by its east face, a peak that was also unclimbed. It's worth noting that it wasn't long ago that locals were still living in caves on the Río Pilla-huasi. Today nobody lives here all year round. This region has the highest volcanoes, active and extinct, in the world, with Ojos del Salado to the north.

Famatina Range, La Rioja

Argentines Griselda Moreno (leader), Ramiro García, Paula Miranda and Lelo Saldaña made the first traverse of all the summits of Nevado de Fama-tina. This traverse was attempted five times in the 1990s without success. The traverse was more interesting because it was done in the southern hemi-sphere winter. The ascents were finished on 28 August after nine days and seven summits. Summits ascended: Cerro Negro Overo (5778m), Cerro 'Pradbhupada' (5842m), Cerro Nevado de Famatina (5821m), Cerro Overo (5930m), Cerro La Mejicana (6094m), Cerro El Gran Riojano (6090m) and Cerro General Belgrano (6122m). They departed from Puesto de las Tres Piedras and finished in the ancient gold and silver mine of La Mejicana. Their camps were: 20 August, Puesto de las Tres Piedras (3200m), 21 August, Cuesta del Tocino (3650m), 22 August, Ridge (4540m), 23 August, Ridge (4820m), 24 August, Leños Ridge (5215m), 25 August Archaeological Ridge (5600m), 26 August, Pradbhupada plateau 5840m, 27 August Highest Summits plateau (6070) and 28 August, La Mejicana mine. High winds destroyed a tent and they passed ancient Inca logs near Negro Overo and Inca ruins at Negro Overo's summit, a sacred mountain where deer-horn offerings were found several decades ago.

Cerro Vallecitos, Cordón del Plata

The area of Vallecitos in Mendoza is a training area with peaks ascended by many climbers each year. It's a good place to climb before going to Aconcagua. Cerro Vallecitos (5435m) is one of the highest and most climbed in the Cordón del Plata. Its first ascent dates back to 8 January 1946. The first team consisted in well known Francisco Ibañez, Ricardo López and Luis Vila.

During September 2016, Matías Hidalgo Nicosia, Agustín Piccolo and Diego Cofone opened a line on the east face of Vallecitos. They named it *Divina Providencia* (1200m, 70°, WI2, D+). They made fast progress up their long route from their base at 4,200m.

Matías Hidalgo Nicosia teamed up with Chicho Fracchia and Matías Sindoni during October 2017 and opened a route on the south face of Valle-citos calling it *Cascadas del Viento* (600m, WI5, MD). This line starts with the crux: two ice pitches some 100m. The second pitch has a 15m section of 90° and another of 95°. After this steep part the difficulties are lower;

Matías Sindoni and Chicho Fracchia just below before the summit ridge on the south face of Vallecitos. *(Matías Hidalgo)*

Climbing the east face on the first ascent of Copla Blanca (4630m) in the Río Tupungato. Although straightforward at PD, the mountains are remote.

they ascended snow gullies up to the summit ridge. They started from a base camp at El Salto (4200m) with two aborted attempts because of high winds. They finally ran out of food because of this with only oatmeal left to eat. Both routes were climbed in the day, with an estimated eight to nine hours to the summit.

Río Tupungato, Mendoza

From 13 to 21 October Ramiro Casas and Glauco Muratti crossed the Tupungato river and hiked up am unnamed creek immediately south-east of Punta de Vacas. First they climbed a peak they named Cerro El Escampe (4570m), at 32°55'36"S 69°38'54"W. The mountain is west of two big cols that link the unnamed creek with Quebrada Colorada. They climbed in snowy conditions, during the second day the weather was bad with easy rotten rock and 50° snow. The two started on the south-west face and then followed the south-south-east ridge before finishing on the upper east face.

The Copla Blanca (4630m), 32°55'11"S 69°42'37"W, is the highest summit in the ridge that separates the unnamed creek and the Quebrada Negra. The route was established on its north-east face up 55° snow slopes and some grade II rotten rock. Because of conditions, they couldn't use crampons or belays. Both these peaks were climbed for the first time.

PERU

Rajuntay

The Cordillera de la Viuda is a very interesting place for exploration and climbing. Next to Lima, it has many 5,000m peaks with moderate ground. The highest summit is Rajuntay (5477m), a beautiful technical mountain.

On 1 May, the French-Peruvian Steve Meder and his Peruvian porters Antonio and Jorge Chinchay climbed a quebrada in the slopes of Nevado Uco, where the Rímac river emerges to camp at 4,930m below the north-east face of Rajuntay. This face was still unclimbed; an attempt the previous year was aborted in bad weather. The next day, with doubtful weather Meder started early, climbing an easy five-metre vertical rock and ice step using crampons and leaving a peg for the descent. He continued up steep terrain with rocks towards the beginning of the snow, the crux. Climbing a 45° snow gully, he made a traverse to a similar gully with a 50° step to a short ridge and from there reached the summit in bad weather. This route was much easier than his previous climb on the more technical west ridge.

On 3 May he attempted an unclimbed summit on the north ridge, a fore-summit of Rajuntay called Pequeño Rajuntay (Little Rajuntay). He climbed a gully of hard ice up to 60°, having seen the route from a previous ascent of Nevado Uco. He protected himself with a 60m rope and reached the north ridge at 5,350m. He continued 20m more (M3). He thought he was standing on the summit but afterwards, studying photos, he realised that the neighbouring top was his objective. He plans to attempt it again up a line of 70° ice and steep loose rock.

The new route on the north-east face of Rajuntay (5477m). *(Steve Meder)*

The north summit of Pico Norte or Rajuntay Norte (c5400m) was one of the last unclimbed peaks of the range. Steve Meder was joined once more by Antonio and Jorge Chinchay. They trekked the Quebrada Uco in a snowstorm, putting base camp at 4,835m on the north-east face of the mountain. Next day he scouted the route and snow conditions of the north-east gully and reached the north ridge. On 6 June he started up alone at 5am, roped-solo, reaching the summit four and a half hours later. The route was 350m, 70°, M3.

Nevado Huayllaco, Cordillera Blanca

Huayllaco (5460m) was first climbed in 1963 by the Brazilian of Italian origin Domingo Giobbi and the Peruvian brothers Eugenio and Macario Angeles. Giobbi was very active in those years in the Cordilera Blanca and surrounding mountains. Huayllaco, located on the south section of the Cordillera Blanca, was very little visited. The first ascent via the south-east ridge route was likely the only route opened for decades.

Argentine Julieta Ferreri and Brazilian Marcelo Motta Delvaux opened a new route during winter 2018, reaching the summit summit on 25 July. They approached the mountain by the Quebrada Huayllaco camping on Laguna Verdecocha (Green Lake) at 4,650m. From there they took the south-west glacier that leads to the col between Huayllaco and Nevado Raria (5576m). Just before the col, they switched right heading to the south-south-east face of Huayllaco, a beautiful face that finishes at the south-east ridge. The route goes directly up the face, at D 60°-70°. Near the summit they reached a rocky section to the left and stopped there, 10m short of the ridge, because of powder snow and dangerous ice cornices with no belays. On June the

View from the north peak towards the summit of Rajuntay. *(Steve Meder)*

same climbers had ascended Raria by the *Giobbi* route but they started from Verdecocha camp and not as *Giobbi* from an advanced camp at 5,150m.

Nevado Tacusiri, Cordillera Vilcanota

On 6 June 2018 a group including Argentine Nehuén Conterno and Peruvians Jorge Sirva and Rodrigo Mendoza departed Pitumarca (3600m), 80km south of Cusco, drove 30km to Alkatauri and then trekked for an hour and a half to the base of Tacusiri (5400m). They took the left couloir on Tacusiri`s south face, climbing eight pitches with a lot of powder snow, some ice and poor rock. They reached the summit ridge rating their route D+ with mixed terrain up to M5. They didn't continue to the summit because of the late hour Unable to rappel the south face, they descended the west face by two 60m abalakov rappels, thence to the north glacier and to the end of the difficulties. They did the round-trip in a nonstop 18 hours and named their route *Expreso de Medianoche* (Midnight Express). They will attempt to finish the route with better weather.

Mount Everest Foundation Expedition Reports

SUMMARISED BY JONNY DRY

The Mount Everest Foundation (*www.mef.org.uk*) was established as a registered charity following the successful ascent of Everest in 1953. It was initially financed using the surplus funds and subsequent royalties from that expedition. It provides financial support for expeditions of an exploratory nature in mountain areas, and is administered by trustees appointed by the Alpine Club and the Royal Geographical Society.

The exploration is mainly of a geographical nature but may also cover disciplines such as geology, botany, zoology, glaciology and medical research. In return for funding the MEF requires only a comprehensive report, and copies of these reports are lodged with the AC and the RGS. The reports can be consulted at these establishments or alternatively online.

The MEF has made total grants of well over £1m to more than 1,600 expeditions with members from the UK and New Zealand. Donations to allow us to continue this work are always welcome. We particularly encourage donations from former beneficiaries of MEF grants.

In 2018 we supported 25 expeditions with grants totalling £70,000. The following notes summarise the reports from these expeditions.

ARCTIC

Greenland North Liverpool Land Expedition – Simon Richardson, James Gregson, Sandra Gregson, Ingrid Baber, Mark Robson and Ron Kenyon (April/May 2018).
In a prolific expedition the team climbed eight new routes and summited 11 new peaks from the Neild Bugt glacier. They found conditions to initially be far colder and under greater snowfall than when they were previously there in 2015. Nonetheless they set about a number of routes on Høngbjerg, Kuldefjeld, and Longridge Peak as well as summits in the Hulya and Seven Dwarfs groups. Their attention then turned to what potential objectives might lie further afield, and struck out on skis. They found a promising number of peaks offering excellent future exploration and discovered significant retreat of the glacier. Returning to camp, the largely excellent weather turned, nearly burying two base camp tents and ultimately heralding the end of the trip. MEF ref 18-14.

Moskus Expedition – Matthew Hay and Louis Chartres (April/May 2018).
The dual aims for this expedition were first ascents of two unclimbed peaks and conducting climate change research on the Roslin glacier. Over 10 days they made the initial approach of 150km from Constable Point to Gurre-

holm Dal. Once established in the area they made two successful ascents and a further two attempts, which were thwarted by a high risk of avalanche. They concluded their expedition after being prevented from doing any further scientific work by storms that kept them in their tent for four days. Despite this they managed a little analysis on Aries glacier close to Karabiner Fjell. This involved photographing the glacier and assessing snowpack level, which was found to be much deeper than that found by previous expeditions in 2017. MEF ref 18-23.

Wegener Halvø Peninsula – Gina Moseley, Robbie Shone, Chris Blakeley, Dario Schwoerer, Sabine Schwoerer, Salina Schwoerer, Andri Schwoerer, Noe Schwoerer, Alegra Schwoerer, Mia Schwoerer, Vital Schwoerer and Mirjam Bruhwiler (July/August 2018).
While the caves on Wegener Halvø peninsula have been known about for some time, little is known about their make up. The team aimed to fill this gap by undertaking exploration and sedimentary and mineral data collection in order to model the caves' changing environment and compare these findings with the wider region. Facing difficult access across steep snow and scree to reach the potential leads they had identified, they instead conducted preliminary assessments of each using a drone. At the first site they discovered the first cave was in actual fact a shelter, while they couldn't locate the second of the leads. Next day they assessed a second site, which was found to be only a shallow cave and did not contain any worthwhile deposits for assessment. With their exploration of both sites completed they returned to Constable Point by helicopter. MEF ref 18-33.

NORTH AMERICA

British Yukon Spring Expedition – Jonathan Wakefield and Glenn Wilks (May 2018).
After previously attempting to access the area around Mount Upton in 2011 and 2014, the team successfully reached the Kluane icefield in 2018 to attempt a number of first ascents. After a day exploring the glacier further, they made their first summit via a long 3,000ft couloir with a grade of Scottish II. Intermittent storms and fine weather over the following days saw them cycle between being tent-bound and ticking off further gullies close to base camp. Two attempts on a further ridgeline were unsuccessful but they made a successful ascent of another peak via a ridge and snowslope traverse to gain the top of a hanging glacier. The area has huge potential for exploration still, with first ascents and repeat ascents still available. MEF ref 18-06.

British Revelations Expedition – Tom Livingstone and Uisdean Hawthorn (March/April 2018).
Using information from Ben Silvestre and Pete Graham, the team planned exploratory attempts on Mount Jezebel's north face and Mount Mausolus.

After diverting due to poor weather, which prevented them from assessing Mount Mausolus, they set up on the Fish glacier to focus solely on Mount Jezebel. They began with an attempt on the N face of Mount Jezebel that ended at an un-climbable chimney section at about half height on the face. Here the snow became powdery with little means of bypassing it or tunnelling through. Equally the top of the deep chimney was capped by a large snow mushroom and given the poor diorite rock they decided to retreat. After a couple of days' rest they turned their attention to Jezebel's E face where they made a first ascent involving technical climbing on fine névé and rock, and in good weather. Returning to camp they found the weather to be turning and with little time left they requested a pick-up.   MEF ref 18-09.

Supraglacial Rock Avalanches – William Smith, Stuart Dunning and Richard Smith (June – July 2018).
As research for William Smith's PhD, the team travelled to Alaska to investigate further how melt-water created during debris deposition onto glaciers affects the glacier's biogeochemistry. The expedition aimed to gather data from fresh debris areas before undertaking laboratory analysis back in the UK. They were dropped initially on the Brady icefield because of better snow conditions for the aircraft and gathered samples from the entire width of the icefield. Despite having a short 10-day window, the expedition was blessed with good weather for five of those days, giving them a chance to gather all the data needed: 20 sediment samples, two water samples, 12 snow samples and 10 clasts. Laboratory analysis is being done in the first quarter 0f 2019. The team noted that relatively little is understood about the Brady icefield and that investigation into the changeable nature of the snowpack could prove an invaluable piece of research, as well as melt-rate research to quantify mass balance and discharge estimates. MEF ref 18-22

SOUTH AMERICA

Avellano Valley – Freja Shannon, Michelle O'Loughlin, Sasha Doyle (January 2018).
Recipients of both the Julie Tullis and Alison Chadwick awards, this team of three women travelled to the Avellano valley in northern Patagonia where they hoped to establish a new line on the Avenali Tower. After overcoming flooded rivers on their approach to base camp from Bahia Murta, the team made an HVS ascent of Aonikenk Peak and an E2 line on Avenali Tower. They went on to attempt a further route on a peak close to Aonikenk but were turned back low on route due to inclement weather. The team notes that while some of the main towers have unclimbed routes available, it is likely they will prove difficult to protect. That said there are still a number of outlying smaller peaks still unclimbed, whilst the east face of the Avenali Tower could still provide real potential.   MEF ref 18-03

PAKISTAN

Broad Peak Expedition – Sandy Allan, Rick Allen, Kacper Tekieli and Stanislav Vrba (June/July 2018).
Following a nine-day approach, the team aimed to complete one of their two expedition objectives: either a new unclimbed line on the steep and technical SW face of the central summit, or an attempt on the unclimbed S ridge. They initially set out to acclimatise on the normal route in unsettled weather and reached camp three at 6,900m. Given the poor weather Sandy Allan decided to retreat whilst Rick Allen decided to push ahead for the summit. After successfully reaching the summit Rick descended, disappearing from view and failing to reappear to the team below. Fearing an accident, the team mobilised a rescue operation, including use of a drone, which located Rick at around 7,300m; he had apparently fallen during the descent. Using the drone as guidance Dan Mazur and accompanying Sherpas located and brought Rick down to base camp. Given Rick's injuries the expedition was halted and Rick flown to hospital. Tekieli and Vrba went on to attempt a shorter line in the following days but were turned around after Stanislav sustained a leg injury during rock fall. MEF ref 18-05

Ultar Expedition – Bruce Normand, Tim Miller and Christian Huber (May/June 2018).
Arriving in late May, the team began by acclimatising on Muchuar glacier and Batokshi peak during the first ten days. Their main objective was to make the first ascent of the SE pillar route on Ultar, which they attempted after awaiting a weather window in base camp for 10 days. In further bad weather they began the route, reaching camp two at 5,900m. Heavy snow continued in the following days, and the team was caught in an avalanche that struck their tent. This sadly resulted in the death of Christian Huber and the team's evacuation by helicopter. MEF ref 18-25

Shuwert Expedition – Peter Thompson and Philip De-Beger (September/ October 2018).
This two person expedition had the primary objective of making a first ascent of any 6,000m peaks around the East Shuwert glacier. They set their initial base camp at the foot of the glacier after approaching from Shuijer-ab and Shuwert villages. ABC was then established at 5,300m from where they then pushed on to reach the summit of 6040m, which they named Banafsheh Sar at the suggestion of their guide. Conditions were generally favourable despite a reasonably high amount of unconsolidated snow. Whilst no permits are required for peaks under 6,500m, they note the need for teams to acquire a new 'No Objection Certificate', which grants permission to climb in the Shimshal region. These are easily available from the assistant commissioner's office in Aliabad provided teams have a guide attached to the expedition. MEF ref 18-32

INDIA

British Kishtwar Expedition – Tom Livingstone, Will Sim and Uisdean Hawthorn (September/October 2018).
The team planned on climbing Barnaj I or II and note a couple of potential lines. After flying in to Leh and arriving at Hagshu base camp however, unseasonably heavy snow led to the team becoming stuck at base camp for their whole three weeks. With their original plan out of the question, an attempt was made on Chiring (6300m) but they only got as far as its foot before having to turn back.   MEF ref 18-07

British Janhukot Expedition – Malcolm Bass, Paul Figg, Guy Buckingham and Hamish Frost (May/June 2018).
Drawing on the previous experience Bass had on the peak, the team's objective was to make a first ascent of Janhukot (6805m) which had first been written about as far back as 1938. After acclimatising on Kedar Dome (6940m) they rested three days waiting for good weather before setting off on 1 June. Progress both onto and across the moraine was slow but improved once on the glacier, and the team set ABC at the confluence of the Gangotri and Maindani glaciers. Their first day on route found climbing of no harder than Scottish IV, with a final short abseil bringing them to the first bivy site. The next day required extensive pitched climbing and progress was slow to their eventual bivy site on a small ledge. With the weather beginning to close in on their third day a secure bivy was found in a palatial scoop; here they sat out the worst of the weather. They summited later that day in wet conditions and descended to ABC the following day.   MEF ref 18-16B

Anglo-New Zealand Kishtwar Expedition – Timothy Elson and Richard Measures (September/October 2018).
The team set themselves two potential objectives of the N spur of Flat Top (6100m) and SW face of Kishtwar Eiger (6000m). After setting base camp at Sattarchin they acclimatised to 5,100m as far as the col of Flat Top. Descending to base camp and a couple of days' rest they struck out for the summit at the beginning of October. The climbing was up to Scottish VI but they had to retreat at 5,300m due to deep snow and increasingly heavy falls. They turned instead to Flat Top's E ridge up which they gained a slightly higher height of 5,400m before their short weather window came to an end and they were forced down. Following three rest days in camp they switched peaks and found excellent climbing on the S face of Kishtwar Eiger. Their summit attempt on the second day failed at what they believe to be 300m short of the top, where they were forced back by increasingly heavy snowfall.   MEF ref 18-19

Chiling II North Face Expedition – Alex Mathie and Matthew Harle (June – July 2018).
The team had the single aim of climbing Chiling II's unclimbed N face.

After a two-day car journey from Leh and a further day accessing ABC, they made an early reconnaissance and acclimatisation trip to the 5,200m plateau between Chiling I and II. They spent two days shuttling and resting between BC and ABC before making a second acclimatisation attempt on Lalung III, bivouacking at the foot of the mountain's E buttress. After a second day's climbing up to 5,600m and a further bivouac, the weather turned and forced retreat. The next two days saw them rest at base camp before striking out for Chiling II's N face on 19 June. Initially the weather looked uncertain but appeared to hold, and the team successfully negoti-ated the lower sections before the being forced to retreat after heavy snow that had settled on the face began to fall as the day warmed. They looked to make a second attempt the following day but the arrival of a significant weather system forced them to end the expedition and return to the road-head. They believe the more stable weather found in September would make a successful attempt more likely but that access could be difficult as previous expeditions have found.   MEF ref 18-21

British Nanda Devi East Expedition – Dave Sharpe and John Crook (September/November 2018).
The objective was to make the first ascent of the NE ridge of Nanda Devi East previously attempted in 2015 by Martin Moran and Mark Thomas. With Dave Sharpe already in India, they arranged to meet at base camp on 5 October, prior to which John Crook made a likely fourth ascent of Nanda Lapak with Sandeep Panwar. The two then continued to acclimatise on Changuch and Nanda Kot but encountered poor snow conditions and were forced to retreat from 5,400m. They then turned to Nanda Devi, where their attempt on the NE ridge began positively. They bivouacked at 5,350m and again at 6,150m. Here they were trapped for three nights in heavy snowfall. This left much of the route impossible to protect and blanketed in unstable and un-surmountable snow and forced a retreat to base camp.
                                                                    MEF ref 18-24

NEPAL

Dye-tracing on Khumbu Glacier – Aberystwyth University (April/May 2018).
Glacial debris, supra-glacial ponds and bare ice cliffs have all been relatively well studied in relation to melt-water flow on glaciers, less is know about how melt water is transported underneath A glacier. The team, led by Katie Miles, travelled to the Khumbu glacier in order to establish whether en-glacial and/or sub-glacial systems exist in the glacier and the relative effects of each. Using fluorescent dye-tracing – the first time this has been success-fully carried out on a high-elevation debris-covered glacier – the team were able to characterise the subsurface drainage of the glacier, with 11 of their 15 traces coming back with successful results. Preliminary results show that subsurface drainage through Khumbu glacier does exist, and is relatively

slow and inefficient at transporting melt water. Looking ahead the team suggest that such a study could be carried out over a longer timescale to look at pre and post-monsoon flow rates.   MEF ref 18-02

Mulung Tokpo Expedition – Derek Buckle, Drew Cook, Mike Fletcher, Adele Long, Gus Morton & Tony Westcott (August/September 2018).
After establishing base camp at the foot of the Mulung glacier, the team ventured further in search of ABC. Establishing this at 5,085m, they decided to switch from their original M15 objective due to poor snow conditions and lack of a close practical camp. Instead they turned to attempting 5631m by its N face. Derek, Drew, Mike and Adele made the attempt but were turned back 300m from the summit by extreme cold and unconsolidated snow. Meanwhile Gus and Tony made the first ascent of 5557m (PD) by its NW ridge. This was repeated next day by the rest of the team, with Derek and Mike climbing the short mixed NE ridge of the adjacent outcrop to make the first ascent of 5537m. Returning to base camp, the expedition was hit with a severe snow storm which crippled three tents and forced a retreat back down the valley.   MEF ref 18-10

British Takphu Himal Expedition – Julian Freeman-Attwood, Nick Colton, Ed Douglas, Christof Nettekoven and Bruce Normand, (October 2018).
Conditions in Takphu Himal area were unseasonably cold for the post-monsoon season. The team's objective was any unclimbed 6,000er in the group. On arrival at base camp Bruce made a repeat of 6153m at the head of Takphu North glacier. Further ascents included the first ascents of Takphu Himal by the W ridge and Til Kang. The latter was reached in a long and committing approach to a snow basin on the Tibetan border below the W face and climbed by Bruce and Ed. Bruce went on to solo four more peaks, including a repeat of Takphu. Nick and Julian made a successful ascent of 6055m from the south gained by negotiating an unstable boulder slope. The expedition encountered no major problems other than minor cold injuries.
                    MEF ref 18-15.

Glaciological Modeling Khumbu Glacier – Dr Martin Kirkbride, Dr Ann Rowan, Dr Duncan Quincey, Dr Evan Miles, Prof Bryn Hubbard, Josephine Hornsey and Katie Miles (April/May 2018).
The team from University of Dundee travelled to Khumbu to undertake data collection that could support theories of glaciological modelling produced by Dr Rowan. The data they collected included debris sources, transport pathways and melt-out processes as well as collecting rock samples to date lateral moraines. The team were in the region from mid April until the end of May and results from the expedition are currently being produced.
                    MEF ref 18-17

CENTRAL ASIA

At-Bashi Expedition, Kyrgyzstan – Marian Krogh, Nicole Mesman and Gabrielle Degagne (January/February 2018).
The team's primary objective was to ski traverse the central At Bashi range and also hoped to ascend and ski three unnamed 4,000m peaks. They found however that many areas they expected to be covered in snow were bare rock and they were forced further north-west where there had been more extensive snowfall. Over four days the team traversed up into the Kon Iylga, reaching a high point of 3,450m. Visibility was poor and snow conditions encountered were unstable and prone to avalanching. A second attempt to reach higher up the valley to Chon Tör was also unsuccessful due to the extreme cold, with one team member suffering frostbite to both feet. The team decided at this point to retreat and seek medical attention. They note however the vast potential the region could offer for ski mountaineering, despite the uncertain snow conditions that can be found from year to year.
MEF ref 18-01

British Minya Konka Expedition – Paul Ramsden and Nick Bullock (September/October 2018).
The team aimed to make an ascent of the impressive central line on Minya Konka's S face in the Daxue range. After waiting and acclimatising for almost a month in base camp they made an attempt on 16 October but were turned back three days later. Whilst they failed to get above 5,800m due to high snowfall, they found the buttress on the south face to be one of the very best unclimbed lines in China. The approach is long and hazardous given that two separate icefalls need to be navigated but a potential expedition could be well rewarded.
MEF ref 18-12

Derjchy Glacier Expedition – David Bird, German Dector-Vega, Charley Hinds, Dante Makin, Dave Milner, Amelia Powys, Isobel Stoddart and Luke Travis (July 2018).
The team had the main objective of exploring 4,000m peaks around the Derjchy valley in Kyrgyzstan. Approaching from Bokonbaevo by truck, the team established base camp at 3,000m with the help of local nomads. Weather was unsettled and temperatures unexpectedly high with much of the glacier and snow cover in a poor and dangerous state. Two groups left camp on 16 July with objectives on 4,500m peaks at the head of the valley. Both parties were turned around, encountering poor snow and loose rock. Upon returning to ABC, and with poor weather forecast, they decided to descend to base camp and request a pick-up.
MEF ref 18-27

Belgorka Valley – Samuel Gillan, Alex Hyde, Tom Drysdale, Louise Reddy and Calum Sowden (June/August 2018).
Alongside investigating the effects of climate change on the Fedorovich glacier in Kyrgyzstan, the team wanted to provide educational training in

first aid, photography and glacial research. Snow and ice melt measurements were taken as well as meteorological data and an assessment of glacial outwash. They also mapped the glacier's drift using prominent landforms such as moraines, trim-lines and eskers to track its movement. Data gathered should enable a reconstruction to be completed, in turn allowing the rate of glacial retreat to be calculated. The team initially approached from Bishkek and spent over 20 days gathering their data as well as an ascent of Shirokaya. The second educational part of their expedition involved students joining the team from the American University of Central Asia. After getting them established in camp the expedition members led a number of activities on expedition craft and took students on guided hikes and glacier walks. The expedition returned to Bishkek at the end of July.

MEF ref 18-28

Reviews

Valley of Lauterbrunnen
John Ruskin, undated
Watercolour, bodycolour, brown ink over pencil.
19.4cm x 25.4cm. Bequest of George D Pratt, 1935,
courtesy of Metropolitan Museum of Art, New York.

Reviews

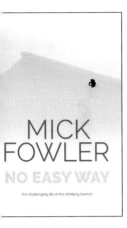

No Easy Way
Mick Fowler
Vertebrate Publishing, 2018, pp272, £24

Mick Fowler's mountaineering accomplishments are bordering on phenomenal. Over the past four decades, he has become one of the most important and influential alpinists in the world. Now into his sixties, he still plans at least one trip to the greater ranges each year. *No Easy Way* covers 11 of these climbs in the past two decades. Almost all are successful, including three Piolets d'Or winners, but he adds a few brilliant failures and exciting near-misses just to prove that getting to the top is not quite everything.

The title, however, covers much more than mere climbing. This partial autobiography also reveals new aspects of Fowler's life: his work as a senior taxman for Her Majesty's Government, his time as president of the Alpine Club, his passion for fell running and, most poignantly, his recent battles with cancer. The conclusion of the first chapter, 'The Competing Priorities of Life', succinctly sums up what this book is about:

> … the ups and downs of and stresses and strains of fitting the little understood urges of a greater-range mountaineer into the well understood challenges of being a family man with a fulltime job.

Fowler saying that the challenges of being a family man with a fulltime job are 'well understood' reveals something more that overconfidence or complacency. Fowler is not trying to simplify the challenges: he is just making an important distinction. It's not that the problems are understood, it's that he understands there are problems. I also worked for a number of years in government and understand the need to get on with the job in the manner that civil servants generally adopt: enabling the policies and laws created by politicians who they meet the 'understood' needs of the majority and thereby ensure they get voted in next time. In the chaos of our current world, I for one find it hard to understand how rapid changes in climate and technology and just about everything else will affect my family. Perhaps only a level headed and stoic civil servant could describe family challenges as 'well understood'.

There are many gleeful moments in this book where Fowler revels in beating the bureaucrats at their own games, getting around obstacles thrown up by foreign permit policies and pointing out the nonsense of perverse policies whereby governments make a hash of things. No more need be said on that subject, except that Mick is a wolf in pinstripe.

The great fun reading *No Easy Way*, and indeed Mick's earlier books, comes from the regular waves of raucous, witty and unique humour. Mick loves to make light of serious moments, especially those where one might expect restraint and decorum. Sometimes the humour reveals his appreciation of the absurdity of both extreme climbing and day-to-day occurrences where the entrance of confident and single-minded climbers changes the whole dynamics of a situation. For example, when Mick with Paul Ramsden climb the crag beneath Nottingham Castle to be caught by a night watchman who becomes increasingly irate and frustrated trying to get the police to arrest the pair. Or when he and Victor Saunders have it out in a boxing match at a rough south London pub known for violent altercations and settlements of differences in the ring. 'Get 'em off and bring on the strippers' come the cries when the audience realise they aren't going to seriously hurt each other.

In one of the more understated chapters, Mick takes on the old guard of the Alpine Club. He wins the first-ever contested presidency in the Club's history. This adds to the stress as he gets on with the job of reforming the Club, a task he stacks precariously on top of the job he is already doing at the tax office. He soon discovers he can't leave the Club to the evenings but must deal with urgent Club business during working hours.

> *Acquiring a smartphone helped in that. But civil service cutbacks meant I no longer had my nice private office with high-back chair and curved mahogany desk. Instead I was ensconced in the corner of an open-plan office visible to all. I felt uncomfortable spending too much time tapping away ... some must have noticed that I spent a lot of time in the toilet.*

Whether it's the day-to-day or extreme alpinism, Fowler uses his sense of fun to great effect. Humour is the perfect tool to explore some of the consequences of those 'little understood urges of the greater range mountaineer.' The climbing adventures are full of slapstick moments: putting an ice axe through the climbing rope on a first pitch; thinking that the red end of a compass must be pointing south because of its colour, since it's hotter in the south; extricating himself from fraught upside-down moments in the dark mayhem of stormy bivouacs; insisting a climbing partner's cup is continuously filled with bitter Tibetan tea knowing how much that partner will gag trying to satisfy the etiquette of local hospitality; being seen behind a bush by a young girl rubbing Vaseline onto his privates before a fell race.

'Daddy look, there's that man again.'

You get the idea. Mick has great fun 'taking the mick' out of his partners and himself. The book sparkles with these moments.

Fowler is a connoisseur of bivouacs, describing especially comfortable and unlikely tent platforms with the same calm resignation as horrendous spindrift-plagued one-cheek perches, knowing that tomorrow will eventually come and with it a new set of challenges. Mealtimes are also often examined in some detail:

… a glorious evening had developed by the time we sat down to brew up and tuck into our evening meal of Chinese baby powder and fruit flavoured sausages. This was one of two menu options, the other being noodles with a flavouring sachet. These were not the meals we had meant to choose, but having decided to buy of food in the shops of Lhasa in order to avoid excess baggage costs, our Chinese and Tibetan had been exposed as woefully inadequate knowing exactly what we were buying. On the bright side, both menu options were very light. And they were sufficiently unappetising for us to frequently fail to finish our meals, so the food was lasting longer than expected.

This is just one of many culinary observations. And although the big and little moments of those 'little understood urges' are described in an apparently casual style, Fowler can also describe perfectly well his depth of feeling for and enjoyment of mountaineering. Pure adventure he defines as a state of uncertainty, but when things come good, which they do for Fowler with impressive regularity, there's a kind of authentic simplicity to his joy. He may at times appear to dismiss risk casually, but his approach to the hardest mountaineering projects are famously well researched and expertly executed. As I write Mick and Victor are planning a new route in Sikkim in the post-monsoon season this year. (Victor is currently on K2.) Mick is working to get fit again after another cancer scare, which was thankfully a false alarm. In a fitting final chapter, he deals with his cancer diagnosis at the very end of a frightening tale out walking his dog. Perhaps I have already given too much away, so I will end by saying that this is an exceptionally fine and entertaining book. For Fowler action and perspective are everything, regardless of whether a situation is little or well understood.

John Porter

The Impossible Climb
Alex Honnold, El Capitan and the Climbing Life
Mark Synnott
Allen & Unwin, 2019, pp403, £20

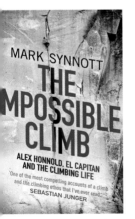

There is an incident in *The Impossible Climb*, recorded by its author, Mark Synnott, which appears to represent all that is reprehensible about the interaction of super-extreme climbing with sponsorship and the media. In June 1999, after several days on the 3,000ft headwall on the west summit of Great Trango, Synnott's teammate Alex Lowe discovered the battery of his laptop computer was drained of power. The laptop was important to their enterprise: it enabled them to write reports on their progress that were to be distributed by their sponsors. The team, comprising Synnott, Lowe and Jared Ogden, had backing to the tune of $12,000 from outdoor brand North Face. An NBC film crew was making a documentary of their ascent with additional funding from Quokka, a social-media start-up with $80m of venture capital and 300 employees. Quokka and its backers saw a lucrative future in sponsoring adventure activities such as theirs: others included round-the-world sailing and grand prix motorcycling. It too had a team at base camp, pumping out the climbers' dispatches, sometimes editing them in a way that magnified disagreements among the team. The climbers were also equipped with radios so they could conduct live interviews, of varying degrees of inanity, with stations in the US.

Synnott was wearying of the demands of the media circus, whose costs had reached $50,000. He therefore felt immensely relieved that he would not have to write any more dispatches, which, he relates, embodied everything he had come to hate about Quokka. But Lowe would not be diverted from the media call and insisted on abseiling down to base camp to have the laptop repaired. He returned two days later and the dispatches resumed.

The story at least has a happy ending, of sorts. The three climbers reached the summit, doing so in sync with four Russians on a parallel route. As for Quokka, on the very same day it made a public share offering, which flopped. The company closed down a year or so later and the 300 jobs were lost, along with the investors' $80m. Lowe, it must be added, died in an avalanche on Shishapangma in October 1999, part of another North Face adventure being filmed for a NBC documentary.

At this point I cannot resist comparing the methods used to convey news of the climb with those I employed during the British Cerro Torre Expedition of 1967-8, when Messrs Haston, Burke, Boysen and Crew were attempting the first authentic ascent. *The Sunday Times*, for whom I was covering the climb, had put up a princely £1500 for the team. After writing my reports in long hand, I walked for six hours to the roadhead where we had parked a pick-up truck. I drove 200 miles across the pampas to the coastal town of Santa Cruz, where I transcribed my report on to a telegram form for transmitting to the paper. I then visited the tiny Santa Cruz airstrip to dispatch our rolls of black-and-white film to London. The round trip took me three days, and several weeks would pass before I learned whether my dispatch and photos had been published.

The point of this old-timer's tale is not hard to grasp: things have moved on since those epic days, and the step change in communications and media sponsorship is matched by the extraordinary levels of technique and audacity at which today's climbers perform. Synnott's book culminates in the astonishing solo ascent by Alex Honnold of *Freerider* on El Capitan in June 2017, accomplished in just 3h 56m. It can thus be seen as the book of the film *Free Solo*, which was the talking point of the AC's London dinner in February 2019, as it had been released a few weeks before.

The *Freerider* ascent occupies just 12 pages near the end of the book, which is also an exposition of the backstory and development of modern extreme climbing. It had a dissident counterculture not so far from the notorious pillaging Chamonix Brits, with groups such as the Stonemasters and the Stone Monkeys pushing standards while leading what Synnott terms 'rebellious feral lives'. Synnott becomes a character in the story as he relates his own accession to this world, graduating to the status of a professional once he has joined the North Face roster. Synnott presents the 1999 Trango episode as a nadir in the drive to fashion a living out of climbing, and the book debates the ethics and pitfalls involved in attempting to do so.

Seen from this side of the Atlantic, there is something unsettling about the way such extraordinary exploits become business ventures. Synnott was present on the day in January 2015 when Tommy Caldwell and Kevin Jorgeson completed their 19-day free ascent of El Cap's *Dawn Wall*. He noted an ABC camerawoman wearing shiny fashionista combat boots, the spraying of champagne like a motor-racing grand prix ceremony, and the public relations minder from Patagonia – Caldwell's sponsors – who shooed away an unauthorised reporter from *Men's Journal*, telling him that Caldwell was 'off limits'. Synnott recalls the pre-internet era when climbers on expeditions 'unplugged' from the outside world. By 2015, sponsored climbers were expected to report their exploits almost hour by hour; their contracts would stipulate how and when they should post, which hashtags they should use, and even creative guidelines to follow. 'It was a rare soul who avoided getting sucked into the vortex.'

It is not until page 144 of the book that the ostensible hero of the story makes his entrance. Synnott's first face-to-face meeting with Honnold takes place at a hotel in Kota Kinabalu in Malaysia in April 2009, when Honnold, then 23, arrives at his door wearing only boxer shorts and Synnott is captivated by his 'deer-in-the-headlights' eyes. Synnott offers him a drink but Honnold says he does not consume alcohol or caffeine, though adding: 'Actually, I do have one vice – fornication.'

This was yet another arranged commercial relationship: Synnott wanted to climb the north face of Kinabalu that rises from the notorious Low's Gully, scene of a British army debacle in 1994, and had been teamed with Honnold by Conrad Anker, then acting as a recruiting sergeant for North Face. Honnold had burst on to the climbing firmament in 2007 with his free solo ascents of two 5.11c routes in Yosemite. Following the Kinabalu ascent, the book weaves multiple paths between their respective careers, and Synnott addresses some of the questions prompted by Honnold's astonishing achievements and ambitions. Does he know fear? This is tested through a scan of his amygdala, a key arousal area in the brain, which proves resolutely normal. Is he a sociopath and/or does he have Asperger's? Here, Honnold concedes he is probably 'somewhere on the autism spectrum'. Honnold is clearly a driven man, but he appears casual in his attitude to celebrity. He is not obsessed with its rewards and donates one third of all his earnings to his own foundation, which funds sustainability projects around the world. He has spent most of his climbing career living in a van.

In the book, as in the film, we catch glimpses of Sanni McCandless, described as his girlfriend, and in several toe-curling encounters we discern that her passion for him is not matched in any way that he is able to express. Honnold appears to find as much fulfilment in the partnership he strikes with Tommy Caldwell, with whom he made the five-day Fitzroy traverse in 2014, followed by several further spectacular ascents including the El Cap Nose in a record 1h 58m in June 2018.

We reach the denouement of the story on page 378, Honnold's *Freerider* attempt. As in the film, it is all over so quickly, which was in the nature of the ascent. What is more, at least half of the description reports the tension among the camera crew and the watchers on the ground, including Synnott. Notably, Honnold had refused to allow camera operators to dangle alongside him on the key pitches, so they strung remote control cameras beside him instead. Even so, we share their relief as Honnold pulls over the final block.

Synnott has pitched his story at a readership beyond the climbing community and his account will be mostly accessible to lay readers. There are however terms and usages that will be new to some AC members: dialled, douchey, sketched, beta, spraying, whose meanings may have to be guessed at. As other reviewers have noted, there is some disturbingly chauvinist language used to refer to women, which is not excused by Honnold's own admission on this score. The chronology can be hard to follow because Synnott is sparing with his dates, and there is no index.

Despite these misgivings, the book is highly readable, intimate and revelatory, on a level with Tommy Caldwell's superb *The Push* in admitting us to this elite world, its culture, attitudes and language. Honnold, we learn, is not the gauche outsider portrayed in his first meeting with Synnott. Nor, for all his extraordinary achievements, is he some alien being. Synnott presents us with someone determined to fulfil his dreams and aspirations, an inspirational figure with whom all can empathise.

Peter Gillman

The Uncrowned King of Mont Blanc
The Life of T Graham Brown, Physiologist and Mountaineer
Peter Foster
Bâton Wicks, 2019, pp205, £14.95

Thomas Graham Brown was a first-class hater, one of the Alpine Club's best, an obdurate Scot happily dedicated to rootling out fresh truffles of gossip to deepen the flavours of his various enmities. The chief object of his loathing was Frank Smythe but, as this excellent, sympathetic but never exculpatory biography makes clear there were others jostling for his attention, most notably Geoffrey Winthrop Young. Graham Brown was also the most successful British alpinist of the interwar years; his season in 1933 must rank among the finest of all, despite the fact he was then 51 years old and had only developed his passion for alpinism in his forties. On top of all that he was a successful research scientist whose

Above: Graham Brown at the Promontoire hut towards the end of his remarkable 1933 season at the age of 51. *(Alpine Club Photo Library)*

Left: Alexander Graven nearing the top of the Pear Buttress in 1933, an immense achievement for the era, the third of Thomas Graham Brown's triptych on the Brenva face. *(Thomas Graham Brown/National Library of Scotland)*

early career was marked by the same intensity and care that he brought to his alpinism. As his friend of 40 years, the lawyer Edwin Herbert, later Lord Tangley, put it: 'His was one of the most complex personalities I have ever known.' Given Herbert's record of public service, I fancy he'd known a fair few of those.

Graham Brown was born in Edinburgh in March 1882, making him four years older than George Mallory, an Edwardian whose best-before date extended deep into the 1930s. His father was a lecturer in neurology who brought up his sons with the sort of bourgeois rectitude that prized position and reputation, determined they should give a good account of themselves. After a wobbly start, Graham Brown knuckled down, graduating in medicine from Edinburgh University, perfecting his German in Strasbourg and gravitating towards a career as a research neurophysiologist in the Liverpool laboratory of his father's great friend, the much-loved future Nobel laureate Charles Sherrington. (Sherrington shared the Nobel with Edgar Adrian, an honorary member of the Club who wrote Graham Brown's obituary for the Royal Society, of which, like Sherrington, he was president.) Allowed to pursue his own direction, Graham Brown conducted experiments in the neural control of movement and had the war not intervened, it's possible he would have stuck to that groove and enjoyed a distinguished scientific career, despite a tendency to write boring papers. In fact, Graham Brown did return to this work in the late 1930s with some ghoulish-looking experiments of decerebrate cats – look it up – on treadmills. This work would inspire the Swedish neuroscientist Anders Lundberg, who revolutionised our understanding of how the brain and spinal column work together. At the outbreak of the First World War, Graham Brown was 32 and at the height of his powers; he worked on the misery of shell shock and was posted to a military hospital in Salonika. Between 1909 and 1920 he produced a huge number of papers, and in a festschrift for Sherrington's 90th birthday wrote how, 'This laboratory life was a continuing adventure with always widening horizons.'

So what happened? How did this bright start, which saw him made a fellow of the Royal Society in 1927, veer off into a life of adventure? Because once he'd pocketed the initials FRS, the fecund research withered on the vine. By then his father, always so hard to please, was dead and Graham Brown was living alone in the Royal Hotel in Cardiff, the professor of physiology at University College, Cardiff's and embroiled in a long-running and bitter scrap over the status of its medical school, a fight for which Graham Brown proved superbly adapted, with his eye for the pedantic and his immense stamina for disputation. Many years later Tom Longstaff would tell him, in a letter following Graham Brown's ill-considered appointment as editor of the *Alpine Journal*: 'you are pathologically sensitive to the exact truth. Speaking – or writing – the exact truth just breeds SWARMS of enemies.' I sympathise, but Graham Brown often struggled to tell the difference between *the* truth and *his* truth.

The scientific and professional parts of Graham Brown's life are dealt with in the first part of Peter Foster's biography, understandably because they are both difficult and quite dry, especially given the juice that comes later, for a mountaineering crowd. But I think he might have structured it differently. I had many questions at the end about Graham Brown's motivation. As the retired Winchester schoolmaster Graham Irving put it, in a private review of Graham Brown's book *Brenva*: 'His meticulousness over times and measurements is almost exasperating and induces the idea that his climbing is the serious business of life, not its refreshment.' Always the scientist, applying the rigour of the laboratory to human affairs, especially something as inconsequential and light as alpinism, made me wonder if the disappointments of Graham Brown's professional life might have been kept a little more in the foreground.

Wholly absent is any reference to Graham Brown's private life. This seems to me the book's only serious omission. No mention is made of sweethearts or indeed the lack of them. From Foster's immense and careful rummage through Graham Brown's papers, a few hints emerge: he seems very much a man's man, tweedy and reeking of pipe tobacco. (In fact, this is a very male book although in a marvellously bitchy way. *Mean Girls* has nothing on 1930s British alpinism.) I can wholly understand why he despised Smythe, who was prone to bouts of insecure petulance and really should have picked his enemies more carefully; but I wondered about Geoffrey Winthrop Young, whom Graham Brown marked down on first acquaintance as a 'poseur'. Is that code for some kind of sexual disapproval? I have no idea, but I'd rather hope such questions were asked. Perhaps Graham Brown was too absorbed in his own life to let anyone else in, but if so, we should be told.

Foster is superb in conjuring the events and atmosphere of Alpine climbing in the late 1920s and 1930s. He doesn't just capture Graham Brown's career, from its late and average inception in the mid 1920s to his fateful first encounter with Frank Smythe in 1927, introduced by his friend Edwin Herbert. Almost 20 years his junior, Smythe was almost anti-matter as far as Graham Brown was concerned, a self-aggrandising romantic who wouldn't hesitate to massage the facts for a better story. They shared two climbs together on the Brenva face, both remarkable, both of them demanding courage and stamina. Smythe's casual misrepresentation of Graham Brown's role on *Route Major* was the start of a bitter and divisive feud that glowered over the Alpine Club for twenty years and only ended with Smythe's premature death in 1949. At which point, as it happened, Graham Brown was serving his choppy stint as *Alpine Journal* editor and had to be adroitly steered away from Smythe's obituary.

Graham Brown's great year was 1933, not coincidentally the year of Smythe on Everest. In the space of a fortnight he climbed Mont Blanc six times, three of the routes new, including the formidable *Via della Pera*, the Pear Route, the final panel in Graham Brown's magnificent triptych of works on the deadly canvas of the Brenva face. The Italian name is important: the French equivalent, *Route de la Poire*, had a double meaning and could be construed as the 'route of the bloody fool'. Graham Brown rarely stopped thinking about how others would regard him. Lindsay Griffin's foreword is a useful reminder of just how impressive this route remains, and its reputation among Europe's finest alpinists. Foster discusses the role of his guides Alexander Graven and Alfred Aufdenblatten in all this: to what extent could these be considered to Graham Brown's routes? He was not technically gifted but had immense drive and strength, and vision too, although I suspect he rather overestimated his talent there. It was very much a 19th century relationship of amateur and guide, the logical conclusion of what was possible in that kind of arrangement. But I would very much like to have sat down with Graven and Aufdenblatten to ask them what they thought of their 'Herr', because Graham Brown made it plain what he thought of them, detailing their shortcomings in his diary, reflecting that perhaps he was asking too much of 'a mere peasant' and accusing Aufdenblatten of cowardice. Contempt was never far away.

After the Pear, Graham Brown was at the Leschaux hut below the north face of the Grandes Jorasses looking up at the Walker spur, a focus for what was the seismic reordering of alpinism away from the guided pattern to partnerships of equals: equally gifted and motivated, sharing the decision making. How else could alpinism progress? On a previous visit to the Leschaux he had made sketches in his notebook of possible lines up the spur, but that's as far as his interest went. The future was not his. Instead he went to the Dauphiné and traversed the Meije, Les Écrins and the Ailfroide and put up a new route on the north face of Les Bans. Strutt, not prone to flattery, called Graham Brown's achievement 'miraculous'. By the end of that season he had literally worn out his gear, not just his clothes, but his crampons too, so often sharpened that the points were too short. In almost eight weeks in the Alps, Graham Brown had five days off, three because of bad weather and two as he travelled between regions. None of the illustrious band on Everest that summer could match his Alpine record.

That begs the question why Graham Brown was not on Everest himself, although the obvious answer is that by then you couldn't have Smythe and Graham Brown in the same room let alone on the same mountain. And anyway, as Foster's portrait makes clear, after 1933 Graham Brown was never really as strong again, despite the first ascent of Foraker in 1934. (The portrayal of his relationship with Charlie Houston, which led to this expedition, is one of this book's great gems.) Graham Brown was not an ideal expedition climber, surprisingly brittle in mood and often sour in a team, indifferent to the needs of others and always determined to get the credit he felt was his due. Bill Tilman kicked himself for sending Graham Brown the proofs of his Nanda Devi book, since it brought down an avalanche of minor corrections aimed at making the Scot look better. 'I have told him,' Tilman wrote to Noel Odell, 'it doesn't accord with his views on being impersonal. They only apply to others apparently.' It's extraordinary how two men, superficially so similar, could be so profoundly different.

Graham Brown stuck at it after an indifferent performance on Nanda Devi, going to Masherbrum on an expedition conceived and organised by James Waller and his fellow army officer Jock Harrison, the latter's close friend Jimmy Roberts and the brilliant rock climber Robin Hodgkin, poised between Oxford and his teaching career. This expedition, which left Hodgkin's hands and feet in ruins, deserves and gets Foster's full attention; it is painful to watch the affection and respect the younger climbers have for Graham Brown curdle as he shows himself to be selfish and deluded about his own performance. Harrison told him to his face 'that from the beginning he had not done a stroke towards helping the expedition along since he joined it and that he was a selfish old man who had no thought beyond his own personal comfort and success.' Anyone who thinks poor behaviour at high altitude is a modern phenomenon needs to read this chapter, although the dignity of Hodgkin, Harrison and the others is a welcome counterweight. Predictably, Graham Brown had a peaceful retirement, beloved by the young climbers of Edinburgh University whose company he sought.

Peter Foster deserves great credit for his cool and reasonable view of Graham Brown. His background as a consultant gives him a valuable extra perspective but it's his judgment as a writer that is most commendable. There were things I disagreed with: he's too harsh I think on Tom Blakeney, but small matter. Thanks to this fascinating study, alongside Tony Smythe's underrated memoir of his father, we now have a much fuller picture of a rich and romantic period of British mountaineering history and one of its most fascinating characters. As for Graham Brown: 'It was a great pity,' Blakeney wrote of his editorship, 'as Graham Brown had great gifts had he chosen to use them well.' That might stand for rather more.

Ed Douglas

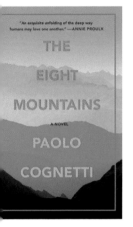

The Eight Mountains
Paolo Cognetti
Harvill Secker, 2018, pp 272, £12.99

For Pietro, the narrator of this lyrical novel, a particular blend of smells defines the mountains: the aroma of the stable, hay, curdled milk, damp earth and wood-smoke. Worldwide it is the smell of the dairies and settlements where pine and juniper give way to summer pasture, threshold to heights of rock and snow.

That same olfactory essence pervades Paolo Cognetti's story of two Italian boys from contrasting backgrounds who meet in a secluded valley somewhere south of Monte Rosa and whose lives remain entwined thereafter. It has melancholic wistfulness that clearly appeals to Italian readers: *The Eight Mountains* spent a full year in the Italian bestseller lists and won the country's Premio Strega as well the French Prix Médicis Étranger. It has been translated into 37 languages, this English version by Simon Carnell and Erica Segre. Carnell is a poet, a sensibility ever present in this captivating book.

Despite its title, *Eight Mountains* is not a climbing novel. Eight mountains are not as such climbed; they are drawn in the dust by a Nepali porter, each mountain at the outer end of a spoke in the wheel of a mandala. At its centre is the tremendously high Sumeru, the heart of the universe. 'Who has learned the most,' the chicken carrier asks Pietro, 'the one who has been to all eight mountains, or the one who has reached the summit of Sumeru?'

Pietro smiles but offers no direct answer. Neither he nor the porter (nor Cognetti) explains that Sumeru (aka Meru) is the meeting place of the gods and above is the pure realm of the Buddha-fields. But Pietro thinks he has understood the meaning. And if I have, it is that while Pietro, the city child turned freelance filmmaker, leads a wandering life, it is his friend Bruno who remains constant to the *alpeggio* and its guardian mountain, the Grenon, at the centre of his world.

To what extent is Pietro's life a reflection on Cognetti's own, divided between Milan and his cabin at 2,000 metres in the Italian Alps? Milan is the city to which Pietro's parents migrate from the countryside, and the Alps their retreat for long family holidays. *Eight Mountains'* place in those bestseller lists may owe something to the fact that this drift to the city and nostalgia for a rural past is a familiar narrative for many Italians.

Set over some four decades, the book is a coming of age story. It is also an elegy for a way of life on the high pastures; one of hard toil and scant economic reward, yet somehow honest and in harmony with nature and the elements. *Eight Mountains* cannot help but put one in mind of abandoned cattle sheds passed on hikes above the treeline and of mountain hamlets with farms converted to swish holiday homes. Yet still in such places a whiff of hay and wood-smoke lingers, just as it does over Cognetti's smouldering tale.

Stephen Goodwin

Free Solo
Directed by Elizabeth Chai Vasarhelyi and Jimmy Chin
National Geographic, 2018, 100 minutes

Dawn Wall
Directed by Peter Mortimer and Josh Lowell
Sender Films, 2017, 100 minutes

I'm gripped. My palms are sweaty and I'm squirming in my seat: it's the UK premiere of *Free Solo* and I've never seen climbing footage this impressive before. I had watched *Dawn Wall* a couple of months earlier, also on the big screen, and on first watch, before I'd seen anything of Free Solo, had been blown away. Now I fear nothing will be as good as Free Solo. Not since the opening of *Mission Impossible 2* have I seen climbing footage so cool, and this could actually be a problem: it looks so impressive you have to wonder how many ill-prepared people will consider giving it a go.

Warren Harding took 47 days to climb El Cap in 1958, using fixed ropes and pitons up the whole of the route, and it's truly inspiring to see how much things have changed. But really, this isn't so much a climbing film as the character study of a very intense person: Alex Honnold. It's about someone who takes such huge risks and the people that love him. It's a staggering film, beautiful but also often visceral to the point where I felt concern, despite knowing how it ends. I *know* I signed up for a questions and answers session with Honnold after the screening. But will he make it off the wall?

Honnold is shown with Tommy Caldwell, of *Dawn Wall* fame, preparing for his solo climb. (The filmmakers chose to leave out footage of training climbs Honnold did with women. These happened, as Honnold makes clear in the Q&A and he expressed displeasure at this.) Otherwise he's solo in everything, eating out of a pan with a spatula seems to capture this perfectly. When my wife is away and left to my own devices, I eat the same way: one pan, one spoon, one cup, one glass. On the other hand, I climb to be with people, seeking adventure and exploring our natural environment with others. I prefer to limit my chances of dying wherever I can. The sheer number of chances Honnold has to die is unfathomable to me, which is why the film works: we still think something could happen, as we watch the close ups of his perfect footwork on penny-sized footholds, even though we know the ending.

Dawn Wall is as unlikely a story as *Free Solo*, really. The suspense is provided by the struggles of Kevin Jorgeson, a boulderer with no big wall and little trad experience either, who finds himself on the project after years of reconnaissance and practice by Caldwell, who needed a partner. (He had also lost a finger along the way, the index finger of his left hand, severed in an accident with a table saw.) Really, all the odds were against them. Caldwell makes it through the hardest pitch first, days before Jorgeson, and decides to suspend his ascent to wait for his partner, even as the media look on, expecting him to continue and complete the project he'd pursued for so many years. For me this was the film that captures the climbing spirit I know and love, and not the ethos displayed in *Free Solo*. It's the pursuit of adventure and finding one's limits and confronting failure time and again that I appreciate climbing for. Above all, it's about the friendships built whilst climbing. The cameras capture Caldwell, who's maybe not the best communicator, struggling to explain this to Jorgeson, that he doesn't want to go ahead without him.

For me, the most difficult part of *Free Solo* wasn't the nerve-wracking climbing but more Honnold's sometimes troubling relationships with those close to him, especially girlfriend Sanni McCandless, and his hyper-masculine approach to life; he frequently compares himself to a warrior or samurai. *Free Solo* often celebrates the 'ardent glory' of war. 'It's about being a warrior. It doesn't matter about the cause necessarily. You face your fear because your path depends on it. That is the goddamn warrior spirit.'

At times, this bubbles over into misogyny, even toxicity. Sanni is perfect for the filmmakers as she appears at the right time to add drama to what otherwise would be *just* a climbing film, and they portray her in a stereotypically cinematic female role: the lover who inserts herself into the 'great man's' life and restricts his achievements, potentially stopping him from achieving his goals. When Ueli Steck's death is announced Sanni responds with appropriate tears and thinks about Ueli's parter. Honnold asks, 'Well, what did she expect?'

The filmmakers offer several of these less than flattering, almost callous moments. Honnold is in the kitchen, saying how he's been waiting for watermelon. Sanni appears, slices some and says, 'It must be nice to have a human slave.' Honnold agrees. There are unnecessary scenes explaining

Sanni's beginner-climber mistakes, and Honnold's statement that he would 'hardly characterise Sanni as a climber,' that convey a belittling disrespect. The message is that to push boundaries, this is how the male athlete/adventurer needs to be – and the women in their lives need to be silenced. Honnold says he 'will always choose climbing over a lady' and the film justifies this prioritisation of his pursuit over those that love and care for him. When things go wrong, Sanni is to blame, for being too clingy. Throughout *Free Solo*, Honnold shows outdated gender roles, leaving Sanni to be 'cute, small in the van' and livening 'the place up', making 'life better in every way', simply there for his pleasure and enjoyment. We're asked to believe that this is the behaviour of an incredibly dedicated athlete. Tommy Caldwell, also a dedicated athlete, tell us that 'a romantic relationship is detrimental to that armour. You can't have both at the same time.' But there are countless athletes, including himself, that do.

I think we're supposed to ask ourselves whether Honnold is right to do these things, but ultimately he achieves his goal and the film celebrates this, as we all do. The film's view is clear: Honnold achieves his impossible goal and his behaviour is consequently justified. But there were ideas I would like to have explored further in *Free Solo*, such as Honnold's MRI brain scan. 'It's not that you don't experience fear,' says the doctor. 'It's just that in your case it takes a lot more to trigger excitement.' Has climbing made him this way through thousands of hours of exposure? Or was his brain always like this, and he's therefore perfectly adapted to take such huge risks?

Free Solo is sufficiently detailed in its description of the technical aspects of climbing and runs through the route's main features: the 'Monster Offwidth', 'Enduro Corner', and the 'Boulder Problem' which is very much the crux of the climb, ending with a move known as the karate kick. Yet *Dawn Wall* is much more of a climbing film, for climbing people. We see the intricacies of climbing: storms lashing the wall, portaledges, climbers cooking and relieving themselves, cutting off rough skin with razor blades, and taping up. The climbing footage again is stunning: perhaps not of the same quality and crispness as *Free Solo*, but it includes the desperation of hard lead climbing, swooping falls and the struggle for the blankest section of El Capitan, the Wall of Early Morning Light, looming 3,000ft above the Valley.

Free Solo is a film that celebrates perfection, admires emotionally inarticulate men, and pursuing goals beyond reason. But for me, one of the beautiful things about climbing is the experience of failure, something that *Dawn Wall* very much celebrates, failing over and over again on a route until you get it right and then not proceeding until you can achieve it with the people that helped make it possible.

'This sucks,' Honnold exclaims near the end of his first abortive attempt. 'I don't want to be here. I'm over it.' Honnold talks to Peter Croft after retreating. 'I failed,' he says.

'Good for you,' Croft replies, before adding: 'You never have to go for it.' This is perfectly put. Climbing is ultimately useless, but it's often sublime, adventurous, and life affirming. Of the two films, *Dawn Wall* captures this the most. *Free Solo* is, in its own 'bro' language, very cool, but it is not a film to follow as an example.

Nigel Buckley

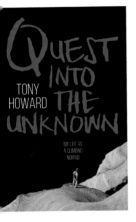

Quest into the Unknown
My Life as a Climbing Nomad
Tony Howard
Vertebrate Publishing, 2018, pp422, £14.95

Is this an autobiography or a diary? It seems to be a bit of both from this respected climber, explorer, adventurer and sometime entrepreneur. Were they publicised, the activities of Tony Howard would put to shame many of the high-profile, so-called adventurers who strut the media these days, but to the mountain community he will already be known for the first ascent of the Troll Wall, Troll climbing equipment and the opening up of Wadi Rum.

There is an awful lot of this book. Though not a slow reader, it has taken me over four weeks to digest the 68 chapters. Admittedly, each occupies only four or five pages, a convenient length for bedtime reading. Split into two parts, the first, comprising 38 chapters, is a fairly organised narrative and to my mind the most interesting. The second I found alluring if confusing, with subjects not necessarily sequential in time or location. Nevertheless the author writes evocatively throughout both parts, conjuring up mood and atmosphere, the sounds and smells of the souk and the frustration of the all too frequent police check-post, while it is evident that he must possess either a prodigious memory or has for years kept a meticulous daily diary, or both.

The author starts at the very beginning: 'The day I was born was a momentous day.' It was indeed, for it was during the evacuation from Dunkirk in May 1940. Having lived through those times myself I was fascinated to read of his wartime and immediate post-war childhood among the western valleys of the Peak District, his discovery of the moors and crags, his early climbing and the birth of the Rimmon Climbing Club. Although as a southerner my own formative years and entry into the mountain world came from a different angle, I can identify with much of it, while I know, or I'm acquainted with, so many of the characters involved, as will be those older AC members.

All climbers have some degree of wanderlust, although until recent times it was most usually restrained by the need to earn a 'proper living'. Where Tony Howard was different was that back in 1958, aged 18, he did something about it. He walked out of school, signed up on a Norwegian whaler and went off hunting the leviathan of the Southern Ocean, thus financing his initial ventures in Norway and his exploration of Romsdal's huge rock walls. Between visits he worked as a deckhand on Icelandic trawlers.

He married a Norwegian girl and in the aftermath of the epic first ascent of the Troll Wall, together with a couple of his Rimmon rope-mates, founded the innovative Troll equipment firm, initially very much a garden shed enterprise centred on the webbing gear they had developed for the climb.

The story continues with trips to anywhere where steep rock might be found or an adventure encountered, especially if the necessary finance could be earned, for instance by labouring throughout the winter at an opencast mine in the Yukon. The lure of putting up a route on a fresh or hitherto unknown crag rather overtook the more disciplined business of entrepreneurship but apart from a foray to Greenland and an epic canoe journey across the Yukon-Alaska marches, Howard veered towards sunnier climes. There were crag-searching visits to Morocco, Algeria, the Sudan and Iran, typically in decrepit vehicles of some kind, often accompanied by his daughter Tannith and Di Taylor, an old friend, a fine climber and eventually his second wife. There were many adventures but all too often red tape, stroppy policemen or the wrong permit got in the way. But essentially part one is about going climbing.

Many of us have been intrigued by the remote mountains of the Sahel, the Hoggar for instance, the Tibesti and the Simien. Here Tony Howard comes into his own, for apart from reconnoitring in Thailand, India's Deccan escarpment and Madagascar, part two is exclusively Middle Eastern. But by now middle age is catching up, the Norwegian marriage has long since failed and it seems that the journey, the exploration, is its own reward, leaving so many promising crags to be 'returned to later with climbing gear.' Armed with a business card for his adventure travel consultancy NOMAD (New Opportunities for Mountaineering, Adventure and Desert Sports), a ploy which sometimes cuts the ice with suspicious officials, the author visits Egypt, Ethiopia, Libya, Mali, Oman, Palestine and Jordan, ostensibly to look for crags and high places, but also delighting in the mere fact of travelling.

In Jordan over Christmas 1983, attracted by the landscapes in David Lean's film *Lawrence of Arabia*, he and Di visited Wadi Rum, and as both rock climbers and mountaineers explored its imposing cliffs, canyons and mountainous mesas. They befriended the local Bedouin, ibex hunters and born climbers themselves, and become persona very much grata to the Jordanian authorities and even Queen Noor. On dozens of subsequent visits they explored virtually the whole of Jordan's extensive wilderness areas, enthused local people to climb and trek and planted the seeds of Jordan not only as a rock-climbing venue but also as an international trekking destination. The culmination of their efforts over more than 30 years was the opening in 2017 of the Jordan Trail, a nine-section, 400-mile trekking route from Um Qais in the far north to Aqaba on the Red Sea, via such evocative places as the crusader castle at Karak, the Dead Sea, Petra, 'a rose-red city, half as old as time', and Wadi Rum.

The detail in part two is so intense that I found it easy to lose track of exactly what was happening, where, when and with whom, while the narrative cries out for small-scale maps to supplement 113 excellently reproduced photographs, most of them in colour. An index would make the book useful. Nevertheless I have to admit that I'm smitten. Were I 10 years younger, I'd be off to Jordan myself as soon as I could pack a rucksack. What a tempting wilderness for a spot of rugged recreation.

John Cleare

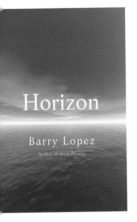

Horizon
Barry Lopez
The Bodley Head, 2019, pp 586. £25

As Barry Lopez sets off from Bull Pass to hike west along the crest of Antarctica's Olympus range he falls prey to a fancy that is a commonplace in mountaineering literature: the idea that one is the first human to tread this particular piece of ground, or, in the climbing version, the first to lay a hand on this expanse of rock.

Since leaving the banks of the Onyx river he had not seen anything like a human footprint. And to the far side of Bull Pass is forbidden territory: the McKelvey valley, one of several dry valleys closed to human entry to preserve them in a completely undisturbed state. He was intoxicated with the sense of the great space about him and that seductive notion of being the first human in that place.

But for Lopez the reverie does not last. Along the ridge he comes upon a camera case and picks it up: the upper half of a black Nikon 35mm SLR case. The climber in such circumstances would, I suspect, have felt cheated of a first ascent. Lopez, however sees it as a deserved chastisement:

I was privately mortified by the fact that I had entertained the illusion that I might be the first to walk this ridgeline. To what degree had this adolescent daydream of mine taken me away from what was actually here?

Two fundamental aspects of Barry Lopez are present in that second sentence: his deep humility, and a meticulous attention to detail of his surroundings. Landscape for Lopez is the great teacher and he does not want to miss a single lesson. He desires to be 'fully present' in whatever place, and in *Horizon*, whether it be the coast of Oregon, Ellesmere Island, the western Lake Turkana uplands, Botany Bay or the central Transantarctic mountains, this intensity of study and thought is manifest.

Let's be clear, Lopez is no climber and there is no mountaineering in this marvellous book. It warrants inclusion among the *Alpine Journal* reviews because, in the words of essayist and poet Mark Tredinnick, 'the wild breathes in the words of Barry Lopez.' And the wild, or what passes for it, is where Lopez' world and that of exploratory mountaineering intersect.

Lopez is best known for his 1986 masterpiece, *Arctic Dreams*. It won the

US National Book Award and gained him a reputation as a kind of sage, steeped in wilderness and native wisdom. He would reject any such notion, just as he rejects the labels 'nature writer' or 'environmentalist'. He accepts only the description 'writer': a writer who travels. And how! Reading *Horizon*, there's no escaping the irony that for someone who is deeply concerned about the trashing of the natural world and effects of climate change, Lopez must have one of the biggest personal carbon footprints on the planet. Polar regions have drawn him repeatedly, but so too has Africa, Australia and the Galápagos.

Offsetting the writer's carbon account are the stories he has brought back. But this is no mere collection of traveller's tales. His approach is one of deep engagement; it's as if he brings together the discipline of an archaeologist, ethnographer, naturalist and geologist, then searches for the spiritual in his findings. Lopez believes the physical land to be sentient and responsive, as informed by its own memory as it is by the weather.

Lopez is now in his mid seventies and *Horizon* is as close as he's likely to come to an autobiography. It is an absorbing reflection on his decades of travel and research: the overall tone is elegiac; he is much concerned with how to live a just life and speculates at length on the fate of modern man. All people, every culture, every country, now face the same problematic future, he says. It is necessary to reconsider human destiny, and in doing so leave behind adolescent dreams of material wealth and the quest for greater economic or military power. And to do so requires 'resituating man in an ecological reality.'

These strictures arise as Lopez relates assisting in a search for hominid fossils in northern Kenya. The time span in these passages is humbling: the first group of primates clearly ancestral to *Homo sapiens*, the gracile australopithecines, appear in the fossil record of the early Pliocene, four to five million years ago. Paleoanthropologists have identified a succession of descendants: in effect our close relatives. Yet only we, *H sapiens*, survive. Why? And for how long?

> The alarming situation here for humanity is that H sapiens, though it has asserted itself as the dominant species on Earth, is at the same time the potential victim of its domination over virtually all Earth's ecosystems. If H sapiens were to become extinct, the event would simply be regarded as evolution continuing to unfold, a biological future for life but not one that any longer included humanity.

You get a sense here of what makes *Horizon* such a deeply thoughtful and challenging book. Its more than 500 pages contain writing of lyrical beauty but also much sadness and suppressed anger, particularly over the disintegration of indigenous societies and the loss thereby of other ways of understanding the world. Of the three tribes of Feugians, unable to cope with a colonizer's culture, each, writes Lopez, 'eventually became another torn prayer flag, snapping in the wind over burned ground.'

Even today one wonders how much of that 'colonizer's culture' mountaineers carry with them in their interactions with expedition crews and hill villagers. Lopez is honest to a fault and wonders whether in his own travels he hasn't unconsciously behaved in some way 'like a grave robber' and given unintended offence: perhaps at an Afghan dinner table or in an Inuit village on Baffin Island. That he hasn't exploited them, seduced them with intoxicants or pressed them with religion, isn't the point.

Often the transgression is no more than that the white guest does not see himself as a guest, but as an emissary. 'Even if he sees himself as only a well-intentioned visitor, he's prone to believe that, in the long run, he knows what's best, whether it's how to sharpen a knife, how to run a bodega, or how to worship the Divine.'

And if that's not sobering thought enough, Lopez drives home the consequence of that 'superior culture' mind-set in three short words: 'It kills people.'

Stephen Goodwin

Waymaking
An Anthology of Women's Adventure Writing, Poetry and Art
Edited by Helen Mort, Claire Carter, Heather Dawe and Camilla Barnard
Vertebrate Publishing, 2018, pp277, £17.99

The Sharp End of Life
A Mother's Story
Deidre Wolownick
Mountaineers Books, 2018, pp253 pages, $24.95

A good deal of mountain writing is concerned with the epic, a word heavily freighted with extremes, both physical and mental. For many climbers, privation seems to be an inevitable part of the experience, even a badge of honour. Ego, the ever-present 'I', is the force that drives adventure; success ensures this brittle inner voice is temporarily quietened, before it all starts again. Sometimes mountain writing dips into the language of combat: laying siege to peaks until they are conquered. There is often the sense of a battle to be fought, that man is pitched against mountain and mountain against man. The mountain is a monster that spits out the ammunition of stone fall or avalanche. This perspective often seems an exclusively male preserve, although I appreciate the debate is more nuanced than that.

Waymaking, a compilation of 57 pieces of women's adventure writing, poetry and art, is the first of its kind and it seeks to present a variety of outdoor experiences which move beyond the insistence of conquest and, in part, towards what Nan Shepherd so memorably described as being 'with the mountain as one visits a friend, with no intention but to be with him.' There is no covert feminist agenda here, instead an opportunity for female adventurers of all kinds to describe their relationships with the landscapes they explore in a variety of ways. The pieces were selected from those which the editors received after an open call for submissions and this volume is intended as the forerunner of future publications.

There are four thematic areas: Vicinity; Heart and Soul; Water; and Union. Each contains a mix of art, poetry and prose. The common themes that emerge are that women adventurers do not feel obliged to conform to stereotypes or to underplay their achievements. Rather, they feel free to simply exist in outdoor environments, sometimes entirely uncoupled from the preoccupations of self and sometimes finding self through the opportunity to detach from the day-to-day litany of tasks and urgencies that beset us all. There is exploration of environmental themes and of family responsibilities, too, and Bernadette McDonald's short story 'Snow' poignantly details the latter as she recalls time spent in the mountains with her father, both before and after his death.

Maria Coffey's autobiographical offering about her fear and sadness at leaving tiny Protection Island on which she and her husband had lived for 20 years beautifully evokes the elements of land and sea. She is inconsolable at the thought of leaving but is advised by a friend to collect beach stones and attach each one to a special moment within the landscape, thus acknowledging her 'deep connection to the ocean and the earth'. This act of gratitude releases her from the burden of sadness and allows her to move on to future adventures with an unfettered heart.

This anthology is a rich experience for readers, rich with variety, rich with insight and rich with inspiration. There is no lack of wild adventure and risk within its pages, but what is absent is the desire to attempt to subdue a landscape, to bend it to one's will, to force it to allow passage. Instead, there are voices to tell us of a different way of considering the interaction between self and landscape. To return to Shepherd: 'On the mountain I am beyond desire. It is not ecstasy … I am not out of myself, but in myself. I am.'

Deidre Wolownick spent a good deal of her life without that immersive sense of self. Her childhood was a dawning realisation that to cause no problems for her parents was the only way to gain their approval. Interactive dialogue did not occur and all decisions about the family were made solely by her parents. Guidance took the form of criticism. Without ever being consulted, a clear life plan was laid out for her: life at home until she married and had children. Little wonder, then, that she escaped to what seemed like an idyllic lifestyle, teaching in California in order to be with the man who had promised to show her a life of adventure.

Her parents had taught her to live by a 'devastating absence of connection' and when, after a year of marriage, her husband began to criticise and, later, to completely withdraw from her she determined to work even harder at a relationship, which, it later became clear to her, was conducted with a man on the autistic spectrum. When the marriage finally ended she was left with close relationships with her son Alex Honnold and her daughter Stasia, both gifted exponents of extreme sports. It was a desire to better understand what they did and why they did it that led her to take up marathon running and climbing.

It was her gradual immersion in climbing which brought her to 'the human sublime': garnered both as a result of the intimate friendships which she had never known elsewhere and the sheer physical, adventurous endeavour of being on beautiful rock. Joy is everywhere in her descriptions of her climbing achievements but it is tempered always by the travails of taking up the sport in her later years. She set her personal bar high, culminating in an ascent of El Cap, visiting the face before her climb to 'touch it, make friends with it,' to make real a 'legend' which otherwise she knew she would inordinately fear.

Determination is woven through every facet of her narrative and her self-deprecating descriptions of her body and initial lack of fitness serve to point up the level of her commitment. Yet this is not just an account of a woman climbing her way out of unhappiness by setting herself new challenges to push her body where she thought it could never go. This is a story of finding freedom from emotional confines, refusing to simply endure whatever life brings-and, perhaps most importantly of all, finding a sense of self.

Her son captures the essence of her story best: it is 'a testament to the transformative power of outdoor adventure.'

Val Johnson

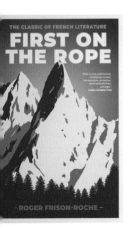

First on the Rope
Roger Frison-Roche
Vertebrate Publishing, 2019, pp256, £8.99

Originally published in 1941, when its author was living in Algiers, this is one of a few climbing novels to have retained a wide readership, having sold over three million copies. Frison-Roche was born in 1906 to parents with Savoyard roots living in Paris where they owned several bars. During the First World War, Frison-Roche visited the family's hometown of Beaufort and developed a passion for the mountains. Leaving school at 14, he worked first for Thomas Cook and then settled in Chamonix. In 1930 he became the first man not born in the valley to become a member of the Compagnie des Guides de Chamonix, the oldest guides' company in the world, formed in 1821, whose members over the years have included some of the best known names in mountaineering history: Payot, Croz, Charlet, Simond, Lachenal, Terray, Rébuffat.

Besides his mountain exploits, Frison-Roche had always wanted be a writer and after publication of some of his stories about being an Alpine guide, became a successful journalist. By the late 1930s he was working in Algeria as a reporter for *La Dépêche*, then an editor. Whilst working in Algeria he made several exploratory trips to the Hoggar mountains. In 1942, following France's 1940 armistice, he was captured at Kairouan in Tunisia by the Germans while reporting on the Allied war effort, transferred to Naples under the control of the Gestapo and condemned to death. Transferred to France, his new commandant was the owner of a hotel in Partenkirchen where Frison-Roche had stayed before the war. The officer arranged papers for his release, and Frison-Roche returned to Chamonix, until Germans replaced the Italian garrison, whereupon he joined the resistance.

Climbing-themed novels are rarely successful, either because they don't sell, or else their stories are less 'true' than real life ones found in books like *Touching the Void*, *The Bond* or *Into Thin Air*. Yet some climbers do tackle this difficult art form, from Wilf Noyce and Dougal Haston to the writing team of Lucy Rees and Al Harris. Five novels have so far won the Boardman Tasker Prize: *Climbers* by M J Harrison, *Mer de Glace* by Alison Fell, *The Ascent* by Jeff Long, *Hazard's Way* by Roger Hubank and *The Fall* by Simon Mawer, of which, for me, *Climbers* is the most outstanding. Although it requires concentration to follow the novel's complex story, it is a well-observed tale of how climbers become obsessed by their lives 'on the rocks', ignoring life's other responsibilities.

There are all sorts of climbing novel genres: science fiction, horror, thrillers and so forth. Two made it onto the big screen as blockbuster adventure movies: *The White Tower* by James Ramsey Ullman and *The Eiger Sanction* by 'Trevenian', the pseudonym of Rodney Whitaker. The former was published in 1945 and is full of racial stereotypes; the latter was written as a satire on James Bond, appearing in 1972 and Whitaker felt the point of the book had been lost in Clint Eastwood's movie of 1975, describing it as vapid. Modern readers would likely struggle with the portrayal of women in both books, but both do explore how wilderness often provides a test of human character.

A book that stands on its own, first published in 1956 after the ascent of Everest and rarely out of print since, is the *The Ascent of Rum Doodle*. Its author Bill Bowman was a Yorkshireman and not a Himalayan mountaineer, but that didn't stop him writing a brilliant satire of expedition climbing. It became so familiar that a bar in Kathmandu is named 'The Rum Doodle', as is a mountain in Antarctica, courtesy of an Australian expedition there in 1959. There are Rum Doodle sleeping bags and it was even recommended in *The Guardian* as part of a list of 1,000 novels everyone must read.

Frison-Roche's novel *First on the Rope* is a much more straightforward story, set in Chamonix and the Mont Blanc range in the 1920s and 1930s, a truly golden period in which to be climbing there. It tells the life of the Servettaz family: the father Jean is a longstanding, well known guide, his son Pierre wishes to follow his father's profession but is being dissuaded from this by his family. In recent winters Jean has been working hard to turn the family's home into a pension, taking in paying guests and working towards something bigger that Pierre will manage.

The novel's action moves swiftly on, and with his knowledge of a mountain guide's life, Frison-Roche draws a compelling and accurate picture of the tragedy that now besets the Servettaz family and its ramifications. As Jean is guiding an American climber down from the summit of Les Drus, he is struck dead by lightning. His porter, in modern parlance *accompagnateur*, George, manages in the teeth of a storm to shepherd the client safely down but suffers severe frostbite in doing so. A team of guides assemble at the Charpoua hut to retrieve Jean's body but to no avail and they retreat. Pierre and his uncle Joseph Ravant, a senior guide, join a second attempt to reach Jean's body. Refusing to turn round despite the route being totally out of condition, Pierre ignores the advice of his seniors and pushes into the lead. He takes a huge fall and badly fractures his skull, with Pierre now the object of a full-scale rescue by his father's friends and guides, who act decisively to save his life but abandoning their attempts to reach Jean's body.

The novel moves on six months. The guides have retrieved Jean's body but Pierre has been both physically and mentally damaged by his accident, and now suffers from vertigo. George the porter is in a nursing home in Geneva having lost all his toes and is learning to walk again in specially constructed short boots, as would happen to Louis Lachenal after Annapurna in 1950. As spring approaches, Pierre takes off by himself up an easy climb on the Brevent. He has a torrid time, suffering from vertigo and nearly falling to his death, and this makes him begin to accept that he will never be able to climb freely again.

There is of course a love interest, an understanding young lady who tries to do her best to comfort him, but he sinks into a black despair spending his days and evenings drinking and keeping low company in Chamonix's less well-known drinking dens. There's a welcome interlude when friends and families meet up to move cattle out and up onto the high Alps to graze for the summer: a time of feasting, singing and a competition between the fighting cows of the area.

George returns from Geneva and he and Pierre meet with friends to celebrate his recovery. He surprises them all by announcing he intends to become a guide despite his injuries, and eventually persuades Pierre to accompany him on some easy outcrop climbs and short routes. Slowly Pierre's vertigo becomes less severe, and they plan a major, secret comeback climb: the north face of the Verte. Leaving separately and meeting up on the Grands Montets, they bivouac near the foot of the route, and early next morning set out. The crossing of the bergschrund almost turns them round but once on the face they find they can cut steps and climb ice as well as before. Pierre tunnels through the cornice at the head of the face and they then spend another night out on the descent before arriving at a refuge early in the morning. Much to the surprise of Pierre's uncle Joseph, who having reached the age of 60 years has retired from the guides' rota and is now in his new profession of hut warden.

So in the end all is happy ever after. Pierre has recovered his health and will shortly marry, and George has shown he can manage major climbs once more. Both can now begin their training to become Chamonix guides. So First on the Rope is not a novel to search within for the meaning of life, but it stands the test of time and its descriptions of life in the Chamonix valley in the 1930s, so different from the modern scene, is obviously so true, as are the descriptions of the routes and mountains. It is an easy read but worthwhile. I first read the book in 1950 as a 14-year-old and later met its translator Janet Adam Smith; as someone who tried to read it in French I must say she made an outstanding job of it.

I cannot finish without mentioning *Mount Analogue*, published in 1952, 11 years after *First on the Rope* in 1952. Written by the poet and surrealist René Daumal, *Mount Analogue* is unlike any other mountaineering book ever published. At only 106 pages it is unfinished, but tells of assembling a team to find and climb a hidden peak that reaches inexorably towards heaven. The film *The Holy Mountain* by Jodorowsky is based on the story. Harold Drasdo sent me his copy urging me to read it and think on its meaning. You don't need to do this with Frison-Roche, but 20 climbers could read Daumal and all come up with a different opinion of its meaning; I read it as an allegory of man's search for himself. So I recommend you to read *First on the Rope* whilst journeying to the mountains, and in your bivouac or tent in the Himalaya study *Mount Analogue* to try to find the meaning of it all.

Dennis Gray

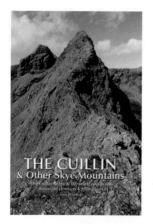

The Cuillin & Other Skye Mountains
The Cuillin Ridge & 100 Select Routes for Mountain Climbers and Hillwalkers
Tom Prentice
Mica, 2019, pp288, £25

For climbers and mountaineers, the Isle of Skye is one of the most sought after destinations in the British Isles. Opportunities for adventure amongst the mountains, sea cliffs and sea stacks abound, but there is no question that the Cuillin peaks are the main attraction. In summer, the traverse of the Cuillin Ridge is one of the most celebrated mountaineering undertakings in the country, and in winter it is a world-class outing.

So it's no surprise that *The Cuillin and Other Skye Mountains*, a new large A5 format guidebook by Tom Prentice, initially focuses on how to succeed on this great challenge. Tom does this by outlining the intricacies of the ridge with a detailed summit-by-summit description illustrated with 23 photo diagrams. There is no doubt, this is the most detailed description of the Cuillin Ridge ever published, and will be a boon for summer visitors intent on traversing the ridge, or making reconnaissance trips prior to a successful traverse, whether it be for summer or winter.

Tom has devoted four pages to ridge planning and tactics. He acknowledges that one-day traverses are frequent, but suggests that for many
climbers, a two-day traverse with prior knowledge from previous visits is
the surest recipe for success. On-sight traverses of the Ridge in summer are
still rare, and likewise, few winter traverses of the ridge occur without prior
knowledge in summer.

It would be a mistake to think this book is just about traversing the Cuillin Ridge however. Tom Prentice goes on to describe ascents and rounds of
peaks throughout Skye, such as the Trotternish Ridge and the mountains of
Kylerhea on the east side of the island, as well as the Cuillin. Many of the
itineraries are well known, such as Pinnacle Ridge on Gillean or the round
of Coire Lagan, but others are less frequented such as the north ridge of
Sgurr na h-Uamha at the northern end of the range. As Tom notes: 'Some
guidebooks suggest Sgurr na h-Uamha as a potential consolation prize after
failing on Sgurr nan Gillean's south-east ridge. Be warned: anyone expecting an "easier day out" will get a very nasty shock.' He goes on to to recommend the route should only be attempted in dry condition and many will
require the security of a rope.

This first hand detailed experience underpins the quality of information
in the book. Tom has spent successive summers on Skye checking all the
routes, and taking hundreds of photographs. The result is a beautiful production, which is almost certainly the most detailed illustrated guidebook
ever published for the Skye mountains. But in many ways it is the balance
of routes included in the book from sub-2,000ft Marilyns to major mountaineering undertakings that sets *The Cuillin and Other Skye Mountains* apart.
Whatever the weather, this book presents a choice of rewarding options that
will make the long trip to the Hebrides worthwhile. Hillwalkers, scramblers,
climbers and winter mountaineers intent on visiting Skye will find it both an
invaluable reference and a source of endless inspiration.

Simon Richardson

Ed Douglas writes: Tom Prentice, for so long publisher for the Scottish Mountaineering Club, has been producing some useful guidebooks under his
Mica imprint in recent years, most notably the hugely popular *Chasing the
Ephemeral*, by Simon Richardson. This book looks as though it will be as
welcome, since it's also born from long and deep experience. Prentice has the
useful skill of inhabiting multiple perspectives – alpinist, rock climber, hill-
walker – in offering advice, particularly when it comes to the Cuillin Ridge.
I finally did this last year, the ridge being the only thing on my wife's climbing to-do list, without ever having been on the northern section, and can see
immediately that I would have benefitted from the excellent photodiagrams
explaining the most awkward sections of route finding. I'm thinking
particularly here of the descent, going south to north, from Bidein Druim
nan Ramh's west peak, whose complexity provoked a scale of marital discord
that might well have ended in the divorce courts had I not finally worked
it out. Photographing these useful diagrams on a phone makes sense, since

the book is too heavy to carry. Prentice offers sound advice on tactics and equipment: my own choice was to catch the boat from Elgol and accept the consequent two-day traverse with a delightful bivy at around halfway. I've no doubt that when I go back, for the Dubhs Ridge say, I'll be taking this excellent book with me. If you have any love for Skye, you need this guide.

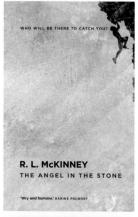

The Angel in the Stone
R L McKinney
Sandstone Press, 2019, pp298, £8.99

Black Car Burning
Helen Mort
Chatto & Windus, 2019, pp324, £12.99

These two novels represent the two poles of climbing fiction. The first is an absorbing novel in which Scottish climbing is in the background of relationship tensions and the second is totally immersed in the Sheffield climbing scene and foregrounds named climbs, although entangled relationship tensions are very much its subject. Each is very readable of its kind, but the two novels also represent two poles of fictional risk-taking. Although R L McKinney looks backward and forwards in time and place in *The Angel in the Stone*, readers always knows where they are, whilst Helen Mort leads her reader into some rather steep moves: crags speak and sex can be complex in *Black Car Burning*.

Calum is a musician whose mother in her Fort William flat does not realise that she has Alzheimer's. He is estranged from his wife and teenage daughter and has sought a quiet life on the west coast where he consoles himself with kayak trips and a noncommittal relationship with a neighbouring sculptor whose studio is in Glasgow. Calum had introduced his younger brother, Finn, to climbing as a distraction from his drug use and manic moods. Finn proves to be very good, although he puts his survival on desperate routes down to the protection of an angel in the rock itself. Calum's mother blames him for the death of Finn when Calum was belaying him and the narrative gradually creeps closer to revealing what really happened. Halfway through the book Calum's daughter arrives at his house and Calum cannot avoid the questions about his past any more. Because Calum's conversations with his mother have been so patient, understanding and witty, the reader is willing him to find a reconciliation with both his troubled daughter and his own past. R L McKinney handles this with great sympathy and narrative economy to suggest that actually each of them knows more than they fully understand.

The open secret of Helen Mort's novel is the Hillsborough football disaster.
The first page of her novel is actually Hillsborough speaking – 'I can speak,
though, if you know how to listen' – watching a climber in his van, parking
and not buying a sandwich, on the way to Wharncliffe Crag, which he thinks
'always felt like a closed room.' So the first pages challenge and engage the
reader with strangely moving detail and the unexpected familiar. The 'He'
turns out to be a former policeman who is haunted and obsessed by the continuing enquiries and inquests. Because everyone in Sheffield is, apparently,
a climber, he is in contact with the three women, Alexa, Caron and Leigh,
whose relationships, of varying degrees of intimacy, are at the centre of this
novel. The publisher suggests that this novel asks, 'How do we trust one another?' but my feeling was that it asks, 'How do we care for one another?'
given the tensions of what Andrew McMillan calls the 'trauma, lust and loss'
underlying those relationships. The title refers to the name of a hard route tar-
geted by Caron, belayed by her new love Leigh, unbeknown to Caron's partner Alexa until Caron ends up in hospital from a fall at Ladybower Quarry.
Ladybower Quarry? Mort certainly knows her crags and this is a contributing
factor to the sense of caring generated by this lyrical and hard-nosed novel.

Terry Gifford

The White Cliff
Epic Tales of Life and Death on the World's Best
Sea Cliff
Edited by Grant Farquhar
Foreword by Stevie Haston
Atlantis Publishing, 2018, 390pp, £35

This is a monster of a book, hard to get to grips
with and initially off-putting: in fact, just like Craig
Gogarth, the fabled sea cliff it describes. But as afi-
cionados of Gogarth, and anyone else revelling in
the world of hard 'out there' trad climbing, knows,
detailed inspection and first-hand experience reap
rewards. I should say from the start that my Gogarth experience was some
time ago and far from comprehensive, but I've been there enough times to
know the fear and respect it engenders: and, if you stick at it, the rewards.
Like many others, I've also been spat off or had an epic when mind and
body were not enough. Johnny Dawes captures this astutely in a quotation
from an early *On The Edge* magazine used as a frontispiece: 'The Gogarth
"look" must not disappear. In the Padarn, say 10 times a year, you'd see a
certain expression – The Look – a manic, almost evil but so very human
picture paint a person's face: Gogarth.'

To say this book is comprehensive is an understatement. It is chock-full of
most of the writing on Gogarth and includes an amazing archive of photographs. It is certainly a labour of love for which we must be in debt to Grant
Farquhar. He started the project when having a long lay-off from climbing,

inspired by Ken Wilson's books. As one of climbers pioneering hard routes on Gogarth in the 1980s, he is well qualified for the job. Crucially, he has drawn in most of the major names across all the decades to provide the definitive account of the cliff, drawing from hundreds of articles, book excerpts but also commissioned writing. It's no mean feat.

It is however frustrating at times. Right from the off, editing issues jump out: Stevie Haston's foreword is spelled 'forward', although perhaps that's just an in-joke from one of the climbing scene's more terrible *enfants terribles*? There's also some kind of weird house style with the use of italics, usefully used to denote subsidiary authorship within the essays, but not in any consistent way. In the acknowledgement he admits that without Smiler Cuthbertson's advice and proofreading, it might have been more sexist and coarser although some will still wince at *Viz*-style references to 'jugs' and 'healthy bouncers': not so hilarious with the benefit of hindsight.

Part way through reading it, I realised two bigger questions had to be asked about the book. Being predominantly a compilation of already published material, albeit from a hugely scattered and arcane set of sources, was it greater than the sum of its parts? And, was there a better way of editing and structuring the book? In my humble opinion, the answers are definitely yes and probably no, or at least, I couldn't see how else to do it. Maybe the final question is would many other people have taken on the task? Again probably not: I, for one, am very glad Farquhar and many others stuck with the project. The passion behind it clearly shows.

Once I got into it, I found I couldn't stop reading. The main pioneers of the 1960s and 1970s were my climbing heroes, the stuff of legends with their hard climbing and hard socialising. Some I knew through the anarchic Liverpool-based Vagabond Mountaineering Club. Some of the stories are well known – Rouse and Minks' epic first ascent of Positron, for example – but I was surprised by how many key early ascents had been done by folk I knew. For mere mortals, like me, the black and white iconography created by John Cleare, Leo Dickinson and Ken Wilson was spellbinding at the time and happily remains so, much of it reproduced throughout the book to great effect. Later colour images are no less impressive.

The book covers the cliff area by area and each section is treated historically, from old to new. Often the text spins away from Gogarth *per se* as it follows the main characters and their other achievements. This 'kitchen sink' approach may infuriate some but generally it makes sense of the myriad contributors to Gogarth's climbing history. In reality it's the history of the modern, bold UK trad ethic with many of its finest exponents also being alpine and super-alpine pioneers: Brown, Boysen, Rouse, Stevie Haston, Fowler and Bullock, to name only a few.

Should you read this book? If you're interested in UK rock climbing in the past five decades, then yes, you should. There's some beautiful writing that goes to the heart of what makes all climbers, from boulderers to alpinists, tick. But it's possibly better for dipping into than reading cover to cover.

Andy Tickle

Obituaries

The Aiguilles du Dru and Mer de Glace, Moonlight
John Ruskin, undated.
Watercolour over pencil, with white bodycolour. 24cm x 35cm.
Gifted to the Alpine Club by Charles Warren.

In Memoriam

The Alpine Club Obituary	Year of Election (including to ACG)
Sue Baldock	1975
Susan Band	Assoc 2012
Donald Barr-Wells	1964
Dave 'Smiler' Cuthbertson	1971
Francois Edwards	1959
Ian 'Pin' Howell	1965
Jack Jackson	1971
Johnny Johnson	1995
Jeff Lowe	Hon 2009
Bruno Messerli	Hon 2008
Alan Pope	Asp 2003
George Rhodes	1974
John Rowlinson	1982
Christopher Simpson	1953
James Cadzow Smith	1990
Ernst Sondheimer	1974
Tony Strawther	1969
Tony Streather	1951
John Temple	1973
Mark Warham	1997
Robin Wilkinson	1979

As usual, the editor will be pleased to receive obituaries for any of those above not included in the following pages.

Robert Fenwick Allen
1936 - 2018

Bob was a man for all seasons, a steady rock climber, a bold and accomplished iceman and an experienced all-round mountaineer. Moreover, he was a talented musician, a landscape artist, a successful businessman and a well-known author of a best-selling series of walking guides covering Snowdonia, the Yorkshire Dales and most extensively, his second home, the English Lake District.

Brought up in the suburbs of north Manchester he took to exploring the crags of the Peak District with his future wife Marjorie Fairclough. Initially equipped, I am reliably informed, with his mother's washing line, they survived early forays on Yellowslacks, since blown up by the

Bob Allen.

local farmer, Windgather and the Roaches. Further experience was gained in the Lake District, North Wales and Scotland but national service in Germany and Korea and reading for a history degree at Cambridge interrupted climbing for several years.

After graduation Bob and Marjorie moved north and their climbing centred on the Lake District, North Wales and Scotland with annual vacations spent in the Alps where they did such climbs as the traverse of La Meije and the north face of the Tour Ronde. Bob did many rock climbs in the HVS and E1 bracket but really came into his own on steep Scottish ice, climbing classics such as *Point Five* and *Zero* gullies with relatively primitive ice tools.

In the early 1960s he joined the Gritstone Club, through which he met Reg Atkins, who had been at School with Trevor Jones (*AJ* 1997, pp355-6). Trevor was a very experienced and enthusiastic rock climber and mountaineer with experience of the Alps and Himalaya: members of a certain age will remember him fondly or otherwise. Bob had many attributes that appealed to Trevor, not the least of which was a company car, and they became regular partners both in the UK and in the Alps. Trevor was a member of the Alpine Climbing Group and was determined to maintain his status as a full member by making at least one significant Alpine ascent each summer.

They formed an unlikely team. Trevor was notorious for his absent-mindedness and chaotic preparations for any climb, whereas Bob was meticulous in all things, frequently customising mountaineering equipment and garments to meet his needs. Despite this they amassed a respectable list of ascents in only a few years, always on the short holidays available to Bob. An early success was on the north-west pillar of Piz Cengalo. The somewhat out-dated AC guide to Bernina and Bregalia states: 'Nowadays it is one of the most desirable objectives in the Bondasca valley,' although it's currently not recommended because of the extremely dangerous approach. On a visit to the Écrins massif with Derek Walker and Ian Roper they made the first British ascent of the Gervasutti route up the south-south-east ridge of the Pic Gaspard. On a lightning visit to Chamonix they made a one-day ascent of the Frendo Spur and later did several climbs in central Switzerland, including the classic *Niedermann* route on the Graue Wand. Climbing with other partners he made ascents of the *Cassin* route on the Piz Badile and the north-east face of the Kingspitz in the Engelhorner.

In 1996 he organised a highly successful Himalayan trip to the Khumbu region of Nepal with a group of friends, average age almost 60, and with the Ladakhi Chewang Motup as sirdar. Four months before they were due to leave he had a coronary by-pass operation and when the artery collapsed this was followed by the insertion of a stent. Despite this he and most of the team trekked to Kala Pattar and made an ascent of Island Peak (6189m) on the way.

Bob was elected president of the Climbers' Club in 1998 and set himself the task of finding a property in the Fort William area that would serve the CC as its hut in Scotland. After much searching and various ultimately futile negotiations, the club bought Riasg, a conveniently situated bungalow in Roy Bridge.

Bob was always a keen walker and early retirement from the carpet trade gave him the time to explore the Lake District thoroughly. *On High Lakeland Fells*, his first guidebook covering both walks and scrambles, illustrated with his own sketches and photographs, sold so well that it displaced James Herriot's books from the top of the *Yorkshire Post's* bestseller list. He followed this with more bestsellers: the inevitable *On Lower Lakeland Fells* and *Walking the Ridges of Lakeland*. Moving further afield he added *Escape to the Dales* and *On Foot in Snowdonia*. After his death, Bob's widow Lin received many letters from readers telling her how much these books had changed their lives.

During the last decade failing health restricted Bob to shorter and shorter days on the fells and he spent much of his time painting; he was particularly proud of being elected president of the Ambleside Art Society. He also became a well-known member of the Grasmere community contributing to its activities. The fact the local parish church was more than full for his funeral service indicates the degree to which he will be missed.

Michael G Mortimer

• Bob Allen was included in the In Memoriam for 2018.

Susan Baldock
1936 - 2018

Susan Margaret Baldock, née Tuke, was born in Newenden, Kent. Her father was a GP who practised in Bournemouth and her mother Australian. She was educated at Cheltenham Ladies College and Girton College Cambridge where she read natural sciences. After Cambridge she became a schoolteacher, primarily of biology but also other sciences. She taught at Sherborne School for Girls for 13 years and then at Bishop Wordsworth's Grammar School for Boys in Salisbury for five years.

Sue Baldock.

Throughout her life, Sue loved the outdoors and travel. In her childhood she sailed with her father in his yacht and at Cambridge won a half blue for sailing. She took up hill walking, skiing and mountaineering, and took full advantage of long school holidays in the 17 years before I met her, spending 43 weeks in the Alps, 13 in summer and 30 in winter. She was a member of Wessex Mountaineering Club, the Fell and Rock Climbing Club, Ski Club of Great Britain and the Eagle Ski Club.

She was a keen skier, particularly ski mountaineering and was prominent in the ski-mountaineering world, organising and leading a number of high mountain ski tours sponsored by the Ski Club of Great Britain including the Haute Route and traverses of the Bernina and the Bernese Oberland. She joined the Eagle Ski Club in 1970 and was awarded 'Golden Eagle' status in 1971. The ESC quickly recognised Sue's organising abilities and made full use of them: she served as their touring secretary from 1976 to 1986. She was particularly keen on organising training, including a training meet for the ESC in the Bernese Oberland and a gritstone meet, remembered by Jay Turner, at a snowy Froggatt Edge for practice in crevasse rescue techniques for which she brought over the well-known Swiss guide Martin Epp from Andermatt. In the summer, Alpine mountaineering was Sue's thing and she climbed extensively in Austria climbing many of the highest peaks.

Sue and I first met on an Alpine Club Welsh meet at Ynys Ettws in February 1975. We were both new members of the Club, with Sue being among the first group of elected female members. As singletons we were arbitrarily paired, the AC equivalent to blind dating. We set off for the Parson's Nose and the pairing stuck for 43 years. Together we had two summer seasons in the Alps in the Bernina and Bregalia and the Dauphiné where our highlights were the Biancograt on Piz Bernina and the traverse of the Meije. She was also a member of John Harding's tragic ski-touring party, which was caught in an avalanche while attempting a traverse of the Pyrenees, burying all but one of the party. John's cousin was lost and Sue was completely buried except for one arm but was rescued. John remembers that Sue was calm, collected and wonderfully helpful throughout this distressing business. She subsequently discovered that at the time she was already pregnant with our son.

With the arrival of Robert our holidays were limited to downhill skiing and camping and hill walking, mainly in the British Isles. The last four years of her life were sadly blighted by Alzheimer's disease and cancer.

David Baldock

Susan Band
1936 - 2018

George and Susan Band in Mumbai harbour for the Kangchenjunga 40th anniversary in 1995. *(Harish Kapadia)*

Susan was born on 7 September 1936 in London. She claimed to be a cockney as she was born within the sound of Bow bells; the rest of the family thought she must have very good hearing. She excelled at school and had three A-levels at 16. Nowadays university would have beckoned but her father did not think it right or necessary for girls to go to university so she had to make do with a year at Grenoble University to perfect her French. She also spent time in Germany learning German and did a secretarial course. Then she joined the Foreign Office and was posted to The Hague where she learnt Dutch. This was where she met George, a young petroleum engineer working for Shell. Romance blossomed and the pair got married in August 1959.

Susan now began the career of an oilman's wife. Their next posting was mid Texas then Lafayette, Louisiana. I was born in 1964 and the family moved to Venezuela shortly after. Louise arrived in 1966 and Rupert in 1969. The family was by now in Chittagong, in what was then East Pakistan. Susan's strength of character was tested here, as she had to make contingency plans for joining the train of refugees heading for Burma with civil war breaking out around them. The family got out and East Pakistan became Bangladesh.

The Band family moved to Oman, which had itself at the time, as George put it, 'a small war waging in the south with Yemeni rebels.' In Oman the family spent a lot of time exploring the deserts and wadis of the interior. Oman was followed by the Netherlands where Susan took the lead role in the Anglo-American theatre group's production of 'The Crucible.

Towards the end of 1976 the family moved to England, first to Holland Park. Here Susan started to do volunteer work with the parole board and started a degree in political history with the Open University. It took a few years but was quite an achievement considering all the other things going on her life. In the summer of 1978 the family moved again to Hartley Wintney, so beginning Susan's great love affair with this Hampshire village and its surrounding area, although one last overseas posting to Sarawak delayed things a little. That autumn Susan accompanied George on the first of her many treks to Nepal.

George was managing director of Shell Sarawak and Sabah; Susan was now hostess in chief. There was an endless round of entertaining, visiting offshore oil platforms and entertaining local dignitaries. She also found time to explore the jungle, water-skied with crocodiles on the Miri river, edit a cook book and produce a play for the local amateur dramatic society. All the time though Susan was aching to get back to Hartley Wintney, which the family did in 1983.

Once back in Hartley Wintney Susan was able to really get stuck in to village life. She seemed to be involved with everything and know everybody. She worked with her friend Lady Sylvia Limerick on a charity researching cot death, commuting up to London up to five days a week and ending up as secretary of the whole organisation. She retired in 1988 but came back in 1989 to organise an international conference on infant deaths involving 22 countries.

While working full time for the foundation she was also involved with local arts groups and accompanied George on more treks in the Himalayas, including one that George nicknamed the Hampshire housewives trek. Susan was starting to get to know the workings of the Himalayan Trust, the charity set up by Sir Edmund Hillary to help the Sherpa people of Nepal with schools and clinics in remote areas.

At the end of the 1980s, another major chapter began in Susan's life. Armed with her degree in political history and worldwide experience, Susan, as she put it, allowed herself to be persuaded to stand for the district council. She campaigned tirelessly. It wasn't enough to put a leaflet through the letter box. She ticked off all those she had spoken to on the electoral roll and then came back a second and sometimes a third time to make sure she spoke to everyone. It was tense at the first count with nobody knowing what to expect and no opinion polls to go on but Susan got in comfortably and did so for another three elections until retiring from the council 20 years later.

Housing was Susan's main interest, preserving the village but champion-ing social housing so the younger generation would not be forced out of the area. From 2001 she served as chair of the council, which meant, to her family's amusement that George could now be referred to as the chair's consort complete with chain of office. Most of all, she remained open and accessible to all throughout her 20 years. Many a Sunday Lunch was interrupted as Susan took a call.

Away from the council Susan was busy in other areas, serving on several local committees. After George died she was made a fellow of the Royal Geographical Society and became a trustee of the Himalayan Trust. In the latter role she helped organise the 60th anniversary celebrations of the first ascent of Everest in the presence of Her Majesty the Queen. She later visited Nepal for the last time, inspecting the schools the charity had built out there.

Sadly the last few years of Susan's life were blighted by dementia. Better to remember her as the vibrant, fun and incredibly busy woman before that.

Nigel Band

Harish Kapadia writes: Most of the later events in the life of Susan Band, née Goodenough, revolved around her husband George, president 1987-9 (*AJ* 2012, pp396-401) and youngest member of the 1953 Everest expedition, who made the first ascent of Kangchenjunga in 1955. 'I had to wait till George finished his mountain climbing,' Susan told me during an oral history recording. She was working at the British embassy at The Hague when George was sent there by his company Shell to train as a petroleum engineer. She says that as George had no mountains to go to, he and friends gravitated towards the young ladies working at the embassy, where they first met. 'I knew nothing about mountains and had not met any mountaineers. When he told me about Everest and Kangchenjunga, I had to imagine what that meant.' She had never climbed a hill and it never occurred to her that a mountain should be climbed, although she did four-inch heels.

Susan, conversant in German and Dutch, worked at the Foreign Office and was posted to The Hague. That's when things began to happen. George proposed and they were soon married in London. The first mountaineer friend she met was Lord Hunt and others soon followed. From then on, mountains became a part of her life albeit in the shadow of George. After the wedding, a Dutch paper interviewed them and asked if she would go climbing: 'I don't know,' was her crisp reply.

Their lives together were certainly full of travels. Soon after their marriage they were sent by Shell to the USA, before returning to the UK to set up their new home. Further postings took them all over the world, first to Malaysia and thereafter to Bangladesh, Oman and Basra. On his return, George became the president of the Alpine Club, responsible for finding a new home for the Club.

Inevitably perhaps, many Himalayan treks followed his retirement, and she especially enjoyed meeting hill people. They were in south-east Nepal in 2005 and at Taplejung, en route to Kangchenjunga base camp, villagers requested they start a school for them, just as Hillary had done for the Sherpas of Khumbu. They worked through the Himalayan Trust, especially Susan, to see it through. She visited Taplejung in 2009 to see the school up and running. Her extensive trekking experience saw Susan elected as an associate member of the Club.

In 1995, Susan and George visited Mumbai to celebrate the 40th anniversary of Kangchenjunga's first ascent. We had a wonderful time together, going on a boat ride in Mumbai harbour, walking in the Western Ghats and sharing the celebrations.

In 2000, George was first diagnosed with prostate cancer and gradually became weaker. Susan was his primary carer and oversaw all his needs, though she told me, 'despite the illness George was self-sufficient almost till his end.' He was obviously keen to attend the 50th anniversary of the first ascent of Everest in 1953 and Susan made it possible for him; it was in a way the climax of their married life.

George passed away in 2011 and was buried in the local churchyard. A few years later I was in London and Susan invited me to visit her home. She walked me round the village, taking me to George's grave, and sat there contemplatively, forbidding me from taking a picture of her there.

Susan was involved in many activities for local village. On Remembrance Day, 11 November, she would attend the local parade proudly wearing the khukri badge of the Gorkha regiment I had presented to her in memory of my son Lt Nawang Kapadia, whom she had met, a Gorkha soldier killed on the same date in the year 2000. Always meticulous, I would receive an email soon after about the parade to tell me she had worn the badge. She will always be in my thoughts on Remembrance Day for this.

Dave Cuthbertson
1948 - 2019

So my old pal Smiler, Dave Cuthbertson, has passed away. His death came suddenly on 2 May after he was admitted to Raigmore hospital with pneumonia, which was soon after diagnosed as caused by lung cancer. He died within a week of admission. His funeral was held at the village of Dores near Inverness where he had lived for the past 23 years. A church service included some heartfelt tributes, and was followed by an open-air lunch at the village pub, in glorious sunshine, looking out over a peaceful Loch Ness.

I first met him when I joined Wolverhampton MC in the late 1960s. Smiler was from Wombourne, a village south-west of the city. It was like meeting a bouncy young dog, full of energy, enthusiasm, and

Smiler Cuthbertson. *(Ian Smith)*

friendliness to all. His nickname says everything. He always had wide climbing interests: he once alarmed some policemen in the West Midlands by his night-time ascent of a disused brick-built factory chimney. Of course, his good-natured charm soon won them round, and the route was completed without further ado.

He was chair of Wolverhampton MC, later becoming president of the Climbers' Club, a stalwart of the Alpine Climbing Group and Alpine Club, a member from 1971 and a member of the SMC and FRCC, as well as an IFMGA mountain guide.

We climbed together throughout the 1970s when he led me struggling and cursing up many hard Welsh and Lakes rock routes, my seconding encouraged by his stream of bubbling optimism, plus an occasional tight rope. Forays north of the border for Scottish ice led to the roles being reversed. Ours was a complementary partnership. His notable Alpine ascents include the Bonatti Pillar, the Walker Spur, the Matterhorn north face and after several abortive attempts, the Eiger north face in 1981. I had a season with him in the Bernese Oberland, resulting in ascents of the Mönch, the first British ascent of a route on the north face of the Lauterbrunnen Breithorn and a new route on the north face of the Ebnefluh.

After this, we sadly drifted apart. He moved into the guiding profession and in 1996 relocated to Scotland with his wife Clare and their children Robyn and Laurie. I concentrated on lightweight trips to the Karakoram, which he was unable to join being committed to summer guiding and the vagaries of the freelance life. His guiding activities included the UK, the Alps, Nepal, Peru, East Africa, and many more locations around the world. More recently, he organised a series of ice climbing visits to Rjukan in Norway for the Climbers' Club.

The author Ernest Hemingway is supposed to have said that 'there are only three sports: bull fighting, motor racing and mountaineering; the others are merely games,' implying a need to put one's life on the line. This quotation underlines an essential feature of our 'sport', the danger involved, which begs the question of where the right balance lies between courage and foolhardiness. This is a matter all climbers must decide for themselves. What is clear with Smiler is that anyone who employed him as a guide would be less subjected to the sort of excessive rule-bound practices followed by some other guides; they would have an active and enjoyable experience, also a fulfilling and exciting one.

Smiler's choices of climbing venues, and styles of climbing show the width of his interests. The sport of athletics has many differing disciplines: sprints, middle and long-distance running, and various jumping and throwing activities. Likewise, our sport also has many disciplines: single and multi-pitch climbing, ice climbing, Alpine and Himalayan mountaineering, and many more, each with its own set of challenges and flavour. Smiler revelled in most of these, so could be likened not to a sprinter or marathon runner, more to a decathlete. He was one of climbing's great characters, and one of its most charming. Those who were guided by Smiler, climbed unguided with him or just met him in the pub all delighted in his company; he will be sorely missed by myself and all in the climbing world who knew him.

Dave Wilkinson

Lt Col Simon Jeremy Hall OBE
1960 - 2017

Simon Hall, Royal Marine and SAS soldier, skier, mountaineer and husband died from pancreatic cancer at the age of 57. Clichés abound within obituaries, but to describe Simon's life as a story from the Boy's Own Paper is no exaggeration.

Simon was educated at Brentwood School, where his future destiny was inspired by two characters: first his father, who as deputy head and CO of the school's combined cadet force introduced him to the

Simon Hall.

mountains of north Wales, and second by a member of the school staff who had been a soldier in the wartime Special Air Service. A Saturday job at Pindisports in London followed, where colleague Jon Tinker recalled Simon was in demand as a model for mountaineering clothing. This was possibly the genesis of Simon's vice for acquiring new kit. Many of us as his friends were frequently subjected to hours of mooching in mountaineering stores, where he had a keen eye for new features and would then invoke the n=x+1 rule, where 'n' is the number of jackets, ice axes or whatever that one needs and 'x' is the number currently held. We feel sure shares in Cotswold Outdoor must have dropped steeply since his passing.

University at Loughborough and Manchester followed, but his PhD in glaciology was left unfinished when he decided to join the Royal Marines. The Corps, as it is affectionately known, was the perfect vehicle for Simon's talent of being able to soldier and perform to the highest standards in hostile environments. He soon volunteered for the Mountain and Arctic Warfare Cadre, qualifying as a mountain leader officer; he was blending two passions: soldiering and the mountains.

I joined 45 Commando as its medical officer in the autumn of 1988, and was immediately befriended by Simon who was commanding the Reconnaissance Troop. With other friends, a small unofficial climbing club evolved within the unit. We were given a fantastic opportunity to take an expedition from 45 Commando to Alaska in 1990. In this era, 'risk assessment' had barely entered the military vocabulary, but to reassure both our CO and ourselves that we were up to the task, we embarked on a binge of winter ascents in Scotland, the Alps and the Lyngen Alps of Norway.

A highlight of this climb-fest was an ascent of the *Kuffner* route on Mont Maudit, followed by a traverse over the summit of Mont Blanc. We did this in three days valley to valley between Christmas and New Year, arriving back in Chamonix just in time to party. In Alaska we made ascents of both the west buttress and the *Cassin* on Denali. We had all had one of the climbs of our lives and Simon's wanderlust had been further stoked.

During the next decade, he wove an intricate path between his desire to advance his military career and simultaneously feed his hunger for mountain adventure. He passed selection for the Special Air Service in 1992 at a time when it was frowned upon within the Royal Marines for an officer to volunteer for the SAS. He saw barriers thrown up to prevent him from volunteering simply as intellectual challenges to be overcome, which he of course did, and predictably was then appointed to command a mountain troop within one of the Sabre squadrons. Reunited within his troop with his *Cassin* climbing partner, who had also taken a sabbatical from the Marines, he swung between operational deployments and training tasks that by design combined mountain adventure with cutting-edge military capability.

Being held to frequent 'very high readiness' commitments, usually supporting counterterrorist operations, meant Simon was at the mercy of a radio pager in the pre-mobile phone era. During an ascent of the *Gabarrou-Albinoni* on Mont Blanc du Tacul, the pager began to vibrate as the final pitch was surmounted, summoning the pair to return to Hereford within 24 hours. A crazily fast abseil was followed by a race on skis back to the Aiguille du Midi and a taxi to Geneva airport for the flight home. The pair made it home to Stirling Lines, the SAS garrison, with six hours to spare and Cheshire Cat grins to boot.

On another occasion Simon's troop re-enacted Operation Gunnerside, subject of the film *Heroes of Telemark*, when in 1943 saboteurs from the Special Operations Executive attacked the heavy-water plant at Vemork, near Rjukan, Norway. Having been inserted at the original wartime drop zone, the troop spent a week patrolling by ski and evading detection until just after the 'objective' had been reached, when the local Rjukan constabulary duly appeared. It transpired there had been a glitch in securing diplomatic clearance for this exercise, and so Simon and his merry band were dispatched to the local nick to wait for some furious political and diplomatic backpedalling.

By 2000, his dalliance with the army became an advantage to him as the hitherto separate Special Air Service and Special Boat Service reorganised under a common command structure. In succession, Simon commanded C squadron of the SBS, became second-in-command of the SBS and then moved back to the army as CO of 23 SAS, one of the UK Special Forces (Reserve) units. This period ushered in the current era of terrorism and the operational tempo was high for the special forces, the details of which are not appropriate for this obituary. Simon's exemplary service was recognised by the award of the OBE in 2004, following both his father and grandfather, who had similarly been recognised for their service. The mountains weren't completely off the agenda, and during an operational interlude in 2002 we shared a ski-mountaineering adventure in the Southern Alps of New Zealand, where I was then living completing higher medical training.

Simon had eschewed a conventional Royal Marines career for one in special forces, to which he had totally and selflessly committed himself. By the law of unintended consequences, a military life lived by necessity largely in the shadows meant his profile didn't fit that required for higher command in the Royal Marines. Picture in your mind's eye a cross between Captain Black from Gerry Anderson's *Captain Scarlet and the Mysterons* TV series and Clint Eastwood's Dirty Harry and that's Simon. When it was suggested to him that a spell as a conventional staff officer in human resources might, the emphasis being on 'might', restore his chances of promotion, Simon read his tea leaves very carefully and changed tack once again.

Characteristically, he identified a gap where he could effect change and assumed command of the Joint Services Mountain Training Centre (JSMTC) at Indefatigable on the Menai Straits, Anglesey. Whilst commanding 23 SAS, he had initiated a Seven Summits project, crediting his 1990 ascents of Denali of course, for eight members of the Special Forces (Reserve), and he completed this with ascents of Everest in 2007 and Vinson in 2010. While commanding JSMTC, he swapped his operational mountaineering role for one in which his organisation promoted mountaineering and ski mountaineering as adventurous training. This is a long-established method of promoting leadership, teamwork and resilience through controlled exposure to the risks inherent in mountaineering. Adventurous training is held to be precious to the military, but it was obvious to Simon that for this to endure against an intrusive climate of risk aversion, there was a need for increased governance of these inherently risky activities without stifling adventure. He achieved this in large part, particularly through the introduction of IFMGA guides into the JSMTC staff and modern guiding techniques into the instructional portfolio.

Hitherto, there had been little time in his schedule for any lasting relationship, but Simon had by now met Gill Burton and they lived together for a number of years. Simon's 50th birthday was held in a packed boathouse at Indefatigable, where during his speech to assembled friends and colleagues he famously referred to Gill as his fiancée, without of course having consulted her on the matter. In the 30 years I knew Simon, the only chink in his armour that I could find – the only lack of otherwise absolute confidence that I could ever detect – was a sort of shyness with women. He and Gill married and lived on Anglesey thereafter.

Moving on from JSMTC, prior to retiring, Simon returned to the security world with one last operational tour in Afghanistan. He concluded his service with the same commitment that he had shown throughout his career and was again decorated for his efforts with a Queen's Commendation for Valuable Service in 2013. He worked freelance in the security reform sector in both Afghanistan and Somalia following retirement until he was diagnosed with his final illness in January 2017. When we met just before his death, I think his one regret was having spent so much time away from Gill during those happy years on Anglesey.

Simon was a consummate professional soldier and a selfless leader, so selfless that it was rumoured he insisted on his rope-mate leading all the pitches on the *Cassin* with Simon as the solid belayer offering encouragement and copious hot drinks when required. He had a great sense of humour, but it was of a particular type: 'acerbic', 'like a sledgehammer' or 'trenchant' are fairly accurate terms. His tendency to be taciturn belied a warm-hearted nature and a deep love of the natural world. He was loyal to his friends and grounded through his parents' influence, and he remained close to his sister Lesley throughout his life. He is epitomised in his obituary published by the Special Boat Service Association: 'His delightfully philosophical perspective on the roles of Special Forces was strongly reminiscent of some of their leading wartime forbears, and he would be well deserving of a place in their hall of fame. We have lost a good friend and an inspirational leader, and, in the hackneyed but totally appropriate language of the eulogy, we can justifiably lament that we will not see his like again.'

Pete Davis

• Simon Hall was included in the In Memoriam for 2018.

Ian Howell
1936 - 2018

There were two climbers named 'Ian' on Whillans' 1964 Gauri Sankar team and Dennis Gray figured that 'Howell' equals 'dowel' equals 'dowel pin', and so Ian Howell became 'Pin'. Inadvertently the team attempted the mountain's Tibetan flank, avoided Chinese patrols – and failed. It was Pin's first expedition and thereafter to his close friends he was known as Pin.

To alpinists the world over Ian was 'Mr Mount Kenya'. By the 1970s he was the acknowledged local guru and his advice and generous assistance were freely available to all who wanted to climb on the mountain he had made his own. 'From the moment I first saw Mount Kenya at the age of 32 I wanted to climb it, and for 33 years I did just that,' he wrote. An ex-BBC engineer, he arrived in Nairobi in 1968 on a two-year contract to establish a countrywide radio net for Kenya's police. At the time there were scarcely a dozen different routes on the mountain massif and in the ensuing 25 years, usually climbing with other expat members of the very active Mountain Club of Kenya (MCK), he put up over 20 new rock and ice climbs of the hardest technical standards on the main peak alone. By 1985 he had reached the summit more than 160 times by dozens of different routes.

The MCK guidebook warns that even the regular route to the twin summits of the mountain should be regarded as a two-day climb; the line, graded IV-, far from obvious and liable to be iced, had been the scene of several accidents to descending parties caught out by the 12-hour equatorial night. Thus

Ian Howell on the summit of Rani Peak, climbed during the 1978 Himalchuli expedition, which ended prematurely following the death of Alison Chadwick-Onyszkiewicz on Annapurna. Her husband Janusz, mathematician and politician, was part of the Himalchuli team. *(John Cleare)*

Ian 'Pin' Howell. *(John Cleare)*

after completing his police contract early in 1970, Pin designed and prefabricated a tiny bivouac hut in his Nairobi garden and arranged for the national park to airdrop it in five loads on to the Lewis glacier below the peak. Then, entirely alone and carrying the loads on his back, he made 13 solo ascents to erect the hut at 5,188m among the summit boulders of Nelion. The tiny Howell hut will accommodate four at a pinch and has ever since proved a godsend to so many climbers. [*Editor's note:* See 404 in AC Notes.]

Born in London and educated at Caterham School in Surrey, Pin had already started work in the Caribbean for his father's employer Cable & Wireless when national service caught up with him in 1958 and posted him to the Royal Signals at Catterick. Here he fell in with Brian Evans, already a well-known climber, who took him out onto the gritstone edges so successfully that climbing soon became the principal motivation of his life.

After a couple of years climbing widely round Britain while working for the BBC's engineering department in Ealing, Pin took a three-month break in 1962 to visit the Alps with Brian and Allan Austin. Starting in the Dolomites they worked their way westwards via an impressive sequence of some 25 hard rock routes including the *Comici* on the Cima Grande, the *Scarf Arete*, the Badile north ridge, the east face of the Grand Capucin and the west faces of both the Noire and the Dru. A shorter holiday the following year added a few more similar achievements and he was elected to the ACG.

Clearly, Aunty Beeb was generous with unpaid leave: the Gauri Sankar attempt followed and then his election to the AC, proposed by Ian Clough, the 'other Ian', and seconded by Peter Crew. Two years later Malcolm Slesser invited Pin to join his team for an abortive attempt on the Amazon face of Yerupajá.

Pin's folks lived on the Isle of Wight and I'd first met him at Swanage in 1965, subsequently sharing a few climbs in Cornwall and elsewhere, but when he returned to Britain after his Kenya police contract, we hit it off as serious rope-mates. He worked for me on several film and photographic assignments, enjoying filming *The Lost River of Gaping Ghyll* but getting jammed tight, deep underground in Ogof y Daren Cilau while we worked on a story entitled 'The Cave from which Rescue is Impossible'. Underground was not quite his scene but we did enjoy a short but very sweet season in the Bernina and Bregaglia, which included the second ascent of Carlo Mauri's direct on the north face of Monte Disgrazia. That autumn he returned with Pete Biven to locate the elusive Pizzo Ligoncio, a facsimile Badile, and make the first British ascent of its comparable north face. That was his style: pioneering, doing a magnificent but unknown route on a fine, little-known peak.

It was 19 years before Pin returned to the Alps while on a business trip to the UK. On the Barre des Écrins I owed him much, perhaps my life. High on the south face, on steep rock, I was swiped by a large rock fall. Despite a suspected broken left arm and leg, with clever rope-work he got me up the final two pitches to the summit and then safely along the summit snow crest and so down the north face to the Glacier Blanc where we were forced to bivouac. Miraculously I was merely very badly bruised and next day, with feeling gradually returning, he roped me safely over the Col des Écrins and back to La Bérarde. It was his final Alpine fling.

During his irregular UK business trips Pin especially enjoyed amphibious explorations on sea cliffs, notable among these the Elugug sea stacks off the Castlemartin coast climbed in wild winter weather, and the Devil's Lime Kiln, that profound blow hole on Lundy, where he and Pete Biven were almost thwarted by an aggressive bull seal.

After Yerupajá his next expedition was as big as they come: we were both selected to join the much publicised 1971 International Everest Expedition attempting the first ascent of the south-west face. BBC sponsored and ill fated, we were groomed to shoot the first synch-sound film from the summit. Needless to say we didn't, and the full story is well covered elsewhere (*AJ* 1972, pp9-20). But preparing for the expedition demonstrated another of Pin's skills; he was handy with a sewing machine, indeed in Kenya he had made much of his own mountain clothing and now, working with BBC technicians, we designed and developed much of the specialised protective gear that was necessary for filming at high altitude and in low temperatures.

Having recovered from Everest (*AJ* 1972, pp80-5) he returned to Kenya to take up the post of sales director of NavCom, a two-man Nairobi firm selling airport radio equipment across Africa. Now new routes on Mount Kenya came thick and fast, usually with one of the two other leading Kenya climbers, Iain Allen and John Temple. When acclimatised and moving fast a route could just be snatched in a weekend. One such was the *Diamond Couloir*, the steep 300m ice gully on the south face between the twin peaks, long considered a death trap since a RAFMA party were avalanched below it in the 1950s. In 1972 Pin and Iain Allen had surmounted all difficulties but on reaching the little Diamond glacier at its head had traversed off to be back at work on Monday morning. Spindrift defeated another attempt in poor weather, this one with Frank Cannings and me. Some weeks later Pin and I zoomed up from Nairobi before dawn one Saturday morning and on Sunday afternoon, high on the final icefall, we each in turn discovered the other had fallen asleep. Too horrified to continue, we swiftly abseiled out. A year later Phil Snyder and Thumbu Mathenge, his African ranger trainee, made the first complete ascent right to the Gate of the Mists but I always felt it was really Pin's route.

He was no stranger to the other great snow mountains of central Africa. He'd ascended the Virunga volcanoes and with Snyder made the first ascent of the remote McConnell's Prong (V, A1) in the Rwenzori. (The obligatory handshake with Idi Amin occurred on a mundane business trip.) He knew Kilimanjaro well having made the first complete traverse of the mountain, west to east, with Snyder, ascending Kibo by the Western Breach and eventually descending the wild, unexplored east face of Mawenzi, enduring nine bivouacs en route. He had ascended each of the southern glaciers and in 1975, with Bill O'Connor and me, made the first direct ascent of the hanging Kersten glacier, a two-day route mostly on steep ice and involving some aid climbing on a large icicle.

Nevertheless, Pin did not relish the cold; he was happiest on sun-warmed rock. With Iain Allen, John Temple and other MCK friends he made regular exploratory climbs on the 'bush crags' and *inselberg* which abound in Kenya, where climbing is spiced by unusual hazards. Descending one day from Lolokwe crag, he and Iain Allen were chased by a rhino, while on the forested Umbwe ridge their tent was ripped in the night by a prowling leopard. A cave on one remote crag held the mummified bodies of what he assumed had been ancient tribal shaman. Benighted below a line of roofs during an attempt on the blank wall of the Ololokwe mesa, we found neither ledge nor protection in the peculiar, crack-less rock, and belayed only to vine stems hanging over the roof we slept perched on mounds of bat guano adhering to the face. In the night the bat guano slid away leaving us held only by the now taut vines. Come daylight we retreated with some difficulty. Favourite crags included Hells Gate, where Pin's brilliant route *Olympian* (600ft, E2 5b) is surely Kenya's most celebrated rock climb. Climbers may well encounter swarming wild bees and face the attentions of aggressive baboons whose antics polish the holds.

Predictably the siege tactics and razzmatazz that Everest ventures attracted left a bad taste in his mouth. Over the next 20 years Pin often returned to the Himalaya, but always with a few trusted friends, determined to climb in better style and to leave no trace on the mountain of their passing. Thus in 1978 he tried a new route without Sherpa support on remote Himalchuli (7893m) and in 1986 he and his two companions were weathered off just below the summit of Ama Dablam. For some reason success eluded him on every 'official' expedition.

However, starting in 1974 he and I with a trusty Sherpa cook, a kitchen boy and Jimmy Roberts' blessing, made a series of lightweight forays into unmapped areas of Nepal where we discovered unknown passes, traversed closed valleys and climbed several good peaks, usually nameless, of around 6,000m, 'because they look interesting and attractive'. Though later we were surprised to discover the highest had been nearer 6,700m. These journeys were probably illegal and official reports were never written. It was mountaineering at its purest, absolutely Pin's style, and years later he claimed that these trips were the most enjoyable ventures in his life.

He had first visited Yosemite in 1966 with the thwarted Yerupajá team, the first British party to do so. When Pin and Davy Bathgate became the first all-British rope to climb the north-west face of Half Dome, Al Steck and several Valley denizens became lifelong friends. Years later, at the age of 61, he toured the American West with Iain Allan, ticking off no less than 18 of the routes in Steck and Roper's *Fifty Classic Climbs in North America*, including the Titan, that frightening 200m monolith of 'solid mud' in the Utah desert whose 'summit changes shape in every thunder storm.' Later, an attempt on the *Cassin* on Denali with fellow Kenya climber Peter Brettle, his last go at a big mountain, was defeated by bad weather. But that was not really his style.

In between all this mountain activity Pin had managed both to earn a living and to find time, in 1975, to marry Ann, a teacher working in Nairobi. In due course, concerned that Kenya was no longer a safe place to bring up a family, they moved back to Britain in the early 1990s and settled near Bath. Now he commuted to Kenya, two weeks on and two weeks off, a gruelling ordeal. He took a fall climbing at Lukenia, a favourite crag outside Nairobi, and his badly damaged ankle was slow to knit; he was diagnosed as coeliac with resultant osteoporosis. Serious dietary planning became essential and so he finally returned home and retired.

A gentle, generous and unassuming man, climbing for Ian Howell was his way of life and mountains his inspiration. He was a safe climber and despite his many successes there were many retreats, for his mountaineering was about exploration, never about conquest. After retirement his explorations continued but in lower key: there was the Groot Spitzkoppe (1728m), the 'Matterhorn of Namibia', at the age of 74, (*CCJ* 2011, pp128-33) and then one final expedition with several old friends to the High Atlas, though here the long ascents of steep snow slopes proved hard work.

He was often to be found on the friendly granite of Cornish sea-cliffs, and occasionally on the bolted limestone crags of the Spanish Costa or taking gentle walking tours with Ann on various Mediterranean islands. At home he tried off-road cycling until a fall on ice outside his home did further damage. He was a volunteer driver for the local hospital car service. As a member of both the Alpine Club and the Climbers' Club he kept in close touch with his climbing friends and with goings-on in the mountain world. But after two knee replacements his fitness gradually declined and he died unexpectedly aged 82, leaving his wife and a daughter, a Cambridge tennis blue who is clinical director of a veterinary practice.

John Cleare

John Temple writes: Ian was king of the mountain. By the time he left Kenya there were few routes he had not climbed. He wore the title lightly, his modesty screening his justifiable pride. He loved the challenge of a new route and had an eye for a line and the skills to follow it. But what he did, he did for fun. He embraced the good fortune of being in the right place at the right time.

Until climate change decimated its glaciers and snowfields, Mount Kenya was the ideal of an alpine peak: shapely, soaring ridges, classic ice-filled couloirs, brutal walls and buttresses, and devoid of any easy way. It was a mountaineer's mountain, high but not too high, accessible from Nairobi in a couple of hours. We'd be up to the road-head above Naro Moru by mid afternoon and in place for a route on Saturday. The comfort of the bivy hut he had built on Nelion, then down on Sunday and hopefully with enough recovery to make it through the working week. The combination of near-perfect, detailed rock, which took protection readily with near-perfect weather in the dry season, made for a fun playground. Ian was fortunate too, as the equipment of the 1960s and 1970s allowed more exacting routes. It was not a malevolent mountain, tolerant rather than homicidal, provided you treated it with respect. Ian did just that.

I had the privilege and pleasure of sharing three of his new routes. I was a middle-aged apprentice after the acquisition of a young family in the 1960s and drifting towards the fringe of the climbing scene. Ian guided the upgrade and expansion of my skills. A model tutor: tolerant, good-humoured, straight. Significantly, I never had anything like an epic in his company. He drew my attention to the realities of the situation when we made an attempt on Kibo's Breach Wall. He'd let me run out the first pitch and joined me at the belay. Here my attention was drawn to the steady rock fall and thickening weather, which, as belayer, had come to his notice. I was too fired up to recognise reality but we abseiled off: a sound mountaineering decision by a sound mountaineer. The only tension between us in those glorious few years was on a rope when I struggled to follow his lead.

Following my departure from Kenya in 1976 we did not climb together for about 20 years. When we did, it felt like 20 days, picking up where we left off: a delightful experience. Our last trip to the hills took us to the Dollies and the shameless use of lifts up and down (knee troubles) let us enjoy the fantastic scenery and the exposure. For Ian it was a return 'to the scene of his climbs'. Almost everywhere we went he would point out some horrendously steep and improbable route that he had ticked back in the 1950s. He had never mentioned them before.

His last years burdened him with ill health but he handled this with characteristic good-humoured fortitude, his cup consistently half full: eyes bright, smile on his face, kind words, big heart. He enhanced my life and that of others. The two days we spent on the Diamond Buttress were the two best days of my life. Thank you Ian.

Derek Buckle writes: I never had the pleasure to climb with Ian, but I fully endorse John's elegant description of Ian's nature. Few people I know embody the mild gentlemanly temperament that characterised Ian. He was an authority on Mt Kenya and was always happy to share his extensive knowledge with others, wishing to explore its beauty and extensive attraction.

John Rodney Johnson
1930 - 2018

Johnny Johnson.

John Johnson was a career diplomat who spent many years in Kenya. He was a passionate walker who climbed all the Munros in Scotland and the Mountain Club of Kenya call all their peaks above 7,000ft 'Johnsons'. He was knighted in 1988 and elected to the Alpine Club in 1995.

John was born in Bihar India and come to the UK when he was seven. Educated at Manchester Grammar School, he followed this with French and German at Keble College, Oxford. On graduation he joined Her Majesty's Colonial Service and was posted to Kenya during the Mau Mau Uprising. He travelled with a revolver and a copy of the Riot Act but recognised some of the British failings that had led to the violence. Later he joined the Foreign Office and was posted variously to Algeria, Lagos and Chad before becoming high commissioner for Zambia. He returned to Kenya as high commissioner in 1986 where he had to deal with issues arising from the murder of Julia Ward, the British wildlife photographer, an issue unfortunately without satisfactory resolution.

On notional retirement in 1990, he returned to UK to become director of the Foreign Service Programme at Oxford and many positions associated with the great outdoors, becoming chair of the Countryside Commission in 1991, president of the Friends of the Lake District in 1995 and vice-president of the YHA from 1995 to 2008.

He married Jean Lewis in 1956, who survives him with two sons and a daughter; a third son died in 2017.

Roderick A Smith

Bruno Messerli
1931 - 2019

Bruno Messerli was, in many ways, a giant of mountain science. In 2007, recognising that climate change and other ecological threats were rising ever higher on the global agenda, he was elected an honorary member of the Alpine Club, to honour his huge contributions to the understanding of mountain environments, which are such delicate indicators of global change.

My involvment with Bruno began in September 1983 when I visited the Institute of Geography at the University of Bern to discuss my possible doctoral research with him. When I walked into his office, I had two surprises. First, he was much taller than I expected. Second, he introduced himself by saying 'I am Bruno.' Formally, he was Herr Professor Doktor Messerli but Bruno was not a formal man.

His father was the stationmaster at Wabern, a village on the edge of Bern; his mother was an innkeeper's daughter. His father loved nature and the mountains; his mother was interested in music and culture. Bruno inherited all these interests. His mother dreamed that he would become a conductor, which, in one sense, he did although his leadership and direction was in science and advocacy rather than music. Although he spent almost all his long academic career, more than six decades from student to professor emeritus, based at the Institute of Geography at the University of Bern, his impacts have gone far beyond Switzerland and geography.

The first stage of Bruno's career followed a reasonably typical course, starting with his undergraduate studies and then proceeding to a doctorate, where his academic focus on mountains became clear. His doctoral and postdoctoral research, from 1958 to 1976, focused on the glacial and post-glacial history of the mountains around the Mediterranean and down into the Sahara, a focus on historic glaciers and arid mountains to which he returned soon before retirement during his last field projects (1988-96) in the high Andes of Chile's Atacama desert.

During his years as a doctoral student and then as a postdoctoral researcher, Bruno also taught and took students on field courses. On one of these he met Béatrice Ruedin. They were married in 1964 and had a happy marriage for 55 years.

While Bruno's roots were in geography he was a great advocate of interdisciplinary research, and played leading roles in many major interdisciplinary projects from quite an early stage in his career. The first of these was the Swiss element of UNESCO's Man and the Biosphere (MAB) Programme, which he directed, together with the unrelated Paul Messerli from 1977 to 1986. This is the context in which I met and first worked with him and learned a few tips for ensuring that scientists from different disciplines work together productively: make sure you have at least two people from each discipline, even if from different parts of the discipline and, during field research, that everyone cooks – and eats! – together.

Overlapping the Swiss MAB project, Bruno was co-manager of the

Above: Bruno Messerli.

Right: Bruno and Beatrice Messerli.

United Nations University's (UNU) project on Highland-Lowland Interactive Systems (later, Mountain Geoecology and Sustainable Development) (1979-1991) with Jack Ives. Jack and Bruno's partnership had started earlier in the International Geographical Union's Mountain Commission; they alternated as chairs from 1972 to 1996. A primary outcome of the UNU work in Nepal was their co-authored book *The Himalayan Dilemma: Reconciling Development and Conservation* (1989), which used detailed field research to analyse the *Myth of Himalayan Degradation*: briefly, that floods in Bangladesh are due to poor farmers in Nepal cutting trees and not maintaining their terraces, and that there would be no forests in Nepal by 2000. Bruno continued this work with Thomas Hofer, resulting in their 2006 book *Floods in Bangladesh: History, Dynamics and Rethinking the Role of the Himalayas.*

The impact of the Messerli-Ives partnership went well beyond academia. The work they led in Nepal showed that many of the myths about Himalayan degradation, often quoted by politicians and in the media, were incorrect. In the early 1990s, their focus turned to the global stage, when they recognised – together with the Swiss Agency for Development and Cooperation – that the UN Conference on Environment and Development (or 'Rio Earth Summit') in 1992 would present a unique opportunity to get mountains on the stage. The result of two years of concerted diplomatic and scientific effort from the growing 'mountain mafia' that they led was Chapter 13 on 'Sustainable Mountain Development' in *Agenda 21*, the plan of action deriving from this global meeting. More detail can be found in Peter Stone's article in *AJ* 2002, 'The Fight for Mountain Environments'. Bruno and the mountain mafia continued to play a key role in keeping mountains on the global agenda, including the publication, again with Jack Ives, of *Mountains of the World: A Global Priority* in 1997 and a series of reports, disseminated at global meetings, until 2002. Key outcomes of these continuing efforts were the declaration of the year 2002 as the International Year of Mountains and, since then, 11 December as International Mountain Day.

In addition to his activities in research and advocacy, Bruno played many other important roles. At the University of Bern, he was a gifted and charismatic teacher and mentor who enthused thousands of students and supervised 35 doctorate and 104 masters theses, and served as rector of the university in 1986-7. He had national roles with the Swiss University Conference, Research Council and Swiss National Science Foundation. After his official retirement in 1996, he became president of the International Geographical Union (1996-2000). In a wider interdisciplinary context, he also became co-director of the International Geosphere-Biosphere Programme's project on Past Global Changes (1996-2001), and then continued in other roles with the International Foundation of Science and the International Centre for Integrated Mountain Development (ICIMOD) in Kathmandu, which he had helped to establish in 1983. He also played important roles in initiating and supporting networks of mountain scientists in Africa and Latin America.

Bruno's significant contributions were recognised in many ways. In Switzerland, he was awarded the Doron Prize and the Marcel-Benoist Prize and, internationally, numerous award, including the Founder's Medal of the Royal Geographical Society, the Mountain Award of the King Albert I Memorial Foundation, and the Prix Vautrin Lud, the 'Nobel' of geography, as well as honorary doctorates from the University of Innsbruck and the Free University of Berlin.

All of the above underlines Bruno's energy, enthusiasm and remarkable professional achievements, which focused mainly on the environments and people of mountain areas around the world: past, present, and future. Yet he was also a man who was deeply committed to his family, his wonderful wife Beatrice, his four children and his nine grandchildren. He enjoyed the mountains, music, and good food and drink. Although his roots were in the Swiss canton of Bern, he was a consummate interdisciplinary scientist who made a real difference to people around the world, especially in mountain areas. Through his publications and the work of his family and everyone else he mentored and worked with, he will continue to do so.

Martin F Price

George Rhodes
1929 - 2019

George Rhodes, who died on 29 March 2019 aged 90, was a longstanding member of the Alpine Club. He was a well known fell runner and set the record for the fastest solo for the three peaks Snowdon, Scafell Pike, Ben Nevis sea level to sea level in 13h 11m, running solo and doing all the driving.

George Rhodes.

The joint record is held by Joss Naylor of Wasdale, who completed the trio in 11hours 56m with Frank Davies of Ambleside driving a rally specified Ford Capri.) He was lent a works Mini Cooper and the record is unlikely to be beaten since there were no speed limits in those days. He won the Dovedale Dash three years in succession as well as many other running achievements. He was on the Olympic shortlist for Melbourne 1956 but had to withdraw due to injury.

George was a member of the Climbers' Club for many years and was prominent running in Skye and other parts of Britain. He later moved on to two-day orienteering. Tony Streather invited him as leader on an Endeavour trip, taking youngsters to Ethiopia, mountaineering and surveying ibex. In addition to climbing in the Alps, he drove to Armenia with Trevor Jones and Eric Beard seemingly to look for remains of the ark on Mount Ararat. Rumour has it they climbed Mount Olympus on the way.

He was managing director of the family motor business in north Staffordshire and regularly supplied cars to the climbing fraternity. In later life he took up golf and fishing, and was often to be seen running on local hills and footpaths. His wife Audrey, sons Chris and Julian, and daughter Fiona still live in the Biddulph area.

Robin Quine

Sir John Shipley Rowlinson
1926 - 2018

John Rowlinson, who died on 15 August 2018 aged 93, had a worldwide reputation as a scientist and engineer. His degree in chemistry from Oxford in 1948 was followed by a D Phil and then John went to the USA as a Fulbright scholar at the University of Wisconsin. On returning to the UK, he became an ICI research fellow at the University of Manchester and was subsequently promoted to lecturer in 1954 and senior lecturer in 1957. In 1961 he was elected to a chair in chemical technology at Imperial College, London and in 1974 was appointed Dr Lee's Professor of Chemistry at Oxford. John was elected a fellow of the Royal Society in 1970 and later became a vice-president. He was knighted in the Queen's Birthday Honours in 2000.

Arriving at Oxford in 1974, John was introduced by fellow academic Brian Smith to the Gorphwysfa Club, based on the exploits of Geoffrey Winthrop Young, in particular his gatherings of like-minded people at the Gorphwysfa Hotel. Brian and a few companions founded the club while

in a tent in driving rain in Glenbrittle, having
used the youth hostel built on the site of the
Gorphwysfa Hotel for their early adventures.
The old-fashioned style of the club was well suited to John's approach to the mountains and he
immediately became a very active member. He is
remembered especially for the Alpine meets he
led, introducing novices to the delights of Alpine
climbing and getting lapsed Alpinists back into
the mountains.

John organised a novices' meet in Zermatt in
1977 which, despite poor weather, was a great
success. Two years later John and I with my
wife, Anne Davis, did the High Level Route in a
period of remarkably fine weather. We rounded
off this trip with an ascent of the Dufourspitze.
Gradually the number of people on John's

John Rowlison.

Alpine meets grew as did the ambitiousness of the climbs. He was particularly fond of *enchaînements*, leading groups from peak to peak on the
frontier ridge above Zermatt. One particular expedition, taking in the
Breithorn and Castor, ended with a dramatic descent of the Schwarztor in
waist deep snow to reach the Monte Rosa hut. Not satisfied with a descent
in loose snow John led me up knee-deep snow nearly to the summit of
Nordend the following day.

On 1 August 1980 John with two companions from the Gorphwysfa
Club climbed the Matterhorn in near winter conditions. He then made a
mini 'spaghetti tour' with Anne and me along the frontier ridge from the
Theodul hut, traversing Castor to the Sella hut before a delicate traverse of
the Naso Dome to the Gnifetti hut, thence across the Lisjoch to the Monte
Rosa hut and so to Zermatt. By now, all our companions had returned home
but John and I had a week left and we decided to have a look at the Finsteraarhorn. We drove to the Grimsel Pass and after a night in the hotel
made our way to the Oberaarjoch hut. Early the next morning we climbed
the Oberaarhorn, which turned out to be an excellent viewpoint. Although
an easy climb, it had a steep little finish to a small summit plateau with a
deceptively large cornice.

We returned to the empty hut but just as we were setting out for the
Finsteraarhorn the telephone rang. John answered it but could barely
understand a very strong German-Swiss accent over a poor connection. The
purpose of the call was not clear and after attempting to make some sense
of what was being said, John simply asked in very simple German: 'Is any-
body hurt?' The answer was a rather puzzled sounding: '*Nein.*' John put the
receiver down, a typical example of his enormously practical nature.

We set off across the Studer glacier and crossed the Gemslücke to reach
the Finsteraarhorn hut. After lunch we sat in the sunshine watching gliders swoop overhead in the clear blue sky. Early next morning it was misty

and a guide taking two clients back down suggested it would not be a good day to climb the mountain. So we stayed in the hut and spent the rest of the day champing at the bit as the weather remained fair but the barometer gradually fell. By evening the hut was full to bursting.

The following morning was not only misty but windy as well. We set off with a huge party of other people but before long nearly everyone had given up and we were left in the company of two other parties of two. I was struggling to make progress up the glacier but John gently urged me on and eventually we reached the Hugisattel where the wind was tremendous; it was as much as we could do to organise ourselves for the final rock ridge with gloves, goggles and so on all threatening to blow away. After much struggling we started on the rock. Good firm stuff but icy, then narrow gullies where we front-pointed, small rock towers and some belaying. We reached the summit plastered in ice, eyelashes frozen, noses numb, no goggles – they had frozen over long ago – and with the worst yet to come. The descent was a whiteout, the wind strong enough to fling 10m of rope into the air in an arc above our heads. Our axes wore a sheath of ice and our anorak drawcords were a centimetre in diameter with ice. We could only find our way back to the hut by careful map and compass work and were both relieved when at last we could see our way to safe ground and we could stop to get rid of some of our icy armour.

We swaggered back into the hut to be faced by tens of already slightly drunk people and could only think to tell them that it had been a typical Welsh day in the mountains. John quietly said to me that in his view 'the importance of good weather for Alpine ascents is grossly exaggerated.' That evening, our third in the hut, John set me a mathematical puzzle to pass the time. I'm still working on it.

Those few days summed up John's mountaineering ethos. He would be the first to acknowledge he was no rock tiger, nor a fierce climber of snow and ice, nor did he aspire to be a hard man; but he had, in abundance, the most important skills for an Alpine climber: fitness, leadership and companionship. Many of us slaved up a steep glacier behind him, mesmerised by his powerful, long gait, not fast but never stopping. Many of his companions have been on the brink of calling a halt in the face of bad weather or fatigue only to be gently urged on a little further: 'just to the next ridge'; or else, 'if it's no better we haven't committed ourselves,' until the climb had been completed. As for companionship, John could spend several days in a hut in terrible weather offering thought-provoking conversation or amusement by way of a mathematical puzzle or similar diversion.

John was a member of the Swiss Alpine Club for many years and came to the Alpine Club late on. He was elected in 1982, proposed by Jeremy Naish, seconded by John Jackson, and supported by David Cox and Mike Baker. His application started with an ascent of the Pic d'Ascobes in 1949 followed by ascents in the Rockies in 1951 when he was at the University of Wisconsin. A developing career put a temporary hold on any Alpine exploits until 1959 saw ascents of the Wildspitze and the Fluchtkogel in the

Ötztal and Piz Palü in the Bernina range. John's great passion was for the Pennine Alps, which he began exploring in the 1970s with ascents of the easier classic routes.

John's climbs included ascents of the Matterhorn, Mont Blanc, the Mönch, the Jungfrau and the Weisshorn, which he regarded as the finest of them all. He climbed extensively in north Wales, the Lake District and Scotland. He also climbed in the Himalaya, making the first ascent of Berthatoli Himal, south peak, New Zealand, where he climbed Mount Tasman and the Tien Shan.

The extremely precise nature of John's academic work did not lend itself to levity but he possessed a gentle sense of humour evident in even the most demanding moments on the mountains. His thoughtful humour was counter-balanced by that of his wife, Nancy, who had a beautiful way of teasing anyone taking themselves too seriously. John met Nancy at a meet in Glen Coe and they married in 1952. They were a devoted couple although John often spent their wedding anniversary in a hut while Nancy remained in the valley pursuing her love of the flora and fauna of the Alps. Nancy died in 2012, after 60 years of marriage. John had long since stopped climbing but still attended the Gorphwysfa New Year meets where his mind was as sharp as ever. He was still publishing papers in his late 80s and remained as perceptive and humorous as ever.

At his memorial service, in Exeter College where he had been a fellow for over 40 years, a colleague's eulogy referred to John's admiration of the American scientist Josiah Willard Gibbs. He particularly enjoyed Gibbs' modest and careful approach to science and scientific writing. In a 1903 obituary one of Gibbs' students wrote that Gibbs was:

Unassuming in manner, genial and kindly in his intercourse with his fellow-men, never showing impatience or irritation, devoid of personal ambition of the baser sort or of the slightest desire to exalt himself, he went far toward realizing the ideal of the unselfish, Christian gentleman. In the minds of those who knew him, the greatness of his intellectual achievements will never overshadow the beauty and dignity of his life.

Those who knew John, academically or on the mountains, would recognise him in those words.

Geoffrey Pocock

Christopher Robert Simpson
1929 - 2018

Christopher Simpson.

Christopher's father was Lt Col Maurice Simpson, a Leicester solicitor and territorial officer, who in 1938 took command of the 115th Field Regiment, Royal Artillery, and led it through much of the Second World War, including Dunkirk. His mother, Renée Laffitte, was born in Bordeaux and came to England where she taught French at a number of girls' schools, including Downe House. She was director of the Leicester Women's Voluntary Services at the start of the war. Christopher attended Hillbrow School and Rugby before reading law at Magdalene College, Cambridge.

As a Leicester lawyer, Christopher was responsible for the expansion of his family firm from Herbert Simpson, Son & Bennett to the firm of Stone & Simpson from which he retired in 1987. He was a passionate early adopter of computers and was very proud of his firm's progress in this area. He briefly continued the academic study of law at Cambridge and was awarded an LLM degree in 1977.

He was a keen rugby player at school and university but the sport that captured his attention in early adulthood was climbing. He became secretary of the Cambridge University Mountaineering Club and was friends with many of the great British climbers of the post-war era; he was a member of the Alpine Club by the age of 22 in 1952. He stopped climbing 'after 25 people I knew well enough to have a drink with had been killed.' Gliding became a huge part of his life instead.

He participated in many regional gliding competitions, winning three of them, as well as flying in the British National Championships. He was assistant manager of the British gliding team at the world championships in the USA in 1970 and Yugoslavia in 1972. He broke two world records and five British records at the South African national championships for two-seaters in 1978. He became chair of the British Gliding Association in 1972 and subsequently chair of the Royal Aero Club, which awarded him its silver medal.

Perhaps because of his French heritage, Christopher was a knowledgeable oenophile. The prize for his win of the Daily Telegraph wine competition provided a welcome boost to one of the best cellars in the country. Food was very important to him, too: he was founding chair of the Leicester Food and

Wine Society. Christopher married Jane Byng in 1955: they were generous hosts. Jane died in 1990; she had been a Leicestershire county councillor for many years. Christopher married Theresa Heath in 1991; she died in 2013.

Christopher was an enthusiast with a keen eye for technical detail. He loved to have the latest technology, be it gliders, cameras or computers. He was a traditionalist who wasn't afraid to say what he thought. He leaves two children and five grandchildren.

David Simpson

James Cadzow Smith
1927 - 2018

One of my earliest childhood memories of being in the hills with my father was sitting on the summit of a Scottish peak in bright sunshine. Looking down, I realised we were surrounded by cloud. This was an amazing experience for a young child and I felt a mixture of awe and fear, as I couldn't fathom how we were going to get down. One look at my father and my fears disappeared. That confidence and faith in him continued for the rest of my life.

He was introduced to scouting early on in life. His scout leader and church minister, Roderick Murchison, had a great influence upon him and through scouting his love for the mountains and outdoors was born, together with his positive attitude towards life. He loved experiencing and learning anything new and this was fed by his love of reading. When he married my mother Moira in 1954, a very special partnership lasting 63 years was created.

As his engineering career developed so did our family life. He always shared his ideals and thoughts with us. So as children we were introduced to walking and skiing in the Scottish mountains, the Swiss Alps and sailing on the Clyde estuary. His enthusiasm was infectious. He didn't consider age as a barrier to experience. So not surprisingly he was mountaineering in the Swiss Alps in his 70s with his good friend George Blades and skiing with the family into his 80s. To celebrate his 70th birthday he organised a family ascent of a 4,000m peak in the Swiss Alps. At 80 he was more than happy to skipper a 50ft yacht in sunny Greece and in his 90th year organised a wild camping trip in Glen Lyon with his son and grandson.

He climbed the Matterhorn in 1952 and had an extensive record of climbing, skiing, walking and camping in the major areas of the Alps and a season's trekking in Nepal in 1981, which included an ascent of Island Peak and a visit to Langtang. He and George became good friends with Roger Payne, for whom my father held a great fondness and huge respect and who guided them many times. He was elected a member of the AC at the relatively senior age of 63 in 1990.

His career saw him switch from seagoing engineer to electrical power generation, perfectly logical as both depended on steam turbines. He joined the forerunner of the South of Scotland Electricity Board in 1952. In 1967 he moved the family to the Midlands where he worked in and was in charge of some of the larger power stations. In his early 40s he took on the post of chief executive of the Northern Ireland Electricity Service with total responsibility for generation, transmission, distribution and sale of electricity during two major political strikes. In 1977 he was appointed by the secretary of state for energy to be chairman of East Midlands Electricity Board and later invited to become chairman of the larger and technically more difficult Eastern Electricity Board.

He was a visionary in so many ways. He believed the basis of this country's wealth is its industry and that electrical engineering is one of the most important contributors to industry's success. He also believed electricity has a huge role to play in the solution of environmental problems. In addition he wanted to see a greater involvement of engineers in public life. 'This must become more prevalent,' he once said, 'if the public is to be made aware of the true worth of the engineering profession. Only improvement in society's valuation of the engineering profession will change the situation.'

He was elected fellow of Royal Academy of Engineering in 1988, was president the Institution of Electrical Engineers (1989-90), and chair of the Natural Environment Research Council (1997-2000). He was appointed CBE in 1989.

To his skills in engineering and administration must be added his commitment to new technologies, his sharpness of mind and not least his common-sense approach to even the most complex of problems. His interest and belief in people and his patent sincerity readily commanded the respect of others. His experience and philosophy of life was fed by the mountains. He always lived his life to the full and this must surely be his legacy.

Elaine Smith

Anthony Strawther
1933 - 2018

Tony was born and brought up in and around Chesterfield, Derbyshire, an only child. After the Second World War, the family moved to Barlow in the Peak District, and it was living here that Tony first discover the great outdoors. He explored the Peak District first with a friend and then with the local YHA group.

After leaving school, Tony was apprenticed as an upholsterer and an older colleague asked if he would like to try rock climbing. At the end of the day at Black Rocks, Cromford, Tony's mentor given him an old 60ft rope. He had many exciting run-outs on that rope because it was far too short for many of the routes he was climbing, bearing in mind that in those days one tied directly onto the rope. In 1951-3 Tony did his national service in the RAF Regiment, and following basic training was stationed in Egypt for two years. He enjoyed his time there, going on training exercises in the desert and in the mountains of Crete. It was when he was returning home by ship to

Trieste and train across Europe that Tony saw the Alps for the first time. Actually seeing what he had read so much about made an influential and lasting impression on him.

Tony Strawther.

Following national service, Tony left his original trade and went to work at Markham and Co, Heavy Engineering Works, in Chesterfield, where he remained until retirement. Work for Tony provided the means to enable him to go away to the mountains as often as possible. In 1959 he had his first Alpine season and joined the Swiss Alpine Club, thereby becoming a member of the ABMSAC (Association of British Members of the Swiss Alpine Club). He remained a full member all his life.

That first season he went to Zermatt, staying in the Hotel Bahnhof and so, like many other climbers of this era, met Bernard Biner and his sister Paula, the owners. The kitchen at Bernard's was the great meeting place for climbers, swapping stories and getting up-to-date knowledge of routes. For Tony, this was one of the great joys of climbing: the diversity of people he met along the way, people from all spheres and walks of life, but with one thing in common, something they all held dear, was their love of the hills. For that reason, climbing clubs were something Tony valued; they were a way of meeting people with the same passions. In 1969, he was elected as a member of the Alpine Club, a huge honour and privilege for him; he was always conscious of the place the AC holds in mountaineering and exploration, and to be part of that meant a great deal to him. In 1987, he joined the Fell and Rock Climbing Club, and enjoyed the warmth and friendship from those he met on meets, in huts and at club dinners. Tony loved going away to the huts; a day out on the tops, followed by sitting round, laughing and chatting in the evening, with friends old and new, was a perfect day for him.

I met Tony in 1971 at a symphony concert in Sheffield. In accepting a coffee in the interval, I little realised at the time what a lifetime of adventures would ensue. Having passed the test of a wet weekend's camping in north Wales, Tony then took the time, trouble and patience to teach and nurture my climbing and mountaineering skills. Our first Alpine season together was in the Bernina, and it did not get off to an auspicious start, when I managed to burn the tent down. Tony was very stoical about it and it was far from the end of a beautiful friendship. We went on to marry a year later and have very many subsequent climbing trips and Alpine seasons.

We repeated many of his previous climbs; he enjoyed taking me on peaks he had enjoyed. But we also explored new areas together. Tony always liked to traverse a peak, to see another valley or pass: we both did. This often led to some very long days. His boast was that we never had to spend the night out, unintentionally, but we came close on a number of occasions.

Tony would never boast about climbs he had done; that was Tony, a very modest man. Bragging wasn't in his nature. If, in the midst of telling a story, he did mention what he had done and where he had been, the listener was often left in amazement at his exploits. On the hills he was a careful climber and a solid partner. He was caring for others less able or competent than himself. He would always ensure that the party stayed together in all weather conditions. He was a great companion in the hills, with the experience for others to rely on and the stability never to get into difficulties.

Away from the hills, we had many shared interests: mountaineering literature, history and art, visiting many exhibitions together, and latterly some of our holidays were taken visiting archaeological sites. Tony was always conscious how vulnerable we were climbing as a husband and wife team. I was the gung-ho, 'let's do it' type, whilst he was the safe one: let's weigh it up. We balanced each other on the hill, as in life.

Suzanne Strawther

Lt Col H R A Streather OBE
1926 - 2018

Tony Streather was a professional soldier, a leader of men but only an accidental, if extraordinary, mountaineer. As such he was an esteemed president of our club, and in both roles his service spanned periods of great change. Tony became president in 1990 during those traumatic days when the Alpine Club, having decamped from South Audley Street, was bivouacking with the Ski Club of Great Britain, searching meanwhile for a new home. Three years later Tony delivered his valedictory address in our new home at Charlotte Road.

Born in London, Tony was educated at University College School in Hampstead and became a keen horseman. With the war in Europe drawing to a close and inspired by tales of the North West Frontier, he volunteered for the Indian army, commissioned into the Rajputana Rifles and was training for jungle warfare in Burma when Japan capitulated. For a while he enjoyed the traditional pursuits of a young officer under the Raj, particularly polo, but on furlough in Kashmir he had seen Nanga Parbat at dawn from the Tragbal Pass and was smitten. Come Partition in 1947, he opted to remain and now under Pakistani command found himself second-in-command of the Chitral Scouts, responsible for a thousand men, 183 horses and 50 camels, an appointment which, he felt, required the gravitas of the moustache which he retained ever after. The regiment was tasked with policing the dangerous tribal territories along the Afghan frontier in the Hindu Kush and this experience of travel in high, rugged and often snow-covered mountain country; his fluency in Pashto and easy way with the locals was to prove invaluable. Already captivated by mountains, the stage was set.

The drama began in 1950, almost by chance, with secondment as transport officer to Arne Naess' Norwegian expedition to the unclimbed

Left and above: Tony Streather.
(John Cleare)

Tirich Mir (7706m), highest peak in the Hindu Kush. The Norwegians were surprised that Tony wore his regulation *chaplis*, or open sandals, on the approach march. They were delighted when Tony, who wasn't expected to go high, powered up the mountain with them in battledress, pyjamas and hob-nailed army boots to reach the summit with Naess and two others. Not only was it a first ascent, it was Tony's first high mountain. With a resting heartbeat in the mid 40s, he was obviously a powerful performer at altitude.

Not surprisingly South Audley Street took notice, and on returning to England later that year to transfer to the British army, Tony was invited to join the AC by Col Tobin, late Indian army himself. 'I'll get Longstaff to second you,' he added. In his innocence Tony assumed the Club to be a typical London gentleman's club where he might dine, entertain friends and spend the night when 'in town': useful for a young officer going places. Only later did he realise the reality of the AC and what an honour had been bestowed on him, especially when the rules were interpreted to allow his years of scrambling around the Hindu Kush to count as viable ascents on his application form.

Meanwhile preparations were afoot for 1953 and Tobin suggested Capt Streather might apply to join the Everest team. After lunching with Shipton, Tony was asked to join four other applicants, all experienced alpinists, in Zermatt for evaluation by Michael Ward and Alf Gregory. Several major peaks were climbed in poor conditions and although he burnt off his colleagues every time, all of whom passed selection, his technical ability did not impress. Later he wrote '… my inept fumbling when putting on crampons let me down.' In retrospect, Ward admitted Tony has been so powerful at altitude that 'he should really have been selected.'

Ironically, Everest rejection arrived at the same time with Charlie Houston's invitation to join his 1953 American team on the considerably more daunting K2, initially as transport officer, but afterwards as a lead climber. The expedition's desperate descent from camp eight at 7,770m, lowering the stricken Gilkey on a makeshift stretcher, the subsequent fall when the entire party was held by Schoening's axe belay, followed by Gilkey's disappearance, by accident or design and without which the party's survival would have been unlikely, was described as 'a Homeric retreat' and 'the finest moment in American mountaineering, and is now legendary (*AJ* 1954, pp391-401).

Tony was thus an obvious choice to join Charles Evans' Kangchenjunga reconnaissance expedition of 1955. The south-west face had never been closely examined before, but so successful was the team that a summit assault was mounted, using oxygen, and Joe Brown and George Band reached the top having surmounted an awkward crack in the summit rock tower. At camp six next morning, before Tony and New Zealander Norman Hardie set off to repeat the climb, Joe quipped, 'No chance Tony! You're hopeless on rock.' Later Hardie dropped an oxygen bottle so Tony gave him one of his own pair before turning his remaining bottle to minimum flow. When eventually they reached the final rock tower they discovered a straightforward snow gully round the corner. Tony became the first climber ever to ascend two peaks above 25,000ft.

All the while Tony was a regular infantry officer serving in the Gloucestershire Regiment, the 'Glorious Glosters' of Korean War fame. In 1957 while a Sandhurst instructor he was invited to lead three young OUMC members to the Karakoram to reconnoitre unclimbed Haramosh (7397m). 'Probably not a wise decision,' he admitted later. 'I'd recently married and had a young baby, but it was tempting to return to Pakistan and look up old friends.' Tragically the expedition turned into a disaster when a small avalanche led to a complex sequence of falls and repeated rescue attempts lasting four days and three nights without food or shelter. It was only Tony's courage and his great strength at altitude that enabled the survival, though horrifically frostbitten, of just one of the young climbers involved. Recognised as one of the most heroic yet poignant survival epics in the annals of mountaineering, the trauma remained with Tony for life. Ralph Barker's book *The Last Blue Mountain* (Chatto & Windus, 1959) records the tragedy in moving detail.

My own great respect for Tony stemmed from its sequel. He was commanding the Glosters in Berlin when in 1970 the BBC inveigled him to Zermatt in the depths of winter as technical adviser for a television 'drama-doc' of *Last Blue Mountain*, which, with a single BBC producer, I was to make. Tony borrowed three leading army climbers to play the various parts while a Glenmore Lodge ice-climbing instructor played Tony himself. Based at the Testa Grigna refuge, we skied to an appropriate location on the Breithorn every day where Tony, a tower of strength, would brew us tea in the igloo he'd constructed, and when falling snow delayed filming he keep us entertained with his stories. When one day I needed some extra gear from the hut, and though it was my responsibility to get it, Tony was adamant that I was not to make the two-hour return trip to do so. He would go himself. It was a selfless gesture that defined the man, one never forgotten. But surprisingly, apart from this one diversion, after the 1952 'evaluation' Tony never again climbed in the Alps.

In 1959, as a captain, he organised and led an official AMA expedition to the Chogo Lungma glacier in the eastern Karakoram with Rev Maj Fred Jenkins (AC) as his deputy. An eastern summit of Malubiting and six small peaks on the Hispar wall above the Kero Lungma glacier were climbed, including 'splendid' Gloster Peak at 5,880m.

Yet the time had come to focus on career and his expanding family, and for 26 years Tony followed his regiment around the world: to Germany, Cyprus and Hong Kong, to Borneo on secondment to the Gurkhas, to Malaysia to command the Jungle Warfare School, to Ulster, and even to Tywyn where he was tasked with rejuvenating the army's Outward Bound School. He still played polo and rugby into his forties. An unusual incident while commanding the regiment demonstrates Tony's leadership qualities and his practical humanity: one of his soldiers went AWOL, fought for a while as a mercenary in the Congo and eventually returned to face serious disciplinary charges. After a thorough grilling, Tony told him, 'The Regiment can do with men of your experience,' and the soldier, suitably chastened and reintegrated with his comrades, continued to give loyal and conscientious service.

There was to be one more major expedition, this time to lead the successful 1976 Army Everest Expedition from camp two in the Western Cwm, before being appointed OBE and retiring the following year. And then Tony was back to Sandhurst for 10 years as estate manager, a 'retired officer' appointment, which he conducted as far as possible on horseback. He'd always believed in the value of adventure and comradeship and working with John Hunt's charity Endeavour; now able to take unpaid leave he led groups of disadvantaged youngsters on expeditions to Greenland and Ethiopia.

Having been elected to honorary membership of the AC, he was not finished with the mountains or with companions with whom he had climbed them. Every few years there were treks with family and AC friends to old haunts in Nepal and the North West Frontier, and team reunions in America and Norway. At the age of 79, Tony paid his third visit to Kangchenjunga with Hardie and Band for the 50th anniversary of their ascent, it transpired that he had arranged, with contributions from others, a pension for Dawa Tenzing, the Kangchenjunga sirdar and a special friend to British climbers, since the old tiger had fallen on hard times. It was recognition of the loyalty and compassion of the local porters, the Hunzas and Sherpas who had tended the survivors of K2 and Haramosh, and made all his expeditions possible.

Tony and Sue, who died in 2005, retired to Hindon, a small village in the south Wiltshire downs, where with his public spirit and old-fashioned courtesy he became an integral part of village life. Here he died, aged 92, and local villagers turned out in force to join family and friends, old soldiers and climbers in Hindon church for his memorial service. Tony is survived by four children and seven grandchildren.

John Cleare

John Temple
1934 - 2018

John was one of life's rich characters. Staying overnight at his house outside Nairobi I discovered a horse in the bathroom. Although it belonged to the then Mrs Temple, it nevertheless suggested John's unconventional ethos.

John was an extremely powerful, and canny, mountaineer, as you might expect for someone born in Yorkshire and bred at Almscliffe, and whose first Alpine season was at 18 and included an ascent of the Matterhorn. He'd already done new routes on Skye with Ian Clough and the outstanding *Vulcan Wall* with Hamish MacInnes. On graduation, John taught geography, marrying in 1959 and moving his growing family to Africa, where he came under the influence of Ian Howell and came to know Mount Kenya very well. In 1970, John was a key player in the difficult rescue of the Austrian, Dr Gert Judmaier, from Shipton's Notch at over 5,000m on the peak. Judmaier had been seriously injured in a fall after descending from the summit. Forty-five years later, John returned to take part in the feature film of the rescue, made by Reinhold Messner, and was reunited with Gert Judmaier and his climbing partner Oswald Oelz.

In 1972, Temple inveigled Frank Cannings and me to join him on Kilimanjaro where he planned to take a close look at the still virgin Great Breach Wall, reputably Africa's highest cliff. We drove down to Tanzania in Temple's battered Land Rover, enjoyed one desert bivouac and three more in convenient caves, and eventually reached the Great Barranco at the foot of the daunting 1,400m wall. An eye-catching 80m icicle at mid-height hung over a band of black cliffs to link a precarious-looking upper ice field to the lower ice-draped crags. The scree suggested awful rock. Suitably chastened, we escaped up the Heim glacier, the steep hanging ice tongue to the east, which had been climbed several times before and is today a recommended grade IV alpine-style ice climb. If it still exists?

One more bivy just below Kibo summit, another down in the Umbwe heather forest, and we were winging our way back to Nairobi, only to be arrested en route by the Tanzanian constabulary on the charge of 'photographing government servants', aka 'cows'. Apparently agriculture was nationalised in Tanzania and while that's another story, it was all part of the guaranteed adventure you had climbing with Temple.

Two years later Temple returned with Tony Charlton and climbed the eastern side of the Breach Wall (V+) in two days and again the following year with Dave Cheesmond when he forced an almost direct route up

Above: 'I can't recommend the hippo.' Temple in the Rwenzori in 1975. *(John Cleare)*

Left: John Temple. *(John Cleare)*

the wall, involving three days of difficult climbing on ice and horrible rock (VI). These two climbs were real tours de force at high altitude on a remote, little known and extremely formidable mountainside, although virtually unknown outside the small local climbing community. They say much for John's commitment and prowess. Later it took Messner to make the *direttissima* straight up the 80m icicle.

In 1975 John invited me to join him in the Rwenzori and naturally I jumped at the chance. Joined by ex-pat climbers Tony Charlton and Jim Slade and botanist John Youngs, we drove 750 miles to far western Uganda in Temple's small Dexion-reinforced and overloaded Toyota jeep. Apart from climbing gear we carried a huge supply of flapjack, which John had been baking and stockpiling for weeks. It was to be our staple diet for the duration: breakfast, lunch and supper, washed down with plenty of tea and a daily soup. Though rather monotonous, flapjack actually worked very well and proved a simple, inexpensive, long-lasting and efficient solution to the problem of expedition catering. Indeed, a typically Temple solution.

Idi Amin was at the height of his power and Uganda was considered inaccessible to Europeans, but John knew how to handle African officials. Scruffy, bearded and wearing his usual flip-flops, he negotiated us safely through the border and the exhaustive customs checks where we watched, somewhat concerned, as an African clerical gentleman, complete with dog collar, was led away in shackles accused of smuggling a bald car tyre. Our sleeping bags were turned inside out but the vehicle's chassis was thankfully ignored, for here John had stashed a quantity of Kenyan banknotes, knowing that petrol would demand a black-market deal.

Our first night in Uganda was spent in comfort, the last for several weeks, at a nunnery whose mother superior happened to be an old chum of John's.

Charm personified, the good lady told me that some years before, when John was teaching in Uganda, he had earned pin money catching snakes and despatching them by air, live, to an American zoo. He had learnt that if grabbed just behind the head snakes were powerless to strike and could safely be dropped into a collecting bag. All went well until one day he grabbed a rare snake he didn't recognise and was bitten. It was apparently the one serpent that is double-jointed and able to bend its head backwards. He was carried out of the bush unconscious, she said, and not expected to survive. But now he was able to identify that particular snake, he had no fear of the others. Not that we encountered any snakes in the Rwenzori, though John did enjoy introducing us to the local three-foot earthworms that he let slither up his arm.

The expedition record itself (see *AJ* 1977, pp12-21) is hardly appropriate to John's obituary, except to mention a few incidents. At a market stall on the shore of Lake Edward, John bought a load of evil-looking dried fish: 'Goes well with flapjack,' he said. 'Very nourishing.' At the Ibanda road-head we unloaded a 100ft coil of plastic hosepipe, unobtainable in Uganda, with which John paid John Matte, the local Bakonjo trader, for organising the 13 porters and shifty-looking headman who would carry our baggage to base camp, the same porters who, three days later, at the notorious Bigo Bog, dropped us in the lurch when they went on strike for double pay. Absolutely unruffled, John dismissed the lot, leaving us sitting beside the piles of baggage as the strikers slunk away down the trail. 'Don't worry,' John said. 'It's par for the course. I expected it.' We brewed up and waited. A couple of hours later the six youngest porters emerged shamefaced from the forest and successfully begged for their jobs. We kept them on for the whole expedition. Happy to make double carries, loyal and cheerful, they worked well and while we enjoyed our climbing they had plenty of spare time to hunt hyrax with their lean yellow dog and their broad-bladed spears. In due course they earned good bonuses.

Some weeks later, tired, dirty and very hungry, we found ourselves nearing Kampala on our drive back to Kenya. It was a Sunday and John recalled that the Sunday buffet lunch at the Imperial Hotel used to be the highlight of the Kampala week and he led us there. There was beer of sorts in the bar and a display of photographs showing Idi Amin himself, in full Highland dress, in action at the previous night's dinner-dance: we kept straight faces with difficulty.

When lunch was served we found ourselves among Amin's top people, immaculate military brass hats, smart civil servants and be-suited cronies with their ladies in full finery, a fascinating riot of colour to which unfortunately the lunch itself would not compare. As the only white faces we were stared at but never investigated. White-coated stewards, some wearing shorts, others camouflage trousers, some wellingtons or barefoot, marched in bearing large silver tureens from which the guests could help themselves. There was just one choice, greasy stew – the massive bones suggested hippo – succulent tomatoes and *matoke*, the national dish of mashed bananas. 'Fill up on the vitamin C, fellows,' John said, 'but I can't recommend the hippo.' Keeping our heads down we were soon safely back on the road.

We'd enjoyed a hugely successful adventure, thanks to John's planning, organisation and indeed leadership. He knew Africa and, never one to stand on ceremony, really had a way with people there. Intrepid, irrepressible, resourceful and always an optimist complete with a knowing chuckle, that's how I shall remember John Temple.

John Cleare

Derek Buckle writes: I first met John when he joined the East Grinstead Climbing Club in early 1994 and our first climbs together were in April the same year on a Club trip to Pembroke. From that time on John and I climbed together on various crags in the UK where he would enthusiastically seek out new routes, or explore hitherto little-known crags. John had pioneered many new routes during his time in east Africa and clearly wanted to continue the tradition when he returned to the UK.

It was never dull climbing with John: you never knew what he would suggest next or what sharp rejoinder would accompany any unguarded remark. A typical example was when we joined a Climbers' Club meet to Llanberis in Wales in June 1999. The weather was brilliant and the crags drier than I have ever seen them. John, however, wanted to do *Waterfall Climb*; the name says it all. I was assigned the first pitch, which set the tone for a very wet day out. Later that year, in November, John set his sights on *Soapgut* on Milestone Buttress, also in Wales. Once again I led the slippery first pitch, having to climb the last part in socks to get any traction. As John and I 'danced' on the slimy rounded stance John set off to climb the second pitch, but eventually conceded defeat when the slime overcame all attempts at upward movement. I will not describe the abseil retreat, except to say that John's nice white trousers were no longer white by the time he got to the bottom.

Some of the best times with John were on expeditions. Having retired late in 1996, John wasted no time in inviting me to climb with him on Mount Kenya over the New Year. Thus, with hardly any time to prepare, I flew to join him in Nairobi. John had been guiding for his friend, Andrew Wielochowski, the director of EWP, and was already well acclimatised. I, on the other hand, was whisked off to 4,000m to nurse a blinding headache. When this eventually dissipated we embarked on some of Mount Kenya's most iconic climbs, all of which John knew by heart. In addition to many classic rock routes we climbed perfect ice on *Point John Couloir* and the *Ice Window*, neither of which continue to exist on account of global warming. After completing the Ice Window route we traversed to Batian, the higher of Mount Kenya's summits, before spending the night like sardines in Ian Howell's tiny bivy hut on Nelion, accompanied by two South Africans who had had an epic multiday climb on Batian.

Our next expedition was not long in coming. In October 1997 John organised an Alpine Club expedition to Mera Peak in Nepal, which he invited me to join. The idea was to attempt a new route on Mera's north face, but this was immediately abandoned after realising that the face was continually swathed by avalanches, and thus lethal. Three of us climbed the normal route to the summit before we all relocated to the south face in order to attempt what was then an unclimbed subsidiary top. This was eventually unsuccessful, but the expedition was a great experience nonetheless.

Our last expedition together was to the Georgian Caucasus in July 1998. John had been to the area previously with Mike Pescod, when they had had an epic retreat from Ushba. This time the objectives were considerably more modest. We climbed a number of the Georgian classics, including Tetnuld, Shchurovsky and Chatyn-tau, but our most memorable experiences were with the less desirable elements of Georgian society. Twice we were robbed at gunpoint by armed bandits, and narrowly missed a third encounter had it not been for friendly locals who invited us to stay in their house overnight. It was during this expedition that John realised his days of high-altitude mountaineering were nearing an end, but he did still go to Kazakhstan with Stuart Worsfold a few years later.

I was particularly glad that my wife, Jill, Steve Humphries and I visited him in hospital in Whitstable just a short while before he died. As was typical for John, he was on good form, joking and reminiscing about old times together. Unfortunately, he knew full well that he would never return home and it is undoubtedly a relief that his suffering was relatively short-lived.

Hugh Alexander writes: I first met John at the Alpine Club in 1996, when he was chair of the wine committee and I was tapping him for information on the Caucasus. We climbed in Switzerland and France, but it was in Italy that we spent most time together.

It was on a trip there in 2002 that we explored a 'new' area, very little known, at least to us. This was the southern part of the Gran Paradiso national park, with access mainly from the Orco valley. After a few days there, we hiked up into the Piantonetto valley, past the dam to the wonderful Rifugio Pontese , then entirely unknown to us. After an overnight storm, we went climbing the next morning and – typically – the first route we climbed was a new route, on the Blanc Giuir.

Even after 50 years of Alpine experience, John described the *Via Malvassora*, on the Becco Meridionale della Tribolazione, as the best route he had climbed in the Alps. And many more superlatives were required on that trip, and those that followed, very many of which were applied to the Rifugio Pontese and its 'gestore', Mara Lacchia. We returned there many, many times and introduced lots of others to the delights of the hut and the area, not least during the SMC meet, the joint Alpine Club, CC and FRCC meet, which John organised (see *AC Newsletter*, Nov 2008), and at John's epic 75th and 80th birthday parties there.

As well as the larger objectives in that area, with Richard Nadin we established a very pleasant 'école d'escalade' at the Piano di Rista, just above the hut, where the routes include *Frutti di Mara*. We also named a 2,800m peak in honour of our hostess. Punta Mara is now well known in the area and is included in the guidebooks. Fortunately, Mara was one of the many friends able to spend time with John in December. John was an enthusiast, an inspiration, the source of a great many stories and a great friend.

Edward W Faure Walker
1946 - 2018

Teddy Faure Walker was a bold and, perhaps, a rather literal-minded mountaineer. On the first occasion he took his boys to the Pyrenees, his wife, Louise, enjoined him not to climb anything so difficult it required a rope. This didn't prevent him from making a number of decent rock routes. He just climbed them un-roped.

Mountains and climbing, although important to Teddy, were only a small part of what was a very varied and rounded life lived to the full by a brave, steadfastly loyal and thoughtful man. After Eton and Sandhurst he was commissioned into the Coldstream Guards and posted into the 2nd Battalion, of which he later became adjutant. Service in Aden, Cyprus, Germany and Northern Ireland was interspersed with mountaineering and parachute courses and 'public duties'. The latter involved providing Guards for state occasions and, routinely, for Buckingham Palace, the Tower of London and elsewhere. Public duties in London were not really to his liking. He regarded them as soulless. Nor was he a natural horseman. On one occasion, when mounted for the Queen's Birthday Parade, he accidentally dropped his sword on the approach to Horse Guards only to be saved from ignominy by a helpful policeman.

Teddy's mountaineering career started with courses on secondment to the Alpini, the École Militaire de Haute Montagne and the French army. He did not keep a climbing journal and, given the considerable time he spent with these experts and his lack of records, it is likely he made many more ascents than those he declared on his AC application form. An Alpine rescue, which he would never discuss, earned him a commander-in-chief's commendation for leadership and courage. A report from the École Militaire summed him up: 'Captain Faure Walker is elegant, phlegmatic and tough. Though his technical standard is still modest he derived the greatest benefit from the course and showed he had a typically British sense of humour.'

In 1974 Teddy left the army and a promising military future to begin the next phase of his life. His father, also a Coldstreamer, had been severely wounded in the evacuation of Dunkirk and needed help on the family farm in North Hertfordshire. A large part of it had been in Teddy's mother's family for, literally, centuries. After a year at the Royal Agricultural College at Cirencester, Teddy became a farmer. His interests and his public service now widened. Over the years he became churchwarden, chair of the village sports club, of the Hertfordshire Association of Youth Clubs, the Hertfordshire Game Conservancy and his local branch of the NFU. He was a parish councillor, an independent district councillor, a trustee of UK Youth and honorary colonel of Hertfordshire Combined Cadet Force. He became a deputy lieutenant of Hertfordshire in 1985, was high sheriff in 2000 and appointed vice-lord lieutenant in 2001.

Shortly before he left the army Teddy met Louise at St James' Palace at a lunch while chief of the guard, so not all public duty was 'soulless'. They fell in love and married in short order and have three children, Mark, Kate and Rob. Family holidays in Scotland and climbing expeditions in the Lake District, the Alps, the Pyrenees, Corsica and the Atlas with their boys gave him enormous pleasure. The youngest, Rob, is a member of the Club. But Teddy's climbing career came to an end in 2000 after a close shave in an electrical storm close to the summit of the Aiguille Croux. He was blown off balance and fell but was rescued by the boys who very efficiently helped him to abseil down to the glacier and thence to the refuge. The hut guardian, who had seen the whole thing, said afterwards that if he had children he hoped they would be like Teddy's. The boys were made to give their mother a heavily redacted account of the event. Teddy later attributed his loss of balance to an early sign of the Parkinson's disease that affected him progressively for the last 15 years of his life.

A hint of the final phase of his career came when Teddy and Louise were exploring one of the remoter parts of Cyprus. They saw a Greek Orthodox priest in his blue robes and tall hat driving a grey Ferguson tractor (typical of Teddy to remember that detail) down a village street.

Being a farmer and a priest struck Teddy then as being a thoroughly good idea though he had no idea that many years later – in 2004 – he would himself be ordained, into the Church of England. After his ordination he was appointed to a curacy in Stevenage where he gained much respect, and many friends, as an evangelist by example rather than by words. He continued to take great pleasure and satisfaction in farming, though in recent years he prepared for his retirement by handing over the running to Kate and determining to move from the farm. Although he was now suffering additionally from cancer he was able to help Louise turn the dilapidated medieval house they bought, aptly named 'Bear House', into a beautiful and welcoming home. It was there, 10 days after having the great satisfaction of moving in, that Teddy died.

Teddy was not well known in the Club but he was very widely known, respected and admired in Hertfordshire as was evidenced by the many hundreds who attended his memorial service which overflowed not only the church but also the large marquee the Faure Walker garden next door.

Mike Baker

• Teddy Faure Walker was included in the In Memoriam for 2018.

Mark Warham
1962 - 2018

Mark Warham was a schoolboy at St Thomas Aquinas grammar in his native Leeds when he suffered the dreadful injury that changed the course of his life. Getting on board the school bus, the doors closed on the 12-year-old as he was only halfway through. Before the driver noticed, Mark had been dragged some distance and seriously injured. The initial diagnosis suggested his left leg would have to be amputated, a devastating loss for a boy growing up in a sporting family with three older brothers.

While doctors were battling to save his leg and Mark was enduring skin grafts, his father Joe, coach of the rugby league team now known as Leeds Rhinos, attended a dinner

Mark Warham. *(Guy Bell)*

where he met Chris Bonington. Bonington wrote a note to Mark on the back of the menu, wishing him a speedy recovery: 'I hope that one day you climb your Everest.' Mark's leg remained badly scarred and somewhat misshapen, but he never concealed it and it seemed to have little impact on his sporting ability. Thirty years later, when Warham had indeed reached the summit of the world's highest peak, he was able to remind Bonington of the story. Once Warham set his mind to something, he was not easily thwarted.

Through his teenage years he started climbing with his brothers, first on the crags around his home and then in Scotland on snow and ice. Later he made several trips to Europe, North and South America and Nepal to climb various mountains and was an experienced mountaineer by his late twenties when he decided to climb Everest. In 1993, when he made his first attempt, only ten Britons had climbed it. Advances in technology and tactics were, however, starting to open the mountain up to a wider group of enthusiasts. He joined a commercial expedition led by Steve Bell but after reaching camp four at the South Col had to turn back with pulmonary oedema.

Four years later, when he was 35, Mark tried again on a trip led by Jon Tinker. When he reached camp four this time a storm was blowing but the wind dropped suddenly and he felt he had a chance at reaching the summit. Climbing through the night, he reached the top in good time: he was the 30th Briton to achieve the feat. He did, however, begin to hallucinate that his ice pick was an old woman and fellow northerners were pinching his gear.

Mark's professional career was even more stellar. From St Thomas Aquinas he went to St Catherine's College, Oxford, to read PPE. Despite his
childhood injury, he played in the first Varsity rugby league match in 1981
at Craven Cottage, Fulham's football ground and was awarded a half-blue.
That same drive also carried him to the top in investment banking. His
career began at 3i, the venture capital company. He then joined Schroders
in 1986 and began to specialise in mergers and acquisitions (M&A). Meticulously organised, in his early years in the City he would come in at dawn
wearing a head torch to let him make a start in the minicab on his reading.

During a stint at Morgan Stanley, where he rose to become head of M&A,
he was seconded to be director-general of the Takeover Panel (PTM), the
regulator run by the finance industry that protects the interests of sharehold-
ers during bids. Traditionally, it has done so to avoid lengthy recourse to law
but Warham's chief challenge during his two-year stint was to put the PTM
on a statutory footing for the first time, implementing a European directive.

At Barclays Capital from 2009, Warham cemented his position as one of
the leading dealmakers in London. He advised Liverpool Football Club on
their sale to John Henry and also had Fiat as a client. He joined Rothschilds
in 2014 as an executive vice-chairman, focusing on UK transactions.

Mark liked to have fun, drawing on a prodigious ability to catnap. He
once bid £10,000 for lunch with the film star Rosamund Pike, although his
favourite food and drink were Yorkshire's curries and ales. He assembled a
lurid collection of shirts that he wore to Glastonbury and Grateful Dead
concerts. Although he took up shooting, he was also a keen ornithologist
and an accomplished wildlife photographer. When he developed throat
cancer he showed the same determination and good humour he had applied
as a young man and then again on Everest before finally succumbing.

In 2000 he had married Olivia Dagtoglou, who became director of
Waging Peace, an organisation that campaigns against human rights viola-
tions in Sudan. She survives him with three daughters, twins Francesca and
Eleanor, and Anna.

Roderick A Smith

Robin Wilkinson
1936 - 2018

When I joined RAF Kinloss mountain rescue team in 1960, Robin or Wilkie
as he was known was already a well-established member of the team and
had also been a leader of the RAF Leeming rescue team that covered
the Lake District. A very experienced mountaineer he was a member of
the Alpine Climbing Group and already had notched up a number of fine
Alpine climbs including an early ascent of the north face of the Dru, which
in the early 1960s was some achievement. He climbed regularly with Ian
Clough who was also at Kinloss doing his national service. He, Ian and
Hamish MacInnes spent a great deal of their time exploring on Skye, the

Robin Wilkinson, first left bottom row, with the rest of the RAF Kinloss MRT in c1960. *(Ian Sykes)*

Cuillin Mountains in those days were fairly devoid of routes.

A regular RAF man, Robin had been made sergeant when he took over RAF Leeming MRT. To me, as a new member of the team and a very low-grade airman, he was a inspiration. It was a great life in those days with virtually free transport, food and accommodation at the expense of HMG. We became good friends and climbed together often. I particularly remember a hilarious tangle of ropes belayed on a terrifying stance under Kilnsey's main overhang that was more or less a peg route in those days. We had so many anchor points and neither of us was willing to unhitch in case we unzipped the lot.

The Kinloss team leader at that time was John Hinde who had a spell in hospital after getting frostbite on Denali and Robin took over as the boss. There were a lot of call-outs in those days and a number of aircraft crashes. The civilian rescue teams were in their infancy and mostly made up of volunteers and shepherds; the RAF were reasonably well equipped and had radios although communications were generally very poor. Most of the calls were lost climbers and walkers and Robin had an uncanny knack of figuring out the most likely place to search.

Robin, Jack Baines and myself planned to open a climbing shop in Fort William when we got demobbed. As it was I was first out but failed to get things started. Robin was next and got involved with a friend and started up Cave & Crag in Settle, still a thriving business, and became involved with Yorkshire cave rescue. Jack started a climbing book business on Anglesey. I finally started Nevisport in Fort William in 1970.

Robin left the RAF in 1966 and entering the next stage of his life, father-hood, he was asked to curb his longing for the mountains for the sake of his two young children, Michael and Kathryn, and so his next career emerged, teaching art at a secondary school in Yorkshire. Robin was a well-respected art teacher until he retired 27 years later. During this time he hired a studio in the Black Horse in Giggleswick and his specialism, sculpture in wood, blossomed. Robin was asked to sculpt for a Jon Finch television series, a task he enjoyed.

Retiring from teaching opened another door for Robin: his wanderlust kicked in again and he found himself loving travel again, spending months at a time in Europe, particularly Portugal where he settled for several years in Tavira. Populated by bohemian artisans, fellow wanderers with fabulous stories of adventure and daring, Robin felt at home immediately and made Tavira his home.

Eventually Robin could see the benefit of 'laying himself in the gentle hands of the NHS' and returned to his roots, to his beloved Yorkshire, where he spent his final few years. It's said that you can tell if you've met a Yorkshireman because he'll tell you within ten minutes of meeting him; this was true of Robin, so proud was he of his county of birth and so fitting that this is where he would spend his last days.

Robin was always on hand with wise words for dealing with life's twists and turns, one such phrase which he would demand of his daughter on many occasion was to 'get above them crawling worms.' And so, with this in mind, his final resting place is on top of Pen-y-ghent, high enough, as high as his daughter could manage, to get him above 'them crawling worms'.

Ian Sykes and Kat Larkham

OFFICERS AND COMMITTEE FOR 2019

Alpine Club Notes

Glacier des Bossons
John Ruskin, 1874. Watercolour over pencil with white bodycolour.
19cm x 31cm. Gifted to the Alpine Club by Charles Warren.

NICHOLAS HURNDALL SMITH

A Mount Kenya Ascent

Two Alpine Club members with strong links to Kenya and east African climbing,
Ian Howell and John Temple, died in the last year, having offered the benefit of
their deep experience to a group of members organising an expedition to Mount
Kenya in February 2019. This is an account from that expedition, including the
installation of a memorial plaque by the Mountain Club of Kenya for Ian Howell
on the bivouac shelter he carried up the mountain in 13 solo ascents for the benefit
of all climbers.

Crawling inside the tiny bivouac hut, a line from the black comedy gangster
film *In Bruges* popped into my head: 'Nooks and crannies, yes! Perhaps this
would be more accurate. Nooks and crannies, rather than alcoves.' This
was not a practical location for an assassin, but there were lots of nooks
and crannies to stow our kit. We were at Baillie's bivy on the south-east
face of Mount Kenya, not to be confused with Ian Howell's hut on the
summit, and after six pitches through thickening swirling mist Nigel
Bassam and I were grateful to find it. We had heard the bivy was seldom
used and possibly full of ice, but also that four SAS men had squeezed into
it at some point in the last year or so. For two, we decided, it would do just
fine. One would have the luxury of lying down, the other sitting up against
a rock with his feet on a block of ice. It had no door, and a strong draft
whistled between its roof and the dry-stone walls supporting it. At 5,000m,
perched on the south-east face of Nelion, this was where we would rest our
heads for the night.

In May 2018, I got a phone call on the way to my book club where we
were due to discuss Felice Benuzzi's *No Picnic on Mount Kenya*, a favourite
of mine. For those who don't know this classic, it tells the tale of Italian
prisoners of war escaping from their 1940s British camp in Nanyuki to
climb the mountain with secretly hand-made gear, before returning to the
camp, simply with the aim of reaffirming their humanity. On the phone was
the AC's Richard Nadin, inviting me to co-lead an expedition to Kenya in
February 2019. Delighted by the coincidence, I needed no time to consider.
The more I read in the following months about the mountain, the more
my delight at the prospect increased. I read of Mackinder's remarkable first
ascent in 1899 with tribal tensions and a caravan of 170 men, including 96
naked Kikuyu, of the entrancing beauty and contrast of the landscape at
different altitudes, and of Shipton and Tilman's exploits in 1929-30. I shared
Shipton's worries prior to his first trip, as I too badly injured my ankle in the
weeks before, not by falling from a cliff into a tree as he did, but by turning
it while running.

Walking towards Mount Kenya via the Chogoria Route. *(Nicholas Hurndall Smith)*

The Baillie bivy, used far less frequently following the construction of the Howell hut. *(Nicholas Hurndall Smith)*

Sunrise from the Baillie bivy over Point Lenana, a popular objective for trekkers. *(Nicholas Hurndall Smith)*

The day of Baillie's bivy hadn't started well. I had woken at 1.30am at the American Camp, on the south-western side of the mountain, with rain drumming on the tent, which was filling rapidly with water. Already there was a 2cm pond around my inflatable mat. I lay there like a mummy, cursing my choice of pitch and shouting at the rain to stop. Eventually, as it died away, I slept again. This was an excuse for a leisurely morning and a hearty breakfast in the warming sun, admiring views of the mountain with its dusting of fresh snow, with any attempt on it far from my mind as my kit dried out. The American Camp is 'one of the loveliest spots I know, it is,' Richard commented. We chatted about the lack of animals we had seen, with the exception of the faithful rock hyrax, distant relative of the elephant, and the receding glaciers. After my recent traverse of the Weisshorn in the Alps, I liked the fact that the Tyndall glacier, with its huge hanging séracs, seemed the most enduring.

As morning passed, Nigel and I slowly resolved to make a start on the mountain after all, and we set off before noon. I was keen to get started, as I knew the niggling feeling of intimidation, which Mount Kenya had instilled in me, would only increase if and when victorious parties from our group of nine returned to camp before us. We had spent a few days over the walk-in via the Chogoria route, climbed Point Lenana, which at 4985m is the third-highest peak on Mount Kenya and the highest point non-technical climbers can reach, and had a good look at the start of the route. We felt ready to have a crack.

After two hours heading up through giant groundsel and contouring around the scree-filled flanks of the mountain to the bottom of the south-east face, we found the starting point, close to the skeleton of a leopard, which we'd been told was nearby but didn't find. Passing two chaps from the Mountain Club of Kenya who had decided to bail, we made quick progress up the first six pitches, climbing Mackinder's Chimney and One O'Clock Gully to Baillie's bivy. Being underway certainly felt good and so did some hot food but the night was endless, with little warmth or sleep. Nigel needed a dose of ibuprofen to alleviate an alarming bout of heavy breathing.

'I just need to tough it out,' he said. I started reading the abseil instructions in case he got worse, but just like last night, when marooned on my sleeping mat, the thought of getting up in the cold dark was horrible. I gave him all the pills I had, which seemed to help. Eventually, from my sitting position by the open doorway, I was rewarded with a beautiful sunrise over Point Lenana and after some breakfast we continued.

We crossed the ridge and, taking the lead, I found myself on increasingly difficult ground as I led us off route, too high and close to the ridge's crest. Here the maxim 'crest is best' does not apply; we should have been climbing easy ground lower down to the left. Lured right by a couple of pegs, I found myself pulling on in-situ gear, before making a belay and listening to Nigel's grunted protests about my choice of line. As he followed 'Smith's Variation', below us appeared Julian Wright, of recent Diamond Couloir fame, and Robyn, making easy work of the correct route, after an early start that morning from our base camp. We began to wonder whether it had been worth the ordeal in Baillie's bivy if, as they pointed out, the rest of our party was hot on their heels.

We tried hard to keep close to them, to spot the route after the steep crux pitch of De Graaf's Variation, but they soon disappeared, as you would expect from a local guide. Mount Kenya is a complicated mountain, and every line of the route description seemed to refer to numerous plausible options made more complicated by the occasional piece of abandoned gear. Shipton himself wrote, 'I know no mountain in the Alps, with the possible exception of Mont Blanc, that presents such a superb complexity of ridges and faces as the twin peaks of Mount Kenya.'

We were blessed with calm and sunny weather and had deliberately left Baillie's late, having read that the crux can be icy, but in fact the rock was dry, superbly grippy and a joy to climb. After 35m of steep, well-protect-

The view back to the summit of Nelion from Batian. *(Nicholas Hurndall Smith)*

ed corner climbing, we reached a ledge from which we spotted the amphitheatre to our right. Here the air opened up beneath our feet as we stepped across to the base of a scree gully. This in turn led to increasingly easy scrambling up the final rocky steps beneath Nelion. Behind us, we caught a fleeting glimpse of Kilimanjaro, which Benuzzi called a 'huge white panettone-shaped mountain', suspended above the clouds.

At 11am on the summit of Nelion (5188m), we met our friends Julian and Robyn enjoying a brief rest next to the Howell hut before their descent. Views back west over the Chogoria Route stretched away below us. Beyond Nelion was Batian. This was the peak on which we had our sights, the true summit of Mount Kenya. An eagle soared far below in the Mackinder valley. My resolve weakened, as the final climb did not look straightforward. Julian pointed out the easiest line and Nigel seemed confident so I pushed my doubts to the back of my mind. Robyn gave me some water as we were in short supply, and we scrambled down to a ledge to abseil 30m into the Gate of the Mists, which separates the twin peaks of Mount Kenya.

Giving little thought to the advice to leave a rope here, we pulled ours down and crossed the Gate, filled with snow. Turning a gendarme on its right, we re-joined the ridge via a pitch of mixed climbing, feeling thankful for the light ice axe we had brought for the purpose. Then, moving together, I took the lead and we discovered the final section was a joy. Beautiful steep granite in a wonderful exposed position led straight up to the summit ridge of Batian, the best climbing on the whole mountain. I felt a surge of relief and satisfaction, as nothing to that point had felt certain, and was delighted by Nigel's comment that 'I stormed up it.' Now at 5,199m, we embraced and beamed across at the summit of Nelion only 11m below us, hoping to see members of our party there, but in vain. We had the mountain to ourselves. Beyond Batian was its west ridge, and I thought of Shipton and Tilman's first ascent of this in 1930, their first climb together and Tilman's first serious mountaineering exploit, one which involved Shipton standing on his shoulders more than once in order to make progress.

Kilimanjaro was no longer visible and the weather looked to be worsening, so we did not tarry long. A few short abseils brought us back down to the Gate of the Mists. I had spotted faint tracks leading up steep snow on the left. We made a good belay, and I started to edge gingerly up around the corner, cutting steps as I went but my light axe made little impression on the hard ice. We had decided to climb without crampons or big boots, and as I edged up I began to regret we had left our one ice screw at base camp. My plan was not a good one: to solo up bullet-hard ice covered in a thin layer of sugary snow with no gear or crampons, kicking or cutting steps as I went, and then to make a belay and lower my axe down for Nigel to follow. Modern alpinists are no longer in the habit of cutting steps, now we are blessed with modern gear. I could only think of Brocherel and Ollier, the Courmayeur guides who had cut steps for Mackinder up the Diamond glacier to the summit in 1899, allegedly at the arduous rate of 130ft in three hours. He had praised them as 'woodmen as well as icemen'. I was sure they would have stormed up this. A woodman I most certainly was not, and as I wondered how I was going to cut the next step, using the axe from which I was hanging, with my two feet on 2 cm foot holds, I turned my attention to the air beneath my feet and Shipton's Camp nearly 1,000m below. I convinced myself quickly that this was a two-axe job and that it might be sensible to turn back before I was committed to an ice climb in my walking boots. Gingerly, I went into reverse. Back at the Gate of the Mists, feeling relieved, I knew I had failed Nigel, who always refers to me as the 'ice specialist' of our team. It had not occurred to us that we might not be able to get back up onto Nelion. Felice Benuzzi would have been better equipped than us, with his hand-made crampons. We looked down at the Darwin glacier below at the foot of the Diamond Couloir, and could just make out our tents beyond, calling to us from the American Camp.

It was over to Nigel to attempt to rock climb out of our predicament. The rock specialist he most certainly is. He disappeared behind a very unpromising corner and began to emit grunting noises, as he forced his way up a steep layback, his determination augmented by the knowledge that he had left his rucksack with all his gear on top of Nelion. Eventually the huffing and puffing died down and Nigel declared himself safe. I had hoped he might go further, but once I saw the corner he had climbed I understood. It rose steeply with no purchase for the feet and when I had done the strenuous moves, I realised we were not out of the woods. Nigel seemed keen to send me down and across right, but my thoughts were only upward, and I could see one bouldery move, which might lead to easier ground. Handing him my rucksack with a nervous smirk, I swung my right foot up and over a

Left: Nigel Bassam and the author at the Howell hut with the memorial plaque brought up by the Mountain Club of Kenya. *(Nicholas Hurndall Smith)*

Right: Ian Howell at Mount Kenya. *(John Cleare)*

featureless round edge, with only a blank smear for my left foot. This was quite a move to undertake at this altitude, I thought, and at least HVS. I scrabbled higher for a hold and was rewarded. Kicking some ice away with my left foot, I returned into balance, and bingo! From here, it was a few more metres of easy climbing back to the abseil point, and then on again, relieved, to the summit of Nelion, three hours after we had left it.

On Nelion, we met Fish and Émmanuel of the Mountain Club of Kenya. They had been behind Julian and Robyn and were concerned that Richard and Neil had not yet joined them. We sat for a while, and used this as an opportunity to admire the hut built by Kenya pioneer and Alpine Club member Ian Howell. Ian had carried the material up over 13 solo ascents in 1970 and his death in November had been a shock to us all as he had been involved in helping us with plans. Not only had Fish and Émmanuel carried up a plaque, which was to be screwed onto the hut in his memory, but Richard was carrying some of his ashes, to be cast to the four winds. I headed across to the top of the final pitch and there, below, were Neil and Richard, happy to find they were close to Nelion, where they would sleep that night. 'Pin' Howell had been the first to climb the Diamond Buttress. 'He was a wonderful man, he was,' as Richard Nadin said.

With 14 equipped abseils ahead of us leading to the base of the route, we accepted gratefully some melted snow from Fish, and forged on down in the hope we might get back before dark. We quickly passed the crux sections and soon found ourselves back at Baillie's bivy, where we retrieved the gear we had left in its nooks and crannies. As we continued, it began to snow heavily and we slowed a little to take more care but we found the abseil points efficiently, with the help of Nigel's eagle eyes, and after just over two hours were back at the base of the route. We reached camp as the last light faded just in time for dinner.

'You're late,' Andrew said, smiling, as we poked our heads into the mess tent.

I have always thought that the best and most memorable climbs are the ones where success in uncertain. The recce we had done had only served to make the route look harder than I expected. We had worked well as a team and suffered none of the constant dangers experienced by our predecessors. I had been particularly struck by the death of the explorer Dr George Kolb, who was killed in 1899 by a charging rhinoceros in the alpine zone. Perhaps he had it coming, as he had tried to shoot it first. The glacier named after him has also perished. Back in my tent, I settled down for what was sure to be a night of dreamy insomnia. We had had Batian to ourselves and stood on the shoulders of the giants who had preceded us. I heard Richard's words, like an echo: 'Ian Howell was only five foot five, he was'.

Alpine Club Library Report 2018

At the AC Library we are never not busy; this year has been no exception. After 13 years, I retired as chair of the Library Council at the Library AGM in September, so this is my last ACL report. Philip Meredith was elected the new chair; he is professor of earth sciences at University College London and has already worked hard as a Library trustee so knows the Library well. Jerry Lovatt has retired as keeper of the artefacts. Nigel Buckley has been appointed in this post.

Jerry remains as a trustee; he had served ACL for 26 years so this now brings his service to a prodigious 27 years and counting. Sue Hare now lives in the French Alps and has retired as a trustee but will remain online as the all-important sales manager for the photographs. Neil Cox joined the Library team as our new hon treasurer and has become a trustee. Trevor Campbell-Davis, hon treasurer of the AC, has become a trustee so we will have plenty of financial knowledge. The RGS has appointed Robin Ashcroft as their trustee and we welcome Robin. Barbara Grigor-Taylor and Kimball Morrison, BMC appointee, both long-term trustees are staying, so the Library Council will have good continuity for Library knowledge and investment management.

John Fairley, keeper of the Paintings, has made improvements to the library facilities. Peter Payne and Philip completed work to re-jig shelving in the basement; our rolling stacks are really wonderful. Also, the AC has fitted new and more fire-detection devices. John has improved the hanging display system for paintings in the lecture room. In the main Library, the visitors' desk is fully functional and shows John's new catalogue of our paintings, with each entry having a small size image of each item. Work is in hand extending this to include the artefacts in the collections. Peter Rowland has photographed 60% of our artefacts at high resolution; more to follow. Peter Payne has scanned 1,000 slides by our member, Harish Kapadia.

Nigel, our new professional Librarian, has brought us excellent database know-how to cataloguing the library and is working with David Lund, chair of the AC's IT group, to implement the first stage of using Koha in place of our ageing AdLib catalogue software. Koha can incorporate images in each Library record, and can be extended to cross-reference to all types of item in the Library. This improved search facility will mean that if, say, we look up Mummery, we will find not only relevant books or archives, but also his

Some of the Library team: Trevor Campbell-Davis, Kimball Morrison, Barbara Grigor-Taylor, Neil Cox, Nigel Buckley, Philip Meredith, Hywel Lloyd and John Fairley.

ice axe and his photographs. This is a large project, likely to take several years to implement fully. The next stage is to include our 240 artefacts where images will be really useful. Of course, many tests and trials must be completed before we move away from AdLib completely.

For insurance purposes, Barbara has led, with assistance from Gordon Turner and Janet Leith, a complete clean-down and inventory of all the book shelves, checking bookplates for ownership; this will confirm recent counts and re-valuation of the book collection: we reckon 30,000 books plus thousands of journals and tracts: over £1m in total.

We are very appreciative of all the members who are donating second-hand books to the Library; the collections gain better and more copies of valued books and the sales of surplus books are an extremely valuable contribution to Library funds. Barbara periodically circulates lists of these to members via email, or by hard copy when requested. Over the last five years, this has generated over £14,000 for the Library, greatly helping conservation of the library stock. Duplicate books have also been donated to other club and school libraries. We can state we have never 'pulped' any book; there is always a new grateful owner who can read interesting mountain stories.

The opportunity arose for the AC Library to participate in the London Book Fair in May, during which 15 prestigious libraries opened their doors to provide a mini-exhibition and lecture, for the public to attend. The AC Library does have a charitable obligation to the public and Barbara planned an exhibition of the treasures of the Alpine Club, billed as 'The Summit of Knowledge, the Pinnacle of Alpine Collections'. This was officially advertised and the press took interest. We had to consider the security of the AC collections, and this necessitated the hiring of lockable glass cases but the minimum period of hire was four weeks; therefore, a programme of three

Visitors from Nagano in the Japanese Alps on their visit to the Club.

further dates were organized for AC members to attend. Unfortunately, this was fixed at very short notice and a number of members responded to say they could not make it. Nevertheless, many members did attend, and enjoyed the event. We hope that this can done again, but with much more notice.

Nigel and Barbara are working with St Paul's School for Girls on a project for their students; they are studying *The White Spider* and are becoming expert about the Eiger north face. Dong Soo Kim from Korea came to see literature on UK Climbers; he is translating many English language mountain books for Korean climbers.

We received a delegation from Nagano in the Japanese Alps who wanted to learn more about an Anglican vicar, Rev Walter Weston, who had been to Japan on three, four-year tours in the 1890s and the early 1900s as a missionary. Fortunately they brought an interpreter, who was very good. We made some presentations to them including slides by Nigel; it was rather strange because each speaker had to wait after each sentence, as it was translated into the other language. Barbara showed books from the collections, written by Weston in 1896, 1918 and 1925 about his trips to the Japanese Alps. Glyn had been digging, and located manuscripts, and Bernie printed a photo. Both Weston and his wife were alpinists; he had joined the AC and his wife joined the Ladies Alpine Club. Our visitors were fascinated to see the original membership application form submitted to the AC by Rev Weston. Below are some photos of the event, including the customary exchange of gifts. An excellent event; the AC is now invited to the Alps in Japan for a celebration of Weston's life.

Discussions have focused on attempts to formulate an AC-ACL custodial agreement, as an earlier text drafted in 2003 has never been confirmed. For

Peter Payne and Janet Johnson at the exhibition of her latest work.

Tatsuya Imai and John Porter.

terms of reference, ACL has used two letters of 1989 between George Band, AC president, and Mike Westmacott, ACL chair. Discussions this year with AC officers agreed that something much more up-to-date was required.

The basis of the AC-ACL relationship is that the AC appoints five of seven ACL trustees as well as the hon librarian, the hon archivist, and the keepers of the artefacts, the photographs and the paintings. Essentially, the AC ultimately controls the Library. It has therefore not been easy to establish how ACL trustees, including those from RGS and BMC, can be empowered to operate an agreement which controls the future of the Library.

However, we have now taken a major step forward in updating the Library structure to meet the original intentions when it was set up in 1971, by the appointment of ACL members. The AC Committee has nominated the first tranche of ACL members, which includes all the keepers and the hon archivist. They will all become full members of the Library in early 2019. We hope that this development will overcome a longstanding anomaly whereby the Library was responsible for the custody of the AC/ACL collections, but the keepers had responsibility only to the AC Committee. This should ensure both a simpler custodial agreement and seamless future custody of all the collections.

In around 2006, it seemed that no significant part of the AC collections was insured; this was at a time of tight finances, not helped by the bank crashes of 2008. But this did concern the trustees who have personal obligations to the charity commissioners and thus the public. The AC was persuaded to insure the books for around £1m and this included some undefined items of fine art. The trustees decided they had to insure the three Ruskin paintings donated to the Library for £0.5m. The Library paid this premium from their funds.

More recently we have begun to worry about being underinsured and the underwriters were pressing for fully itemised lists of what they were insuring. An insurance sub-committee was formed, chaired by John Dempster, which asked two questions: what is the current value of the historic collec-

William Mitchell and Ingram Lloyd at the launch of William's new book on Gabriel Loppé.

tions and who owns what? An estimate of the current value came to around £6m. Now, the keepers have the task of finally itemizing and valuing each item, either individually or by groups; a huge task for everyone.

On the issue of ownership, the Library was formed in 1858 and members have donated items ever since. In 1971, the Library became a charity. In brief terms, this means families of donors do not pay inheritance tax on items donated, these items are held in perpetuity for the benefit of people interested in mountains, the Library pays highly discounted business rates and funding bodies prefer to give grants to registered charities. The question is: which items are to be held in perpetuity? The Library officers took on the task to list what was owned by the Library and we have now completed 'Ownership of the AC Historic Collections'. From this, the insurance premiums payable by the Library are now also calculated.

John Fairley has organized several exhibitions of paintings in the lecture room. Zoe Dickey showed modern canvases that capture the spirit of landscape. Our member Janet Johnson gave a new exhibition of her latest Alpine paintings and member William Mitchell, from the John Mitchell Gallery off Bond Street, gave a lecture on Gabriel Loppé (1825-1913), the artist who was the first French AC member. The AC collections have three of his paintings, which were on show for that evening. William launched his book, the first in English, about Loppé, his life and work.

Peter Rowland and Bernie worked hard with the photos and now have some 6,000 scanned and catalogued. Peter has persuaded our members, who are both excellent mountaineers and photographers, to provide views for this year's AC calendar. All of us must thank the whole Library team for all their efforts to make this year so successful. They care for, catalogue,

The honorary librarian Barbara Grigor-Taylor checking captions for the mini-exhibition held for the London Book fair with some of the Club's featured artefacts.

conserve and arrange access for every item in these historic collections.

Finally, it is for me to say how stimulating is has been working with such marvellous colleagues: always something to learn; someone to meet; an event to make work.

Hywel Lloyd

Boardman Tasker 2018

The Boardman Tasker Award proved as popular as ever in 2018, with 38 entries from eight countries: UK, USA, Canada, Italy, Ireland, South Africa, Austria and Switzerland. This continues the recent high number of submissions from publishers, this being the fourth year in a row we have had more than thirty entries. The 2018 Judges were Peter Gillman, Kate Moorehead and Roger Hubank. Peter and Roger are both past winner of the BT Award. They produced a shortlist of seven books: *Tides*, by Nick Bullock (Vertebrate Publishing); *The Eight Mountains*, by Paolo Cognetti (Harvill Secker); Ed Douglas and John Beatty, *Kinder Scout: The People's Mountain* (Vertebrate Publishing); Christopher Ransmayr, *The Flying Mountain* (Seagull), translated by Simon Pare; David Roberts, *Limits of the Known* (W W Norton); Doug Scott, *The Ogre* (Vertebrate Publishing); Junko Tabei and Helen Rolfe, *Honouring High Places* (Rocky Mountain Books).

The Award was as usual presented at the Kendal festival. Stephen Venables interviewed four of the authors, Nick Bullock, Ed Douglas, Helen Rolfe and Doug Scott and translator Simon Pare, and their were films from John Beatty, David Roberts and Paolo Cognetti. Readings were taken from all seven books and were warmly received by a large audience.

Chair of the judges, Peter Gillman, gave an extensive speech outlining the merits of the shortlisted books and announced the winner for 2018: David Roberts for *Limits of the Known*. This book is an enthralling examination, part history, part memoir of the motivations of mountaineers and other explorers, related by a veteran author and climber.

To quote Peter Gillman: 'We found his writing clear and compelling, with a rich vocabulary and arrestive, figurative language. It is literary in the best sense of the word, at least as we defined it: elegant and lucid, rather than flowery and quasi-poetic.' David was a hugely popular winner, but sadly could not be present to receive the award due to serious health issues. A film of his acceptance speech was greeted with tumultuous applause. Full details of all submissions, film from and of the events including text of Peter Gillman's speech are available at *www.boardmantasker.com*.

Steve Dean

Contributors

MALCOLM BASS has always been fascinated by exploration. At first he focused on caving and cave diving, but his head was turned by a winter trip to Ben Nevis and since then he has been absorbed by the process of trying to climbing new routes in Scotland, Alaska, Pakistan, India and China. He and Paul Figg were nominated for a *Piolet d'Or* for their ascent of the west face of Vasuki Parbat in 2010.

ROBIN CAMPBELL has held every office in the Scottish Mountaineering Club for which administrative competence is not required, including a long stint as editor in the 1960s and 1970s, and as archivist since 1997. Retired from a desultory career as an academic child psychologist, he now wastes his time and money in collecting and studying old drawings and water-colours, particularly those depicting mountains before they were trampled into familiarity by the boots of mountaineers.

JOHN CLEARE has been a freelance professional photographer for over 50 years but a climber for rather longer. Business and many expeditions have taken him all over the world, while he has several dozen books, several films and live TV broadcasts, more than a few new routes and several virgin summits to his credit. An ex-vice president of the AC and an ex-president of the Alpine Ski Club, he lives in remote Wiltshire.

LINDSAY ELMS lives on Vancouver Island and has climbed or travelled on all seven continents including ascents of Mt Logan, Mt Waddington and numerous peaks throughout South America. He has also written two books about the history of mountaineering and exploration on Vancouver Island.

PETER FOSTER is a retired consultant physician. He has been a member of the Alpine Club since 1975. His biography of T Graham Brown is to be published by Vertebrate in January 2019.

TERRY GIFFORD was director of the annual International Festival of Mountaineering Literature for 21 years. Former chair of the Mountain Heritage Trust, he is the author of *The Joy of Climbing* (Whittles, 2004) and *Al Otro Lado del Aguilar* (Oversteps Books, 2011). Visiting professor at Bath Spa University's Centre for Writing and Environment and *profesor honorífico* at the University of Alicante, he celebrated his 70th birthday appropriately on *Wreckers' Slab*.

DENNIS GRAY started climbing on Yorkshire gritstone in 1947. Secretary of the ACG, first national officer, then general secretary of the BMC, Dennis has visited over 60 countries, most recently travelling widely in China. He has written two autobiographies, two books of stories, a novel and a volume of poetry, plays the banjo and sings on three CDs of climbing themed songs.

JIM GREGSON has climbed widely in the Alps since 1972. He is also a telemark ski mountaineer who makes regular trips to Norway. He first visited the Arctic in 1991 and has returned many times, often as an expedition leader, and is one of Britain's leading Arctic mountaineers. His book *Exploring Greenland* documents many of his trips and showcases his photography.

LINDSAY GRIFFIN lives in North Wales, from where he continues to report on developments in world mountaineering. An enthusiastic mind still tries to coax a less than enthusiastic body up pleasant bits of rock and ice, both at home and abroad. He recently completed his term of office as president of the Alpine Club.

GLYN HUGHES is a some-time hon secretary of the Alpine Club, but now carries out the equally important roles of hon archivist and barman: or as the AC quaintly puts it, 'chairman of the Wine Committee'. In 2014 he took on the near-impossible task of following Bill Ruthven as hon secretary of the Mount Everest Foundation.

TOM LIVINGSTONE is a 26-year-old climber and writer based in north Wales. He has a penchant for trad, winter and alpine climbing: the bigger and harder the better. Among his recent successes are ascents of *Divine Providence* (ED3), and a winter ascent of the *Walker Spur* (ED3), but he's still hungry for more. He works as an outdoor instructor, holding the Mountain Leader and Single Pitch Award, and as a rope access technician.

BRUCE NORMAND is a research consultant at the Neutrons and Muons Research Division at the Paul Scherrer Institut in Switzerland, after spending five years as a professor of theoretical physics at Renmin University in Beijing. He has made over 40 first ascents on 6,000m peaks in Nepal, Pakistan, India and China. In 2007 he climbed K2, the first Scotsman to have done so. He won a Piolet d'Or in 2010 and was nominated for a second in 2011.

DONALD ORR is a member of the Scottish Mountaineering Club and recently retired from a career in theology and fine art, which does beg questions. He now spends his time climbing and writing, and being irresponsible with his grandsons. His writings on mountaineering and the mountain environment have contributed over the years to the *Scottish Mountaineering Club Journal*.

SIMON RICHARDSON lives in Aberdeen. Experience gained in the Alps, Andes, Patagonia, Canada, the Himalaya, Caucasus, Alaska and the Yukon is put to good use most winter weekends whilst exploring and climbing in the Scottish Highlands.

C A RUSSELL, who formerly worked with a City bank, devotes much of his time to mountaineering and related activities. He has climbed in many regions of the Alps, in the Pyrenees, East Africa, North America and the Himalaya.

VICTOR SAUNDERS was born in Lossiemouth and grew up in Peninsular Malaysia. He began climbing in the Alps in 1978 and has since climbed in the Andes, Antarctica, Papua, Rockies, Caucasus and across the Himalaya and Karakoram. Formerly a London-based architect, he is now an IFMGA guide based in Chamonix. His first book, *Elusive Summits*, won the Boardman Tasker Prize. In 2007 he received an honorary MA from the University of Stirling for services to Scottish mountaineering.

MARCELO SCANU is an Argentine climber who lives in Buenos Aires. He specialises in ascending virgin mountains and volcanoes in the Central Andes. His articles and photographs about alpinism, trekking, and mountain history, archaeology and ecology appear in prominent magazines in Europe and America. When not climbing, he works for a workers' union.

WILL SIM is a climber and mountain guide from west Cumbria now living in the French Alps. Will regularly seeks out adventurous missions on remote mountains all around the world as well as climbing and skiing in the Alps most days of the year for work and play. He likes crimping just as much as sitting on icy ledges, and will never be able to choose one above the other.

BEN TIBBETTS is a photographer, artist and IFMGA guide based in Chamonix and the UK. He studied Fine Art to postgraduate level and spent almost two years working in the Antarctic and over four months in Greenland. In Europe he is usually preoccupied with climbing long Alpine routes of different styles and difficulty or looking for interesting lines to ski. Over the last few years he has been working on a large format photographic guidebook on the finest routes on the 4,000m peaks of the Alps.

ERIC VOLA is a French climber who lives in Chamonix and Marseille. He spent three years at University College, London, and climbed in the early 1960s with Chris Bonington, Nick Estcourt, Don Whillans and other Brits. In recent years he has translated British mountaineering books, including a selection of Chris Bonington's best stories and Andy Cave's *Learning to Breathe*.

IAN WALL worked at Plas-y-Brenin in the 1960s. Since then he has climbed extensively throughout the UK, the Alps and in Norway. He was involved with the first round of the Kendal Mountain Film Festival in 1980. He has led treks in Africa, Ladakh, Tibet and Nepal, where he now lives and acts as an advisor to the Kathmandu International Mountain Film Festival, Kathmandu Environmental Education Project and in developing and training the Nepal Mountain Leader programme working closely with the Nepal Mountaineering Association.

JONATHAN WESTAWAY is a research fellow in history at the University of Central Lancashire, examining the history of mountaineering, exploration and the outdoor movement, part of a wider interest in the intersections of liberalism, modernity, masculinity, physical culture and imperialism in the late 19th and early 20th century. His research on Eric Shipton's mountain travel writing while in the pay of the British Indian imperial security state, 'That undisclosed world: Eric Shipton's *Mountains of Tartary* (1950)', appears in *Studies in Travel Writing*, vol 18, No4, pp357-373.

SEBASTIAN WOLFRUM is a German writer and mountaineer. He is drawn to remote places and has developed a love affair with the mountains of Iran and its people.

NOTES FOR CONTRIBUTORS

The *Alpine Journal* records all aspects of mountains and mountaineering, including expeditions, exploration, art, literature, geography, history, geology, medicine, ethics and the mountain environment.

Articles Contributions in English are invited. They should be sent to the Hon Editor *The Alpine Journal*, Alpine Club, 55 Charlotte Road, London EC2A 3QF, UK. (**journal.editor@alpine-club.org.uk**) Articles, including images, can be sent as an email attachment, on a disk or memory stick. File-sharing services are also acceptable, by prior arrangement with the editor. With files created in Microsoft Word please confine formatting to italics and bold. A typical article is 2,500 words **and may be edited or shortened at their discretion**. Longer pieces should be discussed with the editor.

The Alpine Journal is unable to offer a fee for articles published, but authors who are not AC members receive a copy of the issue of the *Journal* in which their article appears.

Maps and diagrams These should be well researched, accurate and show the most important place-names mentioned in the text. If submitted electronically, maps and route diagrams should be originated as CMYK .eps files in Adobe Illustrator, InDesign or similar ensuring embedded images are at 300dpi resolution and CMYK. Hard copy should be scanned as a Photoshop compatible 300dpi tiff at A4 finished size. This can be arranged through the editor if required.

Photographs Image files should have unique names or serial numbers **that correspond to the list of captions** appended to the article, as a separate document, or in an email. They should be large jpgs or tiff files. Captions must include the photographer's name. Colour transparencies should be originals. Pre-scanned images should be **300dpi** Greyscale or RGB, tiffs or maximum quality jpegs at A4 final size or larger.

Copyright It is the author's responsibility to obtain copyright clearance for text, photographs, digital images and maps, to pay any fees involved and to ensure acknowledgements are in the form required by the copyright owner.

Summaries A brief summary, listing team members, dates, objectives attempted and achieved, should be included at the end of expedition articles.

Biographies Authors are asked to provide a short autobiography of about 50 words, listing noteworthy highlights in their climbing career and anything else they wish to mention.

Deadline Copy and photographs should reach the editor by **1 February** of the year of publication.

Index 2019

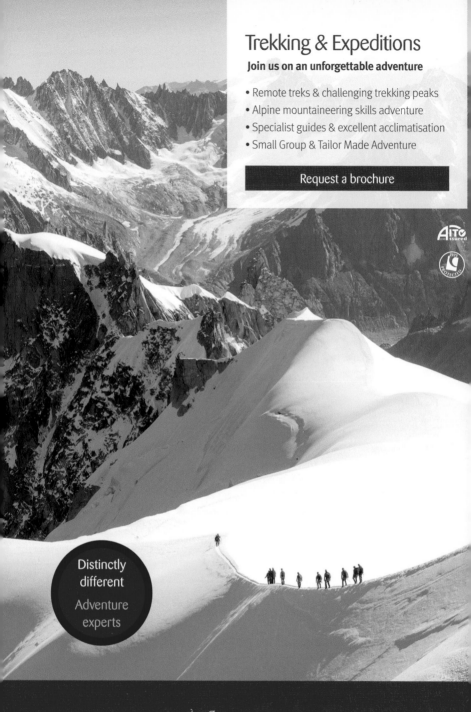

THE BEST ALPINE START YOU CAN GET

Climbing packs the way we want them

For more than fifty years Mountain Equipment has been at the forefront of Himalayan and alpine climbing. We've now taken that experience, passion and opinion to the design of our new range of climbing packs. Lightweight, durable and highly weather resistant, the Tupilak series of packs have been developed specifically for climbers and mountaineers needing the very best in simple, functional design. Excelling on rock, ice and mixed ground, they provide uncompromising functionality for alpinism's leading edge.

MOUNTAIN
EQUIPMENT